Phonics and Reading

Teacher's Guide

Author:
Alan L. Christopherson, M.S.

Editor:
Alan L. Christopherson, M.S.

Alpha Omega Publications, Inc. • Rock Rapids, IA

Horizons Phonics and Reading 2 Teacher's Guide

© MMVI by Alpha Omega Publications, Inc.®
804 N. 2nd Ave. E., Rock Rapids, IA 51246-1759
All rights reserved.

Printed in the United States of America

ISBN 978-07403-1256-4

Table of Contents

Introduction

Introduction

Horizons Phonics and Reading Grade 2 is another addition to the exciting and innovative Horizons curriculum line. Just like the other Horizons materials, there are 160 lessons and 16 tests contained in the two student workbooks. An extensive Teacher's Guide provides plenty of tips and teaching strategies. A reduced student page is included in the Teacher's Guide, along with the instructions and information the teacher will need for the lesson.

Language development begins with listening and is followed by speaking. The listening and speaking skills that a child develops during the first years of life prepare them for learning the skills of reading and writing. The reading and writing skills they learn allow them to communicate the sounds they have heard and spoken. This program will capture the interest of young students with the interesting illustrations and colorful pages. Reading skill develops as the students master the phonics concepts. After its initial presentation, each concept appears a second time as a "review" and is reinforced through a sequentially developing vocabulary which allows previous concepts to be utilized in the practice of new.

Teacher-directed lessons explore the phonetic sounds and guide the students as they practice the concepts. This material will help the student become a proficient and fluent reader one step at a time.

Two readers contain the stories that are recommended for reading after each lesson. These allow the student to apply the phonics concepts that they are learning to reading new stories. Memorization of phonics/spelling rules assists the student in recognizing the relationship between letters and speech sounds—a skill that will enable them to decode new words. The phonics and reading program has three major components: **The Student Workbooks**, **The Readers**, and **The Teacher's Guide**.

The Student Workbooks

Horizons Phonics and Reading Grade 2, Book One contains Lessons 1–80, plus a test after every ten lessons.

Horizons Phonics and Reading Grade 2, Book Two contains Lessons 81–160, plus a test after every ten lessons.

The student workbooks have perforated pages so the lesson sheets can be removed from the book for the student. Removing the pages is essential to promoting good penmanship. It will be impossible for the student to write neatly on the pages if they are only folded back on the binding of the book. After the lesson pages have been completed they can be punched and stored in a 3-ring binder. Completed lessons can be used for drill, review, and preparation for the tests.

The Readers

The Horizons Second Grade Phonics Readers are to be used as a companion to the Horizons Second Grade Student Workbooks. For each lesson in the Student Workbooks there is a corresponding poem, story, or selection from a story in the Readers. Some of the stories are better correlated to the lesson than others but you should always be alert to looking for words that illustrate the lesson concepts.

The stories in the readers were chosen for two primary reasons. First, they needed to have a vocabulary that was comprised mostly of one- and two-syllable words. One focus of Horizons Phonics Grade 2 is to develop skills in reading two-syllable words. Second, they needed to stress the moral values of honesty, industry, courage, kindness, courtesy, and obedience. For many, many years one of the best ways to teach morality and character has been through stories. Stories are used because they give situations and characters that can be identified with and remembered easily. Stories, poems, tales, and essays on character were used in early American education to teach children how to become people with reliable morality and good character. The anchor stories of the readers, *Robinson Crusoe* and *A Little Princess* are electrifying stories that the student will want to read several times. Both clearly illustrate the value of good moral character in becoming a happy individual.

Stories have also been used that carry the student beyond the concrete into an imaginary make-believe world that certainly could not take place. C.S. Lewis saw the imagination as a means of understanding truth more fully. To him, the imagination was a means of knowing something with the heart that the mind or consciousness was not ready to accept. His imagination could recognize a truth that his mind couldn't fully understand or describe. It has been said that as humans we are only able "to see through a glass darkly." Just think for a moment where we would be if people through history had not looked beyond what they could easily see and explain.

The primary goal of the reading is to develop fluency. If the student can decode the words quickly and read them smoothly, his comprehension of the information will be increased. Some of the short poems may seem simple but they are a good measure of how well the student can decode and pronounce words. A few comprehension questions are given in the Teacher's Guide for each story. These questions are not exhaustive of the stories' content but should serve to spark other questions. Always be looking to ask questions like: who are the characters, what are the characters doing, what is the mood of the characters, why are the characters doing what they are doing, what is the order of events, what words are being used, what is the language structure, what new information is being given, and what lesson can be learned?

Look for words that the student will find difficult and review these on the board. The student may require help with some of the words. The teacher or parent should make word cards for the words that the student does not know. The word cards should be reviewed with the student frequently. Some of the stories have a British or old English style and tone. Help the student relate to this style of writing and to the foreign language expressions or colloquial terms that are sometimes used.

The stories in Reader 2 are a little longer than those in Reader 1. This may require that the reading time be divided into two sessions. Read part of the story in the morning and finish it up in the afternoon. A slightly smaller font is also used in Reader 2. If the student has difficulty visually tracking the sentences, let him use a paper strip that can he can slide down the page one line at a time.

The teacher or parent should ask the student questions before and after reading the story. Help the student anticipate what is going to happen in the story by reading the title or looking at the pictures. There are comprehension questions in the Teacher's Guide for each story. The answers to these questions should be discussed. Don't overburden the student with the comprehension questions. It is more important that the student enjoy the reading and become a fluent reader than to face an unnecessary focus on comprehension. The student will receive plenty of comprehension practice in his other subjects.

The Teacher's Guide

The *Horizons Phonics and Reading Grade 2* program contains a total of 160 lessons. Typically, one lesson should be completed each day during the school year. Prepare for each day by carefully reviewing the material provided in the *Teacher's Guide*. The **Lesson Title** highlights the general topic or topics that will be covered in the lesson. The **Overview** is a summary of the concepts and activities that will be covered in the lesson. The **Materials and Supplies** is a list of what will be needed for the lesson. Get these items assembled before starting class with the students. The **Teaching Tips** are classroom teaching procedures that give special instructions for reviewing previous lessons and each activity of the current lesson. Take your time in going over these procedures. Thoroughly think through what you will say and do, so that you have a plan in your mind before teaching the lesson to the student. The **Answer Keys** are reduced student pages with answers. These pages allow you to have both the **Teacher Notes** and the **Student pages** in front of you as you teach the lesson. The **Reader** section has both some general tips for the reading time and some specific comprehension questions for the story or stories.

The student is to complete the activities after you have gone over the instructions, discussed the pictures, and reviewed the words. Allow sufficient time for the student to do each activity before going on to the next. Compliment and encourage the student as he works. The material in this guide has been written in the sense of a singular student. We are fully aware that this material will be used both for an individual student and for classrooms with many students. A choice had to be made over which sense would be used. Please be patient with our choice even though you may have preferred that it be done differently. We simply wanted to avoid the ponderous task of including a parenthesis letter **s** after every word student as in *student(s)*.

Homework

All lessons are presented in a two-page format. Work that is not completed during the scheduled class and seatwork time can be assigned as homework. Send a reading schedule home each week listing the stories that will be covered in the reader. The student should be reading the stories to a parent on a regular basis, so giving the parent a schedule will help them supplement the reading at home. Some of the lessons might be difficult to complete during the scheduled class time. These activities can be completed during seatwork time or sent home as homework. If the lesson sheet is sent home every day for the parent to review, they will get into the habit of checking for incomplete work that needs to be finished at home. Not all of the activities can be done independently, but some can be started during the class time and completed later.

The Daily Schedule

5	minutes	Review homework and previous lesson(s)
3-5	minutes	Drill difficult words, phonics & spelling rules
15-20	minutes	Review the instructions for each activity and give the student time to complete them
1-2	minutes	Review the rules and concepts taught in the lesson
15-20	minutes	Read the story, poem, and/or essay for the lesson

Horizons Phonics & Reading 2 Lesson List

This section of the Teacher's Guide lists the individual lessons and the primary topics that will be covered. At a glance it tells where one is, where one has been, and where one is going. A concise summary of this information is given in the Horizons Phonics & Reading 2 Scope & Sequence.

Phonics & Spelling Rules

This section of the Teacher's Guide lists the phonics and spelling rules that are presented in an ongoing basis through the lessons. Make a set of flashcards for these rules that can be used for instruction and review. Each rule has been given a name for identification. The name and a shortened version of the rule can be placed on the flashcard with a few example words. The rules involve not only pronunciation but also spelling and can be used to enhance the spelling program used for the student.

Curriculum Overview

Curriculum Overview

Horizons Phonics and Reading Grade 2 is a complete, explicit, phonetically based word recognition and reading program. There is a strong emphasis placed on decoding and fluency skills. Students learn to identify the name and sounds of letters and phonemes through picture association and spelling/phonics rules. Dolch sight words are incorporated so that fluency spans the subject areas. Much emphasis is placed on the following:

- fluency
- decoding
- spelling
- auditory skills
- vocabulary development
- alphabetizing
- rhyming
- diacritical marks
- syllabication
- accents
- compound words
- affixes
- contractions

There are several activities associated with each skill. The teacher can choose to expand on the skill by utilizing the accumulation of words for each segment. By using the puzzle approach on the board, a teacher can review and expand the material within the lesson.

Skill presentation in *Horizons Phonics and Reading Grade 2* follows a three-step process:

- Initial presentation
- Review a few lessons later
- Reinforcement of the skill through a sequentially developing vocabulary which allows previous concepts to be utilized in the practice of new.

After every tenth lesson, the student is tested to evaluate his or her mastery of the skills presented.

Horizons Phonics & Reading 2 Lesson List

Lesson 1
Initial consonants b, hard c (cat), soft c (cent), k,
   d, f, hard g (got), soft g (gentle), h, j, l
Short vowels a, e, i, o, u

Lesson 2
Final consonants b, hard c (pac), k, d, f, hard g
   (bag), soft g (Rog), h, j, l
Initial consonants m, n, p, qu, r, s, t
Review short vowels a, e, i, o, u

Lesson 3
Final consonants m, n, p, s, t
Initial v, w, y, z
Initial x as /z/
Review short vowels a, e, i, o, u
Final double consonant ss

Lesson 4
Medial consonants b, hard c (cat), soft c (cent),
   k, d, f, hard g (got), soft g (gentle), h, j, l
Final x as /ks/
Final s
Final s as /z/ as in days and was
Syllable Rule
Final double consonant zz

Lesson 5
Medial consonants m, n, p, qu, r, s as in sad, s
   as in days, t
Review short vowels a, e, i, o, u

Lesson 6
Medial v, w, x, y, z
Review hard and soft c & g
Review short vowels a, e, i, o, u

Lesson 7
Final double consonants ff, ll, ss, zz
Review hard and soft c & g

Lesson 8
Spellings of the /k/ sound: c, k, ck
Initial, Medial and Final consonants

Lesson 9
Short Vowel Rule
Short vowel a

Lesson 10
Comparative ending -er
Suffix -er

Test 1
Lessons 1-4

Lesson 11
Syllables in short vowel a words
Schwa a, e, o
Review Hard and Soft c & g Rule in words with
   syllables

Lesson 12
Short vowel e
Consonant digraph ck

Lesson 13
Consonant digraph th (hard & soft)
Syllables in short vowel e words
Schwa a, e, o

Lesson 14
Consonant digraph sh
Short vowel i

Lesson 15
Consonant digraph ch
Short vowel o

Lesson 16
Consonant digraph tch /ch/

Lesson 17
Review consonant digraphs

Lesson 18
Final consonant blends ct, ft, lt, nt, pt, rt, st, xt
Short vowel u

Lesson 19
Final consonant blends lb, ld, lf, lk, lm, lp
Comparative endings -er & -est

Lesson 20
Final consonant blends mp, nk, nc, nd, rd

Test 2
Lessons 5-14

Lesson 21
Final consonant blends sk, sp, ng, ing

Horizons Phonics & Reading Grade 2 Teacher's Guide

9

Lesson 22
Review final consonant blends

Lesson 23
Initial consonant blends br, cr, dr, fr, gr, pr, tr

Lesson 24
Initial consonant blends sc, sk, sl, sm, sn, sp, st, sw

Lesson 25
Initial consonant blends bl, cl, fl, gl, pl, sl

Lesson 26
Initial consonant blends dw, gw, sw, tw
Final triple consonant blend -dge

Lesson 27
Review initial consonant blends

Lesson 28
Final triple consonant blends with the stable syllables ble, cle, dle, fle, gle, kle, ple, sle, tle, zle

Lesson 29
Final triple consonant blends with lse, lve, nce, nge, nse, ckle

Lesson 30
Final triple consonant blends with nch, lch, nth, rch, rth, tch, mpt, mpse

Test 3
Lessons 15-24

Lesson 31
Medial triple consonant blend tch
Compound words

Lesson 32
Review final and medial triple consonant blends

Lesson 33
Initial triple consonant blends spl, spr, str, shr, squ, scr, thr

Lesson 34
Long a, Final e Rule, a_e

Lesson 35
Long i and e, Final e Rule, i_e, e_e

Lesson 36
Long o, Final e Rule, o_e

Lesson 37
Long u, Final e Eule, u_e

Lesson 38
Review long vowels, Final e Rule

Lesson 39
Long a, spelled a at end of a syllable, VCVopen

Lesson 40
Long a vowel digraphs ai & ay

Test 4
Lessons 25-34

Lesson 41
Long e vowel digraph ee

Lesson 42
Long e, spelled e at end of a syllable, CV & VCVopen
Long e vowel digraph ea

Lesson 43
Long e, spelled -y
Long e vowel digraph -ey

Lesson 44
Long e vowel digraph -ie (i before e Rule)
Long e vowel digraph -ie at the end of a word

Lesson 45
Review spellings of long a & e

Lesson 46
Long i vowel digraph ie
Long i spelled i before two consonants, Wild Colt words

Lesson 47
Long i, spelled y, igh, ey & uy

Lesson 48
Long o vowel digraphs oa & oe

Lesson 49
Long o, spelled o before two consonants, Wild Colt words

Lesson 50
Long o digraphs ow, ou, & ough

Test 5
Lessons 35-44

Lesson 51
Long u as /yoo/, spelled u at end of a syllable

Lesson 52
Long u as /oo/, spelled ue, ui, & u_e

Lesson 53
Review spellings of long i, o, & u

Lesson 54
Plurals with –s, no spelling changes

Lesson 55
Plural with –es, no spelling changes

Lesson 56
Inflected endings –ed & –ing, (no spelling changes)

Lesson 57
Review inflected endings -s & -es (no spelling changes)

Lesson 58
Review inflected endings –ed & -ing (no spelling changes)

Lesson 59
Long a spelled ea, eigh, ei, & ey

Lesson 60
Long u as /oo/, spelled oo & ou

Test 6
Lessons 45-54

Lesson 61
Short oo as in book, spelled u and oo

Lesson 62
Short oo spelled oul
Long u as /oo/, spelled ough
Review long & short oo

Lesson 63
Review long & short oo sound

Lesson 64
Review long & short oo sound

Lesson 65
Initial triple consonant blends with sch & chr

Lesson 66
Vowel diphthongs ou & ow

Lesson 67
Vowel diphthongs oi & oy

Lesson 68
Vowel diphthong ew

Lesson 69
Review diphthongs ew, ou & ow, oi & oy

Lesson 70
Review diphthongs ew, ou & ow, oi & oy

Test 7
Lessons 55-64

Lesson 71
R-controlled ar

Lesson 72
R-controlled er

Lesson 73
R-controlled ur & er with /er/ sound

Lesson 74
R-controlled ir with /er/ sound
Review compound words with R-controlled vowels

Lesson 75
R-controlled /er/ spelled wor, ear, yr, & our

Lesson 76
R-controlled /ir/ spelled eer, ere, ear, ier, & eir

Lesson 77
R-controlled /air/ spelled air, ear, ar, are, eir, & ere

Lesson 78
R-controlled or

Lesson 79
R-controlled /or/ spelled wor, war, ore oar, oor, & our

Lesson 80
Review R-controlled vowels

Test 8
Lessons 65-74

Horizons Phonics & Reading Grade 2 Teacher's Guide

Horizons Phonics & Reading 2
Scope & Sequence

Lessons 1-30

- Consonant, short vowel, and schwa sounds
- Syllables
- Consonant digraphs: ck, th, sh, ch, tch/ch
- Final consonant blends: ct, ft, lt, nt, pt, rt, st, xt, lb, ld, lf, lk, lm, lp, mp, nk, nc, nd, rd, sk, sp, ng, ing
- Comparative endings: -er, -est
- Initial consonant blends: br, cr, dr, fr, gr, pr, tr, sc, sk, sl, sm, sn, sp, st, sw, bl, cl, fl, gl, pl, sl, dw, gw, sw, tw
- Final triple consonant blends: dge, ble, cle, dle, fle, gle, kle, ple, sle, tle, zle, lse, lve, nce, nge, nse, ckle, nch, lch, nth, rch, rth, tch, mpt, mpse

Lesson 31-60

- Medial triple blend tch
- Compound words
- Initial triple consonant blends: spl, spr, str, shr, squ, scr, thr
- Final e and VCVopen long vowels
- Long vowel digraphs: ai, ay, ee, ea, ey, ie, ei, igh, ey, uy, oa, oe, ow, ou, ough, ue, ui, ea, eigh, ei, ey, oo, ou
- Wild Colt long vowels: old, ild, olt, ost
- Plurals: –s, -es, no spelling changes
- Inflected endings: -ed, -ing

Lesson 61-90

- Initial triple consonant blends: sch, chr
- Vowel diphthongs: ou, ow, oi, oy, ew
- R-controlled: ar, ur, er, ir, or, wor, ear, yr, our, eer, ere, ear, ier, eir, air, ear, ar, are, eir, ere, wore, war, ore oar, oor, our
- Digraphs: kn, wr, wh, ng, tch, qu, gu
- Final adjacent clusters: rk, rm, rn, rt
- Medial double letters cc with both hard and soft c

- Short Vowel digraphs: oo, ea, ai, ui
- Digraph /aw/, spelled qua, wa, o, all, alt, alk, au, ough, aw, augh

Lesson 91-120

- Short u, spelled o, o_e, oo, ou
- Silent letters: mn, gm, mb, gh, sc, ps, sw, wh, wr, rh, kn, gn, hn, pn, bt, pt
- Consonant sounds: -ck, -ic, -sk, -rk, -ke, -ge, -dge, -du-, ph, gh, lf, ci, si, ti, ce, s, ss, ex-
- Alphabetical order to the third letter
- Inflected endings -ed, -s, -es, -ing, with spelling changes
- Irregular (Variant) plurals
- Comparative endings -er, -est, with spelling changes

Lesson 121-160

- Possessives: singular, plural
- Suffixes: -ly, -ful, -ness, -less, -y, -en, -able/-ible
- Prefixes: re-, un-, dis-, pre-, mis-, non-
- Syllabication and accents
- Antonyms, synonyms, homographs, and homophones
- Silent t: ten, tle, ter
- Rhyming words
- Two-syllable words with first or second syllable accents
- Three syllable words with various syllable accents
- Difficult and irregular words of one syllable
- Contractions: will, not, have, has, had, am, is, are, us, would

Phonics & Spelling Rules

Short Vowel Rule:

When a word has only one vowel between two consonants, the vowel usually says its short sound as in cat, pet, pin, cod, and cup.

Initial Short Vowel Rule:

The vowels a, e, i, o, and u usually say the short sound when followed by a consonant before the end of a syllable as in at, end, in, odd, and up.

Schwa Rule:

The schwa is the vowel sound in many lightly pronounced unaccented syllables in words of more than one syllable. The vowels a, i, o, u, and e can stand for the schwa sound. It is sometimes signified by the pronunciation "uh" or symbolized by an upside-down rotated e as in fattər. It is the most common vowel sound in the English language. In a strong syllable the vowel is strong, and in a weak syllable the vowel is weak and makes the schwa sound.

Schwa -er Rule:

In many words -er at the end of a word or syllable makes the schwa sound.

Soft c Rule:

When c is followed by e, i, or y, it makes the soft sound as in the word city.

Hard c Rule:

When c is followed by a, u, or o, or a consonant, it makes the hard sound as in the word cat.

Soft g Rule:

When g is followed by e, i or y, it makes the soft sound as in the word giraffe.

Hard g Rule:

When g is followed by a, u, or o, or a consonant, it makes the hard sound as in the word gum.

Soft c or g Rule:

When c or g is followed by e, i, or y, it makes the soft sound.

Hard c or g Rule:

When c or g is followed by a, u, or o, or a consonant, it makes the hard sound.

Initial k Rule:

There are two ways to spell the /k/ sound at the beginning of a word.

> Spell the /k/ sound with k if the sound comes before e, i, or y as in key, king, and Kyle. Spell the /k/ sound with a c if the sound comes before a, o, u, or any consonant as in call, come, curb, and cross.

Final k Rule:

In a one-syllable, short vowel word ending with the /k/ sound, the letters ck are used for correct spelling as in duck and rock.

Digraph qu Rule:

The letters qu make the /kw/ sound that you hear in queen and quick. The letters qu always appear together.

Initial x Rule:

When x comes at the beginning of a word, it often makes the /z/ sound as in xylophone. Very few English words begin with the letter x.

Final x Rule:

When x comes at the end of a word, it usually is pronounced /ks/ as in box and fox.

Final Consonant Doubling Rule: (Twin Consonant Endings Rule)

The letters f, l, s, and z are usually doubled in a one-syllable word that has one vowel followed by only one consonant sound as in muff, stuff, ball, hill, class, kiss, buzz, and fizz. Twin consonants in words are usually treated as a single letter.

Final s Rule:

Sometimes s at the end of a word has the sound of /z/ as in was and has.

Consonant Doubling Rule:

When two consonants are the same in the middle of a word, they are called double medial consonants. To divide the word into syllables, break the word between the double consonants. Double consonant letters do not normally follow long vowels and do not follow non-simple vowels. A double consonant is pronounced singly.

> Letters that double: b c d f g l m n p r s t v z
> Letters that do not double: h j k q w x y

Silent Double Consonant Rule:

When two consonants are the same in the middle of a word, they are called double medial consonants. A double consonant is pronounced singly as in rabbit and daddy.

Final E Rule:

When a syllable ends in a silent e, the silent e is a signal that the vowel in front of it is long as in make, Pete, kite, rope, and use.

v_e Rule:

A vowel followed by a consonant and a "sneaky e" is long; code the vowel with a macron (—) and cross out the "sneaky e." Examples: name, hope, these, like, rule.

Long Vowel Spelling Rule:

Note these common spelling patterns: the spelling a_e is always split as in gate; i_e, o_e, and u_e are very often split as in fine, tone, cute; and ee is rarely split as in feet.

Final y Rule:

Sometimes y can make the long e or i sound. The y is usually at the end of the word when it makes the long e or i sound as in bunny and fly.

Final y Rule:

Sometimes y at the end of a word can make the long ē sound as in funny.

Consonant Blend Rule:

A consonant blend consists of two or more consonants sounded together in such a way that each letter is heard. Their sounds blend together but each sound is heard as in green, frog, tree, drip, bride.

Horizons Phonics & Reading Grade 2 Teacher's Guide

Final Consonant Blends with t Rule:

The ending consonant blends ct, ft, lt, nt, pt, rt, st, and xt work together to make the sounds you hear in fa<u>ct</u>, le<u>ft</u>, be<u>lt</u>, ce<u>nt</u>, ke<u>pt</u>, di<u>rt</u>, be<u>st</u>, and ne<u>xt</u>.

Final Consonant Blends with l Rule:

The ending consonant blends lb, ld, lf, lk, lm, and lp work together to make the sounds you hear in bu<u>lb</u>, he<u>ld</u>, go<u>lf</u>, si<u>lk</u>, fi<u>lm</u>, and gu<u>lp</u>.

Final Consonant Blends Rule:

The ending consonant blends mp, nk nc, nd, and rd work together to make the sounds you hear in ca<u>mp</u>, ba<u>nk</u>, zi<u>nc</u>, se<u>nd</u>, and bi<u>rd</u>.

Final Consonant Blends Rule:

The ending consonant blends sk, sp, and ng work together to make the sounds you hear in du<u>sk</u>, wa<u>sp</u>, and ri<u>ng</u>.

Final Consonant Blend ng Rule:

The /ng/ is a sound that you make in your throat. When you see an ng in a word, you do not say the /n/ sound and the /g/ sound separately. The sound is made at the back of your throat.

Initial Consonant Blends with r Rule:

The beginning consonant blends br, tr, fr, pr, dr, cr, and gr work together to make the sounds you hear in <u>br</u>ead, <u>tr</u>ip, <u>fr</u>og, <u>pr</u>ide, <u>dr</u>ip, <u>cr</u>ab, and <u>gr</u>im.

Initial Consonant Blends with s Rule:

The beginning consonant blends sc, sl, sm, sn, sp, st, and sw work together to make the sounds you hear in <u>sc</u>um, <u>sl</u>op, <u>sm</u>og, <u>sn</u>ob, <u>sp</u>it, <u>st</u>em, and <u>sw</u>im.

Initial Consonant Blends with l Rule:

The beginning consonant blends bl, cl, fl, gl, pl, and sl work together to make the sounds you hear in <u>bl</u>ip, <u>cl</u>ef, <u>fl</u>at, <u>gl</u>ob, <u>pl</u>us, and <u>sl</u>im.

Initial Consonant Blends with w Rule:

The beginning consonant blends dw, gw, sw, and tw work together to make the sounds you hear in <u>dw</u>elt, <u>Gw</u>en, <u>sw</u>ing, and <u>tw</u>in.

Final Consonant Blend dge Rule:

The phonogram dge may be used only after a single vowel that says its short sound as in badge, edge, bridge, lodge, budge.

Consonant Blend sch Rule:

In some words the consonant blend sch- has the sound sk as in school or scheme.

Consonant Blend chr Rule:

In words the consonant blend chr- has the sound kr: Chris, chrome

Triple Consonant Blends Rule:

Triple Consonant Blend nce makes the /ns/ sound that you hear in pounce and bounce.
Triple Consonant Blend nse makes the /ns/ sound that you hear in sense and dense.
Triple Consonant Blend lse makes the /ls/ sound that you hear in false and repulse.
Triple Consonant Blend lve makes the /lv/ sound that you hear in twelve and solve.

Triple Consonant Blend nge makes the /nj/ sound that you hear in range and plunge.
Triple Consonant Blend rch makes the sound that you hear in porch and church.
Triple Consonant Blend nch makes the sound that you hear in bench and inch.
Triple Consonant Blend rth makes the sound that you hear in worth and earth.
Triple Consonant Blend nth makes the sound that you hear in month and ninth.
Triple Consonant Blend mpt makes the sound that you hear in prompt and attempt.
Triple Consonant Blend lch makes the sound that you hear in squelch and mulch.
Triple Consonant Blend scr makes the skr sound that you hear in scream and describe.
Triple Consonant Blend spl makes the sound that you hear in splash and splotch.
Triple Consonant Blend spr makes the sound that you hear in sprint and spray.
Triple Consonant Blend thr makes the sound that you hear in thrash and through.
Triple Consonant Blend shr makes the sound that you hear in shrink and shriek.
Triple Consonant Blend squ makes the skw sound that you hear in squish and squall.
Triple Consonant Blend str makes the sound that you hear in stress and stray.

Final Trigraph tch Rule:

Three letters that come together to make one vowel or consonant sound are called trigraphs. They are underlined and some letters are marked silent. The trigraph tch makes the /ch/ sound at the end of a word and comes after a short vowel as in catch and stretch. Mark the t silent.

Consonant Digraph Rule:

A consonant digraph is two consonants that stay together to make their special sound.

Consonant Digraph ck Rule:

In consonant digraph ck, the k is pronounced and the c is silent as in dock and peck.

Consonant Digraph th Rule:

Consonant digraph th can be used at the beginning, middle, or end of a word as in thank, this, athlete, brother, path, and soothe. To determine if th is soft or hard, place three fingers over your throat and say the word. If you feel vibrations when pronouncing the th, then the th is hard.

Consonant Digraph sh Rule:

Consonant digraph sh can be used at the beginning or end of a word as in shed and hash.

Consonant Digraph ch Rule:

Consonant digraph ch can be used at the beginning or end of a word as in chin, such, sand-wich.

Consonant Digraph tch Rule:

Consonant digraph tch makes the sound you hear in watch and itch. Use ch at the beginning of a word or after a consonant. Use tch at the end of a word after a short vowel.

Consonant Digraph kn Rule:

In consonant digraph kn, the k is silent and n is pronounced as in knife and knot as in know and knelt.

Consonant Digraph wr Rule:

In consonant digraph wr, the w is silent and the r is pronounced as in wrong and write.

Consonant Digraph wh Rule:

In consonant digraph wh, the wh makes the hw sound as in what and when.

Consonant Digraph ng Rule:

In consonant digraph ng, the ng makes a blend of the ng sound as in sing and rung.

Consonant Digraph tch Rule:

In consonant digraph tch, the tch makes the ch sound as in itch and pitcher. It always follows a short vowel.

Initial Consonant Digraph rh Rule:

In consonant digraph rh at the beginning of a word, the h is silent and r is pronounced as in rhino and rhyme.

Consonant Digraph sc Rule:

In the sc consonant digraph before e, i, or y, the c is silent and the s is pronounced as in scene and science.

Consonant Digraph ps Rule:

The s sound is spelled ps as in psalm and psychology.

Consonant Digraph sw Rule:

The s sound is spelled sw as in sword and answer.

Consonant Digraph wh Rule:

The h sound is spelled wh as in whole and who.

Silent Consonants Rule:

Consonants that are not heard are called silent consonants as in wrap, edge, knit, kitchen, lamb, and sigh.

Consonant Digraph mb Rule:

In consonant digraph mb, the b is silent and the m is pronounced as in lamb.

Consonant Digraph gm Rule:

In consonant digraph gm, the g is silent and the m is pronounced as in diaphragm.

Consonant Digraph mn Rule:

In consonant digraph mn, the n is silent and the m is pronounced as in column.

Consonant Digraph lm Rule:

In consonant digraph lm, the l is silent and the m is pronounced as in calm.

Digraph gu Rule:

When the letter g is followed by u, the g makes a hard sound and the u is silent as in guard and guest. The u is not considered a vowel here.

Syllable Rule:

A syllable is a pronounceable part of a word.

Vowel Syllable Rule:

Each syllable in a word has a vowel as in focus (fo/cus) and velvet (vel/vet).

Final le Syllable Rule:

When you have a word that has the old-style spelling in which the -le sounds like -el, divide before the consonant before the -le. For example: a/ble, fum/ble, rub/ble, mum/ble, and thi/stle. The only exceptions to this are ckle words like tick/le.

Final Stable Syllable Rule:

A Final Stable Syllable is a syllable that occurs at the end of a word frequently enough to be considered stable. The final stable syllable is coded first with a bracket (code the e silent) and then code the first syllable of the word. [ble table, [cle uncle, [dle candle, [fle ruffle, [gle goggle, [kle tinkle, [ple staple, [sle hassle, [tle battle, [zle puzzle.

Long Vowel Open Syllable Rule:

Vowels a, e, o, and u usually say their names/long sounds (ā, ē, ō, ū) at the end of a syllable (nā vy, mē, ō pen, mū sic). These are referred to as open syllables.

CVopen Rule:

An open, accented vowel is long; code it with a macron. A macron is a line (—) placed over the long vowel. Examples of words following this rule: no, me, so, we, go, and hi.

VCV Syllable Rule:

VCV means a word has two vowels, so it has two syllables. In the first syllable, the vowel can make a long sound as in ra'/ven, mo'/tor, and pa'/per; a short sound as in riv'/er or de/cide'; or a schwa sound as in a/go', a/way', and po/lite'.

VCVopen Syllable Rule:

When a single consonant comes between two vowels or vowel sounds, it is usually divided before the consonant if the first vowel is long. Long vowels at the end of syllables as in ma'/ker and pi'/lot.

VV Syllable Rule:

Divide between two vowels when they are sounded separately. VV as in di'/et and cru'/el.

VCCV Syllable Rule:

When a word contains more than one vowel, it could follow the VCCV (vowel-consonant-consonant-vowel) pattern. The first step is to mark the vowels by writing a v under each vowel. Then mark the consonants by writing a c under them. Next, divide the word into syllables by drawing a line between the two consonants. Code the vowels and decide which syllable receives the accent ('). Divide between two consonants unless the consonants form a digraph and are sounded together. VCCV as in hap'/py and chil'/dren.

VCCVCCV Syllable Rule:

VCCVCCV means the word has three vowels, so it has three syllables. The syllable lines go between each pair of consonants, then code each syllable as in dif'/fer/ent', sim'/i/lar', and wil'/der/ness'.

Affix Syllable Rule:

The first step in dividing a word into syllables is to check the word for prefixes or suffixes. Prefix/Root/Suffix. When a word has an affix, it is divided between the root and the affix as in mud'/dy and rob'/ber.

Suffix Syllable Rule:

A suffix is a syllable if it contains a vowel sound as in -er, -est, -able/ible, -ful, -y, -en, -ness, -less, -ly, -es, -ing, -ed, and -s. Exceptions are the stable syllables.

Prefix Syllable Rule:

A prefix is always a separate syllable in a word as in re-, un-, dis-, pre-, mis-, and non-.

Compound Word Syllable Rule:

A compound word is a word made from two or more words joined together to make one word. The words that make up a compound word are spelled completely and keep their usual spelling as in cowboy, everybody, spaceman, sidewalk, and bedroom. Most compound words are accented on the first word.

Root Word Rule:

A root word is a word to which a suffix or prefix can be added to make a new word.

Suffix Rule:

A suffix is added to the end of a root words to make a new word.

Comparative Suffix -er Rule:

The suffix -er is used to compare two things as in "His pig is fatter than mine" (comparing two things).

Comparative Suffix -est Rule:

The suffix -est is used to compare more than two things as in "His pigs are the fattest of all" (comparing more than two things).

Suffix -er Rule:

The suffix -er sometimes means "a person who" or "something that." Example: someone who works is a worker. A person who sings is a singer.

Suffix -ing Rule:

When you add -ing, it means something is happening now as in talking and rolling.

Vowel Digraph Rule:

Vowel digraphs are two vowels put together in a word that make a long or short sound or have a special sound all their own.

Long Vowel Digraph Rule:

A vowel digraph is two letters with the first letter making a long sound and the second letter being silent. We call this "The first one does the talking, the second keeps on walking." Examples: ee/sheep, ay/may, ai/paint.

Long Vowel Digraph Rule:

When a word or syllable has two vowels, the first vowel is usually long and the second vowel is usually silent as in kite, pain, weep, blue, and pay.

Long Vowel e Digraph Rule:

Long e vowel digraphs are ee (sheep, see), ea (leaf, meat), ey (key, money), ie (shield, field), and ei (receipt).

Final Long Vowel Digraph ey Rule:

Sometimes ey at the end of a word can make the long ē sound as in key.

Final Long Vowel Digraph ie Rule:

The long e vowel digraph ie says long e at the end of a word as in movie.

i Before e Except After c Rule:

When the sound is ē, write ie except after c. When the sound is other than ē, usually write ei. There are always exceptions as in either, seize, and sheik.

Final Long Vowel Digraph ie Rule:

The long i vowel digraph ie says long i at the end of a word as in pie and tie.

Long i as ign Rule:

Usually when i is followed by gh , the i is long and the gh is silent. Examples: light and night.

Wild Colt Rule:

Wild Colt words contain either the vowels o or i followed by two consonants as in wild, colt, kind, find, and both.

Vowel Diphthong ow Rule:

The vowel diphthong ow can make two sounds: ow as in cow or ow as in snow.

Vowel Digraph ou Rule:

The vowel digraph ou can make the long o sound; ough can make the long o sound.

Long Vowel u Rule:

In some words u has the long yoo sound as in unit and music.

Long Vowel ew, ue, and ui Digraph Rule:

The vowel digraphs ew, ue, and ui form a single long u vowel sound as in statue, tissue, blew, threw, suit, and juice.

Long Vowel ou, ue, and ui Rule:

The vowel digraphs ou, ue, and ui form a single long oo sound as in soup, group, statue, tissue, suit, and juice.

Plurals with -s Rule:

The plural form of most nouns is made by adding -s to the end of a word.
If a words ends in a vowel followed by -y, the plural is formed by adding -s.
The plurals of most nouns ending with -f, -fe, or -ff are formed by adding -s.
If a word ends in a vowel followed by -o, the plural is formed by adding -s and has the /z/ sound.

Plurals with -es Rule:

If a word ends in -s, -sh, -ch, -x, or -z, the plural is made by adding -es and has the /iz/ sound.
If a words ends in a consonant followed by -o, the plural is formed by adding -es and has the /z/ sound.

Suffix -ing Rule:

When you add -ing, it means that something is happening now.
If a words ends in a consonant followed by -y, keep the y when adding the suffix -ing.

Suffix -ed Rule:

In some words, including all verbs ending in a vowel or voiced consonant, the ending -ed has the sound of d. When -ed is added to a word, it means that something has happened in the past.
In some words the ending -ed has the sound of t.
The ending -ed has the sound of ed after t and d.
In some words, including all verbs ending in a vowel or voiced consonant, the ending -ed has the sound of d.

Long Vowel ei, ey, and ea Digraphs Rule:

The vowel digraphs ei, ey, and ea make the long ā sound you hear in vein, they, and great.

Long Vowel Digraph eigh Rule:

The vowel combination eigh makes the long ā sound you hear in weigh.

Vowel Digraph oo Rule:

The vowel digraph oo can stand for the vowel sound heard in book or in pool.

long Vowel Digraph ou Rule:

The vowel digraph ou can stand for the vowel sound heard in soup.

oul as Short oo Rule:

In some words the short oo sound is spelled oul as in should.

ough as Long oo Rule:

In some words the long oo sound is spelled ough as in through.

Letter u Rule:

The letter u can have either the long oo or the short oo sound as in tune, ruby, pull, and put.

Diphthong Rule:

A diphthong is two vowel sounds that come together so fast that they are considered one syllable. Examples: ew, oi and oy, ou and ow.

Diphthong ou & ow Rule:

The diphthongs ou and ow make the sounds you hear in out and how. Diphthongs are coded with an arc (‿) under the letters.

Diphthong oi & oy Rule:

The diphthongs oi and oy make the sounds you hear in coin and boy. Diphthongs are coded with an arc (‿) under the letters.

Diphthong ew Rule:

The diphthong ew makes the sound you hear in new and chew. Diphthongs are coded with an arc (⌣) under the letters.

R-Controlled Vowel Rule:

When a vowel is followed by an r in the same syllable, that vowel is R-controlled. It is neither long nor short. In an R-controlled vowel, an r after the vowel makes the vowel sound different from a
short or long sound. Examples: star, shirt, term, born, burn.

R-Controlled ar Rule:

ar is R-controlled in start, far, and market.

R-Controlled /er/ Rule:

R-controlled er, ir, and ur often sound the same /er/. Examples: term, sir, fir, fur.

R-Controlled wor Rule:

The phonogram or may say /er/ when it follows w (work, worm, worthy);

R-Controlled ear Rule:

ear is R-controlled in heard, learn, and earnest;

R-Controlled yr Rule:

yr is R-controlled in myrrh, myrtle, and martyr.

R-Controlled our Rule:

When the vowel team ou is controlled by a final r at the end of a root, the resulting team, our, can say /er/ as in journey, flourish, and courage.

R-Controlled /er/ Rule:

In an R-controlled vowel, an r after the vowel makes the vowel sound different from a short or long sound—spelled eer as in deer and peer, spelled ere as in here and sincere, spelled ear as in hear and ear, and spelled ier as in fierce.

R-Controlled /air/ Rule:

In an R-controlled vowel, an r after the vowel makes the vowel sound different from a short or long sound—spelled ar as in vary, spelled are as in care, spelled air as in stair, spelled eir as in their, spelled ear as in bear, spelled ere as in there.

R-Controlled /or/ Rule:

In an R-controlled vowel, an r after the vowel makes the vowel sound different from a short or long sound—spelled wor as in worn, spelled war as in wart, spelled ore as in snore, spelled oar as in soar, spelled our as in four, spelled oor as in door.

Short Vowel Digraph ea Rule:

In some words with the cc double consonant, the syllable is split between the consonants and both c's are heard. One has the hard c sound and the other has the soft c as in accent and access.

Short Vowel Digraph ea Rule:

Vowel digraphs are two vowels put together in a word that make a long or short sound or have a special sound all their own. The vowel digraph ea can stand for the short e sound as in head and bread.

Short Vowel Digraph ui Rule:

In some words with the ui vowel digraph, the u is silent and the i makes the short sound as in guilt and build.

Short Vowel Digraph ai Rule:

In some words with the ai vowel digraph, the a is silent and the i makes the short sound as in captain.

Vowel ô Spelled wa or qua Rule:

When the letter a comes after the letters w or qu, it often makes ô or aw sound as in wash and squash.

Vowel ô Spelled al Rule:

The vowel a followed by the letter l often has neither a long nor a short sound but has an ô or aw sound as in small, walnut, salt, and talk.

Vowel ô Spelled o Rule:

In some words the letter o is neither long or short but has an ô or aw sound. Compare the short o sound in cot, top, Tom, and pod to the ô sound in dog, hog, on, and off.

Vowel ô Spelled au or aw Rule:

Vowel digraphs are two vowels put together in a word that make a long or short sound or have a special sound all their own. The vowel digraphs au and aw stand for the ô or aw sound as in saw, lawn, faucet, and auto.

Vowel ô Spelled ough Rule:

The digraph ough is a very special combination of letters and can be very confusing, so we just have to learn it. It helps to really look at the words and remember the ough combination. It can spell the sound of ô or /aw/ as in bought and thought.
The digraph augh can spell the sound of ô or /aw/ as in taught and caught.

Short u Spelling Rule:

Short u can be spelled o as in mother, son, and of.
Short u can be spelled o_e as in none and some.
Short u can be spelled ou as in couple and young.
Short u can be spelled oo as in blood and flood.

Spellings of the /k/ Sound Rule:

If a word ends in sound of /k/ and has a short vowel just before the /k/ sound, we use ck as in back, stack, and rack.
If the vowel is long before the /k/, we use ke as in make and trike.
If there is a vowel and then a sound before the /k/ sound, we use k alone. It does not matter is the vowel is long or short as in dark and bask.

If there are two vowels before the /k/, we use k as in seek and soak.

Some words with two or more syllables end in the /k/ sound that is spelled with a c as in music and picnic.

Silent Vowel Before l Rule:

Vowels before l in unaccented syllables are scarcely heard. Sometimes the vowel sound is dropped altogether, leaving only the sound of l as in fatal, sandal, and mantel.

Spellings of the /z/ Sound Rule:

In some words the sound of /z/ is spelled s or se as in his, has, nose, and noise.

dge and ge Spelling Rule:

When g is followed by e, i, or y, it makes the soft sound as in the word giraffe.

Words that end with the sound of /j/ are spelled with -dge or -ge. Use the letters -dge after short vowels as in bridge, fudge, and badge. Use -ge after anything else as in cage, lounge, and page.

Digraph du Rule:

When d is followed by u in some words, it has the sound of j as in education.

Spellings of the /f/ Sound Rule:

These consonant digraphs can make the f sound: ph as in phonics and graph; gh as in cough and trough; and lf as in calf and half.

Silent gh Rule:

Consonant digraph gh can be silent as in right and nigh.

Spellings of the /sh/ Sound Rule:

When followed by a vowel in the same syllable, ci, si, and ti often have the sound of sh as in nation, action, special, precious, and mission.

The letters s or ss before u say sh as in sure, tissue, and pleasure.

Silent Letter Digraphs Rule:

We call the g, k, h, and p in the digraphs gn, kn, hn, and pn "ghost letters" to help us remember they used to make a sound but now are silent.

    In consonant digraph gn, the g is silent and the n is pronounced as in sign and align.

    In consonant digraph kn, the k is silent and n is pronounced as in know and knob.

    In consonant digraph hn, the h is silent and n is pronounced as in John.

    In consonant digraph pn, the p is silent and n is pronounced as in pneumonia.

Silent Letter Digraph bt Rule:

In consonant digraph bt, the b is silent and the t is pronounced as in doubt and subtle.

Silent Letter Digraph pt Rule:

In consonant digraph pt, the p is silent and the t is pronounced as in ptarmigan.

Digraph ex Rule:

The digraph ex has several sounds: ek as in excel and excite, ek-s as in extra and extend, ek-z as in exact and exist, and eks as in exhale and exchange.

Alphabetical Order Rule:

To put a group of words in ABC order, first read all the words. Next, look at the first letter of each word. If the first letters are the same, you should look at the second letter. If those are both the same, go to the third letter, and so on. Finally, put the words in ABC order.

Plurals with y Rule:

Words (nouns) ending in y preceded by a vowel keep the y and add -s to form the plural as in boy/boys, monkey/monkeys, and turkey/turkeys.

When a word ends in y after a consonant, usually change the y to an i before adding -es as in bunny/bunnies, city/cities, try/tries, and carry/carries.

Consonant Doubling Rule:

If a word with a short vowel sound ends in a single consonant, usually double the consonant before adding a suffix that begins with a vowel as in tag/tagged/tagging, run/running, and dig/digging.

The 1-1-1 Rule:

Words of one syllable (hop), having one vowel followed by one consonant, need another final consonant (hop + ped) before adding endings that begin with a vowel. This rule does not apply to words with x since x has two sounds /ks/.

Drop e Rule:

If a word ends in silent e, drop the e before adding a suffix that begins with a vowel such as -ing or -ed as in bake/baking/baked and slice/slicing/sliced.

Change f to v Rule:

When a word ends in f or fe, change the f to a v and add es to make the word plural as in leaf/leaves, elf/elves, and wife/wives.

Some nouns ending in f or fe do not change their endings to -ves to make the word plural as in cliff/cliffs and safe/safes.

Some nouns ending in f or fe may or may not change their endings to -ves to make the word plural as in dwarf/dwarfs/dwarves.

Irregular Plurals Rule:

Some plurals are irregular and no rule can be made for them. Some add letters as in child and children. Some change internal letters as in tooth/teeth.

Some plurals are irregular and no rule can be made for them. Some do not change as in sheep/sheep, moose/moose, deer/deer.

Doubling Rule:

The suffix -er is used to compare two things as in short/shorter.
The suffix -est is used to compare more than two things as in short/shortest.

Drop e Rule:

When the ending -er or -est is added to words ending in final e, the final e is dropped as in fine/finer/finest and brave/braver/bravest.

Doubling Rule:

When -er or -est is added to some root words that end with one vowel and one consonant, the final consonant is doubled before adding the suffix as in glad/gladder/ gladdest.

Change y to i Rule:

When -er or -est is added to a root word ending in y after a consonant, change the y to i before adding the suffix as in pretty/prettier/prettiest and busy/busier/busiest.

Singular Possessive Nouns Rule:

Nouns that show ownership or possession are called possessive nouns. Place an apostrophe (') and an s after a singular noun to show possession as in girl/girl's and cat/cat's.

Plural Possessive Nouns Rule:

Place an apostrophe after plural nouns ending in s to show possession as in boys/boys' and students/students'. If the plural noun does not end in s, add an apostrophe and s to show possession as in children/children's and men/men's.

Suffix -ly or -ful Rule:

A suffix is an ending that is added to a word to make a new word. Usually when the suffixes -ly or -ful are added, the spelling of the base word does not change as in pain/painful and quick/quickly.

Suffix -less or -ness Rule:

A suffix is an ending that is added to a word to make a new word. Usually when the suffixes -less or -ness are added, the spelling of the base word does not change as in fearless and fullness.

Suffix Rule:

A suffix is an ending that is added to a word to make a new word. When a word ends in a single or a double consonant, the spelling does not usually need to be changed when adding the suffixes -y, -en, or -able/-ible as in frost/frosty, straight/straighten, wear/wearable, and deduct/deductible.

When a word ends with a single consonant that follows a single vowel, the final consonant is usually doubled before the suffix -y is added as in fun/funny and fog/foggy.

Drop e Suffix Rule:

A word that ends in e usually drops the e when adding a suffix beginning with a vowel as in move/movable, force/forcible, and rise/risen.

Prefix re- Rule:

The prefix re- usually means to do again as in redo and repack.

Prefix un- Rule:

The prefix un- usually means not, the opposite, as in unstrung, undress, and unlock.

Prefix dis- Rule:

The prefix dis- usually means not, no, the opposite, as in dishonest and disrepair.

Prefix pre- Rule:

The prefix pre- usually means before, in front of, as in prebake and prescreen.

Prefix mis- Rule:

The prefix mis- usually means bad, badly, wrong, lack, as in misadd and miscolor.

Prefix non- Rule:

The prefix non- usually means not, no, other than, as in nonfat and nonfrozen.

Antonym Rule:

An antonym is a word that means the opposite of another, as in hot – cold.

Synonym Rule:

A synonym is a word having the same or nearly the same meaning as another word, as in big/large, small/little, and closes/shuts.

Homophone or Homonym Rule:

Homophones or homonyms are words that sound the same but have different spellings and different meanings, as in beet/beat, weak/week, and knows/nose.

Homograph Rule:

Homographs are words that are spelled the same, although perhaps pronounced differently as in read/read. Example: We can read the book that we read yesterday.

Rhyme Rule:

Words that rhyme have the same ending sound as in ball/hall and otter/bitter.

Contraction Rule:

A contraction is a word that is made from two words.

Contractions with will Rule:

In contractions formed with the word will, an apostrophe (') is used in place of the letters that are left out as in we + will = we'll and I + will = I'll.

Contractions with not Rule:

In contractions formed with the word not, an apostrophe (') is used in place of the letters that are left out as in cannot = can't and could + not = couldn't.

Contractions with have, has, and had Rule:

In contractions formed with the word have, has, and had, the ha is removed and replaced with an apostrophe (') as in I + have = I've, he + has = he's, and I + had = I'd.

Contractions with am Rule:

In the contraction formed with the word am, the a is removed and replaced with an apostrophe (') as in I + am = I'm.

Contractions with is Rule:

In contractions formed with the word is, the i is removed and replaced with an apostrophe (') as in he + is = he's and she + is = she's.

Contractions with are Rule:

In contractions formed with the word are, the a is removed and replaced with an apostrophe (') as in you + are = you're and they + are = they're.

Contractions with us Rule:

In contractions formed with the word us, the u is removed and replaced with an apostrophe (') as in let + us = let's.

Contractions with would Rule:

In contractions formed with the word would, the woul is removed and replaced with an apostrophe (') as in she + would = she'd.

Contractions with shall Rule:

In contractions formed with the word shall, the sha is removed and replaced with an apostrophe (') as in he + shall = he'll and she + shall = she'll.

Lesson Plans

Lesson 1: Initial Consonant Sounds, Hard & Soft Sounds of c & g, & Short Vowel Sounds

Overview:

- Print beginning consonant letters
- Audio discrimination of consonant sounds
- Print beginning short vowel letters
- Audio discrimination of short vowel sounds
- Complete words by writing the short vowel
- Identify the sound of soft **c** and hard **c** in words
- Identify the sound of soft **g** and hard **g** in words

Materials and Supplies:

- Teacher's Guide & Student Workbook 1
- White board or chalkboard
- Alphabet flashcards
- Reader: *Robinson Crusoe & Other Classic Stories*

Teaching Tips:

Have the student practice printing the upper case and lower case alphabet on lined paper or on the white board. Do one letter at a time by holding up a letter flashcard, asking the student for the name of the letter, asking for the sound that the letter makes, and then asking him to write the letter. Sort the letters into two groups. A group that the student knows well and a group that needs review.

Activity 1. Review the names of the pictures together. Have the student print the upper case and lower case consonant letters for the beginning sound of each picture.

Pictures:
  box, king, door, hand, cat
  gate, lamp, jar, house, fish

Letters:
  Bb, Kk, Dd, Hh, Cc
  Gg, Ll, Jj, Hh, Ff

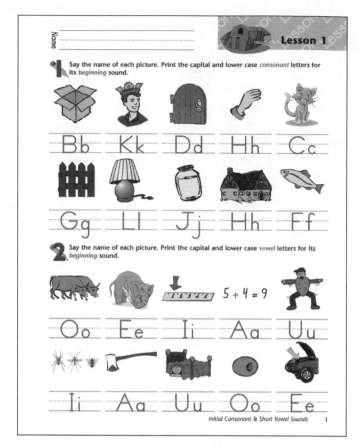

Activity 2. Review the names of the pictures together. Write the vowels on the board. Have the student print the upper case and lower case vowel letters for the beginning sound of each picture.

Pictures:
  ox, elephant, inch, add, umpire
  insect, axe, under, olive, engine

Letters:
  Oo, Ee, Ii, Aa, Uu
  Ii, Aa, Uu, Oo, Ee

Activity 3. Review vowel sounds using flashcards. Write the words *dad*, *fed*, *hit*, *Bob*, and *nut* on the board, leaving out the vowel. Say each word and have a student tell you the letter for the missing vowel. Write the vowel completing the word. Review the pictures in the student book and have the student write the missing letters.

Pictures:
  sun, hot, map, red, dig

Letters:
  u, o, a, e, i

Activity 4. Read and discuss the rule for the hard and soft sounds of **c**. Illustrate the difference in the sounds by writing some words on the board and identifying the words with soft **c** and the words with hard **c**. *Words to teach the concept:* Soft **c** words – cell, cellar, cement, census, center, cinder, civil, cycle. Hard **c** words: can, call, come, camp, could, carry. Discuss the pictures in the activity. Have the student identify each picture and determine whether the hard or soft sound of **c** is heard. Have the student underline all the pictures that begin with the sound of hard **c** first. Go through the activity again and tell the student to circle the pictures that begin with the soft **c** sound.
Pictures:

cold, cent, circus, cut, circle

Hard **c**:

cold, cut

Soft **c**:

cent, circus, circle

Activity 5. Read and discuss the rule for the hard and soft sounds of **g**. Illustrate the difference in the sounds by writing some words on the board and identifying the words with soft **g** and the words with hard **g**. *Words to teach the concept:* Soft **g** words: gem, gentle, germ, genius, gelatin, gypsy, gesture, general. Hard **g** words: go, good, got, gave, get, gun, game, gift, gone. Discuss the pictures in the activity. Have the student identify each picture and determine whether the hard or soft sound of **g** is heard. Have the student underline all the pictures that begin with the sound of soft **g** first. Go through the activity again and draw a square around the pictures that begin with the hard **g** sound.
Pictures:

giraffe, garden, giant, gas, gym

Hard **g**:

garden, gas

Soft **g**:

giraffe, giant, gym

Reading. Read and discuss the maxim for the Lesson.

Read the poem *If a Pig Wore a Wig*. Preview the poem and explain words or sentence structures that are not familiar to the student.

Comprehension questions:

Do the clothes that one wears make a difference?

What is sometimes needed to solve a problem?

Read the story *Familiar Lessons on Animals*. Preview the story and explain words or sentence structures that are not familiar to the student.

Comprehension questions:

What are examples of some of the ways animals are different?

How do the differences in animals help them to live?

What are some of the "useful" animals?

Why are these animals useful?

Assign. Lesson activities or reading that are to be completed as homework.

Lesson 2: Final & Initial Consonant Sounds

Overview:

- Print ending consonant sounds in words
- Print beginning consonant letters
- Audio discrimination of consonant sounds
- Match **qu** pictures to words
- Complete words by writing the short vowel

Materials and Supplies:

- Teacher's Guide & Student Workbook 1
- White board or chalkboard
- Alphabet flashcards
- Reader: *Robinson Crusoe & Other Classic Stories*

Teaching Tips:

Review for Mastery. Discuss and review any work from the previous lesson that was assigned as homework. Check for completion of the activities and orally quiz the student for comprehension. Review any reading that was assigned, discussing the characters, setting, plot, theme, language, sequence, etc.

Strengthen fluency and phonemic awareness by reviewing words and sentences from previous lessons. Build vocabulary skills by using some of the words in sentences.

Review any letters that were found to need extra practice from the previous lesson. Do one letter at a time by holding up a letter flashcard, asking the students for the name of the letter, asking for the sound that the letter makes, and then asking them to write the lower case letter on the white board or on a sheet of paper. This program focuses on phonics so only have the students write the lower case letters and focus on writing skills by using the *Horizons Penmanship* program. Again sort out the letters that need review in future lessons.

Review the sound of the short vowels by having the student read the words in Lesson 1,

Activity 3. Pay special attention to the beginning and ending consonant sounds.

Review the hard and soft sounds of **c** and **g** by having the student review the pictures in Lesson 1, Activities 4 & 5.

Activity 1. Review the names of the pictures together, emphasizing the consonant sound at the end of the word. Have the student print the lower case consonant letters for the ending sound of each picture.

Pictures:
   book, dog, cab, vowel, off
   music, red, work, cub, end

Letters:
   k, g, b, l, f
   c, d, k, b, d

Activity 2. Review the names of the pictures together, emphasizing the consonant sound at the beginning of the word. Have the student print the lower case consonant letters for the beginning sound of each picture.

Pictures:
    night, saw, paper, man, table
    rat, mother, top, sound, picture

Letters:
    n, s, p, m, t
    r, m, t, s, p

Activity 3. Review the **qu** Rule and stress that **q** is always followed by **u**—they always appear together. Have the student write examples of the rule on the chalkboard or white board. Pay special attention to the **/kw/** sound of the **qu** spelling. *Words to teach the concept:* quite, quick, quit, queer, quiet, quack, quail, quake, quiz, quote, quill, quality. Have the student identify the pictures and draw a line to match the pictures with the words.

Pictures:
    quart   queen
    quilt   question mark

Activity 4. Review the names of the pictures together. Have the student print the lower case vowel for the sound of each picture.

Pictures:
    men, ill, cab, up, top
    run, hot, fan, bed, pig

Letters:
    e, i, a, u, o
    u, o, a, e, i

The letters *qu* make the *kw* sound that you hear in *queen* and *quick*.

3 Draw lines to match the pictures with the words.

question
queen
quilt
quart

4 The vowels are *a, e, i, o,* and *u.* Say the name of each picture. Finish the words under each picture with the short vowel sound.

men   ill   cab   up   top

run   hot   fan   bed   pig

4   *Final & Initial Consonant Sounds*

Reading. Read and discuss the maxim for the Lesson.

Read the story *Familiar Lessons on Time*. Preview the story and explain words or sentence structures that are not familiar to the student. With every story ask questions: who are the characters, what are they doing, what are they saying, where does the action take place, what is the order of events, what words are being used, what new information is given, what lesson can be learned?

Comprehension questions:
    What are some of the differences among the seasons?
    What things does time tell us?
    What are some of the things that happen during specific times of the day?
    What are some of the things that happen during specific times of the year?

Assign. Lesson activities or reading that are to be completed as homework.

Lesson 3: Final & Initial Consonant Sounds & Final Double Consonant Sound

Overview:

- Print ending consonant sounds in words
- Audio discrimination of consonant sounds
- Print beginning consonant letters
- Choose ending consonant sounds in words
- Blend consonant-vowel-consonant words
- Audio discrimination of short vowel sounds
- Match pictures to words

Materials and Supplies:

- Teacher's Guide & Student Workbook 1
- White board or chalkboard
- Alphabet flashcards
- Reader: *Robinson Crusoe & Other Classic Stories*

Teaching Tips:

Review for Mastery. Discuss and review any work from the previous lesson that was assigned as homework. Check for completion of the activities and orally quiz the student for comprehension. Review any reading that was assigned, discussing the characters, setting, plot, theme, language, sequence, etc.

Strengthen fluency and phonemic awareness by reviewing words and sentences from previous lessons. Build vocabulary skills by using some of the words in sentences.

Review letters and sounds that were found to need more practice in previous lessons with flashcards.

Review initial consonant sounds with Lesson 2, Activity 1. Review the name for each picture and ask the student to identify the beginning sound that he hears.

Review the sound of the short vowels by having the student read the words in Lesson 2, Activity 4. Pay special attention the beginning and ending consonant sounds.

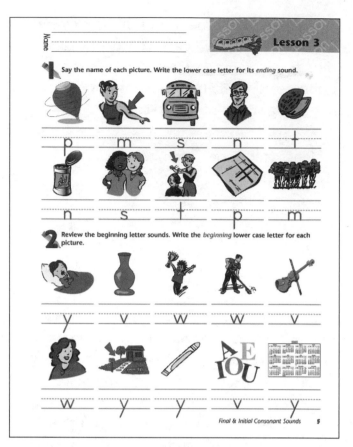

Activity 1. Review the names of the pictures together. Have the student print the lower case consonant letters for the ending sound of each picture.

Pictures:

**top, arm, bus, man, nut
can, us, cut, map, team**

Letters:

**p, m, s, n, t
n, s, t, p, m**

Activity 2. Review the names of the pictures together. Have the student print the lower case consonant for the beginning sound of each picture.

Pictures:

**yawn, vase, win, work, violin
woman, yard, yellow, vowel, year**

Letters:

**y, v, w, w, v
w, y, y, v, y**

Horizons Phonics & Reading Grade 2 Teacher's Guide

Activity 3. Read and discuss the rule for the **z** sound of **x**. *Words to teach the concept:* xerox, xylem, xylene, xenon. Review the names of the pictures together. Have the student fill in the circle by the correct letter for the beginning sound for each picture.

Pictures:

  zoo, week, zipper, van
  xylophone, yam, yak, zero

Letters:

  z, w, z, v
  z, y, y, z

Activity 4. Read and discuss the rule for the spelling of the final **s** sound. *Words to teach the concept:* Bess, bless, boss, brass, class, dress, grass, less, mess, press, truss. Read the words and review the pictures with the student. Have the student draw a line to match the pictures with the words. Have the student draw a slash through the final silent letter.

Pictures:

pass	**hiss**
kiss	**bass**
moss	**miss**
fuss	**loss**

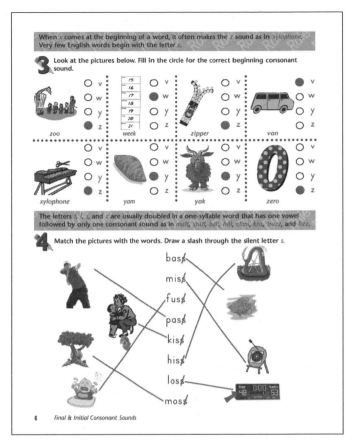

Reading. Read and discuss the maxim for the Lesson.

Read the story *Questions*. Preview the story and explain words or sentence structures that are not familiar to the student. With every story ask questions: who are the characters, what are they doing, what are they saying, where does the action take place, what is the order of events, what words are being used, what new information is given, what lesson can be learned?

Comprehension questions:
  What is similar about all of the questions?
  What is the moral of the story?
  Can the student make up some questions of his own?

Assign. Lesson activities or reading that are to be completed as homework.

Lesson 4: Medial Consonant Sounds, Syllable Rule, & Final Double Consonant Sound

Overview:

- Match pictures to words with final **x** sound
- Audio discrimination of consonant sounds
- Identify words with the final **z** sound
- Use the Syllable Rule to recognize words with more than one syllable
- Choose medial consonant sounds in words
- Audio discrimination of short vowel sounds
- Match pictures to words for final double consonant **zz**

Materials and Supplies:

- Teacher's Guide & Student Workbook 1
- White board or chalkboard
- Alphabet flashcards
- Phonics rules flashcards
- Reader: *Robinson Crusoe & Other Classic Stories*

Teaching Tips:

Review for Mastery. Discuss and review any work from the previous lesson that was assigned as homework. Check for completion of the activities and orally quiz the student for comprehension. Review any reading that was assigned, discussing the characters, setting, plot, theme, language, sequence, etc.

Strengthen fluency and phonemic awareness by reviewing words and sentences from previous lessons. Build vocabulary skills by using some of the words in sentences.

Review letters and sounds that were found to need more practice in previous lessons with flashcards.

Review previous phonics/spelling rules with flashcards.

Review initial consonant sounds with Lesson 3, Activity 1. Review the name for each picture and

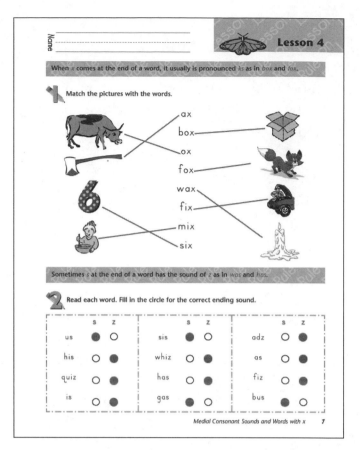

Medial Consonant Sounds and Words with x   7

ask the student to identify the beginning sound that he hears.

Review final consonant sounds with Lesson 3, Activity 2. Review the name for each picture and ask the student to identify the ending sound that he hears.

Activity 1. Review the rule for the sound of **x** at the end of a word. *Words to teach the concept:* tax, fax, relax, hex, lax, vex, prefix, complex, perplex. Read the words in the activity. Review the names of the pictures together and have the student draw a line to match the pictures with the words.

Pictures:

ox	**box**
ax	**fox**
six	**fix**
mix	**wax**

Activity 2. Review the rule for the **z** sound of **s** at the end of a word. *Words to teach the concept:* odds, news, says, suds, yours, tongs, days, ours, eyes. Review the words in each box together. Have the student fill in the circle under the correct letter for the final sound for each word.

Activity 2 continued:

Letters:

s	s	z
z	z	z
z	z	z
z	s	s

Activity 3. Review the Syllable Rule. *Words to teach the concept:* subject, object, problem, because, across, become, monkey, turkey, packing, under, order, idea, after, often, careful, beautiful, behind, unhappy, behave, behold, ahoy, enjoy, banjo, project, rejoice, below, along, follow, family. Review the names of the pictures together. Have the student fill in the circle by the correct letter for the medial sound for each picture.

Pictures:
body, ahead, major, baby
relax, before, broken, second

Letters:
d, h, j, b
l, f, k, c

Activity 4. Read and discuss the rule for the spelling of the final **z** sound. *Words to teach the concept:* pizzazz, razz, frizz, abuzz, whizz (also spelled whiz). Read the words and help the student identify the pictures. Have the student draw a line to match the pictures with the words. Have the student draw a slash through the final silent letter.

Pictures:
fizz	**jazz**
fuzz	**buzz**

Reading. Read and discuss the maxim for the Lesson.

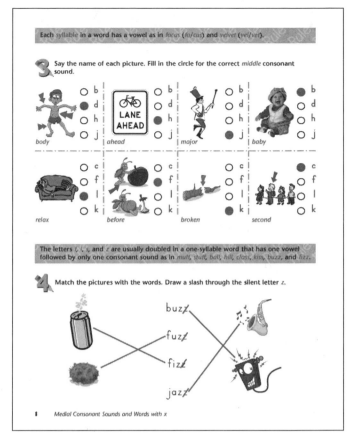

Read the story *The Fox and the Ducks.* Preview the story and explain words or sentence structures that are not familiar to the student.

Comprehension questions:
Where does this story take place?
Who are the characters in the story?
Can a fox really do the things in this story?
Who is this lesson written for?
What are some things that we see and do everyday where there could be some danger?
What are some difficult problems that we can solve by being creative?

Read the poem *Mix a Pancake.* Preview the poem and explain words or sentence structures that are not familiar to the student.

Comprehension questions:
What are the rhyming words in the poem?
What are the different vowel sounds heard in the words of this poem?

Assign. Lesson activities or reading that are to be completed as homework.

Lesson 5: Medial Consonant Sounds

Overview:

- Print medial consonant sounds in words
- Audio discrimination of consonant sounds
- Use the Syllable Rule to recognize words with more than one syllable
- Audio discrimination of short vowel sounds
- Sort words by their short vowel sound

Materials and Supplies:

- Teacher's Guide & Student Workbook 1
- White board or chalkboard
- Alphabet flashcards
- Phonics rules flashcards
- Reader: *Robinson Crusoe & Other Classic Stories*

Teaching Tips:

Review for Mastery. Discuss and review any work from the previous lesson that was assigned as homework. Check for completion of the activities and orally quiz the student for comprehension. Review any reading that was assigned, discussing the characters, setting, plot, theme, language, sequence, etc.

Strengthen fluency and phonemic awareness by reviewing words and sentences from previous lessons. Build vocabulary skills by using some of the words in sentences.

Review letters and sounds that were found to need more practice in previous lessons with flashcards.

Review previous phonics/spelling rules with flashcards.

Review initial and final consonant sounds with Lesson 4, Activity 3. Review the name for each picture and ask the student to identify the beginning and ending sound that he hears.

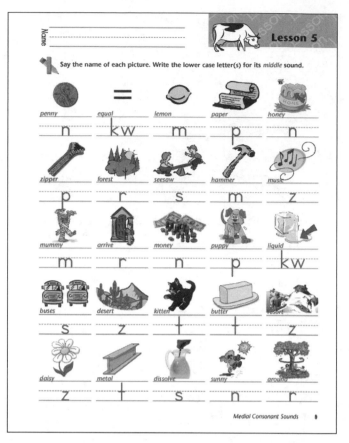

Activity 1. Review the Syllable Rule. Review the rule for the spelling of the **z** sound at the end of a word or syllable. Some of the words used in this activity have a middle **z** sound with the **s** spelling. *Words to teach the concept:* America, complete, tummy, many, country, any, animal, happy, important, liquid, equipment, equator, require, equation, very, merry, berry, also, person, answer, system, himself, easy, present, result, season, after, until, into, city. Review the names of the pictures together. Have the student print the lower case consonant letters for the middle consonant sound heard in each picture.

Pictures:

penny, equal, lemon, paper, honey
zipper, forest, seesaw, hammer, music
mummy, arrive, money, puppy, liquid
buses, desert, kitten, butter, resort
daisy, metal, dissolve, sunny, around

Activity 1 continued:

Letters:

   n, kw (qu), m, p, n

   p, r, s, m, z

   m, r, n, p, kw (qu)

   s, z, t, t, z

   z, t, s, n, r

Note the middle **z** sound spelled **s** in *music*, *resort*, *daisy*, and *desert*.

Note the **kw** sound of **qu** in *equal* and *liquid*.

Activity 2. Have the student read each of the short vowel words in the box. Have the student sort the short vowel words by writing them in the correct box.

Words:

   Short **a**: **tap, bad, rat**

   Short **e**: **den, web, let**

   Short **i**: **big, bid, kit**

   Short **o**: **got, top, sob**

   Short **u**: **put, us, sun**

Reading. Read and discuss the maxim for the Lesson.

Read the story *The Sheep and the Pig*. Preview the story and explain words or sentence structures that are not familiar to the student. With every story ask questions: who are the characters, what are they doing, what are they saying, where does the action take place, what is the order of events, what words are being used, what new information is given, what lesson can be learned?

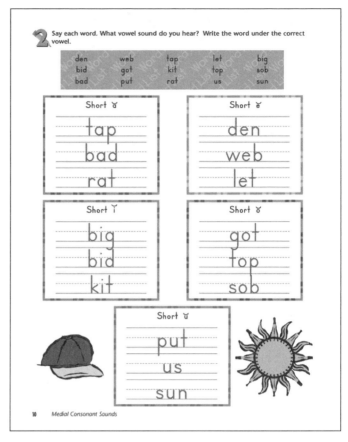

Comprehension questions:

   Where does this story take place?

   Who are the characters of the story?

   What were the animals learning to do?

   Why are the characters working together?

   What thing can you do well that might help someone else?

Assign. Lesson activities or reading that are to be completed as homework.

Lesson 6: Medial Consonant Sounds

Overview:

- Print medial consonant sounds in words
- Audio discrimination of short vowel sounds
- Identify vowels in words
- Identify the number of syllables in words
- Identify soft **c** and hard **c** sounds in words
- Identify soft **g** and hard **g** sounds in words

Materials and Supplies:

- Teacher's Guide & Student Workbook 1
- White board or chalkboard
- Alphabet flashcards
- Phonics rules flashcards
- Reader: *Robinson Crusoe & Other Classic Stories*

Teaching Tips:

Review for Mastery. Discuss and review any work from the previous lesson that was assigned as homework. Check for completion of the activities and orally quiz the student for comprehension. Review any reading that was assigned, discussing the characters, setting, plot, theme, language, sequence, etc.

Strengthen fluency and phonemic awareness by reviewing words and sentences from previous lessons. Build vocabulary skills by using some of the words in sentences.

Review previous phonics/spelling rules with flashcards.

Review initial and final consonant sounds with Lesson 5, Activity 2. Review the sorted words in the activity. Ask the student to form new words by using a different initial or final consonant for the words: tap = map or tan, den = pen or Deb, big = pig or bib, got = hot or gob, put = hut or pup, etc.

Activity 1. Review the Syllable Rule. *Words to teach the concept:* even, never, several, liver, forward, sandwich, aware, unwind, highway,

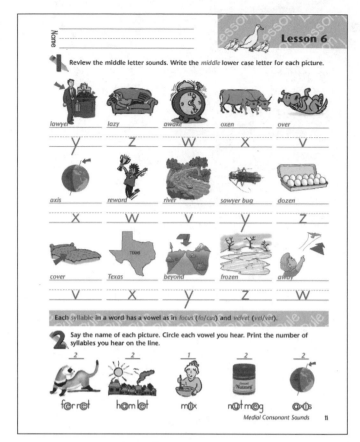

mixture, sixty, expert, Mexico, canyon, courtyard, barnyard, dooryard, backyard, crazy, puzzle, grazing. Review the names of the pictures together. Have the student print the lower case consonant letters for the middle consonant sound heard in each picture. Point out which syllable of each word is to be heard for the activity.

Pictures:
 lawyer, lazy, awake, oxen, over
 axis, reward, river, sawyer bug, dozen
 cover, Texas, beyond, frozen, away

Letters:
 y, z, w, x, v
 x, w, v, y, z
 v, x, y, z, w

Activity 2. Review the Syllable Rule. *Words to teach the concept:* insect, basket. Review the names of the pictures together. Have the student circle the vowels in each word. Have the student write the numbers of vowels each word has on the blank.

Words/Syllables:

ferret(2), hamlet(2), mix(1), nutmeg(2), axis(2)

Activity 3. Read and discuss the rule for the hard and soft sounds of **c**. Words to teach the concept with both a hard and soft **c** in each word: accept, accident, circle, concert, cancel, cyclone, cycle, circus. Discuss the pictures in the activity so the student can identify them correctly. Have the student determine whether the hard or soft sound of **c** is heard. Have the student underline all the pictures with the sound of hard **c** first. Go through the activity again and tell the student to circle the pictures that have the soft **c** sound.

Pictures:

call, face, camp, acid, truce
brace, country, dance, juice, carry

Hard **c**: **call, camp, country, carry**

Soft **c**: **face, acid, truce, brace, dance, juice**

Activity 4. Review the rule for the hard and soft sounds of **g**. *Words to teach the concept:* ginger, gigantic, geologist, geology. Discuss the pictures in the activity so the student can identify them correctly. Have the student determine whether the hard or soft sound of **g** is heard. Have the student underline all the pictures with the sound of soft **g** first. Go through the activity again and tell the student draw a square around the pictures that have the hard **g** sound.

Pictures:

gentle, good, gelatin, germ, game
got, digit, gas, engine, genius

Hard **g**:

good, game, got, gas

Soft **g**:

gentle, gelatin, germ, digit, engine, genius

Reading. Read and discuss the maxim for the Lesson.

Read the story *I Wish to be a Sailor*. This is the first chapter of the *Robinson Crusoe* story which will continue for many lessons. Preview

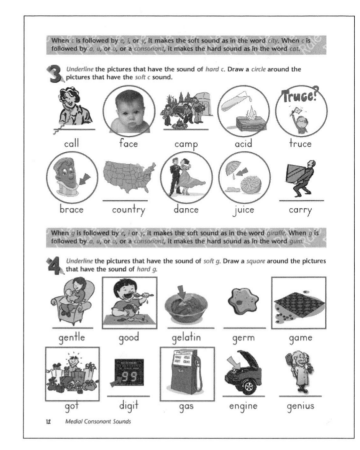

the story and explain words or sentence structures that are not familiar to the student. With every story ask questions: who are the characters, what are they doing, what are they saying, where does the action take place, what is the order of events, what words are being used, what new information is given, what lesson can be learned?

Comprehension questions:

When in Robinson's life does this story take place?
Who are the characters of the story?
Where does the story take place?
Why didn't Robinson's mother want him to go to sea?

Assign. Lesson activities or reading that are to be completed as homework.

Lesson 7: Final Double Consonant Sounds

Overview:

- Match pictures to words for final double consonant **ff**
- Identify the silent consonant in words with final double consonants
- Match pictures to words for final double consonant **ll**
- Identify words with the soft **c** and hard **c** sound
- Identify words with the soft **g** and hard **g** sound

Materials and Supplies:

- Teacher's Guide & Student Workbook 1
- White board or chalkboard
- Phonics rules flashcards
- Reader: *Robinson Crusoe & Other Classic Stories*

Teaching Tips:

Review for Mastery. Discuss and review any work from the previous lesson that was assigned as homework. Check for completion of the activities and orally quiz the student for comprehension. Review any reading that was assigned, discussing the characters, setting, plot, theme, language, sequence, etc.

Strengthen fluency and phonemic awareness by reviewing words and sentences from previous lessons. Build vocabulary skills by using some of the words in sentences.

Review previous phonics/spelling rules with flashcards.

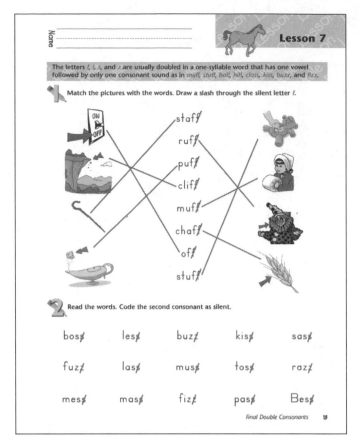

Activity 1. Review the rule for a double consonant after a short vowel. *Words to teach the concept:* stuff, buff, cuff, huff, tuff, Jeff, riff, skiff, stiff, tiff, whiff. Read the words in the activity. Discuss the pictures in the activity so that the student is able to identify them correctly. Have the student draw a line to match the pictures with the words. Have the student draw a slash through the final silent letter.

Pictures:

off	stuff
cliff	muff
staff	ruff
puff	chaff

Activity 2. Read the words in the activity. Identify the vowel in each word. Have the student draw a slash over the final silent letter. This activity reviews concepts from previous lessons.

Activity 3. Review the rule for a double consonant **ll** after a short vowel. *Words to teach the concept:* all, bill, bull, call, cull, dull, dwell, fell, full, grill, hall, hell, hill, hull, kill, mill, mull, poll, shell, skill, skull, stall, still, tall, till toll, wall, will, well. Discuss the pictures in the activity and read the words. Have the student draw a line to match the pictures with the words. Have the student draw a slash through the final silent letter.

Pictures:

ball	**pill**
gull	**roll**
fall	**spill**
bell	**tell**

Activity 4. Review and discuss the rule for the hard and soft sounds of **c** and **g**. Discuss the pictures in the activity so the student can identify them correctly. Have the student determine whether the hard or soft sound of **c** is heard or if the hard or soft sound of **g** is heard. Have the student underline all the pictures with the sound of soft **c** or **g** first. Go through the activity again and tell the student draw a square around the pictures that have the hard **c** or **g** sound.

Pictures:

  mice, can, voice, gallon, genuine

Hard **g**: **gallon**

Soft **g**: **genuine**

Hard **c**: **can**

Soft **c**: **mice**

Reading. Read and discuss the maxim for the Lesson.

Read the story *I Make My First Voyage*. This is another chapter of the *Robinson Crusoe* story which will continue for many lessons. Preview the story and explain words or sentence structures that are not familiar to the student. With every story ask questions: who are the characters, what are they doing, what are they saying, where does the action take place, what

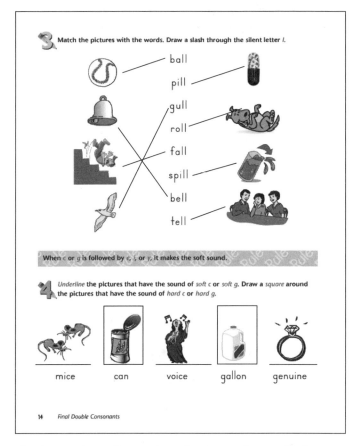

is the order of events, what words are being used, what new information is given, what lesson can be learned?

Comprehension questions:

  When in Robinson's life does this story take place?

  Who are the characters of the story?

  Where does the story take place?

  What event takes place in the story?

Read the poem *The Broken Doll*. Preview the poem and explain words or sentence structures that are not familiar to the student.

Comprehension questions:

  What are the **-ing** words in the poem?

  Who or what is doing the action?

  Where should Molly's attention be focused?

Assign. Lesson activities or reading that are to be completed as homework.

Lesson 8: Spellings of the k Sound

Overview:

- Identify the vowel that determines the spelling of the **k** sound in a word
- Use the spellings of the **k** sound to complete words
- Select the letter for the correct beginning sound of a word
- Select the letter for the correct ending sound of a word.
- Add a middle consonant to complete the spelling of a two-syllable word

Materials and Supplies:

- Teacher's Guide & Student Workbook 1
- White board or chalkboard
- Phonics rules flashcard
- Reader: *Robinson Crusoe & Other Classic Stories*

Teaching Tips:

Review for Mastery. Discuss and review any work from the previous lesson that was assigned as homework. Check for completion of the activities and orally quiz the student for comprehension. Review any reading that was assigned, discussing the characters, setting, plot, theme, language, sequence, etc.

Strengthen fluency and phonemic awareness by reviewing words and sentences from previous lessons. Build vocabulary skills by using some of the words in sentences.

Review short vowel sounds with Lesson 7, Activities 1 & 2. Read the words again and have the student mark the short vowels with a breve.

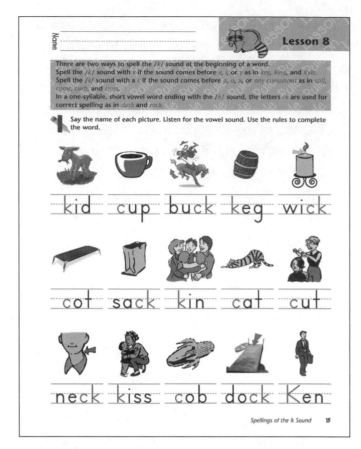

Activity 1. Read and discuss the rule about the spellings of the **k** sound. *Words to teach the concept:* call, come, came, camp, car, color, cold, could, carry, kind, key, kill, king, keep, kite, kitten, kettle, kick, keen, back, deck, Dick, duck, hack, hick, Jack, kick, lack, lick, lock, luck, mock, Nick, pack, peck, pick, puck, rack, Rick, rock, sick, sock, suck, tack, tick, tuck. In the words ending in **ck**, the **k** speaks and the **c** is silent. Ask for examples of other silent letters that have been covered so far (**ff, ll, ss, zz**). Compare the short vowel final **ck** words to long vowel words like bake, take, bike, Mike, poke, joke, puke, Luke. Discuss the pictures in this activity so that the student is able to identify them correctly. The student should use the rules to correctly spell the **k** sound in each word.

Pictures:

    kid, cup, buck, keg, wick
    cot, sack, kin, cat, cut
    neck, kiss, cob, dock Ken

Activity 2. Review initial consonant sounds with flashcards. Discuss the pictures in this activity so that the student is able to identify them correctly. The student will select the consonant for the initial sound heard in each picture.

Pictures:
  hat, fox, jar, dig
  pie, log, rug, mop

Letters:
  h, f, j, d
  p, l, r, m

Activity 3. Review final consonant sounds with flashcards. Discuss the pictures in this activity so that the student is able to identify them correctly. Have the student select the correct consonant for the ending sound heard in each picture.

Pictures:
  bib, pill, buzz, bat
  fox, miss, man, red

Letters:
  b, l, z, t
  x, s, n, d

Activity 4. Review middle consonant sounds with flashcards. Have the student add a consonant letter to complete the two-syllable words.

Words:
  under, oxen or **open, paper** or **pager, women** or **woven, relax**
  Other words may also be used.

Reading. Read and discuss the maxim for the Lesson.

Read the story *I See Much of the World*. This is another chapter of the *Robinson Crusoe* story which will continue for many lessons. Preview the story and explain words or sentence structures that are not familiar to the student. With every story ask questions: who are the characters, what are they doing, what are they saying, where does the action take place, what

is the order of events, what words are being used, what new information is given, what lesson can be learned?

Comprehension questions:
  Where did Robinson go to find a ship on which to sail?
  Where had the old sea captain often traveled?
  What kind of a man was the old sea captain?
  Which direction did the ship travel?
  Was this the only trip that Robinson made?
  Where else did Robinson travel?

Assign. Lesson activities or reading that are to be completed as homework.

Lesson 9: Short Vowel a

Overview:

- Recognize words with the short **a** sound
- Audio discrimination of the short **a** sound
- Complete words with the short **a** sound
- Read words with the short **a** sound

Materials and Supplies:

- Teacher's Guide & Student Workbook 1
- White board or chalkboard
- Phonics rules flashcard
- Reader: *Robinson Crusoe & Other Classic Stories*

Teaching Tips:

Review for Mastery. Discuss and review any work from the previous lesson that was assigned as homework. Check for completion of the activities and orally quiz the student for comprehension. Review any reading that was assigned, discussing the characters, setting, plot, theme, language, sequence, etc.

Strengthen fluency and phonemic awareness by reviewing words and sentences from previous lessons. Build vocabulary skills by using some of the words in sentences.

Review short vowel sounds with Lesson 8, Activity 1. Read the words again and have the student mark the short vowels with a breve (˘).

Review silent letters with the **ck** words from Lesson 8, Activity 1. Have the student code the **c** as silent.

Review the use of **c** or **k** to begin short vowel words by sorting the words from Lesson 8, Activity 1 on a sheet of paper by the initial consonant. After the words have been sorted, list the vowels used in each group. Compare these to the Rule.

Review the final and initial consonant sounds with the words from Lesson 8, Activities 2 & 3. Say the words for each picture and ask the

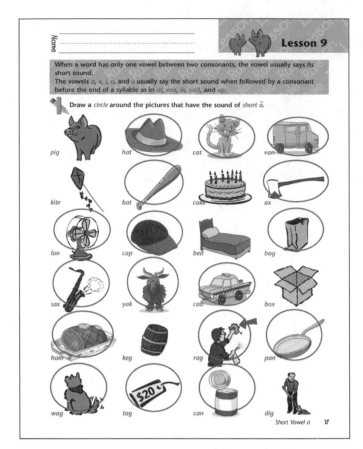

student to identify the final or initial consonant sound that he hears.

Activity 1. Read and discuss the Short Vowel Rule. *Words to teach the concept:* Can the man add? Has the man a tan? The man can gas the van. Dan can wax the cab. Demonstrate the correct diacritical markings for short vowels Discuss the pictures in each activity so that the student is able to identify them correctly. (**Optional:** You may have the students place diacritical markings on the short vowel **a** words.) Discuss each picture and have the student circle each picture with the short **a** sound.

Pictures:

  pig, hat, cat, van
  kite, bat, cake, ax
  fan, cap, bed, bag
  sax, yak, cab, box
  ham, keg, rag, pan
  wag, tag, can, dig

Short **a** words:

  hat, cat, van, bat, ax, fan, cap, bag, sax, yak, cab, ham, rag, pan, wag, tag, can

Note: In some resources, the words with **ag** endings are not considered as short vowel **a** words because they have a slightly different a sound.

Activity 2. Have the student complete the short **a** words given a beginning and ending letter. Not all of them form short **a** words.
Words:
  pat, sap, tab, yap
  bad, has, ban, rap
  gap, was, rat, man
  map, pat, lab, mad

Activity 3. Have the student add a beginning consonant to form a short **a** word. Answers will vary. Have the student read the words that they have formed. They should correct any that are not real words.

Activity 4. Have the student add an ending consonant to form a short **a** word. They can use double consonant letters. Answers will vary. Have the student read the words that they have formed. They should correct any that are not real words.

Reading. Read and discuss the maxim for the Lesson.

Read the story *I Undertake a New Venture*. This is another chapter of the *Robinson Crusoe* story. Preview the story and explain words or sentence structures that are not familiar to the student. With every story ask questions: who are the characters, what are they doing, what are they saying, where does the action take place, what is the order of events, what words are being used, what new information is given, what lesson can be learned?

Comprehension questions:
  Why did Robinson stop sailing?
  Where did Robinson go to open a plantation?
  What was needed for the plantation?
  Where did Robinson intend to go to get the things needed for the plantation?
  What was taken along on the ship?
  How many men went on the ship?

Assign. Lesson activities or reading that are to be completed as homework.

Lesson 10: Comparative ending -er

Overview:

- Define a root word
- Define a suffix
- Define a schwa vowel
- Identify the vowel and consonant of the 1-1-1 Rule
- Apply the 1-1-1 Rule to add the **-er** suffix to a root word
- Write new words with the **-er** suffix
- Compare one item to another with the **-er** suffix
- Read words with the **-er** suffix
- Use the **-er** suffix to indicate someone who

Materials and Supplies:

- Teacher's Guide & Student Workbook 1
- White board or chalkboard
- Phonics rules flashcards
- Reader: *Robinson Crusoe & Other Classic Stories*

Teaching Tips:

Review for Mastery. Discuss and review any work from the previous lesson that was assigned as homework. Check for completion of the activities and orally quiz the student for comprehension. Review any reading that was assigned, discussing the characters, setting, plot, theme, language, sequence, etc.

Strengthen fluency and phonemic awareness by reviewing words and sentences from previous lessons. Build vocabulary skills by using some of the words in sentences.

Review the final and initial consonant sounds with the words from Lesson 9, Activity 1. Say the words for each circled picture and ask the student to identify the final and initial consonant sounds that he hears.

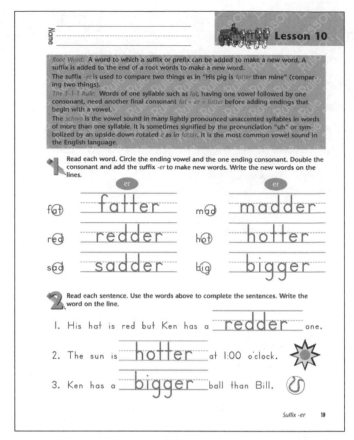

Activity 1. Read and review the rules about root words, suffixes, schwa and adding the **-er** suffix that compares. *Words to teach the concept:* bad-badder, wet-wetter, fit-fitter, fun-funner. Use these words in sample sentences so the student sees how the words compare two things. Have the student read each given word. Have the student circle the single short vowel and the single ending consonant in each word. Have the student write the new words with the **-er** suffix. Remind him to double the final consonant.

Words:
  fatter, madder
  redder, hotter
  sadder, bigger

Activity 2. Make up some sentences out of the root and the new word that compares in Activity 1. For example: "This ball is fat but the red one is fatter." Complete the sentences by choosing a word from Activity 1. Read the sentences that have been formed.

Activity 2 continued:

Sentences:

His hat is red but Ken has a <u>redder</u> one.

The sun is <u>hotter</u> at 1:00 o'clock.

Ken has a <u>bigger</u> ball than Bill.

Activity 3. Read and review the rules about root words, suffixes, schwa, and adding the **-er** suffix that means "a person who." *Words to teach the concept:* zap–zapper, gas–gasser, cap–capper, bid–bidder, fan–fanner, win–winner, tip–tipper, sip–sipper, tug–tugger. Use these words in sample sentences so the student sees how the words change to "a person who." Have the student read each given word. Have the student circle the single short vowel and the single ending consonant in each word. Have the student write the new words with the **-er** suffix.

Words:

batter, patter

tanner, tagger

runner, bagger

gunner, fogger

logger, tinner

sinner, tapper

lagger, rapper

fanner, napper

yapper, mapper

canner, banner

Make sentences out of the root and the new word that compare. For example: "Here is a bat but where is the batter?" "A tinner is one who works with tin." Do this for all of the words.

Review for Test. The instructor should plan to use some time at the end of the class to review and prepare for the test that follows this lesson. Review the objectives for the test and then look over the lessons that it will cover. If the student has struggled with any of the concepts that will be included in the test, some additional drill, practice, or review may be needed to adequately prepare him for the test.

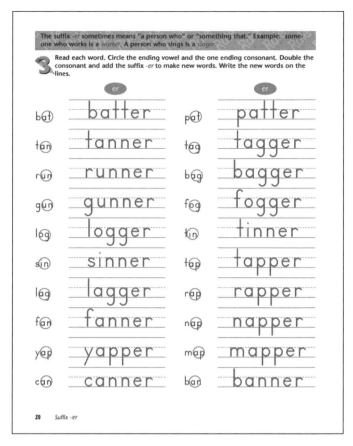

Reading. Read and discuss the maxim for the Lesson.

Read the story *I Am Shipwrecked*. This is another chapter of the *Robinson Crusoe* story. Preview the story and explain words or sentence structures that are not familiar to the student. With every story ask questions: who are the characters, what are they doing, what are they saying, where does the action take place, what is the order of events, what words are being used, what new information is given, what lesson can be learned?

Comprehension questions:

How many years had Robinson been away from his family?

Was Robinson happy to go to sea again?

How was the weather for the first few days that they were sailing on the sea?

What did they do during the storm?

What happened after land was sighted?

What happened to the small boat?

Assign. Lesson activities or reading that are to be completed as homework.

Test 1
Lessons 1–4

Overview:

- Audio discrimination of short vowel sounds
- Match pictures having the same vowel sound
- Audio discrimination of initial and final consonant sounds
- Audio discrimination of the **z** sound
- Read short vowel words with a silent final double consonant
- Read and sort words by the hard or soft sound of **c**
- Read and sort words by the hard or soft sound of **g**
- Write words given picture clues and letter choices

Materials and Supplies:

- Teacher's Guide & Student Workbook 1

Instructions:

Assessment Start-up. Have the student name all of the pictures in the test to make sure that he/she can identify them. Review the positions of beginning, middle, and end in words to make sure that the student understands the concept. Help the student pronounce all of the words in the test. Answer any questions the student may have. This test should not be timed.

Activity 1. Read the instruction with the student. Review the pictures, making sure the student can correctly identify them. Instruct the student to match the pictures that have the same vowel sound.

Pictures:

men	pen
pan	ax
off	hot
bus	up
pin	inch

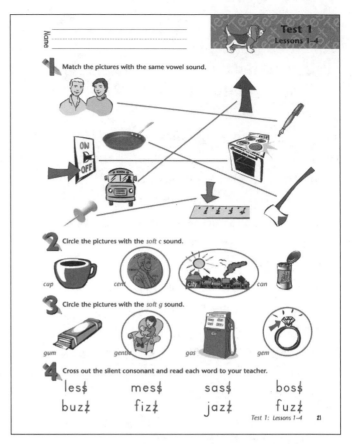

Activity 2. Read the instructions and the review the pictures with the student. Tell the student to circle the pictures that have the soft **c** sound.

Pictures:
   cup, cent, city, can

Hard **c**:
   cup, can

Soft **c**:
   cent, city

Activity 3. Read the instructions and the review the pictures with the student. Tell the student to circle the pictures that have the soft **g** sound.

Pictures:
   gum, gentle, gas, gem

Hard **g**:
   gum, gas

Soft **g**:
   gentle, gem

Activity 4. Read the instruction with the student. Instruct the student to cross out the silent letter in each word and listen as they read they words aloud.

Words:
  less, mess, sass, boss
  buzz, fizz, jazz, fuzz

Activity 5. Read the instruction with the student. Review the pictures, making sure the student can correctly identify them. Have the student select the initial consonant sound, the vowel sound, and the final consonant sound for each picture by filling in the circle by the letters. Finally, have the student write the word on the line.

Pictures:
  sun, box, mom, bed
  top, cat, dig, man

Activity 6. Read the instruction with the student. Review the pictures, making sure the student can correctly identify them. Instruct the student to circle the pictures that have the z sound.

Pictures:
  xylophone, fox, zoo
  zipper, news, quiz,
  ship, fizz, eyes

Words with z:
  xylophone, zoo
  zipper, news, quiz,
  fizz, eyes

Assessment Follow-up. Every test is an important assessment of both the student's comprehension of the concepts and the instructional process. This makes follow-up after each test essential to the learning process. Review all of the errors made on the test with the student. Check for understanding of the concepts and of the problem instructions. Compare the errors made on the test to the test objectives to identify specific areas of weakness. If weak areas of understanding are detected it might be necessary to go back to those lessons to devise some enrichment activities for the concept.

The test results can be used to determine what concepts are reviewed during the daily time of classroom instruction. Devise enrichment activities that will provide development in those areas.

If time permits, choose a selection and have the student read it again. This can also be used as a catch-up time to complete unfinished selections.

Lesson 11: Syllables in Short a Words

Overview:

- Identify short vowel **a** in words
- Identify the number of syllables in words
- Code the short **a** in words with a breve
- Identify the vowel in the second syllable of a word
- Read words with a schwa vowel
- Complete words with a short **a**
- Identify hard and soft **c** & **g** in two-syllable words

Materials and Supplies:

- Teacher's Guide & Student Workbook 1
- White board or chalkboard
- Phonics rules flashcards
- Reader: *Robinson Crusoe & Other Classic Stories*

Teaching Tips:

Review for Mastery. Discuss and review any work from the previous lesson that was assigned as homework. Check for completion of the activities and orally quiz the student for comprehension. Review any reading that was assigned, discussing the characters, setting, plot, theme, language, sequence, etc.

Strengthen fluency and phonemic awareness by reviewing words and sentences from previous lessons. Build vocabulary skills by using some of the words in sentences.

Review comparative ending **-er** with words from Lesson 10, Activity 1. Make up some sentences out of the root and the new word that compares.

Review ending **-er** with words from Lesson 10, Activity 2. Make up some sentences out of the root and the new word that tells "a person who."

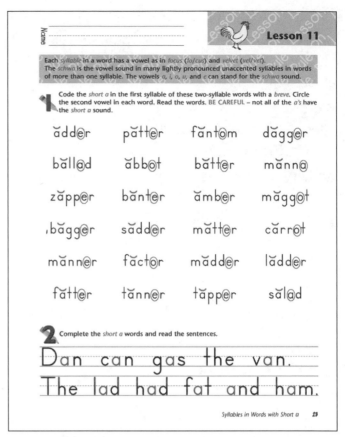

Activity 1. Review the Syllable Rule. Review the schwa sound and how it can be spelled. *Words to teach the concept:* patter, jabber, badder, banner, canner, hammer, tapper, hatter, latter, batter, lagger, nagger, tagger, fanner, canner, rapper, napper, mapper, fanner wagger. Have the student code the short **a** in the first syllable of the words with a breve. Remind them that an **a** in the second syllable of these words is a schwa sound. Next, have the student circle the second vowel in the words. Have the student read all of the words. Pay special attention to the slightly different sounds of the schwa as the words are read.

Activity 2. Complete the words by writing a letter **a** in the space. Read the sentences that have been formed.

Sentences:
  Dan can gas the van.
  The lad had fat and ham.

Activity 3. Review the Soft **c** or **g** Rule. Review the pictures and the words. Have the student *circle* the soft **c** or **g** found in the words. Have the student draw a *square* around the hard **c** or **g** in the words. These words can be difficult, so have the student focus on one syllable of the word at a time.

Words (hard sounds are underlined, the rest are soft):

geologist gigantic ginger Georgia geology
circle accept concert circus
cancel accident cycle cyclone

Activity 4. Complete the words by writing a letter a in the space. Read the sentences that have been formed.

Sentences:

The man can pat the cat.
Nat ran at the lab.

Reading. Read and discuss the maxim for the Lesson.

Read the story *I Am Cast Upon a Strange Shore*. This is another chapter of the *Robinson Crusoe* story. Preview the story and explain words or sentence structures that are not familiar to the student. With every story ask questions: who are the characters, what are they doing, what are they saying, where does the action take place, what is the order of events, what words are being used, what new information is given, what lesson can be learned?

Comprehension questions:

What does the word *cast* mean?
Where did Robinson find himself after the boat had turned over?
How did Robinson reach safety on the dry land?
Was Robinson able to see the ship from the shore?
What things did Robinson find along the shore?
What happened to the other men?

Assign. Lesson activities or reading that are to be completed as homework.

Lesson 12: Short e Words & Consonant Digraph ck

Overview:

- Recite the Short Vowel Rule
- Identify words that have the short **e** sound
- Complete words with a short **e** vowel
- Give an example of a consonant digraph
- Complete words with a final **ck** consonant digraph
- Read words that end with the **ck** consonant digraph

Materials and Supplies:

- Teacher's Guide & Student Workbook 1
- White board or chalkboard
- Alphabet flashcards
- Phonics rules flashcards
- Reader: *Robinson Crusoe & Other Classic Stories*

Teaching Tips:

Review for Mastery. Discuss and review any work from the previous lesson that was assigned as homework. Check for completion of the activities and orally quiz the student for comprehension. Review any reading that was assigned, discussing the characters, setting, plot, theme, language, sequence, etc.

Strengthen fluency and phonemic awareness by reviewing words and sentences from previous lessons. Build vocabulary skills by using some of the words in sentences.

Review phonetic sounds using alphabet flashcards.

Activity 1. Read and discuss the Short Vowel Rule. *Words to teach the concept:* beg, egg, gem, led, less, mess, met, peck, pen, sell, Ted, tell, web, wed, well, yell, yes, Zed. Discuss each picture so that the student can correctly identify them. Instruct the student to draw a square around the pictures that have the short **e** sound.

Pictures:
  **bed, fed, hen, shed, desk
  red, vet, net, rat, wet
  tent, peg, hat, ten, jet**

Answers:
  **bed, fed, hen, shed, desk
  red, vet, net, wet
  tent, peg, ten, jet**

Activity 2. Have the student complete the short **e** words given an beginning and ending letter. Not all of them form short **a** words. Read the words to the teacher.

Words:
  **pet, set, den, yet
  Ned, Ben, get
  let, leg, Wes, bet, men**

Activity 3. Review the rule for the spelling of the **k** sound at the end of a short vowel word. "In a one-syllable, short vowel word ending with the /**k**/ sound, the letters **ck** are used for correct spelling." Review the definition for a consonant digraph and the rule for pronouncing the **ck** digraph. *Words to teach the concept:* buck, deck, Dick, duck, hack, kick, lack, muck, neck, Nick, pick, rack, Rick, sack, sick, sock, suck, tack, tuck, wick. Discuss each picture so that the student can correctly identify them. Have the student complete the words by adding a **ck** ending. Read the words.

Pictures:
  back, dock, lick, attack
  tick, jack, rock, deck
  pack, peck, puck, lock
  duck, hack, luck, rack

Reading. Read and discuss the maxim for the Lesson.

Read the story *I Find a Strange Lodging Place*. This is another chapter of the *Robinson Crusoe* story. Preview the story and explain words or sentence structures that are not familiar to the student. With every story ask questions: who are the characters, what are they doing, what are they saying, where does the action take place, what is the order of events, what words are being used, what new information is given, what lesson can be learned?

Comprehension questions:
  What was the time of day?
  What questions did Robinson asked himself?
  Why was Robinson afraid?
  Where did Robinson fix a place to sleep?
  What did Robinson make to protect himself?
  How well did Robinson sleep in the tree?

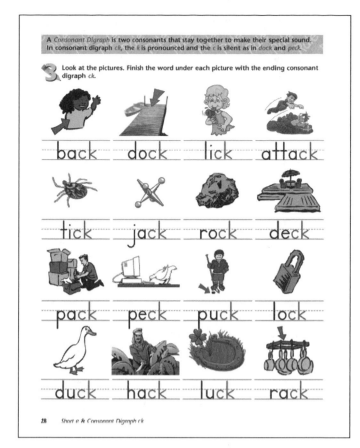

A *Consonant Digraph* is two consonants that stay together to make their special sound. In consonant digraph *ck*, the *k* is pronounced and the *c* is silent as in *dock* and *peck*.

Look at the pictures. Finish the word under each picture with the ending consonant digraph *ck*.

back   dock   lick   attack
tick   jack   rock   deck
pack   peck   puck   lock
duck   hack   luck   rack

28   *Short e & Consonant Digraph ck*

Read the poem *The Kitchen Clock*. Preview the poem and explain words or sentence structures that are not familiar to the student.

Comprehension questions:
  What words in the poem say the **k** sound?
  What things does the clock tell besides time?
  What are the rhyming words in the poem?

Assign. Lesson activities or reading that are to be completed as homework.

Lesson 13: Hard & Soft Digraph th & Syllables in Short e Words

Overview:

- Define the term "consonant digraph"
- Complete words that begin, end, or have a middle **th** consonant digraph
- Read words that begin, end, or have a middle **th** consonant digraph
- Identify the hard or soft **th** sound heard in a word
- Identify vowels in words
- Identify the number of syllables in words
- Code the short **e** in words with a breve
- Identify the vowel in the second syllable of a word
- Read words with a schwa vowel

Materials and Supplies:

- Teacher's Guide & Student Workbook 1
- White board or chalkboard
- Word cards (as necessary)
- Phonics rules flashcards
- Reader: *Robinson Crusoe & Other Classic Stories*

Teaching Tips:

Review for Mastery. Discuss and review any work from the previous lesson that was assigned as homework. Check for completion of the activities and orally quiz the student for comprehension. Review any reading that was assigned, discussing the characters, setting, plot, theme, language, sequence, etc.

Strengthen fluency and phonemic awareness by reviewing words and sentences from previous lessons. Build vocabulary skills by using some of the words in sentences.

Review the **ck** ending in short vowels words from Lesson 12, Activity 3. Have the student code the short vowel with a breve and draw a slash over the silent **c** in each word. Say the words and use them in a sentence.

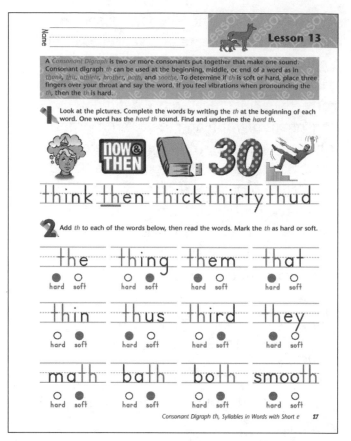

Consonant Digraph th, Syllables in Words with Short e   17

Activity 1. Review the Consonant Digraph Rule. Review the rule for the soft or hard **th** sound. *Words to teach the concept:* (voiceless **th**: thank, thought, thumb, thunder, thaw, thief, thigh, thistle, thorn, thump) (voiced **th**: this, there, than, these, thee, those, their). Review the pictures with the student. Have the student complete the words in the activity by adding a beginning **th** consonant digraph. Then have the student underline the **th** in the word with the hard sound.

Words:

  think, <u>then</u>, thick, thirty, thud

Activity 2. Review the Consonant Digraph Rule. Review the rule for the soft or hard **th** sound. *Words to teach the concept:* (voiceless **th**: Beth, booth, breath, broth, cloth, death, fifth, lath, moth, mouth, myth, ninth, path, south, teeth, tooth, truth, with, worth, wrath, wreath) (voiced **th**: teethe, soothe). Have the student add the consonant digraph **th** to the beginning or ending of the words. Read the words that have been formed. Select whether the **th** heard in each word is hard or soft.

Horizons Phonics & Reading Grade 2 Teacher's Guide

Activity 2 continued:

Words:
  the, thing, them, that
  thin, thus, third, they
  math, bath, both, smooth

Hard **th**:
  the, them, that, thus, they, smooth

Soft **th**:
  thing, thin, third, math, bath, both

Activity 3. Review the Consonant Digraph Rule. Review the rule for the soft or hard **th** sound. *Words to teach the concept:* (voiceless **th**: something, athlete, breathing, faithful, python) (voiced **th**: brother, father, although, clothing, either, weather, rhythm, farther, leather, northern, feather, weather). Discuss compound words as being two words put together to form a new word. *Words to teach the concept:* bathhouse, bathmat, bathwater, toothache, toothpaste, toothpick. Have the student add the consonant digraph **th** to the middle of the words. Read the words that have been formed. Select whether the **th** heard in each word is hard or soft.

Words:
  mother, bathtub, bother
  author, other, gather
  nothing, toothbrush

Hard **th**:
  mother, bother, other, gather

Soft **th**:
  bathtub, author, nothing, toothbrush

Activity 4. Review the Syllable Rule. Review the rule for the schwa sound. *Words to teach the concept:* member, tenter, cellar, elder. Have the student code the short **e** in the words with a breve. Remind them that an **e** in the second syllable of these words is a schwa sound. Next, have the student circle the second vowel in the words. Have the student read all of the words.

Reading. Read and discuss the maxim for the Lesson.

Read the story *I Visit the Wreck*. This is another chapter of the *Robinson Crusoe* story. Preview the story and explain words or sentence structures that are not familiar to the student. With every story ask questions: who are the characters, what are they doing, what are they saying, where does the action take place, what is the order of events, what words are being used, what new information is given, what lesson can be learned?

Comprehension questions:
  What was the weather like when Robinson woke up?
  What had happened to the ship?
  How far away was the ship?
  What would have happened if the men had stayed on the ship?
  How did Robinson get onto the ship?
  Where did Robinson go on the ship?

Assign. Lesson activities or reading that are to be completed as homework.

Lesson 14: Consonant Digraph sh & Short Vowel i

Overview:

- Define the term "consonant digraph"
- Complete words that begin or end with the **sh** consonant digraph
- Read words that begin or end with the **sh** consonant digraph
- Auditory discrimination of the **sh** sound
- Recite the Short Vowel Rule
- Identify words that have the short **i** sound
- Complete words with a short **i** vowel
- Read words with a short **i** vowel

Materials and Supplies:

- Teacher's Guide & Student Workbook 1
- White board or chalkboard
- Word cards (as necessary)
- Phonics rules flashcard
- Reader: *Robinson Crusoe & Other Classic Stories*

Teaching Tips:

Review for Mastery. Discuss and review any work from the previous lesson that was assigned as homework. Check for completion of the activities and orally quiz the student for comprehension. Review any reading that was assigned, discussing the characters, setting, plot, theme, language, sequence, etc.

Strengthen fluency and phonemic awareness by reviewing words and sentences from previous lessons. Build vocabulary skills by using some of the words in sentences.

Review soft and hard **th** by reviewing the words in Lesson 13, Activities 1, 2, & 3. Read all of the words again and listen for the **th** sound.

Activity 1. Review the Consonant Digraph Rule. Teach the **sh** consonant digraph. *Words to teach the concept:* she, shall, short, shape, shirt, sheet, shoe, blush, crash, flash, fresh, hush, trash. Review the pictures with the student. Have the student complete the words in the activity by adding a beginning or ending **sh** consonant digraph.

Words:

wash, rush, shed, shot, shut

Activity 2. Review the pictures with the student. Have the student select whether there is a beginning or ending **sh** consonant digraph in each picture.

Pictures:

shack, fi**sh**, **sh**ip, ma**sh**, **sh**op

Activity 3. Have the student add the consonant digraph **sh** to the beginning or ending of the words. Read the words that have been formed.

Words:

shad, sham, shep, cash
Nash, shag, shell, gush

Activity 4. Review the Short Vowel Rule and the short **i** sound. *Words to teach the concept:* bib, bid, big, chin, chip, did, dim, dip, fin, fit, fix, hid, him, hip, his, hit, in, ink, into, Jill, lip, mix, pig, rib, rip, sin, six, thin, thin, will, win. Discuss each picture so that the student can correctly identify them. Instruct the student to draw a square around the pictures that have the short **i** sound.

Pictures:
  hill, dig, ill, miss, mitt
  mill, fish, rat, wig, six
  ink, sip, spin, net, bib

Answers:
  hill, dig, ill, miss, mitt
  mill, fish, wig, six
  ink, sip, spin, bib

Activity 5. Have the student complete the short **i** words given ending and/or beginning letter(s). Not all of the letters can be used to form short **i** words. Then read the words that have been formed.

Words:
  it, rip, sin
  if, wish, Bill, is
  exit, until, with, gig
  this, will hiss, miss

Note: Always remind the student of how rules previously covered apply to new words that are being introduced. In this activity there are several short vowel words that use the Doubling Rule for consonants **f**, **l**, **s**, and **z** at the end of a word.

Reading. Read and discuss the maxim for the Lesson.

Read the story *I Make Me a Raft*. This is another chapter of the *Robinson Crusoe* story. Preview the story and explain words or sentence structures that are not familiar to the student. With every story ask questions: who are the characters, what are they doing, what are they saying, where does the action take place, what is the order of events, what words are being used, what new information is given, what lesson can be learned?

Comprehension questions:
  What did Robinson find to eat on the ship?
  Why couldn't Robinson easily take the items from the ship the shore?
  How did Robinson solve the problem of getting supplies to the shore?
  What things were loaded onto the raft?
  What heavy item was loaded onto the raft?

Assign. Lesson activities or reading that are to be completed as homework.

Lesson 15: Consonant Digraph ch & Short Vowel o

Overview:

- Define the term "consonant digraph"
- Identify words that begin or end with the **ch** consonant digraph
- Read words that begin or end with the **ch** consonant digraph
- Match words with the **ch** consonant diagraph to the picture
- Recite the Short Vowel Rule
- Identify words that have the short **o** sound
- Complete words with a short **o** vowel
- Read words with a short **o** vowel

Materials and Supplies:

- Teacher's Guide & Student Workbook 1
- White board or chalkboard
- Word cards (as necessary)
- Phonics rules flashcards
- Reader: *Robinson Crusoe & Other Classic Stories*

Teaching Tips:

Review for Mastery. Discuss and review any work from the previous lesson that was assigned as homework. Check for completion of the activities and orally quiz the student for comprehension. Review any reading that was assigned, discussing the characters, setting, plot, theme, language, sequence, etc.

Strengthen fluency and phonemic awareness by reviewing words and sentences from previous lessons. Build vocabulary skills by using some of the words in sentences.

Review the short vowels **a** & **e** with words from Lesson 14, Activity 3. Code the vowels with a breve and read the words.

Review the short vowel **i** with words from Lesson 14, Activity 5. Code the vowels with a breve and read the words.

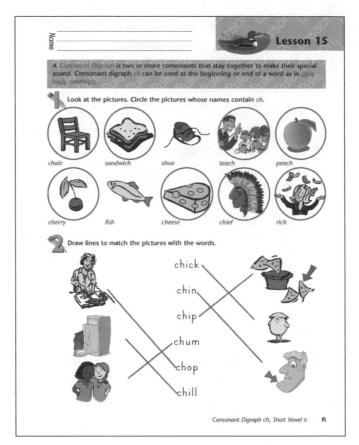

Activity 1. Review the Consonant Digraph Rule. Review the **ch** Consonant Digraph Rule. *Words to teach the concept:* child, church, chart, change, chance, chest, cheer, chain, chair, check, chase, which, each, branch, touch, reach. Review the pictures with the student. Have the student circle the pictures with a beginning or ending **ch** consonant digraph.

Pictures:
chair, sandwich, shoe, teach, peach
cherry, fish, cheese, chief, rich

Answers:
chair, sandwich, teach, peach
cherry, cheese, chief, rich

Activity 2. Review the pictures with the student. Have the student read the words. Then have the student match the picture to the correct word.

Pictures:
chop	chip
chill	chick
chum	chin

Note: The word *chick* reviews the **ck** spelling of the **k** sound at the end of a short vowel word.

Activity 3. Review the Short Vowel Rule and the short **o** sound. *Words to teach the concept:* Bob, bond, box, chop, cob, cot, Don, fox, from, God, got, hog, job, jot, lot, mom, nod, not, odd, pop, sob, Tom. Discuss each picture so that the student can correctly identify them. Instruct the student to draw a circle around the pictures that have the short **o** sound.

Pictures:
   lock, fox, cob, mop, shot
   dock, pop, rat, on, top
   sock, pot, hog, net, dog

Answers:
   lock, fox, cob, mop, shot
   dock, pop, on, top
   sock, pot, hog, dog

Activity 5. Have the student complete the short **o** words given an ending and/or a beginning letter(s). Then read the words that have been formed.

Words:
   shock, moss, shop, shot, oxen
   hock, tock, doll, Bob, odd
   Ross, hotdog, popup, cannot

Note the compound words formed in this activity.

Reading. Read and discuss the maxim for the Lesson.

Read the story *I Carry Some Things Ashore*. This is another chapter of the *Robinson Crusoe* story. Preview the story and explain words or sentence structures that are not familiar to the student. With every story ask questions: who are the characters, what are they doing, what are they saying, where does the action take place, what is the order of events, what words are being used, what new information is given, what lesson can be learned?

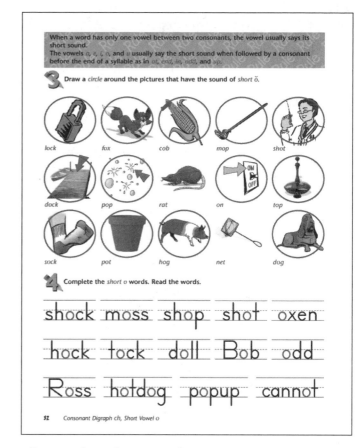

When a word has only one vowel between two consonants, the vowel usually says its short sound.
The vowels *a, e, i, o,* and *u* usually say the short sound when followed by a consonant before the end of a syllable as in *at, end, in, odd,* and *up.*

3 Draw a *circle* around the pictures that have the sound of *short ŏ.*

lock · fox · cob · mop · shot
dock · pop · rat · on · top
sock · pot · hog · net · dog

4 Complete the *short o* words. Read the words.

shock · moss · shop · shot · oxen
hock · tock · doll · Bob · odd
Ross · hotdog · popup · cannot

51   *Consonant Digraph ch, Short Vowel o*

Comprehension questions:
   What time was it?
   What did Robinson realize was missing from the things he had loaded on the raft?
   What was the weather like?
   What helped carry the raft toward the shore?
   Where did the tide first carry the raft?
   What left the raft high and dry on the land?

Assign. Lesson activities or reading that are to be completed as homework.

Lesson 16: Consonant digraph tch

Overview:

- Identify words that have the **tch** sound
- Auditory discrimination of the **tch** sound
- Complete words that end with **tch**
- Apply the rule to correctly spell the **ch** sound
- Read words with the **tch** ending
- Complete sentences with **tch** words
- Unscramble words with the **tch** ending

Materials and Supplies:

- Teacher's Guide & Student Workbook 1
- White board or chalkboard
- Word cards (as necessary)
- Phonics rules flashcards
- Reader: *Robinson Crusoe & Other Classic Stories*

Teaching Tips:

Review for Mastery. Discuss and review any work from the previous lesson that was assigned as homework. Check for completion of the activities and orally quiz the student for comprehension. Review any reading that was assigned, discussing the characters, setting, plot, theme, language, sequence, etc.

Strengthen fluency and phonemic awareness by reviewing words and sentences from previous lessons. Build vocabulary skills by using some of the words in sentences.

Review the short vowels **a**, **e**, and **i** with words from Lesson 15, Activity 2. Code the vowels with a breve and read the words.

Review the short vowel **o** with words from Lesson 15, Activity 4. Code the vowels with a breve and read the words.

Activity 1. Go over the rule and the examples. Have the student think of additional examples of the rule. Make word cards for the words in the lesson as necessary. *Words to teach the concept:* clutch, crutch, glitch, sketch, snatch, snitch, stitch, stretch, switch, wretch. Compare some words that begin or end with ch to ones that end in **tch**. *Words to teach the concept:* chair, cherry, cheese, chief, chin, chip, chum, chop, teach, sandwich, peach, rich. Review the **tch** Consonant Digraph Rule. Review the pictures with the student. Have the student circle the pictures with an ending **tch** consonant digraph.

Pictures:
   watch, catch, cup, pitch, sock
   fetch, match, patch, latch, itch

Answers:
   watch, catch, pitch
   fetch, match, patch, latch, itch

Activity 2. Have the student complete the words ending in **tch**. Read the words that are formed. Emphasize the short vowel sound heard in the words.

Horizons Phonics & Reading Grade 2 Teacher's Guide

Activity 2 continued:

Words:

batch, witch, ditch, hatch
retch, Mitch, hitch, botch
etch, Dutch, notch, hutch
nuthatch

Activity 3. Have the student read each of the **tch** words in the box. Assist the student as needed to read and complete the sentences.

Sentences:

1. I use a <u>watch</u> to tell time.
2. We store our plates in a <u>hutch</u>.
3. I like to <u>catch</u> the ball when it is thrown to me.
4. Most of my socks <u>match</u>.
5. Mom made a <u>batch</u> of cookies

Activity 4. Have the student read each of the **tch** words in the box. The student is to unscramble the words and write them on the line.

Words:

notch	match
ditch	itch
watch	hitch

Reading. Read and discuss the maxim for the Lesson.

Read the story *I Learn That I Am On an Island*. This is another chapter of the *Robinson Crusoe* story. Preview the story and explain words or sentence structures that are not familiar to the student. With every story ask questions: who are the characters, what are they doing, what are they saying, where does the action take place, what is the order of events, what words are being used, what new information is given, what lesson can be learned?

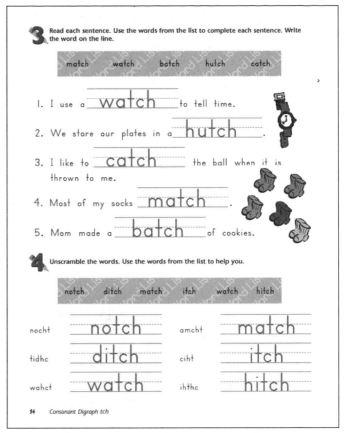

Comprehension questions:

What is the meaning of the phrase, "the sun was still two hours high?"

Where did Robinson go to explore?

What did Robinson take along when he went to explore?

What did Robinson see from the top of the hill?

How big was the island?

Why did Robinson feel sad?

Where did Robinson sleep the second night?

Assign. Lesson activities or reading that are to be completed as homework.

Lesson 17: Review Consonant Digraphs, ck, th, sh, ch & tch

Overview:

- Complete words for a picture by adding the correct consonant digraph
- Read words with initial and final consonant digraphs
- Read words with inflected endings
- Match words with consonant digraphs to the picture

Materials and Supplies:

- Teacher's Guide & Student Workbook 1
- White board or chalkboard
- Word cards (as necessary)
- Phonics rules flashcards
- Reader: *Robinson Crusoe & Other Classic Stories*

Teaching Tips:

Review for Mastery. Discuss and review any work from the previous lesson that was assigned as homework. Check for completion of the activities and orally quiz the student for comprehension. Review any reading that was assigned, discussing the characters, setting, plot, theme, language, sequence, etc.

Strengthen fluency and phonemic awareness by reviewing words and sentences from previous lessons. Build vocabulary skills by using some of the words in sentences.

Review the short vowels **a**, **e**, **i**, and **o** with words from Lesson 16, Activity 2. Code the vowels with a breve and read the words.

Review words and rules from Lessons 12-16 to prepare the student for this lesson. Pay special attention to the digraph rules covered in previous lessons and the soft and hard sound of the **th** digraph. Use the white board to illustrate examples of all rules.

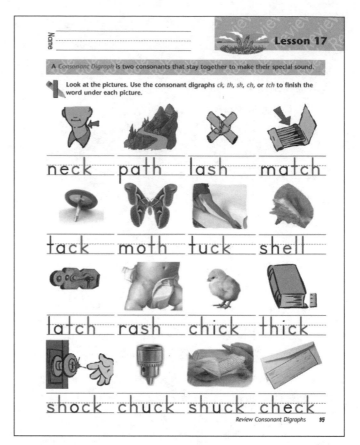

Activity 1. Review the pictures with the student. Review the digraphs that can be used to complete the words. Have the students complete the words using the digraphs listed in the instructions.

Words:
   neck, path, lash, match
   tack, moth, tuck, shell
   latch, rash, chick, thick
   shock, chuck shuck, check

Note the voiceless **th** in *path*, *moth*, and *thick*.

Activity 2. Review inflected ending **-er** which is used in these words. Inflection: An alteration of the form of a word by the addition of an affix, as in English *dogs* from *dog*, or by changing the form of a base, as in English *spoke* from *speak*, that indicates grammatical features such as number, person, mood, or tense. Review the pictures with the student. Have the student read the words. Then have the student match the picture to the correct word.

Pictures:

sacker	sucker
brother	mother
shatter	pitcher
kicker	musher
pusher	catcher
gather	father
	shutter

Note the voiced **th** in *gather*, *father*, *mother*, and *brother*.

Note: The **u** sound of **o** has not been covered in *mother* and *brother*. It will be covered in a later lesson.

Reading. Read and discuss the maxim for the Lesson.

Read the story *I Have a Strange Visitor*. This is another chapter of the *Robinson Crusoe* story. Preview the story and explain words or sentence structures that are not familiar to the student. With every story ask questions: who are the characters, what are they doing, what are they saying, where does the action take place, what is the order of events, what words are being used, what new information is given, what lesson can be learned?

2 Read the words. Draw lines to match the pictures with the words.

catcher
pitcher
kicker
shutter
pusher
musher
sucker
sacker
gather
father
mother
brother
shatter

96   *Review Consonant Digraphs*

Comprehension questions:
   When did Robinson return to the ship?
   What was the first thing Robinson did on his second visit to the ship?
   What did Robinson load onto the raft?
   What unusual thing did Robinson find when he got back from the ship?
   What did Robinson do after he got back from the ship?

Assign. Lesson activities or reading that are to be completed as homework.

Lesson 18: Final Consonant Blends & Short Vowel u

Overview:

- Define a consonant blend
- Select the ending consonant blend for the sound of a word
- Complete words with the correct ending consonant blend
- Read words with ending consonant blends
- Complete words by adding a consonant and a vowel to an ending blend
- Complete words with the short **u** sound
- Read words with the short **u** sound

Materials and Supplies:

- Teacher's Guide & Student Workbook 1
- White board or chalkboard
- Word cards (as necessary)
- Phonics rules flashcards
- Reader: *Robinson Crusoe & Other Classic Stories*

Teaching Tips:

Review for Mastery. Discuss and review any work from the previous lesson that was assigned as homework. Check for completion of the activities and orally quiz the student for comprehension. Review any reading that was assigned, discussing the characters, setting, plot, theme, language, sequence, etc.

Strengthen fluency and phonemic awareness by reviewing words and sentences from previous lessons. Build vocabulary skills by using some of the words in sentences.

Review the short vowels **a**, **e**, **i**, and **o** with words from Lesson 17, Activity 1. Code the vowels with a breve and read the words.

Activity 1. Discuss the rule for the consonant blends with **t** and the sample words. *Words to teach the concept:* attract, conduct, deduct, direct, erect, react, strict, tract, cleft, craft, draft, drift, swift, theft, fault, insult, knelt, result, count,

flint, grant, joint, meant, paint, plant, stunt, leapt, slept, blurt, concert, court, desert, flirt, heart, skirt, least, blast, east, feast, host, most, trust, wrist. Discuss the pictures in this activity so that the student is able to identify them correctly. The student will select the consonant blend for the final sound heard in each picture.

Pictures:
  raft, duct, dent, belt
  dart, wept, next, nest

Letters:
  ft, ct, nt, lt
  rt, pt, xt, st

Activity 2. Have the student complete the words ending in **nt**. Read the words that have been formed.

Words:
  cent, hint, pant, chant
  hunt, sent, ant, bent

Note the consonant digraph **ch** at the beginning of the word *chant*.

Note the **s** sound of **c** in *cent* and the homonym *sent*.

Horizons Phonics & Reading Grade 2 Teacher's Guide

Activity 3. Have the student complete the words ending in **lt**. Read the words that have been formed.

Words:
  gilt, hilt, pelt, silt
  felt, cult, kilt, welt

Activity 4. Review the pictures with the student. Review the consonant blends that are being used to complete the words. Have the students complete the words using a consonant or consonant blend and a short vowel. Read the words that have been formed.

Words:
  rust, rest, soft, act, best
  gift, fast, shift, pact, last

Activity 5. Have the student complete the words ending in **st**. Read the words that have been formed.

Words:
  lest, pest, west, zest, test

Activity 6. Review the Short Vowel Rule and the short **u** sound. *Words to teach the concept:* until, ugly, uncle, usher, upset, umbrella, must, just, sudden, funny, hunt. Have the student complete the short **u** words given an ending and/or beginning letter. Not all of them form short **u** words. Read the words that have been formed.

Words:
  us, run, sum
  up, shut, bull, rub
  but, gull, thus, hull
  upper, cutter, buzzer
  mugger, rubber

Reading. Read and discuss the maxim for the Lesson.

Read the story *I Find a Great Store of Things*. This is another chapter of the *Robinson Crusoe* story. Preview the story and explain words or sentence structures that are not familiar to the student. With every story ask questions: who

are the characters, what are they doing, what are they saying, where does the action take place, what is the order of events, what words are being used, what new information is given, what lesson can be learned?

Comprehension questions:
  How many times did Robinson return to the ship?
  What was left on the ship?
  What did Robinson find on this trip to the ship?
  What made Robinson return to the shore?
  What happened after Robinson got back to the shore?

Assign. Lesson activities or reading that are to be completed as homework.

Lesson 19: Final Consonant Blends & Comparative Endings -er & -est

Overview:

- Define a consonant blend
- Select the ending consonant blend for the sound of a word
- Complete words with the correct ending consonant blend
- Read words with ending consonant blends
- Identify root words
- Use the 1-1-1 Rule to add comparative endings to single syllable words
- Compose sentences using words that have comparative endings
- Read words with comparative endings -er & -est

Materials and Supplies:

- Teacher's Guide & Student Workbook 1
- White board or chalkboard
- Word cards (as necessary)
- Phonics rules flashcards
- Reader: *Robinson Crusoe & Other Classic Stories*

Teaching Tips:

Review for Mastery. Discuss and review any work from the previous lesson that was assigned as homework. Check for completion of the activities and orally quiz the student for comprehension. Review any reading that was assigned, discussing the characters, setting, plot, theme, language, sequence, etc.

Strengthen fluency and phonemic awareness by reviewing words and sentences from previous lessons. Build vocabulary skills by using some of the words in sentences.

Review the short vowels **a**, **e**, **i**, **o**, and **u** with words from Lesson 18, Activities 2, 3, and 4. Code the vowels with a breve and read the words.

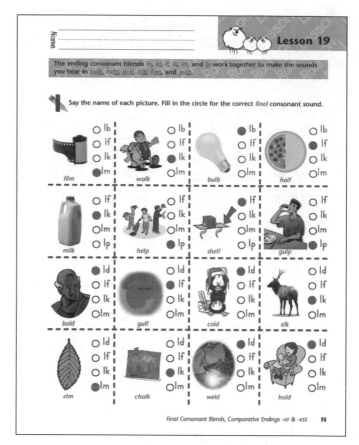

Final Consonant Blends, Comparative Endings -er & -est **78**

Activity 1. Discuss the rule for the consonant blends with **l** and the sample words. *Words to teach the concept:* flashbulb, lightbulb, bold, child, could, fold, mild, old, wild, elf, self, folk, hulk, silk, talk, helm, real, kelp, scalp, yelp. Discuss the pictures in this activity so that the student is able to identify them correctly. The student will select the consonant blend for the final sound heard in each picture.

Pictures:
  film, walk, bulb, half
  milk, help, shelf, gulp
  bald, gulf, cold, elk
  elm, chalk, weld, hold

Letters:
  lm, lk, lb, lf
  lk, lp, lf, lp
  ld, lf, ld, lk
  lm, lk, ld, ld

Note the initial consonant blends in the words *shelf* and *chalk*.

Note: The Wild Colt words ending in **ild** and **old** have a long vowel sound.

Activity 2. Have the student complete the words ending in **lp**. Read the words that have been formed.

Words:
  gulp, help, kelp, yelp

Activity 3. Read and review the rules about root words, suffixes, schwa and adding the **-er** suffix. Have the student read each given word. Have the student circle the single short vowel and the single ending consonant in each word. Have the student write the new words with the **-er** and **-est** suffixes.

Words:
  bigger, biggest
  fatter, fattest
  madder, maddest
  sadder, saddest

Make sentences out of the root and the new words that compare. For example: "This ball is big but a basketball is bigger." "I was sad when I lost my pencil and sadder when I skinned my knee; but the saddest day of my life was when my pet dog broke his leg." Do this for all of the words.

Reading. Read and discuss the maxim for the Lesson.

Read the story *I Build Me a Castle*. This is another chapter of the *Robinson Crusoe* story. Preview the story and explain words or sentence structures that are not familiar to the student. With every story ask questions: who are the characters, what are they doing, what are they saying, where does the action take place, what is the order of events, what words are being used, what new information is given, what lesson can be learned?

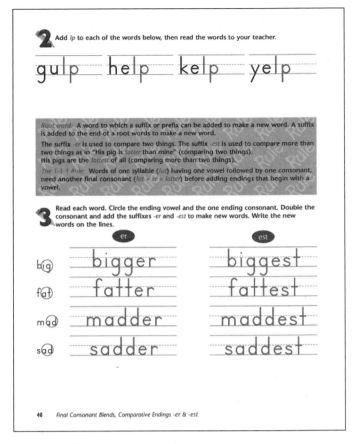

Comprehension questions:
  What did Robinson see in the morning?
  Why was Robinson somewhat afraid?
  Why did Robinson need to find a better place to stay?
  Where did Robinson chose to fix another place?
  What did Robinson call his new place?

Assign. Lesson activities or reading that are to be completed as homework.

Lesson 20: Final Consonant Blends

Overview:

- Define a consonant blend
- Read words with final consonant blends
- Match words to pictures
- Write words with final consonant blends
- Complete words with final consonant blends

Materials and Supplies:

- Teacher's Guide & Student Workbook 1
- White board or chalkboard
- Word cards (as necessary)
- Phonics rules flashcards
- Reader: *Robinson Crusoe & Other Classic Stories*

Teaching Tips:

Review for Mastery. Discuss and review any work from the previous lesson that was assigned as homework. Check for completion of the activities and orally quiz the student for comprehension. Review any reading that was assigned, discussing the characters, setting, plot, theme, language, sequence, etc.

Strengthen fluency and phonemic awareness by reviewing words and sentences from previous lessons. Build vocabulary skills by using some of the words in sentences.

Review the comparative endings in Lesson 19, Activity 2, circle the root in each word.

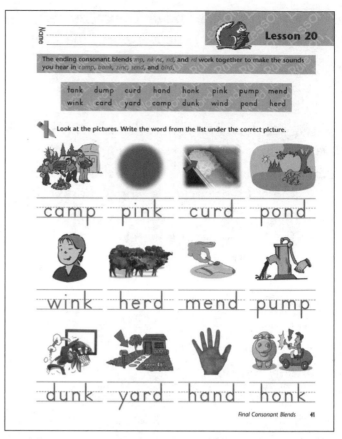

Activity 1. Review the final consonant blends and sample words in the rule box. *Words to teach the concept:* amp, blimp, blank, drink, frank, thank, franc, Banc, blind, brand, hound, mind, sound, spend, board, gourd, hear, lord, sword, third, weird. Have the student read each of the words in the box with final consonant blends. Discuss the pictures in this activity so that the student is able to identify them correctly. The student will write the correct word on the line. This exercise is continued on the next page of the student lesson.

Words:
  camp, pink, curd, pond
  wink, herd, mend, pump
  dunk, yard, hand, honk
  dump, card, wind, tank

Note the R-controlled words *curd*, *herd*, *yard*, and *card*. Help the student pronounce those words. They will be covered in more detail in later lessons.

Activity 2. Have the student complete the words ending in **nk**. Read the words that have been formed.

Words:
    junk, bonk, link, dank
    mink, bunk, rank, honk

Activity 3. Have the student complete the words ending in **nd**. Read the words that have been formed.

Words:
    bind, bond, find, land
    mind, fund, band, fond

Activity 4. Have the student complete the words ending in **nc**. Read the words that have been formed.

    Words: **zinc, franc, Banc**

franc—A silver coin of France, and since 1795 the unit of the French monetary system. It has been adopted by Belgium and Switzerland.

Banc—A bench; a high seat, or seat of distinction or judgment; a tribunal or court.

Review for Test. The instructor should plan to use some time at the end of the class to review and prepare for the test that follows this lesson. Review the objectives for the test and then look over the lessons that it will cover. If the student has struggled with any of the concepts that will be included in the test, some additional drill, practice, or review may be needed to adequately prepare him for the test.

Reading. Read and discuss the maxim for the Lesson.

Read the story *I Build Me a Castle (continued)*. This is another chapter of the *Robinson Crusoe* story. Preview the story and explain words or sentence structures that are not familiar to the student. With every story ask questions: who are the characters, what are they doing, what are they saying, where does the action take

place, what is the order of events, what words are being used, what new information is given, what lesson can be learned?

Comprehension questions:
    How long did it take Robinson to move his stuff?
    What planning did Robinson do for the building of his castle?
    How did Robinson build the walls of his castle?
    How did Robinson build a shelter from the rain?
    What was the "kitchen?"

Assign. Lesson activities or reading that are to be completed as homework.

Test 2
Lessons 5–14

Overview:

- Define a consonant blend
- Read words with initial consonant blends
- Read words with final consonant blends
- Match words to pictures
- Auditory discrimination of the final **s** sound
- Auditory discrimination of the soft **g** sound
- Auditory discrimination of the **k** sound
- Correctly spell the initial or final **k** sound in short vowel words
- Read short vowel words with a silent final double consonant
- Apply the Syllable Rule to determine the number of syllables in words

Materials and Supplies:

- Teacher's Guide & Student Workbook 1

Instructions:

Assessment Start-up. Read through the test with the student. Help the student with any words that he is still unsure of. The teacher should be available to answer any questions that the student may have during the test.

Activity 1. Read the instruction for the activity with the student. Review the pictures in the activity so the student can correctly identify them. Instruct the student to circle all of the pictures that have the final **s** sound.

Pictures:
   mix, juice, pass, bass
   buzz, lace, mess, brace

Final **s**:
   juice, pass, bass
   lace, mess, brace

Activity 2. Read the instruction for the activity with the student. Review the pictures in the activity so the student can correctly identify them. Instruct the student to circle all of the pictures that have the soft **g** sound.

Pictures:
   engine, gas, genius, wagon
   giant, girl, ginger, garden

Soft **g**:
   engine, genius, giant, ginger

Hard **g**:
   gas, wagon, girl, garden

Activity 3. Read the instruction for the activity with the student. Review the words in the activity so the student can correctly read them. Instruct the student to fill in the circle for the number of syllables in each word.

Words:
   engine–2, garden–2, dock–1, oxen–2
   rack–1, fatter–2, dozen–2, paper–2
   bigger–2, shell–1, cover–2, taller–2

Activity 4. Read the instruction with the student. Instruct the student to cross out the silent letter in each word and listen as they read they words aloud.

Words:
 puff, less, bell, gull
 off, pill, razz, ruff

Activity 5. Read the instruction for the activity with the student. Review the pictures in the activity so the student can correctly identify them. Instruct the student to circle all of the pictures that have the **k** sound.

Pictures:
 cup, sack, ship, neck,
 duck, tick, keg, tack

Sound of **k**:
 cup, sack, neck, duck, tick, keg, tack

Activity 6. Read the instruction for the activity with the student. Review the pictures in the activity so the student can correctly identify them. Instruct the student to fill in the circle for the consonant blend that he hears.

Pictures:
 think, rush, third, bath,
 shell, thin, south, cash,
 tooth, shed, fish, ship

Sound of **th**:
 think, third, bath, thin, south, tooth

Sound of **sh**:
 rush, shell, cash, shed, fish, ship

Activity 7. Read the instruction for the activity with the student. Review the pictures in the activity so the student can correctly identify them. Instruct the student to complete the words by writing the spelling for the **k** sound on each blank.

Pictures:
 peck, cab, cot, dock, puck

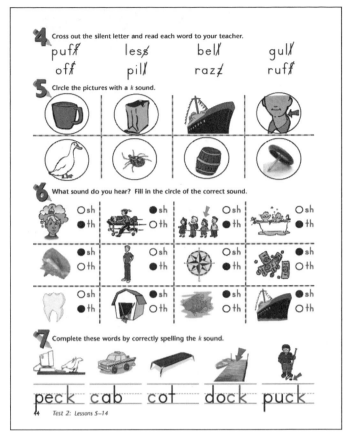

Assessment Follow-up. Every test is an important assessment of both the student's comprehension of the concepts and the instructional process. This makes follow-up after each test essential to the learning process. Review all of the errors made on the test with the student. Check for understanding of the concepts and of the problem instructions. Compare the errors made on the test to the test objectives to identify specific areas of weakness. If weak areas of understanding are detected it might be necessary to go back to those lessons to devise some enrichment activities for the concept.

The test results can be used to determine what concepts are reviewed during the daily time of classroom instruction. Devise enrichment activities that will provide development in those areas.

If time permits, choose a selection and have the student read it again. This can also be used as a catch-up time to complete unfinished selections.

Lesson 21: Final Consonant Blends, Suffix -ing

Overview:

- Define a consonant blend
- Read words with final consonant blends
- Match words to pictures
- Write words with final consonant blends
- Complete words with final consonant blends
- Add the suffix **-ing** to words with no spelling changes
- Read words with suffix **-ing** ending

Materials and Supplies:

- Teacher's Guide & Student Workbook 1
- White board or chalkboard
- Word cards (as necessary)
- Phonics rules flashcards
- Reader: *Robinson Crusoe & Other Classic Stories*

Teaching Tips:

Review for Mastery. Discuss and review any work from the previous lesson that was assigned as homework. Check for completion of the activities and orally quiz the student for comprehension. Review any reading that was assigned, discussing the characters, setting, plot, theme, language, sequence, etc.

Strengthen fluency and phonemic awareness by reviewing words and sentences from previous lessons. Build vocabulary skills by using some of the words in sentences.

Review the short vowels **a**, **e**, **i**, **o**, and **u** with words from Lesson 20, Activities 2, 3, and 4. Code the vowels with a breve and read the words.

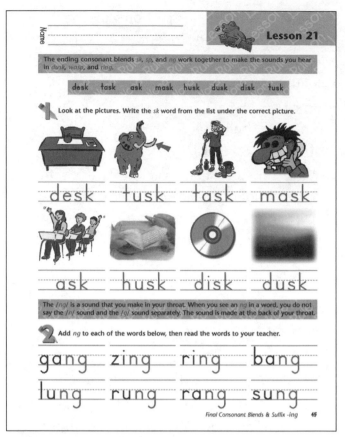

Activity 1. Review the rule and the sound for the **sk** consonant blend. *Words to teach the concept:* bask, basket, frisk, risk, whisker. Have the student read each of the words in the box with final consonant blends. Discuss the pictures in this activity so that the student is able to identify them correctly. The student will write the correct word on the line.

Words:
  desk, tusk, task, mask
  ask, husk, disk, dusk

Activity 2. Review the rule and the sound for the **ng** consonant blend. *Words to teach the concept:* bring, clang, cling, ding, hang, king, ping, sang, sing, thing, wing. Have the student complete the words ending in **ng**. Read the words that have been formed.

Words:
  gang, zing, ring, bang
  lung, rung, rang, sung

Activity 3. Review the rule and the sound for the **sp** consonant blend. *Words to teach the concept:* crisp, grasp. Have the student complete the words ending in **sp**. Read the words that have been formed.

Words:

gasp, lisp, wisp, hasp
rasp, cusp, wasp, clasp

Note the word *clasp* with the **cl** initial consonant blend.

Activity 4. Review the Suffix Rule and the meaning of the **-ing** suffix. Words to teach the concept can be taken from Lessons 19 & 20. Many of those words can have the **-ing** suffix. Read the words with final consonant blends given for the exercise. The student will add the **-ing** suffix to each of the words. Read the words that have been formed.

Words:

asking, ringing, rasping
husking, pinging, singing
gasping, banging, winging
disking, dinging, zinging
risking, masking, basking
landing, linking, dumping
camping, winking, mending

Make up some sentences that use the words.

Reading. Read and discuss the maxim for the Lesson.

Read the story *I Go A-hunting*. This is another chapter of the *Robinson Crusoe* story. Preview the story and explain words or sentence structures that are not familiar to the student. With every story ask questions: who are the characters, what are they doing, what are they saying, where does the action take place, what is the order of events, what words are being used, what new information is given, what lesson can be learned?

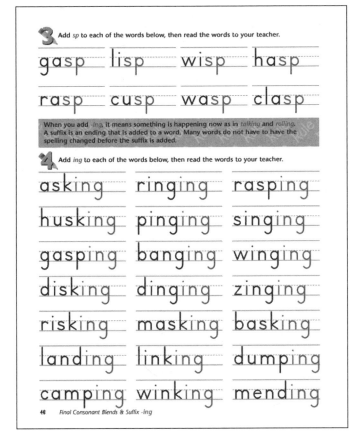

Comprehension questions:

How long did it take Robinson to finish his castle?
What did Robinson get for food?
Why did Robinson kill the baby goat?
What did Robinson do with the injured goat?
What was Robinson's plan for the injured goat?

Assign. Lesson activities or reading that are to be completed as homework.

Lesson 22: Review
Final Consonant Blends

Overview:

- Define a consonant blend
- Read short vowel words
- Form words with consonant blend endings
- Read words with consonant blend endings
- Select the ending consonant blend for the sound of a word

Materials and Supplies:

- Teacher's Guide & Student Workbook 1
- White board or chalkboard
- Word cards (as necessary)
- Reader: *Robinson Crusoe & Other Classic Stories*

Teaching Tips:

Review for Mastery. Discuss and review any work from the previous lesson that was assigned as homework. Check for completion of the activities and orally quiz the student for comprehension. Review any reading that was assigned, discussing the characters, setting, plot, theme, language, sequence, etc.

Strengthen fluency and phonemic awareness by reviewing words and sentences from previous lessons. Build vocabulary skills by using some of the words in sentences.

Review the short vowels **a**, **e**, **i**, **o**, and **u** with words from Lesson 21, Activities 1, 2, and 3. Code the vowels with a breve and read the words.

Activity 1. Review the final consonant blends and rules from previous lessons. Read the short vowel words. The student will drop the final consonant on the short vowel word and form a new word using the consonant blends listed in the instructions. Have the student write the new word on the line. Read the words that have been formed.

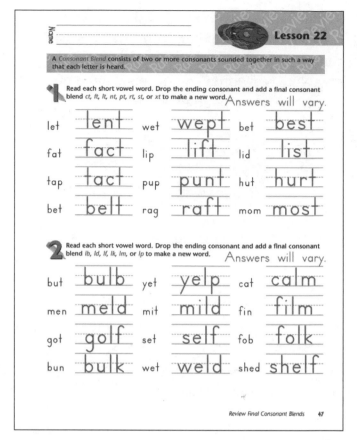

Activity 1 continued.

Words:
  lent, wept, best
  fact, lift, list
  tact, punt, hurt
  belt, raft, most

Note: Student answers can vary.

Activity 2. Read the short vowel words. The student will drop the final consonant on the short vowel word and form a new word using the consonant blends listed in the instructions. Have the student write the new word on the line. Read the words that have been formed.

Words:
  bulb, yelp, calm
  meld, mild, film
  golf, self, folk
  bulk, weld, shelf

Note: Student answers can vary.

Activity 3. Read the short vowel words. The student will drop the final consonant on the short vowel word and form a new word using the consonant blends listed in the instructions. Have the student write the new word on the line. Read the words that have been formed.

Words:
  ramp, bank, camp
  task, bunk, bing
  hasp, bend, pond
  land, funk, pink

Note: Student answers can vary.

Activity 4. Discuss the pictures in this activity so that the student is able to identify them correctly. The student will select the consonant blend for the final sound heard in each picture.

Pictures:
  silk, sift, vest, mink
  helm, bend, ford, fort
  salt, pint, kelp, jump

Letters:
  lk, ft, st, nk
  lm, nd, rd, rt
  lt, nt, lp, mp

Note the R-controlled vowels heard in *ford* and *fort*.

Reading. Read and discuss the maxim for the Lesson.

Read the story *I Keep Myself Busy*. This is another chapter of the *Robinson Crusoe* story. Preview the story and explain words or sentence structures that are not familiar to the student. With every story ask questions: who are the characters, what are they doing, what are they saying, where does the action take place, what is the order of events, what words are being used, what new information is given, what lesson can be learned?

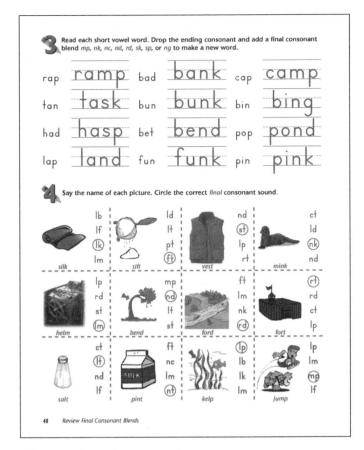

Comprehension questions:
  What things had Robinson brought from the ship that he hadn't mentioned before?
  What things of his own had Robinson brought from the ship?
  Why did Robinson have to stop writing?
  What furniture did Robinson build?
  What did Robinson's cave look like?
  What did Robinson make for moving dirt?

Assign. Lesson activities or reading that are to be completed as homework.

Lesson 23: Initial Consonant Blends br, cr, dr, fr, gr, pr, & tr

Overview:

- Define a consonant blend
- Read words with initial and final consonant blends
- Match words with initial consonant blends to the picture
- Complete sentences using words with initial consonant blends
- Read sentences that contain words with initial consonant blends

Materials and Supplies:

- Teacher's Guide & Student Workbook 1
- White board or chalkboard
- Word cards (as necessary)
- Phonics rules flashcards
- Reader: *Robinson Crusoe & Other Classic Stories*

Teaching Tips:

Review for Mastery. Discuss and review any work from the previous lesson that was assigned as homework. Check for completion of the activities and orally quiz the student for comprehension. Review any reading that was assigned, discussing the characters, setting, plot, theme, language, sequence, etc.

Strengthen fluency and phonemic awareness by reviewing words and sentences from previous lessons. Build vocabulary skills by using some of the words in sentences.

Review final consonant blends with the words for Lesson 22, Activities 1, 2, and 3. Try to form some additional words from the word beginnings and consonant blend endings.

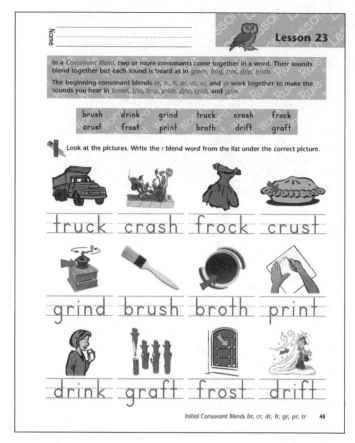

Activity 1. Differentiate between an initial consonant blend and a final consonant blend. A consonant blend is two letters that blend together but both sounds are heard. Illustrate examples on the board. Review the consonant blends in the rule box. *Words to teach the concept:* bring, brass, brash, brand, brisk, craft, crest, crisp, crush, crust, crutch, drill, drug, dress, drop, drug, frog, Fred, fresh, frill, frizz, grass, grin, grab, gram, grim, grub, pram, prom, prop, proper, trim, trip, trap, trot, trip, trim. Help the student read the words in the list. Discuss the pictures in this activity so that the student is able to identify them correctly. The student will write the words under the correct picture.

Words:
  truck, crash, frock, crust
  grind, brush, broth, print
  drink, graft, frost, drift

Note that these words also have final consonant blends.

Activity 2. Help the student read the words in the activity. Discuss the pictures in this activity so that the student is able to identify them correctly. The student will match the words to the correct picture.

Pictures:

grand (piano)	**grist** (mill)
press	**track**
frisk	**trick**

Note that some of these words also have final consonant blends.

Activity 3. Help the student read each sentence and the two choice words. Have the student select the word that fits the sentence and write it on the line. Read the sentences again with the correct word.

Sentences:

1. **Drop the red <u>brick</u> in the back of the truck.**
2. **Brad can <u>crack</u> the crisp crab leg.**
3. **Fred <u>drank</u> his fresh can of pop.**
4. **Trust the end of the <u>crutch</u> to grab the deck.**
5. **Print the <u>prank</u> on a press.**

Note the other words in the sentences with initial or final consonant blends. Have the student circle the consonant blends in these words.

Reading. Read and discuss the maxim for the Lesson.

Read the story *I Have a Great Fright*. This is another chapter of the *Robinson Crusoe* story. Preview the story and explain words or sentence structures that are not familiar to the student. With every story ask questions: who are the characters, what are they doing, what are they saying, where does the action take place, what is the order of events, what words are being used, what new information is given, what lesson can be learned?

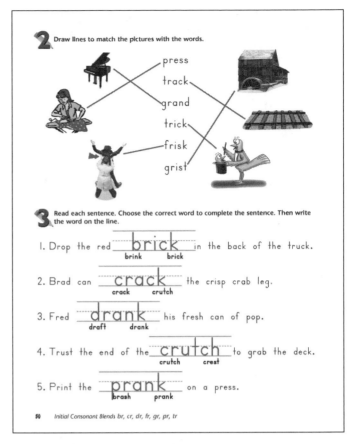

Comprehension questions:
  What frightened Robinson?
  Where did Robinson go during the earth-quake?
  What did Robinson say during the earth-quake?
  What happened to the weather after the earthquake?
  Where was Robinson during the hurricane?
  Where did Robinson go after the hurricane?

Assign. Lesson activities or reading that are to be completed as homework.

Lesson 24: Initial Consonant Blends sc, sl, sm, sn, sp, st, & sw

Overview:

- Define a consonant blend
- Read words with initial and final consonant blends
- Match words with initial consonant blends to the picture
- Complete words with initial consonant blends
- Complete sentences using words with initial consonant blends
- Read sentences that contain words with initial consonant blends

Materials and Supplies:

- Teacher's Guide & Student Workbook 1
- White board or chalkboard
- Word cards (as necessary)
- Reader: *Robinson Crusoe & Other Classic Stories*

Teaching Tips:

Review for Mastery. Discuss and review any work from the previous lesson that was assigned as homework. Check for completion of the activities and orally quiz the student for comprehension. Review any reading that was assigned, discussing the characters, setting, plot, theme, language, sequence, etc.

Strengthen fluency and phonemic awareness by reviewing words and sentences from previous lessons. Build vocabulary skills by using some of the words in sentences.

Review final consonant blends with Lesson 23, Activities 1 & 2. Read the words and have the student circle the final consonant blends.

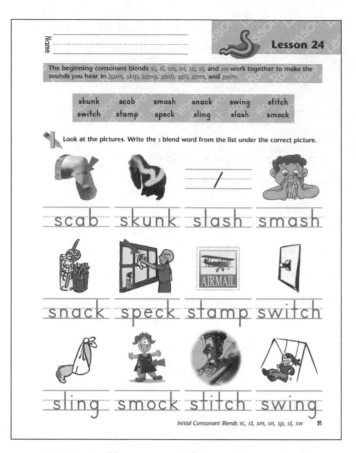

Activity 1. Differentiate between an initial consonant blend and a final consonant blend. A consonant blend is two letters that blend together but both sounds are heard. Illustrate examples on the board. Review the consonant blends in the rule box. *Words to teach the concept:* scare, scam, scamp, scarf, scent, skin, skill, skirt, skim, slip, slid, slap, slim, slug, slum, smell, small, smog, smut, snug, snip, snap, snob, snub, snuff, spell, spot, spin, spud, stop, step, still, staff, stag, swim, swell, swan, swap, swat. Help the student read the words in the list. Discuss the pictures in this activity so that the student is able to identify them correctly. The student will write the words under the correct picture.

Words:
   scab, skunk, slash, smash
   snack, speck, stamp, switch
   sling, smock, stitch, swing

Note that these words also have final consonant blends.

Activity 2. Review the Consonant Blend Rule. Have the student add the given consonant blend to each of the word endings and read them aloud.

Words:
    swift, stand, smack, slink
    swamp, stink, smith, slant
    swish, stack, smart, slack
    swept, stuck, smell, slept

Note the R-controlled vowel in the word *smart*.

Activity 3. Help the student read each sentence and the two choice words. Have the student select the word that fits the sentence and write it on the line. Read the sentences again with the correct word.

Sentences:
    1. Snack on the <u>scant</u> grub.
    2. Stop and <u>stand</u> on the top step.
    3. Swap the <u>swing</u> for a swift swan.
    4. Spot spun a spud at the <u>speck</u>.
    5. The slug will not <u>smell</u> the slim skunk.
    6. Stan will skip the <u>swift</u> swim.

Note the other words in the sentences with initial or final consonant blends. Have the student circle the consonant blends in these words.

Reading. Read and discuss the maxim for the Lesson.

Read the story *I Explore My Island*. This is another chapter of the *Robinson Crusoe* story. Preview the story and explain words or sentence structures that are not familiar to the student. With every story ask questions: who are the characters, what are they doing, what are they saying, where does the action take place, what is the order of events, what words are being used, what new information is given, what lesson can be learned?

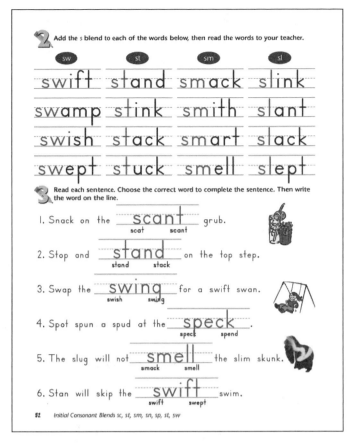

Comprehension questions:
    What had the earthquake and hurricane done to the castle?
    How long had Robinson been on the island?
    Where did Robinson go on a walk?
    What plants did Robinson find on the island?
    What problem did Robinson wonder about after his walk?
    What did Robinson find on his second walk?
    What happened to the first fruit that Robinson brought back to the cave?
    What happened to the grapevines?

Assign. Lesson activities or reading that are to be completed as homework.

Lesson 25: Initial Consonant Blends bl, cl, fl, gl, pl, & sl

Overview:

- Define a consonant blend
- Read words with initial and final consonant blends
- Match words with initial consonant blends to the picture
- Determine the initial consonant blend that is heard in a word
- Classify words with the same initial consonant blend
- Complete words with initial consonant blends
- Auditory recognition of consonant blends

Materials and Supplies:

- Teacher's Guide & Student Workbook 1
- White board or chalkboard
- Word cards (as necessary)
- Reader: *Robinson Crusoe & Other Classic Stories*

Teaching Tips:

Review for Mastery. Discuss and review any work from the previous lesson that was assigned as homework. Check for completion of the activities and orally quiz the student for comprehension. Review any reading that was assigned, discussing the characters, setting, plot, theme, language, sequence, etc.

Strengthen fluency and phonemic awareness by reviewing words and sentences from previous lessons. Build vocabulary skills by using some of the words in sentences.

Review final consonant blends with Lesson 24, Activities 1 & 2. Read the words and have the student circle the final consonant blends.

Activity 1. Review the initial consonant blends with **l** and the sample words in the Rule Box. Ask for examples of each. *Words to teach the*

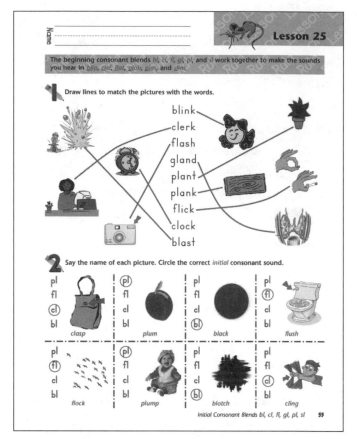

concept: blot, blab, bled, bless, blimp, bliss, bluff, climb, cloth, class, cliff, clap, cling, clip, flat, flap, flax, flop, glad, glass, gloss, plan, plus, plot, plug, plum, slip, slap, sled, slam, slim, slumber. Help the student read the words in the activity. Discuss the pictures in this activity so that the student is able to identify them correctly. The student will match the words to the correct picture.

Pictures:

blast	plant
clock	blink
clerk	flick
flash	plank
	gland

Note that these words also have final consonant blends. The word *clerk* has an R-controlled vowel.

Activity 2. Discuss the pictures in this activity so that the student is able to identify them correctly. The student will select the consonant blend for the initial sound heard in each picture.

Activity 2 continued:

Pictures:

clasp, plum, black, flush

flock, plump, blotch, cling

Letters:

cl, pl, bl, fl

fl, pl, bl, cl

Note that these words also have final consonant blends.

Activity 3. Help the student read the words in the list. Help the student read the given words and to identify the initial consonant blend. Have the student write a word with the same initial consonant blend on the line.

Words:

glass	clump
blunt	pluck
flank	slash

Activity 4. Review the Consonant Blend Rule. Have the student add the given consonant blend to each of the word endings and read them aloud.

Words:

slim, sled, slum, slop

glib, glen, glut, glob

plan, pled, plump, plot

cluck, clang, clump, clutch

fling, flesh, flub, flag

blip, blest, bluff, block

Reading. Read and discuss the maxim for the Lesson.

Read the story *I Get Ready for Winter*. This is another chapter of the *Robinson Crusoe* story. Preview the story and explain words or sentence structures that are not familiar to the student. With every story ask questions: who are the characters, what are they doing, what are they saying, where does the action take place, what is the order of events, what words are being used, what new information is given, what lesson can be learned?

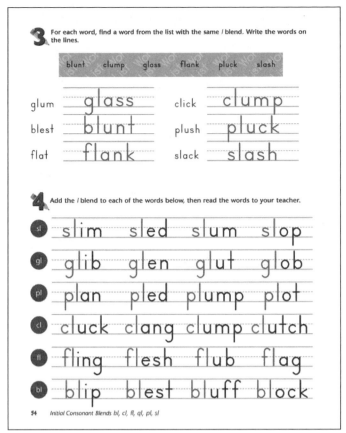

Comprehension questions:

What did Robinson build in the valley that he had discovered?

Did Robinson's fence around his cottage have a gate?

What did Robinson pick and dry for food?

What happened everyday during the winter?

What foods did Robinson find to eat?

What were the ways that Robinson made for getting into his castle?

What improvements did Robinson make to his castle?

Assign. Lesson activities or reading that are to be completed as homework.

Lesson 26: Initial Consonant Blends dw, gw, tw, sw, & Final Consonant Blend -dge

Overview:

- Define a consonant blend
- Read words with initial and final consonant blends
- Match words with initial consonant blends to the picture
- Complete words with final consonant blend **-dge**
- Complete words with initial consonant blends

Materials and Supplies:

- Teacher's Guide & Student Workbook 1
- White board or chalkboard
- Word cards (as necessary)
- Phonics rules flashcards
- Reader: *Robinson Crusoe & Other Classic Stories*

Teaching Tips:

Review for Mastery. Discuss and review any work from the previous lesson that was assigned as homework. Check for completion of the activities and orally quiz the student for comprehension. Review any reading that was assigned, discussing the characters, setting, plot, theme, language, sequence, etc.

Strengthen fluency and phonemic awareness by reviewing words and sentences from previous lessons. Build vocabulary skills by using some of the words in sentences.

Review final consonant blends with Lesson 25, Activities 1 & 3. Read the words and have the student circle the final consonant blends.

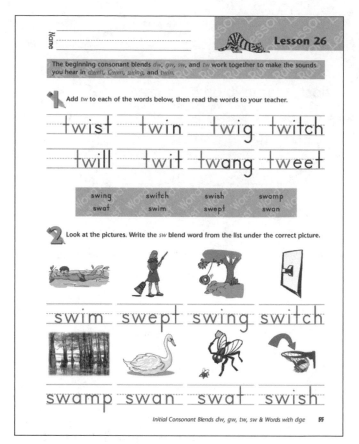

Activity 1. Review the rule and the sound for the **tw** consonant blend. Stress the difference between consonant digraphs and consonant blends. *Words to teach the concept:* twelve, twenty, twice, twine, twinkle, twirl. Have the student complete the words beginning with **tw.** Read the words that have been formed.

Words:

  twist, twin, twig, twitch
  twill, twit, twang, tweet

Note that several of these words also have final consonant blends.

Activity 2. Review the rule and the sound for the **sw** consonant blend. *Words to teach the concept:* swam, swan, swap, swell, swift, swill, swallow. Help the student read the words in the list. Discuss the pictures in this activity so that the student is able to identify them correctly. The student will write the words under the correct picture.

Words:

  swim, swept, swing, switch
  swamp, swan, swat, swish

Horizons Phonics & Reading Grade 2 Teacher's Guide

Activity 2 continued:

Note that several of these words also have final consonant blends.

Activity 3. Review the rule for the **dge** phonogram. *Words to teach the concept:* budge, dodge, edge, grudge, ledge, lodge, nudge, ridge. Help the student read the words in the activity. Discuss the pictures in this activity so that the student is able to identify them correctly. The student will match the words to the correct picture.

Pictures:

badger	hedge
badge	judge
bridge	pledge
fudge	sledge
	wedge

Note that a few of these words also have initial consonant blends.

Activity 4. Have the student complete the words ending in the **dge** triple consonant blend. Read the words that have been formed.

Words:
**budge, ridge, nudge, badge
edge, ledge, hodgepodge
Madge, dodge, grudge, lodge**

Activity 5. Review the rule and the sound for the **dw** and **gw** consonant blends. Have the student complete the words beginning in **dw** and **gw**. The **gw** ending is very rare. Only the words Gwen, Gwendolyn, and gweduck (a large saltwater clam) begin with the **gw** consonant blend. Read the words that have been formed.

Words:
dwell, dwelt, Gwen

Reading. Read and discuss the maxim for the Lesson.

Read the story *I Make Me a Calendar*. This is another chapter of the *Robinson Crusoe* story. Preview the story and explain words or sentence structures that are not familiar to the

student. With every story ask questions: who are the characters, what are they doing, what are they saying, where does the action take place, what is the order of events, what words are being used, what new information is given, what lesson can be learned?

Comprehension questions:
How long had Robinson been on the island?
How did Robinson keep track of time?
What did Robinson do to celebrate being on the island for a year?
What was Robinson thankful for?
How were the seasons on the island different from the seasons in England?

Assign. Lesson activities or reading that are to be completed as homework.

Lesson 27: Review Initial Consonant Blends

Overview:

- Word/picture matching
- Form words with consonant blend beginnings
- Read words with consonant blend beginnings
- Auditory recognition of initial consonant blends

Materials and Supplies:

- Teacher's Guide & Student Workbook 1
- White board or chalkboard
- Word cards (as necessary)
- Phonics rules flashcards
- Reader: *Robinson Crusoe & Other Classic Stories*

Teaching Tips:

Review for Mastery. Discuss and review any work from the previous lesson that was assigned as homework. Check for completion of the activities and orally quiz the student for comprehension. Review any reading that was assigned, discussing the characters, setting, plot, theme, language, sequence, etc.

Strengthen fluency and phonemic awareness by reviewing words and sentences from previous lessons. Build vocabulary skills by using some of the words in sentences.

Review the short vowels **a**, **e**, **i**, **o**, and **u** with words from Lesson 26, Activities 1, 2, 3, and 4. Code the vowels with a breve and read the words.

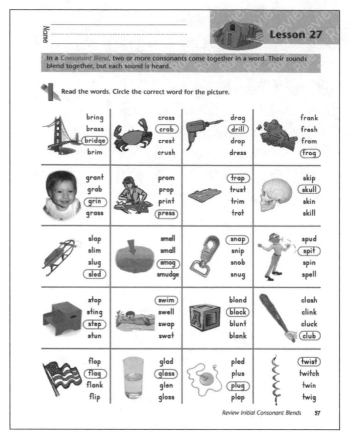

Activity 1. This activity will review initial consonant blends **br, cr, dr, fr, gr, pr, tr, sk, sl, sm, sn, sp, st, sw, bl, cl, fl, gl, pl, tw.** Review these blends with words from previous lessons as is needed. Help the student read all of the words in each box and identify the pictures. Instruct the student circle the word to match the picture with the word.

Words:
   **bridge, crab, drill, frog
   grin, press, trap, skull
   sled, smog, snap, spit
   step, swim, block, club
   flag, glass, plug, twist**

Activity 2. This activity will review initial consonant blends with r: **br, cr, dr, fr, gr, pr, tr.** Review these blends with words from previous lessons as in needed. Read the short vowel words. The student will drop the initial consonant on the short vowel word and form a new word using the consonant blends listed in the instructions. Have the student write the new word on the line. Read the words that have been formed.

Horizons Phonics & Reading Grade 2 Teacher's Guide

Activity 2 continued:

Words:
**crash, trip
brush, prank
trim, drab
drag, drop**

Note that the student answers can vary.

Activity 3. This activity will review initial consonant blends with **s**: **sk, sl, sm, sn, sp, st, sw.** Review these blends with words from previous lessons as needed. Read the short vowel words. The student will drop the initial consonant on the short vowel word and form a new word using the consonant blends listed in the instructions. Have the student write the new word on the line. Read the words that have been formed.

Words:
**snap, spill
slam, slot
skip, scab
snug, sting**

Note that the student answers can vary.

Activity 4. This activity will review initial consonant blends with **l**: **bl, cl, fl, gl, pl, sl.** Review these blends with words from previous lessons as in needed. Read the short vowel words. The student will drop the initial consonant on the short vowel word and form a new word using the consonant blends listed in the instructions. Have the student write the new word on the line. Read the words that have been formed.

Words:
**flank, floss
clash, clod
slop, flap
glass, slink**

Note that the student answers can vary.

Reading. Read and discuss the maxim for the Lesson.

Read the story *I Sow Some Grain*. This is another chapter of the *Robinson Crusoe* story.

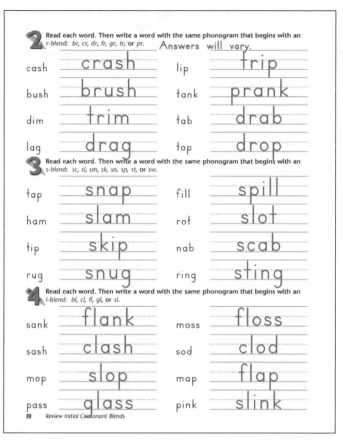

Preview the story and explain words or sentence structures that are not familiar to the student. With every story ask questions: who are the characters, what are they doing, what are they saying, where does the action take place, what is the order of events, what words are being used, what new information is given, what lesson can be learned?

Comprehension questions:
When did the first wet season begin?
When did the second wet season begin?
How did Robinson keep track of the seasons?
What had happened to the barley that was in the bag that Robinson brought from the ship?
What happened to the chaff that Robinson shook onto the ground?
What grew from the chaff besides the barley?

Assign. Lesson activities or reading that are to be completed as homework.

Lesson 28: Final Stable Syllable Triple Consonant Blends

Overview:

- Define a Final Stable Syllable
- Read words with Final Stable Syllables
- Code words with Final Stable Syllables
- Match words with Final Stable Syllables to the picture
- Complete words with Final Stable Syllables
- Auditory recognition of the sound of a Final Stable Syllable

Materials and Supplies:

- Teacher's Guide & Student Workbook 1
- White board or chalkboard
- Word cards (as necessary)
- Phonics rules flashcards
- Reader: *Robinson Crusoe & Other Classic Stories*

Teaching Tips:

Review for Mastery. Discuss and review any work from the previous lesson that was assigned as homework. Check for completion of the activities and orally quiz the student for comprehension. Review any reading that was assigned, discussing the characters, setting, plot, theme, language, sequence, etc.

Strengthen fluency and phonemic awareness by reviewing words and sentences from previous lessons. Build vocabulary skills by using some of the words in sentences.

Review the short vowels **a**, **e**, **i**, **o**, and **u** with words from Lesson 27, Activities 1, 2, 3, and 4. Code the vowels with a breve and read the words.

Review initial consonant blends with the words from Lesson 27, Activity 1. Read the words that are not identified by the pictures.

Activity 1. Review the Final Stable Syllable rules. Go over examples of each rule using the chalkboard or white board. *Words to teach the concept:* babble, Bible, gobble, hobble, ramble, syllable, bicycle, cycle, icicle, tricycle, bridle, cradle, poodle, baffle, muffle, shuffle, whiffle, beagle, eagle, gargle, Google, struggle, crinkle, rankle, sparkle, tinkle, ample, cripple, sample, staple, tussle, gristle, hustle, jostle, little, rattle, rustle, dazzle, fizzle, puzzle, swizzle. Help the student code the Final Stable Syllable in each word with a bracket. Have the student put a slash over the final silent **e** in each word and code the short vowel with a breve. Read the words.

Words:

> gob[ble, un[cle, dwin[dle
> scuf[fle, sin[gle, crin[kle
> grap[ple, has[sle, lit[tle
> fraz[zle, ram[ble, twin[kle

Activity 2. Help the student read the words in the activity. Discuss the pictures in this activity so that the student is able to identify them correctly. The student will match the words to the correct picture.

Activity 2 continued:

Pictures:

stubble	apple
ankle	jungle
turtle	bottle
dribble	thistle

Note the R-controlled vowel in the word *turtle*.

Activity 3. Discuss the pictures in this activity so that the student is able to identify them correctly. The student will select the Final Stable Syllable for the sound heard in each picture.

Pictures:

twinkle, puzzle, circle, muzzle
thimble, fiddle, bubble, temple
nozzle, shuttle, whistle, ruffle
crinkle, tangle, tussle, tinkle

Letters:

kle, zle, cle, zle
ble, dle, ble, ple
zle, tle, tle, fle
kle, gle, sle, kle

Reading. Read and discuss the maxim for the Lesson.

Read the story *I Sow Some Grain (continued)*. This is another chapter of the *Robinson Crusoe* story. Preview the story and explain words or sentence structures that are not familiar to the student. With every story ask questions: who are the characters, what are they doing, what are they saying, where does the action take place, what is the order of events, what words are being used, what new information is given, what lesson can be learned?

Comprehension questions:
What did Robinson do with the harvest of barley and rice?
How many times did Robinson harvest the barley before he dared to use any of it for bread?
What made the summer house very beautiful?
How did Robinson add more protection to his castle?

Read the poem *Hey Diddle, Diddle*. Preview the poem and explain words or sentence structures that are not familiar to the student.

Comprehension questions:
What are the stable syllable words in the poem?
What words rhyme in the poem?
Does the poem make any sense?

Assign. Lesson activities or reading that are to be completed as homework.

Lesson 29: Final Triple Consonant Blends

Overview:

- Define a Final Stable Syllable
- Identify the exception to the Final Stable Syllable Rule.
- Read words with a final **ckle** syllable
- Code words with a final **ckle** syllable
- Match words with a final **ckle** syllable to the picture
- Complete words with triple consonant blend endings
- Auditory recognition of the sound of triple consonant blends

Materials and Supplies:

- Teacher's Guide & Student Workbook 1
- White board or chalkboard
- Word cards (as necessary)
- Phonics rules flashcards
- Reader: *Robinson Crusoe & Other Classic Stories*

Teaching Tips:

Review for Mastery. Discuss and review any work from the previous lesson that was assigned as homework. Check for completion of the activities and orally quiz the student for comprehension. Review any reading that was assigned, discussing the characters, setting, plot, theme, language, sequence, etc.

Strengthen fluency and phonemic awareness by reviewing words and sentences from previous lessons. Build vocabulary skills by using some of the words in sentences.

Activity 1. Review the Final Stable Syllable rules. Go over examples of each rule using the chalkboard or white board. Go over the exception to the Final Stable Syllable Rule and give examples on the board. *Words to teach the concept:* fickle, freckle, grackle, honeysuckle, knuckle, outsparkle, prickle, shackle, sickle, spackle, speckle, stickler, suckle, turnbuckle. Pay special attention to how

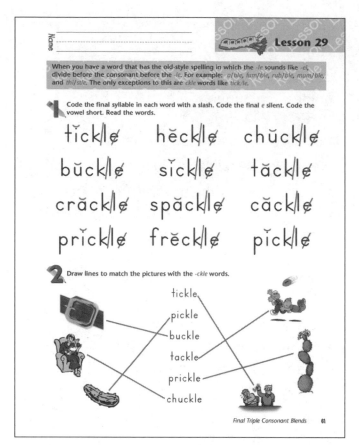

the words are divided into syllables. Help the student code the final syllable in each word with a slash. Have the student put a slash over the final silent **e** in each word and code the short vowel with a breve. Read the words.

Words:

   tick/le, heck/le, chuck/le
   buck/le, sick/le, tick/le
   crack/le, spack/le, cack/le
   prick/le, freck/le, pick/le

Activity 2. Help the student read the words in the activity. Discuss the pictures in this activity so that the student is able to identify them correctly. The student will match the words to the correct picture.

Pictures:

buckle	tackle
chuckle	prickle
pickle	tickle

Activity 3. Review the rule and the sound for the **nce** triple consonant blend. Go over examples using the chalkboard or white board. *Words to teach the concept:* science, fragrance, guidance, patience. Have the student complete the words

Horizons Phonics & Reading Grade 2 Teacher's Guide

ending in triple consonant blend **nce** with the /ns/ sound. Read the words that have been formed.

Words:
   fence, since, mince, prince
   advance, penance, hindrance
   entrance, riddance, distance

*A short vowel sound is not a requirement for the **nce** ending.

Activity 4. Review the rule and the sound for the **nse** triple consonant blend. Go over examples using the chalkboard or white board. *Words to teach the concept:* condense, defense, expense, license, incense, offense, suspense. Have the student complete the words ending in triple consonant blend **nse** with the /ns/ sound. Read the words that have been formed.

Words:
   rinse, dense, sense, tense

Activity 5. Review the rule and the sound for the **lse** triple consonant blend. Go over examples using the chalkboard or white board. *Words to teach the concept:* repulse, impulse. Have the student complete the words ending in triple consonant blend **lse** with the /ls/ sound. Read the words that have been formed.

Words:
   false, else, pulse, dulse

Activity 6. Review the rule and the sound for the **lve** triple consonant blend. Go over examples using the chalkboard or white board. *Words to teach the concept:* revolve, shelves, dissolve, ourselves, resolve, salve. Have the student complete the words ending in triple consonant blend **lve** with the /lv/ sound. Read the words that have been formed.

Words:
   valve, shelve, solve, twelve

Activity 7. Review the rule and the sound for the **nge** triple consonant blend. Go over examples using the chalkboard or white board. *Words to teach the concept:* change, lounge, orange, strange. Have the student complete the words

Triple Consonant Blends: *nce* as in *pounce* and *bounce*; *nse* as in *sense* and *dense*; *lse* as in *false* and *repulse*; *lve* as in *twelve* and *solve*; *nge* as in *range* and *plunge*.

3 Add *nce* which has the *ns* sound to each of the words below, then read the words to your teacher.

fence   since   mince   prince
advance   penance   hindrance
entrance   riddance   distance

4 Add *nse* which has the *ns* sound to each of the words below, then read the words to your teacher.

rinse   dense   sense   tense

5 Add *lse* which has the *ls* sound to each of the words below, then read the words to your teacher.

false   else   pulse   dulse

6 Add *lve* which has the *lv* sound to each of the words below, then read the words to your teacher.

valve   shelve   solve   twelve

7 Add *nge* which has the *nj* sound to each of the words below, then read the words to your teacher.

tinge   cringe   fringe   hinge
singe   plunge   challenge

62   Final Triple Consonant Blends

ending in triple consonant blend **nge** with the /nj/ sound. Read the words that have been formed.

Words:
   tinge, cringe, fringe, hinge
   singe, plunge, challenge

Note: A short vowel sound is not a requirement for the **nge** ending.

Reading. Read and discuss the maxim for the Lesson.

Read the story *I Make a Long Journey*. This is another chapter of the *Robinson Crusoe* story. Preview the story and explain words or sentence structures that are not familiar to the student.

Comprehension questions:
   What did Robinson take with him as he explored the island?
   What did Robinson see that was far off in the distance?
   What did Robinson find on this side of the island?
   What animals did Robinson catch and take back with him?

Assign. Lesson activities or reading that are to be completed as homework.

Lesson 30: Final Triple Consonant Blends

Overview:

- Read words with a final **-rch** consonant blend
- Match words with a final **-rch** consonant blend to the picture
- Read words with the **-nch** triple consonant blend ending
- Match words with a final **-nch** consonant blend to the picture
- Read words with a final **-rth** consonant blend
- Match words with a final **-rth** consonant blend to the picture
- Complete words with triple consonant blend endings
- Read words with a final triple consonant blend endings

Materials and Supplies:

- Teacher's Guide & Student Workbook 1
- White board or chalkboard
- Word cards (as necessary)
- Phonics rules flashcards
- Reader: *Robinson Crusoe & Other Classic Stories*

Teaching Tips:

Review for Mastery. Discuss and review any work from the previous lesson that was assigned as homework. Check for completion of the activities and orally quiz the student for comprehension. Review any reading that was assigned, discussing the characters, setting, plot, theme, language, sequence, etc.

Strengthen fluency and phonemic awareness by reviewing words and sentences from previous lessons. Build vocabulary skills by using some of the words in sentences.

Activity 1. Review the rule and the sound for the **rch** triple consonant blend. Go over examples using the chalkboard or white board. *Words to teach the concept:* march, research.

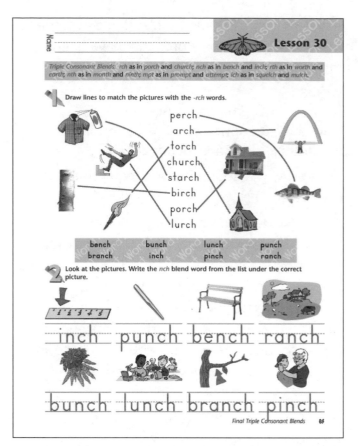

Read the R-controlled words with the **rch** triple consonant blend endings. Identify the pictures, and have the student draw lines from the pictures to the correct words.

Pictures:

starch	**arch**
lurch	**porch**
birch	**perch**
torch	**church**

Activity 2. Review the rule and the sound for the **nch** triple consonant blend. Go over examples using the chalkboard or white board. *Words to teach the concept:* bench, blanch, brunch, clinch, crunch, finch, French, grinch, launch, punchball. Help the student read the words in the word list. Identify the pictures, and have the student write the word for the picture on the line.

Pictures:

  inch, punch, bench, ranch
  bunch, lunch, branch, pinch

Activity 3. Review the rule and the sound for the **rth** triple consonant blend. Go over examples using the chalkboard or white board.

Words to teach the concept: Bertha, birthday, earth. Read the R-controlled words with the **rth** triple consonant blend endings. Identify the pictures, and have the student draw lines from the pictures to the correct words.

Pictures:

girth	mirth
berth	worth
birth	north

Activity 4. Review the rule and the sound for the **mpt**, **mpse**, and **nth** triple consonant blends. Go over examples of each blend, using the chalkboard or white board. *Words to teach the concepts:* exempt, tempt, collapse, elapse, eclipse, hyacinth, eighteenth, seventh. Have the student add the given triple consonant blend to each of the word beginnings and read them aloud.

Words:

   prompt, glimpse, tenth, plinth

Note: The word *glimpse* is the only word with the **mpse** ending. There are a few words that end in **pse** as listed in the samples.

Activity 5. Review the Triple Consonant Blend rules. Go over examples of each blend using the chalkboard or white board. Have the student add the given triple consonant blend to each of the word beginnings and read them aloud.

Words:

   zilch, belch, mulch, gulch
   catch, batch, latch, hatch
   switch, Scotch, crutch, Dutch
   snitch, sketch, clutch, snatch
   crunch, quench, hunch, trench
   French, stench, drench, clench

Review for Test. The instructor should plan to use some time at the end of the class to review and prepare for the test that follows this lesson. Review the objectives for the test and then look over the lessons that it will cover. If the student has struggled with any of the concepts that will be included in the test, some

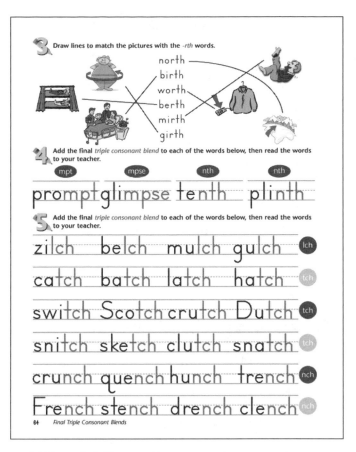

additional drill, practice, or review may be needed to adequately prepare him for the test.

Reading. Read and discuss the maxim for the Lesson.

Read the story *I Harvest My Grain*. This is another chapter of the *Robinson Crusoe* story. Preview the story and explain words or sentence structures that are not familiar to the student. With every story ask questions: who are the characters, what are they doing, what are they saying, where does the action take place, what is the order of events, what words are being used, what new information is given, what lesson can be learned?

Comprehension questions:

   How long had Robinson been away from the castle exploring the island?
   What kept Robinson from being lonely?
   Why did Robinson build a fence around his barley?
   What took the barley after the fence was built?
   How were the birds kept out of the barley?

Assign. Lesson activities or reading that are to be completed as homework.

Test 3
Lessons 15-24

Overview:

- Define a consonant blend
- Complete words with final consonant blends
- Complete sentences using words with final consonant blends
- Use picture clues to complete words with final consonant blends
- Complete words with both an initial and final consonant blend

Materials and Supplies:

- Teacher's Guide & Student Workbook 1

Instructions:

Assessment Start-up. The teacher should be available to answer any questions that the student may have during the test.

Activity 1. Read the instruction for the activity with the student. Review the pictures in the activity so the student can correctly identify them. Instruct the student to complete the word with the a letter from the list for the sound that he hears.

Pictures:

shelf, bulb, chalk, belt
weld, film, help, salt

Activity 2. Review the instructions and assist the student in reading any difficult words in the sentences. Instruct the student to complete the sentence with one of the word choices and underline it.

Sentences:

1. Will he pass the <u>test</u>?
2. I <u>slept</u> in the pink bed.
3. Did he <u>crash</u> the truck?
4. The bell is <u>ringing</u>.
5. <u>Bring</u> the raft to the camp.
6. Help stack the junk on the <u>desk</u>.

Activity 3. Read the instruction for the activity with the student. Review the pictures in the activity so the student can correctly identify them. Instruct the student to complete the word with a short vowel for the sound that he hears.

Pictures:

lift, gulp, elk, moth, half

Horizons Phonics & Reading Grade 2 Teacher's Guide

Activity 4. Read the instruction for the activity with the student. Review the pictures in the activity so the student can correctly identify them. Instruct the student to complete the word with a letter from the list for the sound that he hears.

Pictures:
    nest, dent, cent, slept
    duct, gift, cart, next

Activity 5. Read the instruction for the activity with the student. Review the pictures in the activity so the student can correctly identify them. Instruct the student to complete the word by selecting from the letters beside the word.

Pictures:
    snack, speck, stamp, stitch
    swing, sling, brick, prank
    skunk, crutch, frost, grind

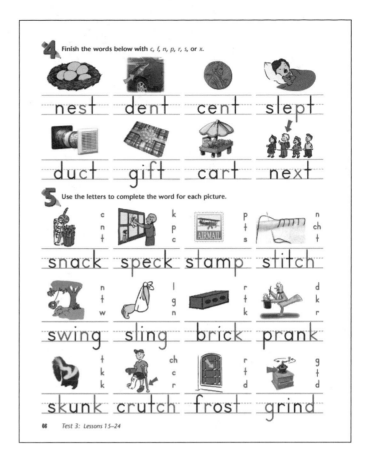

Assessment Follow-up. Every test is an important assessment of both the student's comprehension of the concepts and the instructional process. This makes follow-up after each test essential to the learning process. Review all of the errors made on the test with the student. Check for understanding of the concepts and of the problem instructions. Compare the errors made on the test to the test objectives to identify specific areas of weakness. If weak areas of understanding are detected it might be necessary to go back to those lessons to devise some enrichment activities for the concept.

The test results can be used to determine what concepts are reviewed during the daily time of classroom instruction. Devise enrichment activities that will provide development in those areas.

If time permits, choose a selection and have the student read it again. This can also be used as a catch-up time to complete unfinished selections.

Lesson 31: Medial Triple Consonant Blend tch & Compound Words

Overview:

- Read words with the medial **tch** trigraph
- Cross out silent letters
- Divide words into syllables
- Unscramble words with medial **tch**
- Match words to form compound words
- Read two-syllable and compound words with the **tch** trigraph

Materials and Supplies:

- Teacher's Guide & Student Workbook 1
- White board or chalkboard
- Word cards (as necessary)
- Phonics rules flashcards
- Reader: *Robinson Crusoe & Other Classic Stories*

Teaching Tips:

Review for Mastery. Discuss and review any work from the previous lesson that was assigned as homework. Check for completion of the activities and orally quiz the student for comprehension. Review any reading that was assigned, discussing the characters, setting, plot, theme, language, sequence, etc.

Strengthen fluency and phonemic awareness by reviewing words and sentences from previous lessons. Build vocabulary skills by using some of the words in sentences.

Review syllable rules for words with affixes and for compound words.

Activity 1. Review the rule for the **tch** consonant blend and the sample words in the rule box. *Words to teach the concept:* ditching, snatching, snitching, Dutchman, notchback, switchman, watchman. Divide these words into syllables and code the tch consonant blend. Review compound words. Have the student identify the pictures and read the words. Help the student with pronunciation. Have the student draw a line under the **tch** trigraph in the words and cross out the silent letter.

Words:

stitch/ing, match/ing, patch/ing, hatch/ing
pitch/ing, snatch/ing, catch/ing, sketch/ing
hatch/back, latch/ing, clutch/ing, hitch/ing
hop/scotch, nut/hatch, ketch/up, switch/back

Horizons Phonics & Reading Grade 2 Teacher's Guide

Activity 2. Review the rule and the **er** ending for the **tch** words. *Words to teach the concept:* itcher, latcher, patcher, switcher, watcher. Divide these words into syllables. Have the student read each of the **tch** words in the box. Point out the suffixes for each words. The student is to unscramble the words and write them on the line.

Words:

switching	butcher
catcher	etching
twitching	pitcher

Activity 3. Review the rule for compound words. Have the student read the words in each word list. The student will match a word from the first list to one in the second to form a compound word. Then the student will match a word from the center list to the words on the right to form compound words. Some words can be used more than once.

Words:

hatchback	lockstitch
matchup	hopscotch
ketchup	nuthatch
notchback	topnotch
	topstitch
	backstitch

Reading. Read and discuss the maxim for the Lesson.

Read the story *I Work Under Many Difficulties*. This is another chapter of the *Robinson Crusoe* story. Preview the story and explain words or sentence structures that are not familiar to the student. With every story ask questions: who are the characters, what are they doing, what are they saying, where does the action take place, what is the order of events, what words are being used, what new information is given, what lesson can be learned?

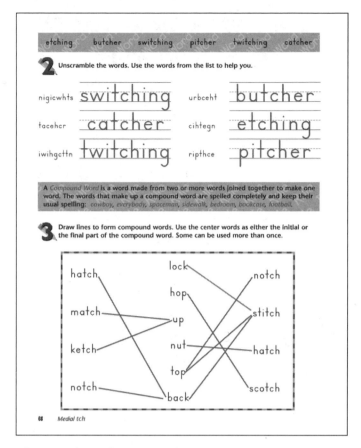

Comprehension questions:

What problem did Robinson face when the barley got ripe?

How was the problem solved?

What other problems did Robinson face and solve?

How was the old crowbar bent to make a pickax?

How were the tools sharpened?

Assign. Lesson activities or reading that are to be completed as homework.

Lesson 32: Review Final & Medial Triple Blends

Overview:

- Read words with triple consonant blends
- Recognize triple consonant blends in words
- Identify words with triple consonant blends
- Complete sentences with words having triple consonant blends
- Select words with triple consonant blends to complete sentences
- Read sentences

Materials and Supplies:

- Teacher's Guide & Student Workbook 1
- White board or chalkboard
- Word cards (as necessary)
- Phonics rules flashcards
- Reader: *Robinson Crusoe & Other Classic Stories*

Teaching Tips:

Review for Mastery. Discuss and review any work from the previous lesson that was assigned as homework. Check for completion of the activities and orally quiz the student for comprehension. Review any reading that was assigned, discussing the characters, setting, plot, theme, language, sequence, etc.

Strengthen fluency and phonemic awareness by reviewing words and sentences from previous lessons. Build vocabulary skills by using some of the words in sentences.

Review the **tch** triple consonant blend with Lesson 31, Activity 2. Divide the words into syllables and mark the silent **t** in the **tch** consonant blend.

Review the triple consonant rules from previous lessons.

Activity 1. Have the student read the words with triple consonant blends. Circle the consonant blend in each word and write it on the blank.

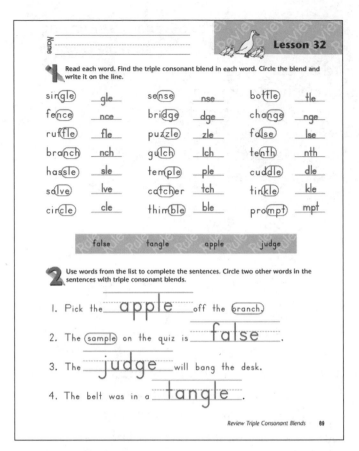

Activity 1 continued:

Blends:

gle	nse	tle
nce	dge	nge
fle	zle	lse
nch	lch	nth
sle	ple	dle
lve	tch	kle
cle	ble	mpt

Activity 2. Help the student read the word choices and the sentences. Instruct the student to select the word that will correctly complete each sentence and write the word on the line.

Sentences:

1. Pick the <u>apple</u> off the branch.
2. The sample of the quiz is <u>false</u>.
3. The <u>judge</u> will bang the desk.
4. The belt was in a <u>tangle</u>.

Have the student find the other two words used in the sentences with a triple consonant blend.

Words:

branch   sample

Horizons Phonics & Reading Grade 2 Teacher's Guide

Activity 3. Help the student read the sentences and the word choices. Instruct the student to circle the words that will correctly complete each sentence.

Sentences:
1. A <u>bubble</u> left the <u>nozzle</u> of the can.
2. His <u>uncle</u> sent him a <u>fiddle</u>.
3. Did the fall <u>cripple</u> his <u>ankle</u>?
4. <u>Rattle</u> the <u>little</u> <u>latch</u> on the <u>fence</u>.
5. Patrick put <u>twelve</u> cans in the bag.
6. The <u>distance</u> to the <u>bench</u> is an <u>inch</u>.
7. <u>Plunge</u> the <u>nozzle</u> in the <u>puddle</u>.
8. <u>Bundle</u> the twigs in the trash.
9. <u>Solve</u> the <u>puzzle</u> with a <u>sketch</u>.
10. <u>Rinse</u> the dish with the <u>nozzle</u>.
11. <u>Catch</u> a <u>glimpse</u> of the <u>shuttle</u> in the <u>distance</u>.
12. <u>Solve</u> the <u>riddle</u> with a <u>match</u>.
13. <u>Circle</u> the <u>dense</u> <u>jungle</u> with a <u>fence</u>.
14. The <u>catcher</u> can <u>fumble</u> the <u>pitch</u>.
15. Brad had a <u>pickle</u> at <u>lunch</u>.
16. A <u>gulch</u> is in the path of the <u>entrance</u>.
17. A <u>buckle</u> can <u>clench</u> the <u>ruffle</u> of the <u>bustle</u>.

Reading. Read and discuss the maxim for the Lesson.

Read the story *I Become a Potter*. This is another chapter of the *Robinson Crusoe* story. Preview the story and explain words or sentence structures that are not familiar to the student. With every story ask questions: who are the characters, what are they doing, what are they saying, where does the action take place, what is the order of events, what words are being used, what new information is given, what lesson can be learned?

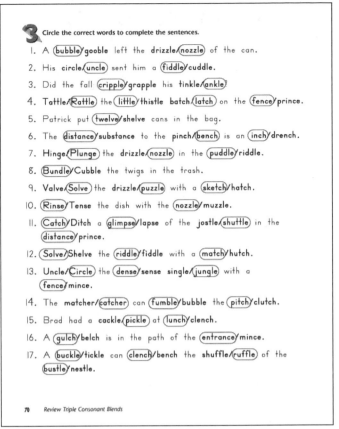

Comprehension questions:
What did Robinson need to make bread?
How was the problem solved?
What was used to make pots or jars?
How were the first clay items hardened?
What did Robinson discover in the coals of the fire?
How did Robinson make better pots?

Assign. Lesson activities or reading that are to be completed as homework.

Lesson 33: Initial Triple Consonant Blends spl, spr, str, shr, squ, scr, thr

Overview:

- Picture naming
- Word completion and reading
- Adding initial triple consonant blends **scr**, **spl**, **thr**, **shr**, **squ**, and **str** to words
- Auditory recognition of beginning consonant blends **scr**, **spl**, **thr**, **shr**, **squ**, and **str**
- Sentence reading

Materials and Supplies:

- Teacher's Guide & Student Workbook 1
- White board or chalkboard
- Word cards (as necessary)
- Phonics rules flashcards
- Reader: *Robinson Crusoe & Other Classic Stories*

Teaching Tips:

Review for Mastery. Discuss and review any work from the previous lesson that was assigned as homework. Check for completion of the activities and orally quiz the student for comprehension. Review any reading that was assigned, discussing the characters, setting, plot, theme, language, sequence, etc.

Strengthen fluency and phonemic awareness by reviewing words and sentences from previous lessons. Build vocabulary skills by using some of the words in sentences.

Build vocabulary skills by using some of the words from Lesson 32, Activity 1 in sentences.

Assist the student as needed in identifying the pictures and reading the words in the lesson. Review the rules for consonant digraphs and consonant blends. Ask students for examples of consonant digraph **wh** and consonant blends **pl**, **sl**, and **sm**.

Activity 1. Review the rule and the sample words for the **scr** consonant blend. *Words to teach the concept:* scrabble, scream, screech, scroll, scramble. Help the student identify each picture. Have the student complete the words underneath each picture. Read the words that have been formed.

Pictures:

scrub, scrap, scratch, scram

Activity 2. Review the rules and the sample words for the **spl** and **spr** consonant blends. *Words to teach the concept:* spleen, splice, splurge, sprawl, spread, sprout, spruce. Help the student identify each picture. Have the student complete the words underneath each picture. Read the words that have been formed.

Pictures:

splint, spring, sprig, splash

Activity 3. Help the student read the riddles. Instruct the student to underline the initial triple consonant blends in the questions.

Activity 3 continued:

Blends:

1. spl, spl, spl, spl
2. spr, spr, spr, spr
3. scr, scr, scr

Activity 4. Review the rules and the sample words for the **thr** and **shr** consonant blends. *Words to teach the concept:* thread, treat, three, throat, throne, shriek, shrew, shrill. Help the student identify each picture. Have the student complete the words underneath each picture. Read the words that have been formed.

Pictures:

throb, shred, shrimp, thrush

Activity 5. Review the rules and the sample words for the **squ** and **str** consonant blends. *Words to teach the concept:* squad, square, squat, squeak, squirrel, straight, straw, stream, street, strike, stroll. Help the student identify each picture. Have the student complete the words underneath each picture. Read the words that have been formed.

Pictures:

squid, strut, squint, string

Activity 6. Help the student read the riddles. Instruct the student to underline the initial triple consonant blends in the questions.

Blends:

1. thr, thr, thr, thr
2. squ, squ, squ
3. str, str, str, str, str
4. shr, shr, shr

Reading. Read and discuss the maxim for the Lesson.

Read the story *I Build a Big Canoe*. This is another chapter of the *Robinson Crusoe* story. Preview the story and explain words or sentence structures that are not familiar to the student. With every story ask questions: who are the characters, what are they doing, what

are they saying, where does the action take place, what is the order of events, what words are being used, what new information is given, what lesson can be learned?

Comprehension questions:

Although Robinson was quite happy on the island, what was one wish that he had?

What was Robinson's plan for the canoe?

How long did Robinson work on making the canoe?

What problem did Robinson have with the canoe?

What moral did Robinson remember from building the canoe?

How did Robinson cheer himself up?

What did Robinson wish he could trade for his gold?

Assign. Lesson activities or reading that are to be completed as homework.

Lesson 34: Long Vowel a, Final E Rule

Overview:

- Auditory recognition of long **a** sound
- Picture naming
- Apply the Final E Rule to read long vowel words
- Code long vowel words
- Word completion
- Match words to form compound words
- Reading long **a** words

Materials and Supplies:

- Teacher's Guide & Student Workbook 1
- White board or chalkboard
- Word cards (as necessary)
- Phonics rules flashcards
- Reader: *Robinson Crusoe & Other Classic Stories*

Teaching Tips:

Review for Mastery. Discuss and review any work from the previous lesson that was assigned as homework. Check for completion of the activities and orally quiz the student for comprehension. Review any reading that was assigned, discussing the characters, setting, plot, theme, language, sequence, etc.

Strengthen fluency and phonemic awareness by reviewing words and sentences from previous lessons. Build vocabulary skills by using some of the words in sentences.

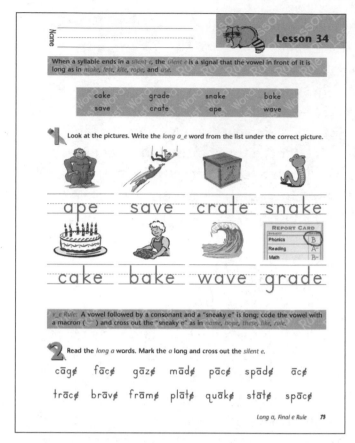

Activity 1. Review the Silent **e** Rule and the sample words. *Words to teach the concept:* ache, make, wave, space, gave, same, came, state, place, name, cake. Ask the student for some examples of short a words to write on the board. Add a silent **e** to these words and pronounce them with a long **a**. Point out any that are not real words. *Words to teach the concept:* pan–pane, man–mane, tan–tane, etc. Have the student read the words and help them identify the pictures. Have them write the words on the line under the picture.

Pictures:

ape, save, crate, snake
cake, bake, wave, grade

Activity 2. Review the **v_e** Rule with the student. Help the student read the words. Instruct the student to code the long vowel and the silent **e**. Review the **qu** Rule for the word *quake* and any other consonant blends that the student may find difficult.

Horizons Phonics & Reading Grade 2 Teacher's Guide

Activity 3. Help the student read the instructions and do some samples on the board. Have the student complete the words and then read them.

Answers will vary:

Look for real words and different words in each column.

Activity 4. Review the rule for compound words. Have the student read the words in each word list. The student will match a word from the first list to one in the second to form a compound word. The student will then write the words on the lines and read them.

Words:

wakeup
snakeskin
facelift
spaceman
nameplate
shipmate
bakeshop

Reading. Read and discuss the maxim for the Lesson.

Read the story *I Make an Umbrella*. This is another chapter of the *Robinson Crusoe* story. Preview the story and explain words or sentence structures that are not familiar to the student. With every story ask questions: who are the characters, what are they doing, what are they saying, where does the action take place, what is the order of events, what words are being used, what new information is given, what lesson can be learned?

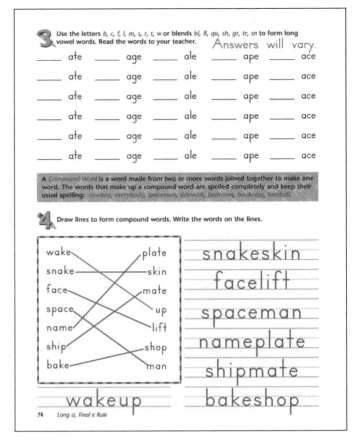

Comprehension questions:

What happened to the things brought from the ship?
What had Robinson saved from the animals?
What did Robinson first make from a skin?
What other clothes did Robinson make?
What did Robinson want to protect him from the sun?
What was Robinson's schedule of things to do for each day?

Assign. Lesson activities or reading that are to be completed as homework.

Lesson 35: Long Vowels i & e, Final E Rule

Overview:

- Auditory recognition of long **i** sound
- Auditory recognition of long **e** sound
- Apply the Final E Rule to read long vowel words
- Picture naming
- Code long vowel words
- Word completion
- Reading long **i** words
- Reading long **e** words

Materials and Supplies:

- Teacher's Guide & Student Workbook 1
- White board or chalkboard
- Word cards (as necessary)
- Phonics rules flashcards
- Reader: *Robinson Crusoe & Other Classic Stories*

Teaching Tips:

Review for Mastery. Discuss and review any work from the previous lesson that was assigned as homework. Check for completion of the activities and orally quiz the student for comprehension. Review any reading that was assigned, discussing the characters, setting, plot, theme, language, sequence, etc.

Strengthen fluency and phonemic awareness by reviewing words and sentences from previous lessons. Build vocabulary skills by using some of the words in sentences.

Review the Final E Rule. Write examples on the board. Review word cards as necessary.

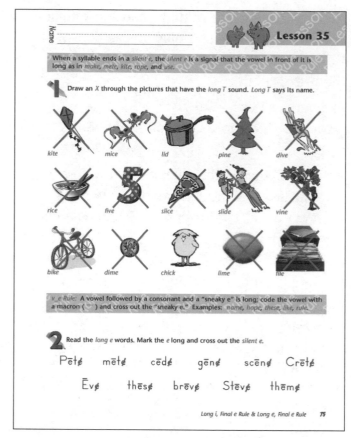

Activity 1. Review the Silent **e** Rule and the sample words. *Words to teach the concept:* five, white, fire, life, side, line, mile, while. Ask the student for some examples of short **i** words to write on the board. Add a silent **e** to these words and pronounce them with a long **i**. Point out any that are not real words. *Words to teach the concept:* pin–pine, sin–sine, tin–tine, bin–bine, etc. Review each of the pictures and have the student draw an **X** over the pictures for the long vowel words.

Pictures:
   kite, mice, lid, pine, dive
   rice, five, slice, slide, vine
   bike, dime, chick, lime, file

Answers:
   kite, mice, pine, dive
   rice, five, slice, slide, vine
   bike, dime, lime, file

Activity 2. Review the v_e Rule with the student. *Words to teach the concept:* Swede, scheme, theme, convene, obese, these, athlete, delete, trapeze. There are not very

Horizons Phonics & Reading Grade 2 Teacher's Guide

many long **e**_silent **e** words, most are spelled with vowel digraphs. Help the student read the words in the activity. Instruct the student to code the long vowel and the silent **e**. Review any consonant blends that the student may find difficult.

Activity 3. Help the student to read the word choices. Instruct the student to draw a square around the words with the long **i** sound.

Words:
   spite, trike
   glide, pike, prize, slime
   site, prime, smile
   pride, shine

Activity 4. Review the **v_e** Rule with the student. Help the student read the words. Instruct the student to code the long vowel and the silent **e**. Review any consonant blends that the student may find difficult.

Activity 5. Help the student read the instructions and do some samples on the board. Have the student complete the words and then read them.

Answers will vary:
   Look for real words and different words in each column.

Reading. Read and discuss the maxim for the Lesson.

Read the story *I Have a Perilous Adventure*. This is another chapter of the *Robinson Crusoe* story. Preview the story and explain words or sentence structures that are not familiar to the student. With every story ask questions: who are the characters, what are they doing, what are they saying, where does the action take place, what is the order of events, what words are being used, what new information is given, what lesson can be learned?

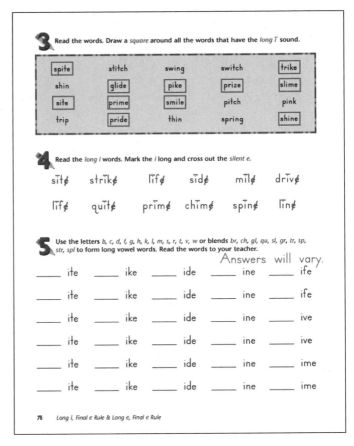

Comprehension questions:
   How did Robinson better prepare for building his second canoe?
   How long did it take to make the canoe?
   How long did it take to dig the ditch to launch the canoe?
   Was the canoe suitable for a long journey?
   Where did Robinson hope to travel in the canoe?
   What made Robinson's voyage harder that expected?
   How did Robinson overcome his problems in sailing the canoe?

Assign. Lesson activities or reading that are to be completed as homework.

Lesson 36: Long Vowel o, Final E Rule

Overview:

- Auditory recognition of long **o** sound
- Apply the Final E Rule to read long vowel words
- Picture naming
- Code long vowel words
- Word completion
- Reading long **o** words

Materials and Supplies:

- Teacher's Guide & Student Workbook 1
- White board or chalkboard
- Word cards (as necessary)
- Phonics rules flashcards
- Reader: *Robinson Crusoe & Other Classic Stories*

Teaching Tips:

Review for Mastery. Discuss and review any work from the previous lesson that was assigned as homework. Check for completion of the activities and orally quiz the student for comprehension. Review any reading that was assigned, discussing the characters, setting, plot, theme, language, sequence, etc.

Strengthen fluency and phonemic awareness by reviewing words and sentences from previous lessons. Build vocabulary skills by using some of the words in sentences.

Review the Final E Rule. Write examples on the board. Review word cards as necessary.

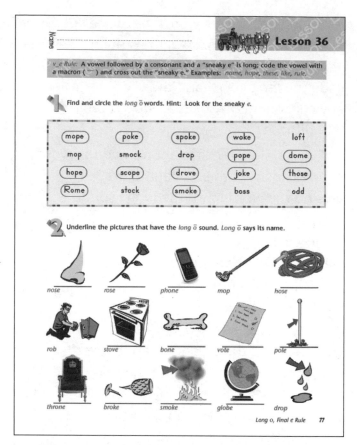

Activity 1. Review the Silent **e** Rule and the sample words. *Words to teach the concept:* mole, spoke, tone, woke, spoke, slope. Ask the student for some examples of short **o** words to write on the board. Add a silent **e** to these words and pronounce them with a long **o**. Point out any that are not real words. *Words to teach the concept:* ton–tone, bon–bone, son–sone, etc. Help the student to read the word choices. Instruct the student to draw a circle around the words with the long **o** sound.

Words:
   mope, poke, spoke, woke
   pope, dome
   hope, scope, drove, joke, those
   Rome, smoke

Activity 2. Review each of the pictures and have the student underline the pictures for the long vowel words.

Pictures:
   nose, rose, phone, mop, hose
   rob, stove, bone, vote, pole
   throne, broke, smoke, globe, drop

Horizons Phonics & Reading Grade 2 Teacher's Guide

Activity 2 continued:

Answers:
    nose, rose, phone, hose
    stove, bone, vote, pole
    throne, broke, smoke, globe

Activity 3. Help the student read the instructions and do some samples on the board. Have the student complete the words by choosing the correct letter.

Words:
    bone, cone, dome, hope
    joke, lone, mole, note
    poke, rope, stone, broke
    those, grove, scope, woke

Activity 4. Review the **v_e** Rule with the student. Help the student read the words. Instruct the student to code the long vowel and the silent **e**. Review any consonant blends that the student may find difficult.

Reading. Read and discuss the maxim for the Lesson.

Read the story *I Am Alarmed By a Voice*. This is another chapter of the *Robinson Crusoe* story. Preview the story and explain words or sentence structures that are not familiar to the student. With every story ask questions: who are the characters, what are they doing, what are they saying, where does the action take place, what is the order of events, what words are being used, what new information is given, what lesson can be learned?

    What were the first things Robinson did after getting back to land?
    Instead of sailing some more what did Robinson do?
    What did Robinson hear in the darkness?
    Who was doing the talking?
    Why didn't Robinson sail the canoe back to the little river?
    How did Robinson know that Poll the parrot loved him?

Assign. Lesson activities or reading that are to be completed as homework.

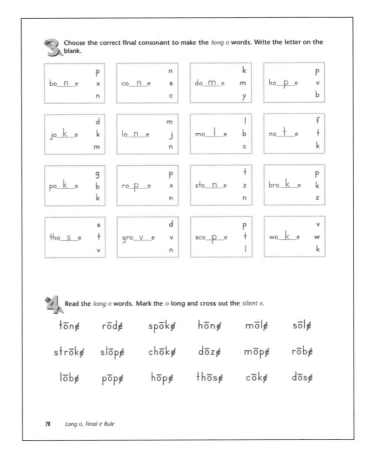

Lesson 37: Long Vowel u, Final E Rule

Overview:

- Auditory recognition of long **u** sound
- Apply the Final E Rule to read long vowel words
- Picture naming
- Code long vowel words
- Word completion
- Sentence reading
- Reading long **u** words

Materials and Supplies:

- Teacher's Guide & Student Workbook 1
- White board or chalkboard
- Word cards (as necessary)
- Phonics rules flashcards
- Reader: *Robinson Crusoe & Other Classic Stories*

Teaching Tips:

Review for Mastery. Discuss and review any work from the previous lesson that was assigned as homework. Check for completion of the activities and orally quiz the student for comprehension. Review any reading that was assigned, discussing the characters, setting, plot, theme, language, sequence, etc.

Strengthen fluency and phonemic awareness by reviewing words and sentences from previous lessons. Build vocabulary skills by using some of the words in sentences.

Review the Final E Rule. Write examples on the board. Review word cards as necessary.

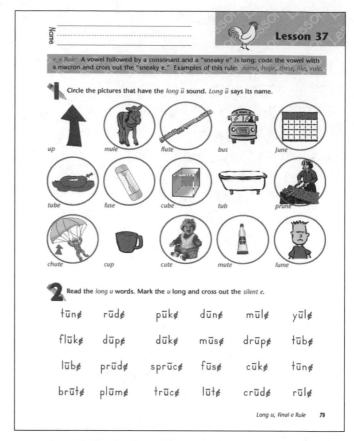

Activity 1. Review the Silent **e** Rule and the sample words. *Words to teach the concept:* acute, compute, conclude, excuse, produce, volume. Ask the student for some examples of short **u** words to write on the board. Add a silent **e** to these words and pronounce them with a long **u**. Point out any that are not real words. *Words to teach the concept:* cub–cube, cut–cute, tun–tune, etc. Have the student identify the pictures and draw a circle around the pictures with the long **u** sound.

Pictures:
  up, mule, flute, bus, June
  tube, fuse, cube, tub, prune
  chute, cup, cute, mute, fume

Answers:
  mule, flute, June
  tube, fuse, cube, prune
  chute, cute, mute, fume

Activity 2. Review the **v_e** Rule with the student. Help the student read the words. Instruct the student to code the long vowel and the silent **e**. Review any consonant blends that the student may find difficult like the **spr** in *spruce*.

Activity 3. Help the student read the instructions and do some samples on the board. Have the student complete the words by choosing the correct initial consonant sound or blend.

Words:
  brute, fuse, prune, prude
  duke, mule, fume, drupe
  tube, jute, tune, crude
  nuke, plume, cute, spruce

Activity 4. Assist the student as needed in reading the sentences where most of the words are long **u** words.

Reading. Read and discuss the maxim for the Lesson.

Read the story *I Am Happy as a King*. This is another chapter of the *Robinson Crusoe* story. Preview the story and explain words or sentence structures that are not familiar to the student. With every story ask questions: who are the characters, what are they doing, what are they saying, where does the action take place, what is the order of events, what words are being used, what new information is given, what lesson can be learned?

Comprehension questions:
  How many goats were in Robinson's herd?
  What supplies did Robinson get from the goats?
  What would a picture of Robinson look like?
  How did Robinson feel about his life?
  Who kept Robinson company?
  What did Robinson compare his life to?

Assign. Lesson activities or reading that are to be completed as homework.

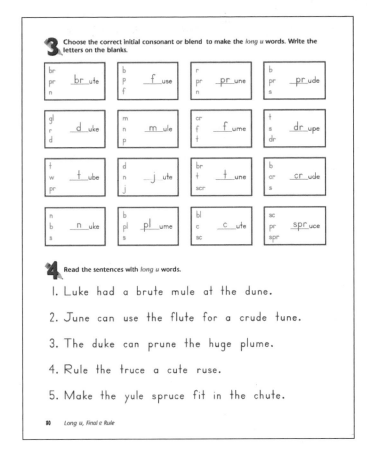

3 Choose the correct initial consonant or blend to make the *long u* words. Write the letters on the blanks.

br pr n	_br_ute	b P f	_f_use	r pr n	_pr_une	b pr s	_pr_ude
gl r d	_d_uke	m n P	_m_ule	cr f t	_f_ume	t s dr	_dr_upe
t w pr	_t_ube	d n j	_j_ute	br t scr	_t_une	b cr s	_cr_ude
n b s	_n_uke	b pl s	_pl_ume	bl c sc	_c_ute	sc pr spr	_spr_uce

4 Read the sentences with *long u* words.

1. Luke had a brute mule at the dune.
2. June can use the flute for a crude tune.
3. The duke can prune the huge plume.
4. Rule the truce a cute ruse.
5. Make the yule spruce fit in the chute.

80 *Long u, Final e Rule*

Lesson 38: Review Final E Long Vowel Words

Overview:

- Read short vowel words
- Read long vowel words
- Code long vowel words
- Auditory recognition of long vowel sound
- Apply the Final E Rule to read long vowel words
- Identify long vowel words in a word find
- Sentence completion with long vowel words

Materials and Supplies:

- Teacher's Guide & Student Workbook 1
- White board or chalkboard
- Word cards (as necessary)
- Reader: *Robinson Crusoe & Other Classic Stories*

Teaching Tips:

Review for Mastery. Discuss and review any work from the previous lesson that was assigned as homework. Check for completion of the activities and orally quiz the student for comprehension. Review any reading that was assigned, discussing the characters, setting, plot, theme, language, sequence, etc.

Strengthen fluency and phonemic awareness by reviewing words and sentences from previous lessons. Build vocabulary skills by using some of the words in sentences.

Review long **u_e** words with Lesson 37, Activity 4. Circle the long **u** words in the sentences, code the vowel long and make a slash over the silent **e** in each word.

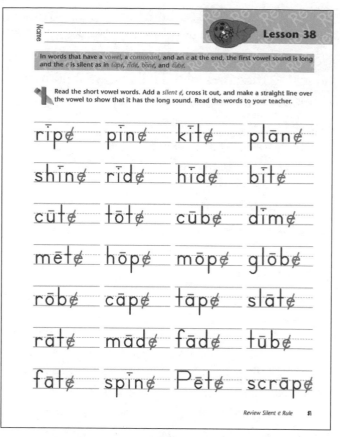

Activity 1. Have the student read all of the short vowel words in the activity. Instruct the student to change the short vowel words to long vowel words by adding a silent **e**. Have the student code the words and read them out loud.

Words:
  ripe, pine, kite, plane
  shine, ride, hide, bite
  cute, tote, cube, dime
  mete, hope, mope, globe
  robe, cape, tape, slate
  rate, made, fade, tube
  fate, spine, Pete, scrape

Activity 2. Help the student read the questions and the word choices in the box. Instruct the student to write the correct words on the line.

Sentences:

1. In what <u>state</u> do you <u>live</u>?
2. Can Nate <u>wave</u> at the man in <u>space</u>?
3. On what <u>side</u> of the <u>page</u> is the <u>name</u>?
4. Will <u>those</u> buses run <u>five</u> <u>miles</u>?
5. Can Pete <u>take</u> the <u>same</u> bike ride?
6. Did June find a <u>life</u> <u>line</u>?

Activity 3. Have the student read all of the words in the activity. Give them some tips for finding words in a puzzle like looking for the first letter of the word, etc. Instruct the student to find and circle each of the words in the puzzle.

Reading. Read and discuss the maxim for the Lesson.

Read the story *I Learn to Bake and Am Prosperous*. This is another chapter of the *Robinson Crusoe* story. Preview the story and explain words or sentence structures that are not familiar to the student. With every story ask questions: who are the characters, what are they doing, what are they saying, where does the action take place, what is the order of events, what words are being used, what new information is given, what lesson can be learned?

Comprehension questions:

What was Robinson's great wish?
What did Robinson use for a flour mill?
What was the hardest part to learn about bread making?
How did Robinson bake his first biscuits?

Assign. Lesson activities or reading that are to be completed as homework.

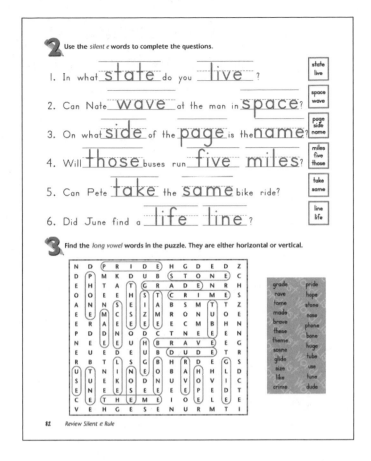

Lesson 39: Long Vowel a at the End of a Syllable, VCVopen

Overview:

- Auditory recognition of long vowel **a**
- Syllabications of two-syllable words
- Read VCVopen words
- Code VCVopen words
- Sentence completion with VCVopen words

Materials and Supplies:

- Teacher's Guide & Student Workbook 1
- White board or chalkboard
- Word cards (as necessary)
- Phonics rules flashcards
- Reader: *Robinson Crusoe & Other Classic Stories*

Teaching Tips:

Review for Mastery. Discuss and review any work from the previous lesson that was assigned as homework. Check for completion of the activities and orally quiz the student for comprehension. Review any reading that was assigned, discussing the characters, setting, plot, theme, language, sequence, etc.

Strengthen fluency and phonemic awareness by reviewing words and sentences from previous lessons. Build vocabulary skills by using some of the words in sentences.

Review long vowel silent **e** words with Lesson 38, Activity 2. Circle the other long vowel words in the sentences, code the vowel long and make a slash over the silent **e** in each word.

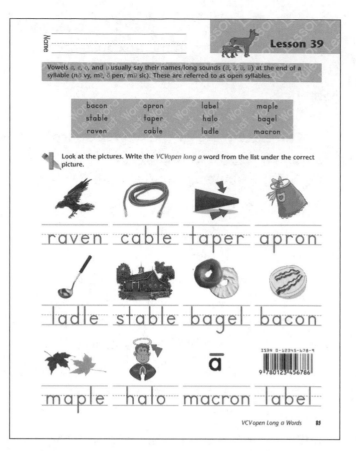

Activity 1. Review the Syllable Rule from previous lessons. Use the white board or chalkboard to illustrate. Review the VCVopen Syllable Rule and examples from this lesson. *Words to teach the concept:* Asia, lady, baby, radio, crazy, tomato, navy, station, equator, hazy, potato, vacation. Ask the student for examples. Read the words in the box. Review the pictures, and instruct the student to listen as you say the name of each picture. Have the student write the correct word under the picture.

Pictures:
  raven, cable, taper, apron
  ladle, stable, bagel, bacon
  maple, halo, macron, label

Activity 2. Review the definition of VCVopen words. Label the vowels and middle consonants in the example words used in Activity 1. Read the VCVopen words in this activity. Point out the coding in the first word. Have the student mark the vowels in all of the words. Then have the student mark the consonant between the vowels. Next, have the student divide each word into syllables. Finally, have the student mark the open vowel long.

Words:

A/pril, pa/per, ba/sic, ma/tron
ba/sis, sa/cred, na/sal, fa/tal, ga/la
va/por, ha/ven, a/gent, ha/tred, va/cant
ga/ble, fla/vor, sa/ble, pa/gan, ba/sic

Activity 3. Help the student read the words in the sentences. The student should use words from Activity 2 to complete the sentences. Read the completed sentences.

Sentences:

1. Put the pig in the <u>vacant</u> shed.
2. The fish had a bad <u>flavor</u>.
3. The home had a <u>gable</u> on the top.
4. Will the <u>agent</u> catch the bad man?
5. The <u>vapor</u> will make a smell in the home.

Note: Many words with an initial vowel **a** are pronounced with a schwa. Examples: *above*, *about*, *around*, and *ajar*. The student should not assume that every word that begins with **a** has a long sound.

Reading. Read and discuss the maxim for the Lesson.

Read the story *I Learn to Bake and Am Prosperous (continued)*. This is another chapter of the *Robinson Crusoe* story. Preview the story and explain words or sentence structures that are not familiar to the student. With every story ask questions: who are the characters, what are they doing, what are they saying, where does the action take place, what is the order of events, what words are being used, what new information is given, what lesson can be learned?

Horizons Phonics & Reading Grade 2 Teacher's Guide

VCVopen words: Long vowels at the end of syllables as in *clover, bacon, glider, fever, Friday, meter,* and *solo.*

2 Read the *VCVopen long a* words. Mark the vowels in each word with a *V*. Mark the consonant between the vowels in each word with a *C*. Divide each word into syllables. Mark the long open vowel at the end of the first syllable with a *macron*. The first one has been done for you.

a/ble   A/pril   pa/per   ba/sic   ma/tron
ba/sis   sa/cred   na/sal   fa/tal   ga/la
va/por   ha/ven   a/gent   ha/tred   va/cant
ga/ble   fla/vor   sa/ble   pa/gan   ba/sic

3 Use the words above to complete the sentences.

1. Put the pig in the _vacant_ shed.
2. The fish had a bad _flavor_.
3. The home had a _gable_ on the top.
4. Will the _agent_ catch the bad man?
5. The _vapor_ will make a smell in the home.

54   *VCVopen Long a Words*

Comprehension questions:
What made the bread baking successful?
What were the differences between the two plantations?
Where did Robinson often sleep when he was at the summer home?
How did Robinson keep the goats from running away?

Assign. Lesson activities or reading that are to be completed as homework.

Lesson 40: Long Vowel a Spelled ai & ay

Overview:

- Auditory recognition of long **a** sound
- Define a vowel digraph
- Read words with long **a** digraphs
- Apply the rule to read vowel digraphs
- Word completion
- Match pictures to words
- Code long vowel digraphs

Materials and Supplies:

- Teacher's Guide & Student Workbook 1
- White board or chalkboard
- Word cards (as necessary)
- Phonics rules flashcards
- Reader: *Robinson Crusoe & Other Classic Stories*

Teaching Tips:

Review for Mastery. Discuss and review any work from the previous lesson that was assigned as homework. Check for completion of the activities and orally quiz the student for comprehension. Review any reading that was assigned, discussing the characters, setting, plot, theme, language, sequence, etc.

Strengthen fluency and phonemic awareness by reviewing words and sentences from previous lessons. Build vocabulary skills by using some of the words in sentences.

Review VCVopen words with Lesson 39, Activity 1 by labeling the vowels with a **v**, labeling the consonant between the vowels with a **c**, dividing the words into syllables, and marking the open vowel long.

Review word cards as necessary.

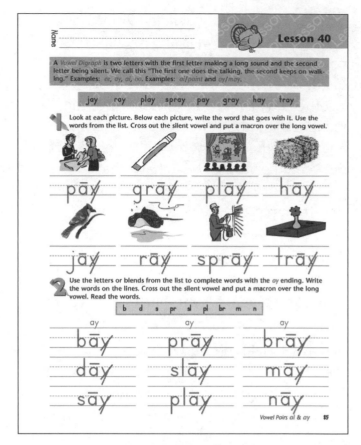

Activity 1. Review the definition of a vowel digraph and the examples. *Words to teach the concept:* gay, maybe, say, anyway, bay stay, pray, birthday, today. Help the student read the words in the box. Review the pictures. The student will write the correct word under each picture. Have the student code the vowel digraph by crossing out the silent vowel and placing a macron over the long vowel.

Words:
   pay, gray, play, hay
   jay, ray, spray, tray

Activity 2. The student is to use the word beginnings from the list and the word ending to write words on the lines. Code the words. Read the words.

Words:
   bay, pray, bray
   day, slay, may
   say, play, nay

Activity 3. Review the definition of a vowel digraph and the examples. *Words to teach the concept:* aid, wait, tail, pain, strait, afraid, claim, detail, explain, main, obtain, paid, plain, rail. Help the student read the words in the box. Review the pictures. The student will write the correct word under each picture. Have the student code the vowel digraph by crossing out the silent vowel and placing a macron over the long vowel.

Words:

  aim, train, chain, jail
  brain, nail, braid, maid

Activity 4. The student is to use the word beginnings from the lists and the word endings to write words on the lines. Code the words. Read the words.

Words:

train	chain	mail
brain		trail
grain		bail
main	fail	sail

Review for Test. The instructor should plan to use some time at the end of the class to review and prepare for the test that follows this lesson. Review the objectives for the test and then look over the lessons that it will cover. If the student has struggled with any of the concepts that will be included in the test, some additional drill, practice, or review may be needed to adequately prepare him for the test.

Reading. Read and discuss the maxim for the Lesson.

Read the story *I See Something in the Sand*. This is another chapter of the *Robinson Crusoe* story. Preview the story and explain words or sentence structures that are not familiar to the student. With every story ask questions: who are the characters, what are they doing, what are they saying, where does the action take place, what is the order of events, what words are being used, what new information is given, what lesson can be learned?

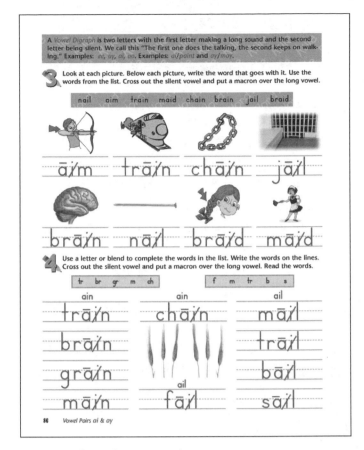

Comprehension questions:
  What gave Robinson great pleasure when he was at his summer house?
  What did Robinson see one morning as he walked to his canoe?
  How did Robinson react to seeing a footprint?
  How many days did Robinson hide in his castle?
  Who missed Robinson while he was hiding?
  What did Robinson do to better protect himself?
  How long did Robinson live in fear?

Assign. Lesson activities or reading that are to be completed as homework.

Test 4
Lessons 25-34

Overview:

- Define a consonant blend
- Complete words with initial consonant blends
- Match words to pictures with final triple consonant blends
- Match words to pictures with medial triple consonant blends
- Match words to pictures with initial triple consonant blends
- Complete words with both an initial and final consonant blend

Materials and Supplies:

- Teacher's Guide & Student Workbook 1

Instructions:

Assessment Start-up. Review the definitions of consonant blends and consonant digraphs.

Read through the test with the student. Identify the pictures, and help the student with any words that he is still unsure of. The teacher should be available to answer any questions that the student may have during the test.

Activity 1. Review the short vowel words and make sure the student can read them. Instruct the student to drop the initial consonant from the given word and to use the given consonant blends to write three new words. The student will read the words to the teacher.

Words:

pink	sock	rank
blink	block	blank
clink	clock	plank
plink	flock	clank
wing	cash	bush
cling	flash	flush
fling	clash	blush
sling	slash	plush

Activity 1 continued:

Note: Answers will vary as these are suggested answers.

Activity 2. Instruct the student to use the given consonant blends to form words with the word endings. The student will read the words to the teacher.

Words:

twist   swim   twitch or switch   dwelt

Activity 3. Help the student read the words in the box. Review the pictures. The student will write the correct word under each picture.

Pictures:

scrub   spring
shrimp   string

Activity 4. Read the instruction with the student. Review the pictures, making sure the student can correctly identify them. Instruct the student to match the picture to the word.

Pictures:

f. judge e. fiddle g. pickle c. castle j. thimble
i. ruffle a. apple b. bugle h. puzzle d. circle

Horizons Phonics & Reading Grade 2 Teacher's Guide

Activity 5. Read the instruction with the student. Review the pictures, making sure the student can correctly identify them. Instruct the student to match the picture to the word.

Pictures:

b. fence   **g.** torch   **c.** ketchup   **e.** north
a. church   **f.** stitching   **d.** lunch   **h.** twelve

Assessment Follow-up. Every test is an important assessment of both the student's comprehension of the concepts and the instructional process. This makes follow-up after each test essential to the learning process. Review all of the errors made on the test with the student. Check for understanding of the concepts and of the problem instructions. Compare the errors made on the test to the test objectives to identify specific areas of weakness. If weak areas of understanding are detected it might be necessary to go back to those lessons to devise some enrichment activities for the concept.

The test results can be used to determine what concepts are reviewed during the daily time of classroom instruction. Devise enrichment activities that will provide development in those areas.

If time permits, choose a selection and have the student read it again. This can also be used as a catch-up time to complete unfinished selections.

Lesson 41: Long Vowel e Spelled ee

Overview:

- Auditory recognition of long **e** sound
- Define a vowel digraph
- Complete words with long **e** digraphs
- Word completion
- Match words to form compound words
- Code long vowel digraphs

Materials and Supplies:

- Teacher's Guide & Student Workbook 1
- White board or chalkboard
- Word cards (as necessary)
- Phonics rules flashcards
- Reader: *Robinson Crusoe & Other Classic Stories*

Teaching Tips:

Review for Mastery. Discuss and review any work from the previous lesson that was assigned as homework. Check for completion of the activities and orally quiz the student for comprehension. Review any reading that was assigned, discussing the characters, setting, plot, theme, language, sequence, etc.

Strengthen fluency and phonemic awareness by reviewing words and sentences from previous lessons. Build vocabulary skills by using some of the words in sentences.

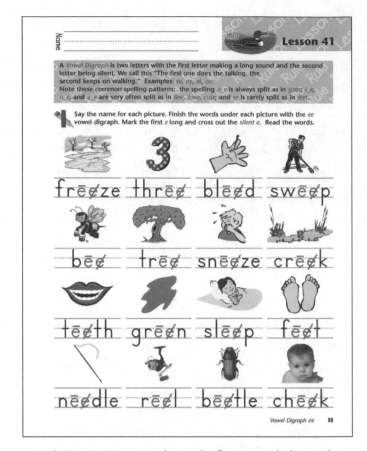

Activity 1. Discuss the rule for vowel digraphs. Use the white board or chalkboard to illustrate. Discuss the note in the rule for the spellings of the long vowel sound. Remind the student that there are not many long **e** words with the final **e** spelling. Compare the meanings and spelling of these long **e** words: mete–meet. *Words to teach the concept:* sleep, street, sweet, week, screen, succeed, see, degree, flee, goatee, freedom, breeze, canteen. Point out the **ee** spelling of the final **ee** long vowel sound. Review the pictures with the student. Have the student complete the words and code the vowel digraph. Read the words.

Words:
  freeze, three, bleed, sweep
  bee, tree, sneeze, creek
  teeth, green, sleep, feet
  needle, reel, beetle, cheek

Activity 2. Have the student complete the words by adding a consonant or blend to the root words. Read the words.

Words:

bee	fee	see	tee
beep	feed	seed	teen
beet	feeble	seem	teeth
beef	feel	seek	flee
beech	feet	seen	fleece
beetle	pee	seep	fleet
free	peek	lee	wee
freed	peel	leech	weed
freeze	peep	leek	week

Activity 3. Review the rule for compound words. Have the student read the words in each word list. The student will match a word from the first list to one in the second to form a compound word.

Words:

beekeep	canteen
teepee	nineteen
beebee	sixteen
freebee*	beeline
peewee	upkeep

Freebee is an alternate spelling for *freebie*, which is more common.

Note: Lines of matching will vary.

Reading. Read and discuss the maxim for the Lesson.

Read the story *I Am Again Alarmed*. This is another chapter of the *Robinson Crusoe* story. Preview the story and explain words or sentence structures that are not familiar to the student. With every story ask questions: who are the characters, what are they doing, what are they saying, where does the action take place, what is the order of events, what words are being used, what new information is given, what lesson can be learned?

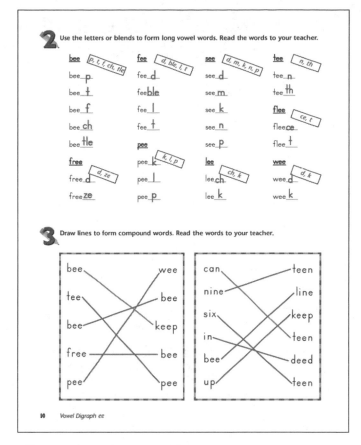

Comprehension questions:

How many years had it been since Robinson had seen the footprint?

Why did Robinson continue to be cautious?

What did Robinson think he saw in the water?

What made Robinson's heart stand still?

What is a cannibal?

Is cannibalism right?

Has cannibalism happened in the past?

Does cannibalism happen today?

How did Robinson react to the scene on the beach?

What did Robinson do after he ran to safety?

How long had Robinson lived on the island safely?

What helped Robinson to sleep without fear?

Assign. Lesson activities or reading that are to be completed as homework.

Lesson 42: Long Vowel e, at the End of a Syllable, CV & VCVopen, & Spelled ea

Overview:

- Auditory recognition of long **e** sound
- Apply the CV Rule to long **e** words
- Read CV words
- Code CV words
- Apply the VCVopen Rule to long **e** words
- Read VCVopen words
- Code VCVopen words
- Auditory recognition of long or short vowel sound
- Syllabications of two-syllable words
- Define a vowel digraph
- Apply the rule to read vowel digraphs
- Read words with long **e** digraph spelled **ea**
- Code digraph **ea** words
- Sentence completion with **ea** words

Materials and Supplies:

- Teacher's Guide & Student Workbook 1
- White board or chalkboard
- Word cards (as necessary)
- Phonics rules flashcards
- Reader: *Robinson Crusoe & Other Classic Stories*

Teaching Tips:

Review for Mastery. Discuss and review any work from the previous lesson that was assigned as homework. Check for completion of the activities and orally quiz the student for comprehension. Review any reading that was assigned, discussing the characters, setting, plot, theme, language, sequence, etc.

Strengthen fluency and phonemic awareness by reviewing words and sentences from previous lessons. Build vocabulary skills by using some of the words in sentences.

Review the **ee** long vowel digraph with Lesson 41, Activity 2. Have the student make a slash

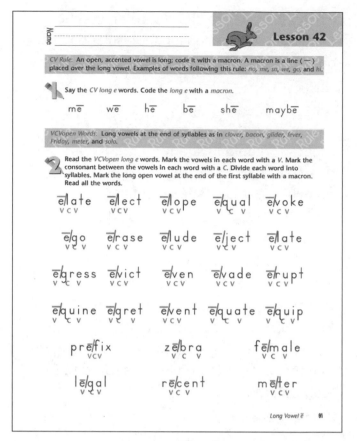

through the silent letter and code the vowel long. Review the "first vowel does the talking while the second keeps walking" rule.

Review the **ee** long vowel digraph with Lesson 41, Activity 3. Have the student write the compound words on a separate sheet of paper. Code the **ee** vowel digraph(s) in each word. Read each word and use it in a sentence.

Review the CV and CVCopen rules for the long **e** sound. Use the white board or chalkboard as necessary to demonstrate. Ask the student for additional examples of long **e** words. Assist the student as necessary in reading the words and identifying the pictures in the lesson.

Activity 1. Review the CV Rule for the long **e** sound. Use the white board or chalkboard as necessary to demonstrate. Ask the student for additional examples of long **e** words. There are only a few. *Words to teach the concept:* adobe, acme. Have the student read the CV long **e** words. Code the vowel long.

Activity 2. Review the CVCopen Rule for the long **e** sound. Use the white board or chalkboard as

Horizons Phonics & Reading Grade 2 Teacher's Guide

necessary to demonstrate. *Words to teach the concept:* equal, Egypt, ether. Point out the coding in the first word. Have the student mark the vowels in all of the words. Then have the student mark the consonant between the vowels. Next, have the student divide each word into syllables. Read the VCVopen words in the activity.

Words:

e/late, e/lect, e/lope, e/qual, e/voke
e/go, e/rase, e/lude, e/ject, e/late
e/gress, e/vict, e/ven, e/vade, e/rupt
e/quine, e/gret, e/vent, e/quate, e/quip
pre/fix, ze/bra, fe/male
le/gal, re/cent, me/ter

Note: The initial open vowel in some of these words is considered a schwa sound or a short **i** sound in some dictionaries.

Activity 3. Review the definition of a vowel digraph and the Long **e** Vowel Digraph Rule. *Words to teach the concept:* read, east, easy, Easter, neat, beat, clean, meat, peach, tea, flea, pea, beacon, beaker, defeat, squeak. Help the student read the words in the box. Review the pictures. The student will write the correct word under each picture. Have the student code the vowel digraph by crossing out the silent vowel and placing a macron over the long vowel.

Words:

eagle, beach, eat, beak
peanut, seal, team, leash
weasel, bleach, beaver, peacock

Activity 4. Help the student read the words in the sentences and the word choices in the instruction. The student should use the words to complete the sentences. Read the completed sentences. Have the student identify the other words used in the sentences with the **ea** digraph.

Sentences:

1. **The eagle will <u>eat</u> the teal in his beak.**
2. **The <u>weasel</u> will leave the feast.**
3. **Please pass the <u>meal</u> to Dean.**

Horizons Phonics & Reading Grade 2 Teacher's Guide

Reading. Read and discuss the maxim for the Lesson.

Read the story *I Make a Surprising Discovery*. This is another chapter of the *Robinson Crusoe* story. Preview the story and explain words or sentence structures that are not familiar to the student.

Comprehension questions:

What things was Robinson afraid to do?
Where did Robinson discover the cave?
What did Robinson make to do his cooking with?

Read the poem *If all the Seas Were One Sea*. Preview the poem and explain words or sentence structures that are not familiar to the student.

Comprehension questions:

What vowel digraphs can be found in the words?
Do all of the **ea** digraphs have the same sound?

Assign. Lesson activities or reading that are to be completed as homework.

Lesson 43: Long Vowel e Spelled -y and -ey

Overview:

- Auditory recognition of long **e** sound
- Read words with final long **e** spelled **-y** ending
- Match words with a final long **e** spelled **-y** to the picture
- Read words with final long **e** spelled **-ey** ending
- Match words with a final long **e** spelled **-ey** to the picture
- Sentence completion with final **-y** or **-ey** words
- Identify long vowel words in a word find

Materials and Supplies:

- Teacher's Guide & Student Workbook 1
- White board or chalkboard
- Word cards (as necessary)
- Phonics rules flashcards
- Reader: *Robinson Crusoe & Other Classic Stories*

Teaching Tips:

Review for Mastery. Discuss and review any work from the previous lesson that was assigned as homework. Check for completion of the activities and orally quiz the student for comprehension. Review any reading that was assigned, discussing the characters, setting, plot, theme, language, sequence, etc.

Strengthen fluency and phonemic awareness by reviewing words and sentences from previous lessons. Build vocabulary skills by using some of the words in sentences.

Pass out Lesson 42 and review the rules and words covered in the lesson.

Activity 1. Review the rule for the **y** spelling of long **e** at the end of some words. *Words to teach the concept:* baggy, candy, crazy, empty, hurry, plenty, skinny, worry, lucky. Read the words with the long **e** spelled **-y** endings. Identify the

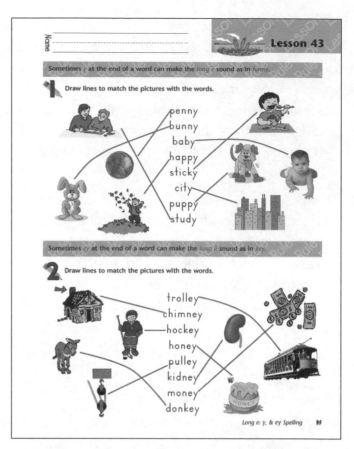

pictures, and have the student draw lines from the pictures to the correct words.

Pictures:

study	**sticky**
penny	**puppy**
bunny	**baby**
happy	**city**

Activity 2. Review the rule for the **ey** spelling of long **e** at the end of some words. *Words to teach the concept:* abbey, alley, baloney, galley, journey, turkey, key. Note that in a few words the **ey** spelling has a long **a** sound as in *survey*, *they*, *lamprey*, and *grey*. Read the words with the long **e** spelled **-ey** endings. Identify the pictures, and have the student draw lines from the pictures to the correct words.

Pictures:

chimney	**money**
hockey	**kidney**
donkey	**trolley**
pulley	**honey**

Activity 3. Help the student read the words in the sentences. Instruct the student to underline the word that completes the sentence and write it on the line. Read the sentences after they have been completed. Have the student identify the other words used in the sentences with the long **e** spelled with **-y** or **-ey** endings.

Sentences:
1. We need to get up <u>early</u>.
2. He will give the man the <u>money</u>.
3. Keith will eat in the <u>galley</u>.
4. The lady will read us a <u>story</u>.
5. I felt <u>sleepy</u> at the hockey game.
6. Amy will play an easy <u>medley</u> of the music.

Note the long **e** in the words *We, need, He, Keith, eat, lady, read, hockey, Amy,* and *easy.*

Activity 4. Have the student read all of the words in the activity. Give him some tips for finding words in a puzzle like looking for the first letter of the word, etc.

Reading. Read and discuss the maxim for the Lesson.

Read the story *I Make a Surprising Discovery (continued).* This is another chapter of the *Robinson Crusoe* story. Preview the story and explain words or sentence structures that are not familiar to the student. With every story ask questions: who are the characters, what are they doing, what are they saying, where does the action take place, what is the order of events, what words are being used, what new information is given, what lesson can be learned?

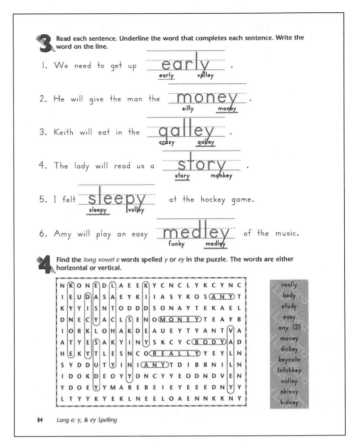

Comprehension questions:
Why did Robinson scramble out of the cave?
Why did Robinson go back into the cave?
What was making the noises in the cave?
How did Robinson treat the old goat?

Read the poem *What They Do.* Preview the poem and explain words or sentence structures that are not familiar to the student.

Comprehension questions:
What vowel digraphs can be found in the words?
How does the baby get the honey?

Assign. Lesson activities or reading that are to be completed as homework.

Lesson 44: Long Vowel e, as i Before e Rule & -ie at the End of a Word

Overview:

- Auditory recognition of long **e** sound
- Read words with final long **e** spelled **-ie** ending
- Match words with a final long **e** spelled **-ie** to the picture
- Define a vowel digraph
- Apply the rule to read vowel digraphs
- Apply the **i** Before **e** Rule to read vowel digraphs
- Read words with long **e** digraph spelled **ie**
- Code digraph **ie** words
- Sentence completion with **ie** digraph words

Materials and Supplies:

- Teacher's Guide & Student Workbook 1
- White board or chalkboard
- Word cards (as necessary)
- Phonics rules flashcards
- Reader: *Robinson Crusoe & Other Classic Stories*

Teaching Tips:

Review for Mastery. Discuss and review any work from the previous lesson that was assigned as homework. Check for completion of the activities and orally quiz the student for comprehension. Review any reading that was assigned, discussing the characters, setting, plot, theme, language, sequence, etc.

Strengthen fluency and phonemic awareness by reviewing words and sentences from previous lessons. Build vocabulary skills by using some of the words in sentences.

Activity 1. Review the definition for vowel digraphs. Illustrate on the chalkboard or white board, if desired. Review the rule for the **ie** digraph at the end of a word. This is an exception to "The first vowel does the talking while the second keeps on walking" rule. *Words to teach*

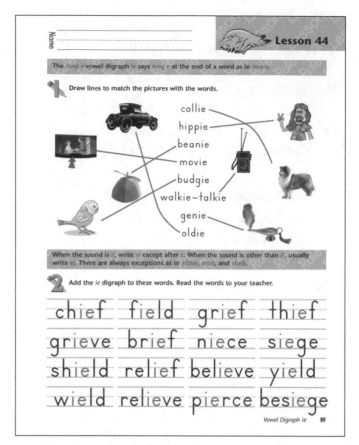

the concept: Brownie, cookie, goalie, lassie, prairie, rookie, sweetie. Read the words. Have the student identify the pictures and draw a line to match the pictures with the words.

Pictures:

oldie	hippie
movie	walkie-talkie
beanie	collie
budgie	genie

Activity 2. Review the rule for the **ie** digraph as **i** before **e** except after **c**. Again these are exception to "The first vowel does the talking while the second keeps on walking" rule. *Words to teach the concept:* achieve, diesel, hygiene, piece, priest, shriek. Have the student complete the words. Read the words.

Words:

chief, field, grief, thief
grieve, brief, niece, siege
shield, relief, believe, yield
wield, relieve, pierce, besiege

Note the short **i** sound of **e** in the first syllable of *relief*, *believe*, *relieve*, and *besiege*.

Horizons Phonics & Reading Grade 2 Teacher's Guide

Activity 3. Help the student read the sentences and the word choices. Assist the student with the meanings of unknown words. Instruct the student to complete each sentence. Read the sentences.

Sentences:

1. Give his <u>sweetie</u> a <u>piece</u> of the <u>brownie</u>.
2. The <u>hippie</u> had a <u>budgie</u> in his hand.
3. The <u>collie</u> was in a <u>movie</u> with the title of <u>Lassie</u>.
4. The <u>chief</u> put the <u>thief</u> in jail.
5. Bring the <u>priest</u> to <u>grieve</u> with the <u>niece</u>.
6. With a <u>shield</u> he will keep off the <u>fierce</u> attack of the <u>fiend</u>.
7. The <u>shriek</u> will <u>pierce</u> the calm of the <u>movie</u>.

Note the long **e** digraph **ee** in *sweetie*, the VCVopen long **o** in *movie*, and the **ai** digraph in the word *jail*.

Reading. Read and discuss the maxim for the Lesson.

Read the story *I Explore My Cave Further*. This is another chapter of the *Robinson Crusoe* story. Preview the story and explain words or sentence structures that are not familiar to the student. With every story ask questions: who are the characters, what are they doing, what are they saying, where does the action take place, what is the order of events, what words are being used, what new information is given, what lesson can be learned?

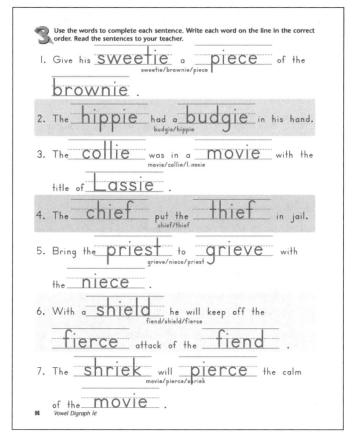

Comprehension questions:

How did Robinson make his candles?

What unpleasant task did Robinson do in the cave?

What did the large area of the cave remind Robinson of?

What use did Robinson see for the cave?

What was the one thing that made Robinson unhappy?

What animal supplied Robinson with eggs?

Assign. Lesson activities or reading that are to be completed as homework.

Lesson 45: Review Spellings of Long Vowels a & e

Overview:

- Auditory recognition of long vowel **a** & **e**
- Syllabications of two-syllable words
- Read VCVopen words
- Define a vowel digraph
- Read words with long **a** & **e** digraphs
- Code words with long vowel digraphs
- Apply the rule to read vowel digraphs
- Read words with final long **e** spelled **-y** ending
- Read words with final long **e** spelled **-ey** ending
- Read words with long **e** digraph spelled **ie**
- Classify words with long vowel sounds
- Match words to form compound words
- Unscramble words with long vowel **a** & **e** sounds

Materials and Supplies:

- Teacher's Guide & Student Workbook 1
- White board or chalkboard
- Word cards (as necessary)
- Phonics rules flashcards
- Reader: *Robinson Crusoe & Other Classic Stories*

Teaching Tips:

Review for Mastery. Discuss and review any work from the previous lesson that was assigned as homework. Check for completion of the activities and orally quiz the student for comprehension. Review any reading that was assigned, discussing the characters, setting, plot, theme, language, sequence, etc.

Strengthen fluency and phonemic awareness by reviewing words and sentences from previous lessons. Build vocabulary skills by using some of the words in sentences.

Review the **ie** vowel digraph with Lesson 44, Activities 1 & 2. Code the vowel digraphs in the activities. Cross out the silent **i** and code the **e** with a macron. These are exceptions to "The first vowel does the talking while the second goes on walking" rule.

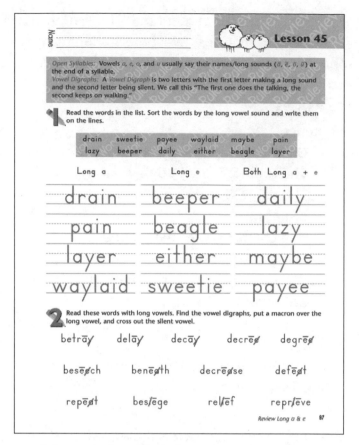

Build vocabulary skills by using some of the words from Lesson 44 in sentences.

Activity 1. Review the rules and vowel digraphs covered in Lessons 39-44. Help the student read the words in the box. The **ei** digraph as in the word *either* has not been covered. This is an example of a few words that do not follow the **i** Before **e** Rule. *Words to teach the concept:* caffeine, codeine, Holstein, Keith, neither, protein, receipt, seizure, Sheila. The student will classify the words by the long vowel sound and then write them on the line.

Words:
  drain, beeper, daily
  pain, beagle, lazy
  layer, either, maybe
  waylaid, sweetie, payee

Activity 2. Help the student read the long vowel words. Have the student find and code the long vowel digraph in each word.

Activity 2 continued:

Words:

betr<u>ay</u>, del<u>ay</u>, dec<u>ay</u>, decr<u>ee</u>, degr<u>ee</u>
bes<u>ee</u>ch, ben<u>ea</u>th, decr<u>ea</u>se, def<u>ea</u>t
rep<u>ea</u>t, bes<u>ie</u>ge, rel<u>ie</u>f, repr<u>ie</u>ve

Note the "first vowel does the talking" exceptions in *besiege*, *relief*, and *reprieve*.

Activity 3. Review the rule for compound words. Have the student read the words in each word list. The student will match a word from the first list to one in the second to form a compound word. Read the compound words that are formed.

Words:

leeway
mainstream
maybe
freeway
waylaid

Activity 4. Have the student read the words in the box. The student is to unscramble the words and write them on the line.

Words:

daisy, needy
zany, dainty
trainee, crazy

Activity 5. Help the student read the sentences. Instruct the student to read the sentences again and circle the words with the long **a** or **e** sound. The student may wish to focus on one vowel sound at a time.

Sentences:

1. <u>Faith</u> is a <u>trait</u> of a <u>saint</u>.
2. <u>Delay</u> will <u>raise</u> the <u>decay</u>.
3. The <u>trainee</u> is a <u>greedy</u> <u>payee</u>.
4. <u>Maybe</u> the <u>beagle</u> is <u>beneath</u> the <u>drain</u>.
5. <u>Be</u> a <u>sweetie</u> and <u>retrieve</u> the <u>beanie</u> for the <u>baby</u>.
6. <u>Either</u> <u>he</u> will <u>seize</u> the <u>crayfish</u> or <u>paint</u> the <u>steeple</u>.
7. The <u>pathway</u> was <u>beneath</u> the <u>main-stream</u> of the <u>speedy</u> <u>freeway</u>.
8. <u>Neither</u> the <u>beeper</u> nor the <u>radio</u> did <u>raise</u> the <u>sleeper</u>.

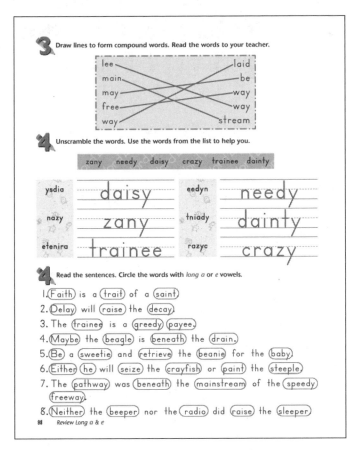

Note: Some words have both a long **a** and long **e** sound.

Note the long **o** final syllable in *radio*.

Reading. Read and discuss the maxim for the Lesson.

Read the story *I See Savages*. This is another chapter of the *Robinson Crusoe* story. Preview the story and explain words or sentence structures that are not familiar to the student. With every story ask questions: who are the characters, what are they doing, what are they saying, where does the action take place, what is the order of events, what words are being used, what new information is given, what lesson can be learned?

Comprehension questions:

Why did Robinson get up early to do his work?
What did Robinson see in the darkness?
How did Robinson react to the fire?
Where did Robinson go when he left his castle?

Assign. Lesson activities or reading that are to be completed as homework.

Lesson 46: Long Vowel i Spelled ie & Wild Colt i Before ld

Overview:

- Auditory recognition of long vowel **i**
- Matching pictures to words
- Complete words with **ie** long **i** digraph
- Read words with **ie** long **i** digraph
- Apply the rule to read long **i** Wild Colt words
- Auditory discrimination of long and short **i**
- Sentence completion with long **i** Wild Colt words

Materials and Supplies:

- Teacher's Guide & Student Workbook 1
- White board or chalkboard
- Word cards (as necessary)
- Phonics rules flashcards
- Reader: *Robinson Crusoe & Other Classic Stories*

Teaching Tips:

Review for Mastery. Discuss and review any work from the previous lesson that was assigned as homework. Check for completion of the activities and orally quiz the student for comprehension. Review any reading that was assigned, discussing the characters, setting, plot, theme, language, sequence, etc.

Strengthen fluency and phonemic awareness by reviewing words and sentences from previous lessons. Build vocabulary skills by using some of the words in sentences.

Review long vowel digraphs by coding the vowels in Lesson 45, Activities 1, 4, and 5. Note that some of the words have two digraphs.

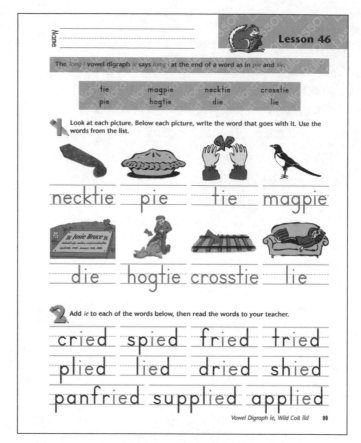

Activity 1. Review the Long **i** Rule for the **ie** digraph. *Words to teach the concept:* cowpie, die, untie. Help the student read the words in the box. Review the pictures. The student will write the correct word under each picture.

Words:
  necktie, pie, tie, magpie
  die, hogtie, crosstie, lie

Activity 2. Review the rule for the **ie** digraph with the long **i** sound. Have the student complete the words. Read the words.

Words:
  cried, spied, fried, tried
  plied, lied, dried, shied
  panfried, supplied, applied

Activity 3. Review the Wild Colt Rule. *Words to teach the concept:* bind, behind, blind, hind, mind, childhood, wildfire, wildflower, godchild. Point out the different consonant blends for these words. Have the student read the words aloud in each row. Then ask the student to circle the word in the row with the long **i** sound.

Words:

child, mild, rind, wild, kind, find, pint

Activity 4. Help the student read the sentences and the word choices. Instruct the student to circle the word that completes the sentence and to write it on the line. Read the sentences again.

Sentences:
1. The <u>stepchild</u> went to his mom.
2. He saw a <u>wildcat</u> in the woods.
3. She stopped to <u>find</u> a rare leaf.
4. Beth will <u>grind</u> the peanut.
5. The <u>grandchild</u> ran to see the magpie.

Reading. Read and discuss the maxim for the Lesson.

Read the story *I See Savages (continued)*. This is another chapter of the *Robinson Crusoe* story. Preview the story and explain words or sentence structures that are not familiar to the student. With every story ask questions: who are the characters, what are they doing, what are they saying, where does the action take place, what is the order of events, what words are being used, what new information is given, what lesson can be learned?

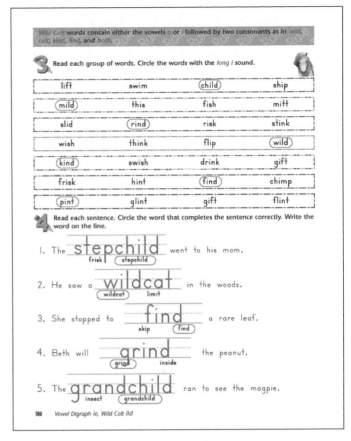

Comprehension questions:
  What did Robinson see from his lookout?
  When did Robinson feel the savages would leave?
  Where did the savages go after they got back into their canoes?
  Where did Robinson go after the savages left?
  How many canoes did Robinson see?
  What did Robinson see in the sand?
  What was Robinson always planning and dreaming about?

Read the poem *Simple Simon*. Preview the poem and explain words or sentence structures that are not familiar to the student.

Comprehension questions:
  What are the long **e** words in the poem?
  What are the rhyming words in the poem?

Assign. Lesson activities or reading that are to be completed as homework.

Lesson 47: Long Vowel i Spelled y, igh, ey, & uy

Overview:

- Auditory recognition of long vowel **i**
- Matching pictures to words
- Complete compound words with **y** and **uy** long **i** sound
- Read words with **uy** long **i** digraph
- Apply **igh** Silent **gh** Rule to read long **i** words
- Code words with long **i** silent **gh**

Materials and Supplies:

- Teacher's Guide & Student Workbook 1
- White board or chalkboard
- Word cards (as necessary)
- Reader: *Robinson Crusoe & Other Classic Stories*

Teaching Tips:

Review for Mastery. Discuss and review any work from the previous lesson that was assigned as homework. Check for completion of the activities and orally quiz the student for comprehension. Review any reading that was assigned, discussing the characters, setting, plot, theme, language, sequence, etc.

Strengthen fluency and phonemic awareness by reviewing words and sentences from previous lessons. Build vocabulary skills by using some of the words in sentences.

Review the **ie** long **i** digraphs with Lesson 46, Activity 1. Have the student code the vowel digraph by crossing out the silent vowel and placing a macron over the long vowel.

Review the **i** sound of **y** and **ie** with Lesson 46, Activity 2. On the board start with the base word and then add the **-ed** ending by changing the final **y** to **i** and adding **-ed**: cry–cried, spy–spied.

Activity 1. Review and illustrate the rule on the board. *Words to teach the concept:* dry, my, shy, try, why, apply, July, reply, deny. Instruct the

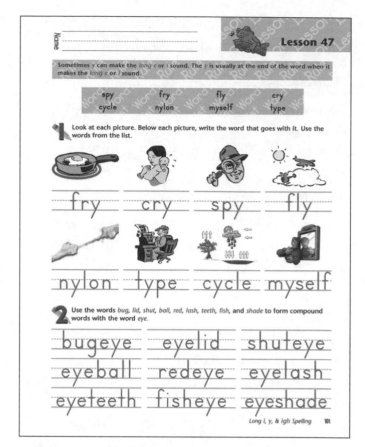

student to read each of the words in the box. Review the pictures with the student. Have the student write the correct word under each picture.

Words:

fry, cry, spy, fly
nylon, type, cycle, myself

Activity 2. Only one word with the long **i** sound is spelled **ey**, it is the word *eye*. Use each of the words listed in the instruction to form compound words with the word *eye*. The words either begin or end with the word *eye*. Have the student write the words on the line.

Words:

bugeye, eyelid, shuteye
eyeball, redeye, eyelash
eyeteeth, fisheye, eyeshade

Note: These words can be in any order.

Activity 3. Discuss the **i** Followed by Silent **gh** Rule. *Words to teach the concept:* blight, flight, sight, tight, highland, knight, lightning, midnight, bullfight, highlight. Assist the student in reading the words. Have the student code the words. Then have the student read the words again.

Activity 3 continued:

Words:

high, light, nigh, bright, sigh
fight, right, fright, night, thigh
catfight, upright, slight, penlight, insight
fistfight, alright, highjack, delight, skylight

Activity 4. Only two words with the long **i** sound are spelled **uy**; they are the words *buy* and *guy*. Use each of the words listed in the instruction to form compound words with the word *buy*. Have the student write the words on the line. Read the words.

Words:

buyback, buyout, underbuy

Note: These words can be in any order.

Activity 5. Only two words with the long **i** sound are spelled **uy**; they are the words *buy* and *guy*. Use each of the words listed in the instruction to form compound words with the word *guy*. Have the student write the words on the line. Read the words.

Words:

guyline, wiseguy

Note: These words can be in any order.

Activity 6. Only one word with the long **i** sound is spelled **ey**; it is the word *eye*. Use each of the words listed in the instruction to form compound words with the word *eye*. Have the student write the words on the line.

Words:

buckeye, eyepiece, oxeye
walleye, pinkeye, eyeglass
eyelid, eyebrow, eyesight

Notes: These words can be in any order. Note the **ight** in the word *sight*. This activity is parallel to Activity 2 in this lesson and can be assigned as homework or done for review to start the next class period.

Reading. Read and discuss the maxim for the Lesson.

Read the story *I Discover a Wreck*. This is another chapter of the *Robinson Crusoe* story. Preview the story and explain words or sentence structures that are not familiar to the student.

Comprehension questions:

Where was Robinson during the storm?
What did Robinson hear that caused him to leave the safety of his castle?
Where did he go to check on the noise?
What did Robinson do in hopes of saving the men on the ship?
What did Robinson see in the morning?

Read the poem *Fly Away, Fly Away*. Preview the poem and explain words or sentence structures that are not familiar to the student.

How is the sound of long **i** spelled in this poem?
What are the rhyming words in the poem?

Assign. Lesson activities or reading that are to be completed as homework.

Lesson 48: Long Vowel o Spelled oa & oe

Overview:

- Auditory recognition of long vowel **o**
- Complete words with **oa** and **oe** long **o** sound
- Read words with **oa** long **o** digraph
- Matching pictures to words
- Apply Long **o** Digraph Rule to words
- Complete sentences with long **o** digraphs

Materials and Supplies:

- Teacher's Guide & Student Workbook 1
- White board or chalkboard
- Word cards (as necessary)
- Phonics rules flashcards
- Reader: *Robinson Crusoe & Other Classic Stories*

Teaching Tips:

Review for Mastery. Discuss and review any work from the previous lesson that was assigned as homework. Check for completion of the activities and orally quiz the student for comprehension. Review any reading that was assigned, discussing the characters, setting, plot, theme, language, sequence, etc.

Strengthen fluency and phonemic awareness by reviewing words and sentences from previous lessons. Build vocabulary skills by using some of the words in sentences.

Activity 1. Review the rule for long vowel **oa** digraph. *Words to teach the concept:* coat, soap, coast, toast, roast, coach, railroad. Have the student complete the words. Read the words.

Words:
   toad, float, Joan, road
   coax, boast, soak, throat

Activity 2. Review the rule for long vowel **oe** digraph. Have the student complete the words. Read the words.

Words:
   toe, hoe, Joe, doe

Activity 3. Review the rule for long vowel **oa** digraph. Read the words. Have the student identify the pictures and draw a line to match the pictures with the words.

Pictures:

goat	oat
soap	loaf
boat	roast
oath	oak

Activity 4. Review the words in the list. Help the student read the crossword puzzle clues. Assist the student as necessary with the crossword puzzle.

Across:
3. goal
5. cockroach
8. coast
10. coach
13. railroad
14. load
15. cloak

Down:
1. foal
2. coal
4. broach
6. oatmeal
7. moat
9. toad
11. coat
12. croak

Activity 5. Help the student read the words in the sentences. Instruct the student to circle the word that completes the sentence and write it on the line. Read the sentences after they have been completed.

Sentences:
1. **The bank will give a <u>loan</u> to his mom.**
2. **At lunch we had <u>toast</u> and jam.**
3. **<u>Poach</u> the egg in the water.**
4. **Rub <u>soap</u> on the muddy <u>toe</u>.**
5. **The <u>doe</u> ran along the <u>road</u>.**

Reading. Read and discuss the maxim for the Lesson.

Read the story *I Discover a Wreck (continued).* This is another chapter of the *Robinson Crusoe* story. Preview the story and explain words or sentence structures that are not familiar to the student. With every story ask questions: who are the characters, what are they doing, what are they saying, where does the action take place, what is the order of events, what words are being used, what new information is given, what lesson can be learned?

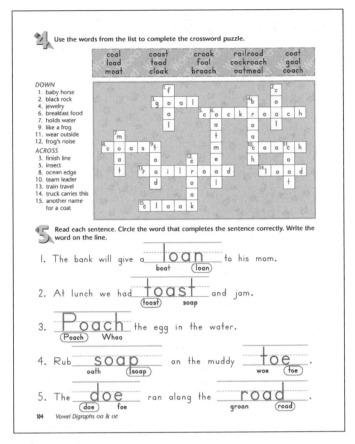

Comprehension questions:
What could Robinson see through his spyglass?
What was Robinson's wish after seeing the wrecked ship?
What plans did Robinson make?
What made Robinson worry if he could reach the ship?
How did Robinson react to seeing the current?

Read the poem *I Had a Little Pony.* Preview the poem and explain words or sentence structures that are not familiar to the student.

Comprehension questions:
How is the sound of long **i** spelled in this poem?
How is the sound of long **o** spelled in this poem?
What lesson is taught by the poem?
What are the rhyming words in the poem?

Assign. Lesson activities or reading that are to be completed as homework.

Lesson 49: Long Vowel o as Wild Colt o before st and ld

Overview:

- Word/picture match
- Auditory discrimination of long vowel **o**
- Apply Wild Colt Rule to read long **o** words
- Classify words by the vowel sound
- Code Wild Colt words
- Sentence completion

Materials and Supplies:

- Teacher's Guide & Student Workbook 1
- White board or chalkboard
- Word cards (as necessary)
- Phonics rules flashcards
- Reader: *Robinson Crusoe & Other Classic Stories*

Teaching Tips:

Review for Mastery. Discuss and review any work from the previous lesson that was assigned as homework. Check for completion of the activities and orally quiz the student for comprehension. Review any reading that was assigned, discussing the characters, setting, plot, theme, language, sequence, etc.

Strengthen fluency and phonemic awareness by reviewing words and sentences from previous lessons. Build vocabulary skills by using some of the words in sentences.

Review the **oa** vowel digraph with Lesson 48, Activity 1 & 2. Have the student code the long vowel and put a slash over the silent vowel.

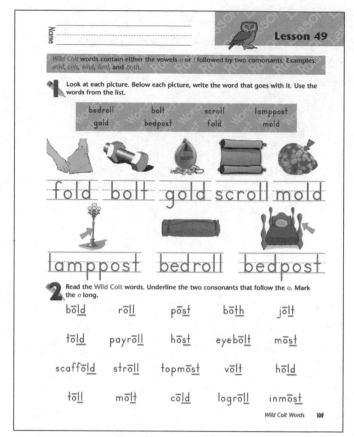

Activity 1. Review the rule for Wild Colt words. *Words to teach the concept:* behold, billfold, blindfold, bold, cold, scold, uphold, bankroll, enroll, knoll, unroll, guidepost, goalpost, most, signpost, colt, jolt, volt, both. Have the student read the words in the box aloud. Have the student name the pictures. Have the student write the correct word under each picture.

Words:

**fold, bolt, gold, scroll, mold
lamppost, bedroll, bedpost**

Activity 2. Have the student read the words aloud. The student will underline the two consonants that follow the long vowel **o** and code the **o** as long.

Activity 3. Have the student read the words aloud. The student will classify the words and write them under the correct category of vowel sound.

Words:

both	loss
bolt	rock
uphold	body
drumroll	cloth

Activity 4. Help the student read the words in the sentences and all of the Wild Colt word choices. Instruct the student to circle the words that complete the sentence and write them on the lines. Read the sentences after they have been completed.

Sentences:

1. <u>Both</u> Joan and Rolly rode the black <u>colt</u>.
2. Take a <u>stroll</u> past the next <u>milepost</u>.
3. <u>Fold</u> the sheet and put it by the <u>bedpost.</u>
4. The boss kept the <u>payroll</u> in his <u>billfold</u>.
5. He <u>sold</u> the <u>eyebolt</u> at his shop.

Reading. Read and discuss the maxim for the Lesson.

Read the story *I Make Another Voyage*. This is another chapter of the *Robinson Crusoe* story. Preview the story and explain words or sentence structures that are not familiar to the student. With every story ask questions: who are the characters, what are they doing, what are they saying, where does the action take place, what is the order of events, what words are being used, what new information is given, what lesson can be learned?

Comprehension questions:

How did Robinson avoid getting pulled out to sea?

What was Robinson's reaction to seeing the wrecked ship?

What living things did Robinson see on the wreck?

What was the sad sight on the wreck?

What did Robinson load into his canoe?

What made Robinson's trip back to land successful?

What did Robinson find in the chests?

What things in the chests were of no value?

How was Robinson watchful on a daily basis?

Assign. Lesson activities or reading that are to be completed as homework.

Lesson 50: Long Vowel o Spelled ow, ou, & ough

Overview:

- Word/picture match
- Auditory discrimination of long vowel **o**
- Apply the Diphthong Rule to read **ow** long **o** words
- Classify words by the vowel sound
- Apply the Digraph Rule to read **ou** & **ough** long **o** words
- Sentence reading

Materials and Supplies:

- Teacher's Guide & Student Workbook 1
- White board or chalkboard
- Word cards (as necessary)
- Phonics rules flashcards
- Reader: *Robinson Crusoe & Other Classic Stories*

Teaching Tips:

Review for Mastery. Discuss and review any work from the previous lesson that was assigned as homework. Check for completion of the activities and orally quiz the student for comprehension. Review any reading that was assigned, discussing the characters, setting, plot, theme, language, sequence, etc.

Strengthen fluency and phonemic awareness by reviewing words and sentences from previous lessons. Build vocabulary skills by using some of the words in sentences.

Review Wild Colt words with Lesson 49, Activity 4. Have the student make up a sentence for each of the unused words.

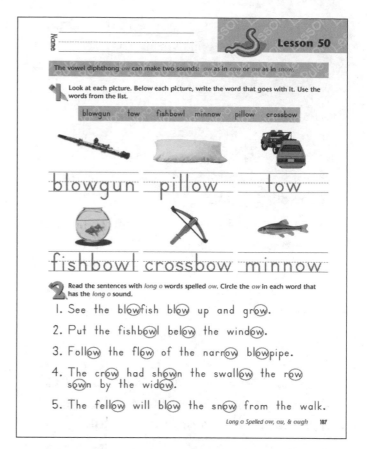

Activity 1. Review the **ow** Diphthong Rule. Cover examples of the **ow** vowel diphthong on the board. *Words to teach the concept:* snow plow, slow cow. This activity will focus on the **ow** diphthong with a long **o** sound. Have the student read the words in the box aloud. Have the student name the pictures. Have the student write the correct word under each picture.

Words:

  blowgun, pillow, tow
  fishbowl, crossbow, minnow

Activity 2. Help the student read the sentences. Instruct the student to circle the words that have the **ow** long **o** sound in each sentence.

Sentences:

  1. See the bl<u>ow</u>fish bl<u>ow</u> up and gr<u>ow</u>.
  2. Put the fishb<u>ow</u>l bel<u>ow</u> the wind<u>ow</u>.
  3. Foll<u>ow</u> the fl<u>ow</u> of the narr<u>ow</u> bl<u>ow</u>pipe.
  4. The cr<u>ow</u> had sh<u>ow</u>n the swall<u>ow</u> the r<u>ow</u> s<u>ow</u>n by the wid<u>ow</u>.
  5. The fell<u>ow</u> will bl<u>ow</u> the sn<u>ow</u> from the walk.

Activity 3. Review the rules for spellings of the long **o** sound. *Words to teach the concept:* soul, four, court, although, doughboy, sourdough. Have the student read the words in the box aloud. Have the student name the pictures. Have the student write the correct word under each picture.

Words:

> boulder, dough, poultry
> doughnut, shoulder

Activity 4. Help the student read the sentences. Instruct the student to circle the words that have the **ow**, **ou**, or **ough** long **o** sound in each sentence.

Sentences:

1. Sh**ow** the d**ough**nut to the fell**ow**.
2. Kn**ow** that the d**ough** will gr**ow**.
3. Sh**ou**lder the b**ow**line and t**ow** the boat from the will**ow**s.
4. M**ow** the grass bel**ow** the b**ou**lder.
5. The d**ough** will gr**ow** th**ough** the b**ow**l is cold.
6. Thr**ow** the d**ough** bel**ow** the sh**ou**lder of the fell**ow**.

Note the long **o** digraph **oa** in *boat* and the Wild Colt long **o** in *cold*. The **k** in the word *know* is silent.

Review for Test. The instructor should plan to use some time at the end of the class to review and prepare for the test that follows this lesson. Review the objectives for the test and then look over the lessons that it will cover. If the student has struggled with any of the concepts that will be included in the test, some additional drill, practice, or review may be needed to adequately prepare him for the test.

Reading. Read and discuss the maxim for the Lesson.

Read the story *I Have a Queer Dream*. This is another chapter of the *Robinson Crusoe* story.

The vowel digraph *ou* can make the *long o* sound; *ough* can make the *long o* sound.

3 Look at each picture. Below each picture, write the word that goes with it. Use the words from the list.

shoulder   dough   boulder   doughnut   poultry

boulder   dough   poultry

doughnut   shoulder

4 Read the sentences with *long o* words spelled *ow*, *ou*, or *ough*. Circle the *ow*, *ou*, or *ough* in each word that has the *long o* sound.

1. Sh**ow** the d**ough**nut to the fell**ow**.
2. Kn**ow** that the d**ough** will gr**ow**.
3. Sh**ou**lder the b**ow**line and t**ow** the boat from the will**ow**s.
4. M**ow** the grass bel**ow** the b**ou**lder.
5. The d**ough** will gr**ow** th**ough** the b**ow**l is cold.
6. Thr**ow** the d**ough** bel**ow** the sh**ou**lder of the fell**ow**.

108   *Long o Spelled ow, ou, & ough*

Preview the story and explain words or sentence structures that are not familiar to the student. With every story ask questions: who are the characters, what are they doing, what are they saying, where does the action take place, what is the order of events, what words are being used, what new information is given, what lesson can be learned?

Comprehension questions:
How much time has gone by?
What thoughts were going though Robinson's mind as he tried to sleep?
What did Robinson see in his dream?
What now occupied Robinson's thoughts?
What goal made Robinson look forward to each new day on the island?

Assign. Lesson activities or reading that are to be completed as homework.

Test 5
Lessons 35-44

Overview:

- Auditory discrimination of long vowel sounds
- Match long vowel words to pictures
- Match short vowel words to words with a final silent **e**
- Auditory discrimination of long **a** in words with open syllables and vowel digraphs
- Code long **a** & **e** vowel digraphs
- Auditory discrimination of the long **e** sound

Materials and Supplies:

- Teacher's Guide & Student Workbook 1

Instructions:

Assessment Start-up. Read through the test with the student. Help the student with any words that he is still unsure of. The teacher should be available to answer any questions that the student may have during the test.

Activity 1. Read the instruction with the student. Make sure the student understands how to match the words. After the student has matched the words listen as he reads them to you.

Words:

rob	robe
rod	rode
mop	mope
pop	pope
hop	hope
slop	slope
spit	spite
slim	slime
shin	shine
sit	site

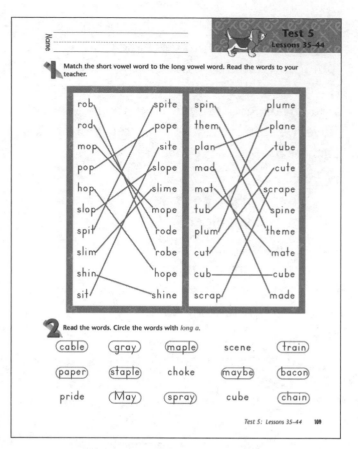

Activity 1 continued:

spin	spine
them	theme
plan	plane
mad	made
mat	mate
tub	tube
plum	plume
cut	cute
cub	cube
scrap	scrape

Activity 2. Read the instruction with the student. The student is to read the words and circle the words with a long **a** sound.

Words:
 cable, gray, maple, train
 paper, staple, maybe, bacon
 May, spray, chain

Activity 3. Read the instruction with the student. The student is to read the words and circle the words with a long **e** sound.

Words:

movie, peanut, even, money
beetle, she, believe, penny

Activity 4. Read the instruction with the student. Review the pictures, making sure the student can correctly identify them. Instruct the student to match the picture to the word.

Pictures:

rosebud	bike
snake	driveway
cupcake	kite

Activity 5. Read the instruction with the student. The student is to read the words and code the long vowel and silent letter in each vowel digraph.

Words:

pay, nail, feet, honey
say, maid, sleep, donkey
team, seal, chief, piece

Assessment Follow-up. Every test is an important assessment of both the student's comprehension of the concepts and the instructional process. This makes follow-up after each test essential to the learning process. Review all of the errors made on the test with the student. Check for understanding of the concepts and of the problem instructions. Compare the errors made on the test to the test objectives to identify specific areas of weakness. If weak areas of understanding are detected it might be necessary to go back to those lessons to devise some enrichment activities for the concept.

The test results can be used to determine what concepts are reviewed during the daily time of classroom instruction. Devise enrichment activities that will provide development in those areas.

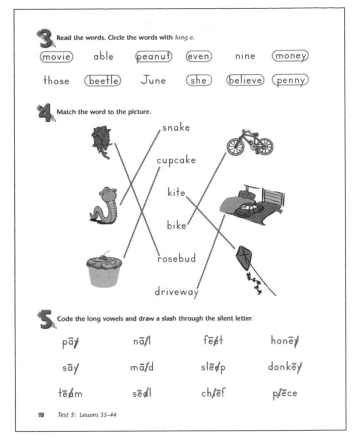

If time permits, choose a selection and have the student read it again. This can also be used as a catch-up time to complete unfinished selections.

Lesson 51: Long Vowel u, yoo Sound at the End of a Syllable

Overview:

• Auditory recognition of long **u** sound
• Word/picture match
• Apply the VCVopen Rule to long **u** words
• Read VCVopen words
• Word completion with long **u** words

Materials and Supplies:

• Teacher's Guide & Student Workbook 1
• White board or chalkboard
• Word cards (as necessary)
• Phonics rules flashcards
• Reader: *Robinson Crusoe & Other Classic Stories*

Teaching Tips:

Review for Mastery. Discuss and review any work from the previous lesson that was assigned as homework. Check for completion of the activities and orally quiz the student for comprehension. Review any reading that was assigned, discussing the characters, setting, plot, theme, language, sequence, etc.

Strengthen fluency and phonemic awareness by reviewing words and sentences from previous lessons. Build vocabulary skills by using some of the words in sentences.

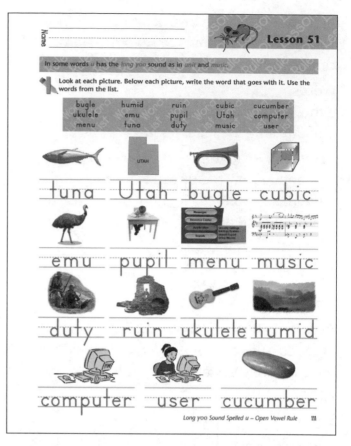

Activity 1. Review the "If two vowels go walking, the first usually does the talking and says its long sound" rule. *Words to teach the concept:* cube, tube, lube, cute. Review the rule for the long **yoo** sound of the **u** open syllable. *Words to teach the concept:* united, uniform, usual, unify, funeral, future, valuable, museum, humor. Have the student read the words in the box aloud. Review the pictures so the student can identify them. The student will write the word under the picture.

Words:
  tuna, Utah, bugle, cubic
  emu, pupil, menu, music
  duty, ruin, ukulele, humid
  computer, user, cucumber

Activity 2. Have the student complete the words. Help the student read words using the picture as clues.

Words:

    computer user
    human duty
    bugle pupil
    cubic unit
    ukulele music duet
    tuna menu
    Utah ruin
    emu duel

Note: Most of these words are review from the previous activity.

Reading. Read and discuss the maxim for the Lesson.

Read the story *I Get Hold of a Savage*. This is another chapter of the *Robinson Crusoe* story. Preview the story and explain words or sentence structures that are not familiar to the student. With every story ask questions: who are the characters, what are they doing, what are they saying, where does the action take place, what is the order of events, what words are being used, what new information is given, what lesson can be learned?

Comprehension questions:
    How much time has gone by?
    How many canoes did Robinson see on the beach?
    How many men did Robinson estimate came in the canoes?
    How did Robinson react to seeing the canoes?
    How many prisoners were pulled from the canoes?
    In what direction did the one prisoner try to escape?
    Did Robinson think his dream would come true?

Assign. Lesson activities or reading that are to be completed as homework.

Lesson 52: Long Vowel u, oo Sound Spelled ue, ui, & u_e

Overview:

- Auditory recognition of long vowel **u**
- Word/picture match
- Code words with **ue**, **u_e**, and **u** long **u** sound
- Read words with **ue**, and **ui** long **u** digraph
- Matching pictures to words
- Apply Long **u** Digraph Rule to words
- Complete compound words with **ui** long **u** sound

Materials and Supplies:

- Teacher's Guide & Student Workbook 1
- White board or chalkboard
- Word cards (as necessary)
- Phonics rules flashcards
- Reader: *Robinson Crusoe & Other Classic Stories*

Teaching Tips:

Review for Mastery. Discuss and review any work from the previous lesson that was assigned as homework. Check for completion of the activities and orally quiz the student for comprehension. Review any reading that was assigned, discussing the characters, setting, plot, theme, language, sequence, etc.

Strengthen fluency and phonemic awareness by reviewing words and sentences from previous lessons. Build vocabulary skills by using some of the words in sentences.

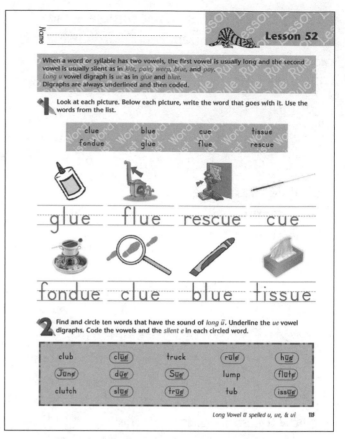

Activity 1. Review the "If two vowels go walking, the first usually does the talking and says its long sound" rule. Review the rule for the long **u** digraphs. *Words to teach the concept:* due, argue, blueprint, avenue, revenue. Have the student read the words in the box aloud. Discuss the pictures and make sure the student can identify them. The student will write the word under the correct picture.

Words:
  glue, flue, rescue, cue
  fondue, clue, blue, tissue

Activity 2. Have the student read aloud the words in the box. The student will circle the words with the long **u** sound. Then have the student code the circled words.

Words:
  clue, rule, hue
  June, due, Sue, flute
  slue, true, issue

Horizons Phonics & Reading Grade 2 Teacher's Guide

Activity 3. Review the rule for vowel digraph **ui**. Write examples on the board. *Words to teach the concept:* pantsuit, pursuit, recruit, swimsuit, juicy, starfruit. Have the student read the words in the box aloud. Discuss the pictures and make sure the student can identify them. The student will write the word under the correct picture.

Words:

   fruit, bruise, suit, cruise

   spacesuit, suitcase, fruitcake

Activity 4. Review the vowel sounds and spellings in the words *play*, *snow*, *body*, and *law*. Use each of the words listed in the instruction to form compound words with the word *suit*. Have the student write the words on the line.

Words:

   pantsuit, playsuit, snowsuit

   spacesuit, sunsuit, tracksuit

   wetsuit, swimsuit, lawsuit

   jumpsuit, bodysuit

Note: These words can be in any order.

Reading. Read and discuss the maxim for the Lesson.

Read the story *I Get Hold of a Savage (continued)*. This is another chapter of the *Robinson Crusoe* story. Preview the story and explain words or sentence structures that are not familiar to the student. With every story ask questions: who are the characters, what are they doing, what are they saying, where does the action take place, what is the order of events, what words are being used, what new information is given, what lesson can be learned?

Comprehension questions:

   How many savages followed the prisoner?

   What is Robinson doing as the prisoner is running away?

   When did Robinson leave his castle?

   How did Robinson communicate with the prisoner?

   How did Robinson protect the prisoner?

   How did Robinson show the prisoner that he would not harm him?

   How did the prisoner react?

Assign. Lesson activities or reading that are to be completed as homework.

Lesson 53: Review Long Vowels

Overview:

- Auditory recognition of long vowels
  a, e, i, o, & u
- Word/picture match
- Code words with long vowels
- Read words with long vowel digraphs
- Read sentences with long vowel words
- Identify long vowel words in sentences
- Apply the Open Vowel Rule to read words with long vowels
- Find long vowel words in a puzzle

Materials and Supplies:

- Teacher's Guide & Student Workbook 1
- White board or chalkboard
- Word cards (as necessary)
- Phonics rules flashcards
- Reader: *Robinson Crusoe & Other Classic Stories*

Teaching Tips:

Review for Mastery. Discuss and review any work from the previous lesson that was assigned as homework. Check for completion of the activities and orally quiz the student for comprehension. Review any reading that was assigned, discussing the characters, setting, plot, theme, language, sequence, etc.

Strengthen fluency and phonemic awareness by reviewing words and sentences from previous lessons. Build vocabulary skills by using some of the words in sentences.

Review the **ue** digraph with Lesson 52, Activity 1. Code the vowel long and draw a slash through the silent vowel.

Review the **ui** digraph with Lesson 52, Activities 3 and 4. Code the vowel long and draw a slash through the silent vowel.

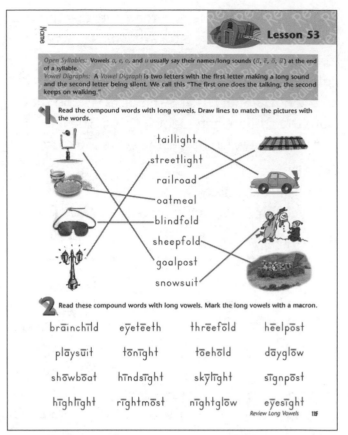

Activity 1. Review the Open Syllable Rule and the Vowel Digraph Rule with words from previous lessons. Have the student read the words in this activity aloud. Discuss the pictures and make sure the student can identify them. The student will draw a line to match the picture to the word.

Pictures:

goalpost	**railroad**
oatmeal	**taillight**
blindfold	**snowsuit**
streetlight	**sheepfold**

Note: All of these compound words have a digraph, diphthong, or Wild Colt long vowel.

Activity 2. Have the student read aloud the words in the activity. The student will code the long vowels in each word.

Note: All of these compound words have a digraph, diphthong, or Wild Colt long vowels.

Activity 3. Help the student read the sentences. Instruct the student to circle all of the words with long **i**, **o**, or **u** vowel sounds in each sentence.

Sentences:
1. <u>Hold</u> the <u>hoe</u> <u>by</u> <u>my</u> <u>shoulder</u>.
2. <u>Glue</u> the <u>ruby</u> <u>to</u> the <u>gold</u> <u>bolt</u>.
3. <u>Why</u> is the <u>sky</u> <u>blue</u>?
4. The <u>guy</u> <u>tried</u> <u>to</u> <u>roll</u> the <u>dough</u>.
5. <u>Joe</u> has a <u>slight</u> <u>cold</u> in his <u>throat</u>.
6. <u>Find</u> the <u>dried</u> <u>fly</u> <u>by</u> the <u>boat</u>.
7. <u>Stow</u> the <u>yellow</u> <u>pillow</u> <u>by</u> the <u>bedpost</u>.

Activity 4. Help the student read the words in the list. Instruct the student to find and circle each word in the puzzle.

Reading. Read and discuss the maxim for the Lesson.

Read the story *I Am Pleased With My Man Friday*. This is another chapter of the *Robinson Crusoe* story. Preview the story and explain words or sentence structures that are not familiar to the student. With every story ask questions: who are the characters, what are they doing, what are they saying, where does the action take place, what is the order of events, what words are being used, what new information is given, what lesson can be learned?

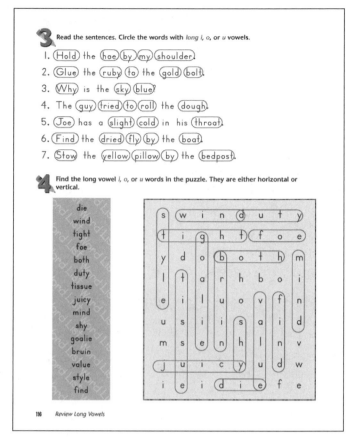

Comprehension questions:
How long had it been since Robinson had heard another human voice?
What puzzled the prisoner?
What request did the prisoner make to Robinson with signs?
Where did Robinson take the prisoner?
How did Robinson treat the prisoner?
How did the prisoner look?

Assign. Lesson activities or reading that are to be completed as homework.

Lesson 54: Plurals with -s

Overview:

- Write singular words as plurals
- Apply the rules to read plural words with the correct sound
- Apply the Vowel Followed by **y** Rule to make singular words plural
- Apply the Nouns that End in **f** or **fe** Rule to make singular words plural
- Apply the Vowel Followed by **o** Rule to make singular words plural
- Identify the base word in plurals

Materials and Supplies:

- Teacher's Guide & Student Workbook 1
- White board or chalkboard
- Word cards (as necessary)
- Phonics rules flashcards
- Reader: *Robinson Crusoe & Other Classic Stories*

Teaching Tips:

Review for Mastery. Discuss and review any work from the previous lesson that was assigned as homework. Check for completion of the activities and orally quiz the student for comprehension. Review any reading that was assigned, discussing the characters, setting, plot, theme, language, sequence, etc.

Strengthen fluency and phonemic awareness by reviewing words and sentences from previous lessons. Build vocabulary skills by using some of the words in sentences.

Review long vowel digraphs, diphthongs or Wild Colt long vowels with Lesson 53, Activity 1. Have the student identify the vowel structure in each word. Since they are compound words they each have two vowel structures.

Review long vowel digraphs, diphthongs or Wild Colt long vowels with Lesson 53, Activity 3. Have the student identify the vowel structure in each circled word.

Pronunciation Rules for Plurals:

In American English, the sound of "s" depends on which sound comes before it.

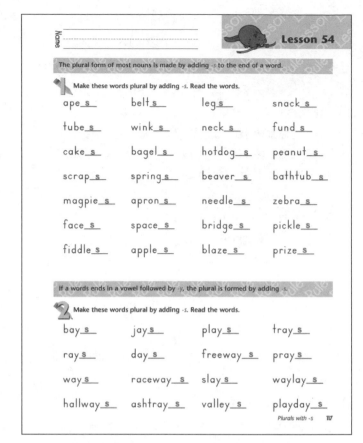

1. If the noun ends in an unvoiced consonant sound: **/f/, /k/, /p/, /t/, /th/-**(thin), pronounce "s" as **/s/**.
2. When it ends in a voiced consonant sound, **/b/, /d/, /g/, /l/, /m/, /n/, /ng/, /r/** or with a vowel sound, **/a/, /e/, /i/, /o/, /u/,** pronounce "s" as **/z/**.
3. If it ends with a sibilant **/s/, /z/, /sh/, /ch/-**chair, **/zh/-**the second "g" in garage, **/dz/-**(j), pronounce "s" or "-es" as **/iz/**.

Activity 1. Review the rule for forming plurals from nouns. *Words to teach the concept:* agents, backs, banks, batters, beaks, bites, blocks, bolts, braids, daggers, dances, eagles, grades, letters, lungs, meters, plates, posts, races, ravens, runners, salads, shells, sinners, stables, stamps, swans, toes, trains, trees, waves, winks. Note the **/s/, /z/,** and **/iz/** sound in these plurals. Have the student read the words aloud and add **(-s)** to each word to make it plural. Read the plural words.

Words: **apes, belts, legs, snacks**
        tubes, winks, necks, funds
        cakes, bagels, hotdogs, peanuts
        scraps, springs, beavers, bathtubs

Horizons Phonics & Reading Grade 2 Teacher's Guide

Activity 1 continued:

> magpies, aprons, needles, zebras
> faces, spaces, bridges, pickles
> fiddles, apples, blazes, prizes

Activity 2. Review the rule. *Words to teach the concept:* always, bays, boys, essays, highways, keys, railways, weekdays. Pay special attention to the ending /**z**/ sound and the vowel before the **y** ending. Have the student read the words aloud. Have the student add (**-s**) to each word to make it plural. Read the plural words.

Words: **bays, jays, plays, trays**
rays, days, freeways, prays
ways, raceways, slays, waylays
hallways, ashtrays, valleys, playdays

Activity 3. Review the rule with the student. *Words to teach the concept:* beliefs, briefs, cliffs, payoffs, showoffs, cafes, giraffes, safes. Help the student read the words aloud. Have the student underline the **f** or **fe** ending in each word. Then add (**-s**) to each word to make it plural. Read the plural words.

Words: **che<u>f</u>s, fi<u>fe</u>s, gul<u>f</u>s, cle<u>f</u>s**
loa<u>f</u>s, sni<u>ff</u>s, tipo<u>ff</u>s, sa<u>fe</u>s
sta<u>ff</u>s, cu<u>ff</u>s, spino<u>ff</u>s, cha<u>fe</u>s

Note that some of these words have another plural form that will be covered later.

Activity 4. Review the rule. *Words to teach the concept:* audios, cockatoos, igloos, patios, trios, studios. Help the student read the words aloud. Have the student underline the vowel before the final **o** in each word. Then add (**-s**) to each word to make it plural. Read the plural words with a /**z**/ sound.

Words: **bamb<u>o</u>os, vid<u>e</u>os, shamp<u>o</u>os, z<u>o</u>os**
boob<u>o</u>os, waz<u>o</u>os, yah<u>o</u>os, jackar<u>o</u>os

Activity 5. Help the student read the words aloud. Have the student underline the base word in each plural. Read the base words. Review the rule used to make each word plural.

Words: **<u>abbot</u>s, <u>maple</u>s, <u>bluejay</u>s, <u>sendoff</u>s**
<u>subway</u>s, <u>snake</u>s, <u>brain</u>s, <u>boohoo</u>s
<u>payday</u>s, <u>sail</u>s, <u>roof</u>s, <u>toad</u>s
<u>strife</u>s, <u>bugaboo</u>s, <u>spray</u>s, <u>temple</u>s

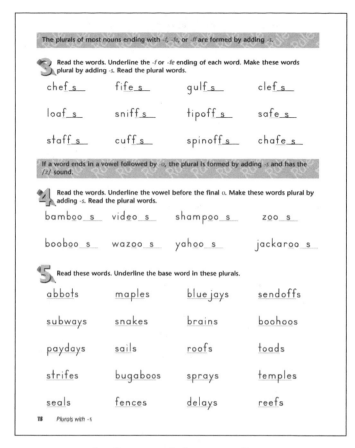

<u>seal</u>s, <u>fence</u>s, <u>delay</u>s, <u>reef</u>s

Reading. Read and discuss the maxim for the Lesson.

Read the story *I Am Pleased With My Man Friday (continued)*. This is another chapter of the *Robinson Crusoe* story.

Comprehension questions:

What was Robinson doing when the prisoner woke from his nap?

What did the prisoner do again?

What name did Robinson give to the prisoner?

What did Robinson find on the beach?

How did Robinson react to what was on the beach?

What did Robinson make for Friday?

Read the poem *The Wind*. Preview the poem and explain words or sentence structures that are not familiar to the student.

What plurals can be found in the poem?

Which lines in the poem rhyme?

Assign. Lesson activities or reading that are to be completed as homework

Lesson 55: Plural with -es

Overview:

- Write singular words as plurals
- Apply the rules to read plural words with the correct sound
- Apply the Word Ending Rule to make singular words plural
- Apply the Consonant Followed by **o** Rule to make singular words plural
- Match pictures with plural words

Materials and Supplies:

- Teacher's Guide & Student Workbook 1
- White board or chalkboard
- Word cards (as necessary)
- Phonics rules flashcards
- Reader: *Robinson Crusoe & Other Classic Stories*

Teaching Tips:

Review for Mastery. Discuss and review any work from the previous lesson that was assigned as homework. Check for completion of the activities and orally quiz the student for comprehension. Review any reading that was assigned, discussing the characters, setting, plot, theme, language, sequence, etc.

Strengthen fluency and phonemic awareness by reviewing words and sentences from previous lessons. Build vocabulary skills by using some of the words in sentences.

Review plurals with Lesson 54, Activities 1-5. Write headings of the Pronunciation Rules for Plurals on the board and sort some of the words from the activities into the proper category by writing them under the heading. Have each student pick a word and then come to the board and write it under the correct list.

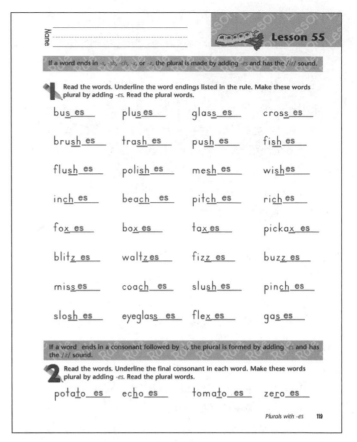

Activity 1. Review the rule, the word endings, and the sound made by the plural. *Words to teach the concept:* bosses, classes, kisses, losses, tosses, ashes, bushes, leashes, toothbrushes, washes, arches, belches, blotches, branches, crunches, crutches, hutches, leeches, lunches, perches, stitches, searches, axes, duplexes, fixes, prefixes, suffixes, waxes, fizzes. Have the student read the words aloud. Instruct the student to underline the ending in each word from the rule. Then add (**-es**) to each word to make it plural. Read the plural words.

Words:
buses, pluses, glasses, crosses
brushes, trashes, pushes, fishes
flushes, polishes, meshes, wishes
inches, beaches, pitches, riches
foxes, boxes, taxes, pickaxes
blitzes, waltzes, fizzes, buzzes
misses, coaches, slushes, pinches
sloshes, eyeglasses, flexes, gases

Note: The words chosen for this activity review consonant blends and vowel patterns from previous lessons.

Activity 2. Review the rule and the sound made by the plural. *Words to teach the concept:* cargoes, heroes. Have the student read the words aloud. Instruct the student to underline the consonant followed by **o** ending of each word. Then add (**-es**) to each word to make it plural. Read the plural words.

Words:

pota<u>t</u>oes, ec<u>h</u>oes, toma<u>t</u>oes, ze<u>r</u>oes

Activity 3. Review the rule from Activity 1. Discuss the pictures so the student can identify them. Instruct the student to look for the base word in each plural and then fill in the circle by the word that has correctly been made into a plural. Read the plural words.

Words:

mailboxes, radishes
sunglasses, benches
goldfishes, buses
tuxes, crosses
peaches, saxes

Note: The words chosen for this activity review consonant blends and vowel patterns from previous lessons.

Reading. Read and discuss the maxim for the Lesson.

Read the story *I Teach Friday Many Things*. This is another chapter of the *Robinson Crusoe* story. Preview the story and explain words or sentence structures that are not familiar to the student. With every story ask questions: who are the characters, what are they doing, what are they saying, where does the action take place, what is the order of events, what words are being used, what new information is given, what lesson can be learned?

Comprehension questions:
  How did Robinson teach Friday about a gun?
  What other things was Robinson teaching Friday to do?
  What items were given to Friday?
  How did Robinson feel about his life?

Assign. Lesson activities or reading that are to be completed as homework.

Lesson 56: Inflected Endings -ed & -ing

Overview:

- Add suffixes to base words
- Read words with inflected endings
- Add suffix **-ing** to a base word for things that are happening now
- Apply the rules to add suffix **-ed** to words
- Correctly pronounce words with **-ed** endings

Materials and Supplies:

- Teacher's Guide & Student Workbook 1
- White board or chalkboard
- Word cards (as necessary)
- Phonics rules flashcards
- Reader: *Robinson Crusoe & Other Classic Stories*

Teaching Tips:

Review for Mastery. Discuss and review any work from the previous lesson that was assigned as homework. Check for completion of the activities and orally quiz the student for comprehension. Review any reading that was assigned, discussing the characters, setting, plot, theme, language, sequence, etc.

Strengthen fluency and phonemic awareness by reviewing words and sentences from previous lessons. Build vocabulary skills by using some of the words in sentences.

Review plurals with Lesson 54, Activities 1-5. Write headings of the *Pronunciation Rules for Plurals* on the board and sort some of the words from the activities into the proper category by writing them under the heading. Have each student pick a word and then come to the board and write it under the correct list.

Activity 1. Review the rule with the student. Inflection: An alteration of the form of a word by the addition of an affix, as in English *dogs* from *dog*, or by changing the form of a base, as in English *spoke* from *speak*, that indicates gram-

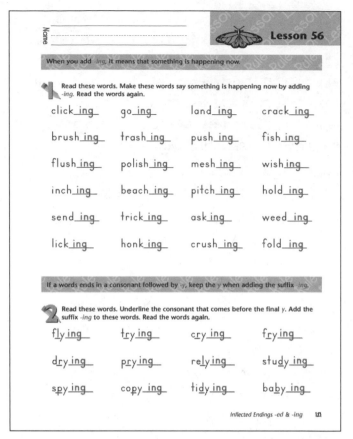

matical features such as number, person, mood, or tense. *Words to teach the concept:* aiding, mending, sanding, bathing, cashing, mashing, hatching, clashing, matching stashing, weighing, bucking, licking. Have the student read the words aloud. The student will write new words by adding **-ing** to the end of each base word. Read the new words. Use some of the words in a sentence to say something is happening now.

Words:
clicking, going, landing, cracking
brushing, trashing, pushing, fishing
flushing, polishing, meshing, wishing
inching, beaching, pitching, holding
sending, tricking, asking, weeding
licking, honking, crushing, folding

Activity 2. Review the rule. Have the student read the words aloud. Underline the consonant that comes before the final **y**. The student will write new words by adding **-ing** to the end of each base word. Read the new words and use some of then in a sentence to say something is happening now.

Activity 2 continued:

Words:

flying, trying, crying, frying
drying, prying, relying, studying
spying, copying, tidying, babying

Activity 3. Review the rule. *Words to teach the concept:* billed, grilled, killed, weighed, zeroed, decayed, clanged, pulled, rolled. Have the student read the words aloud. The student will write new words by adding **-ed** to the end of each base word. Read the base word and the new word with the ending sound of **d**.

Words:

called, banged, filled, bailed
opened, cleaned, delayed, echoed

Activity 4. Review the rule with the student. *Words to teach the concept:* cashed, mashed, hatched, clashed, matched, stashed, bucked. Have the student read the words aloud. The student will write new words by adding **-ed** to the end of each base word. Read the base word and the new word with the ending sound of **t**.

Words:

brushed, trashed, pushed, fished
flushed, polished, meshed, wished
pitched, tricked, asked, licked
honked, crushed, leaked, masked

Activity 5. Review the rule. *Words to teach the concept:* aided, ended, mended, avoided, molded, baited, blended. Have the student read the words aloud. The student will write new words by adding **-ed** to the end of each base word. Read the base word and the new word with the ending sound of **-ed**.

Words:

added, folded, tended, loaded
needed, bended, landed, handed
coated, jolted, hunted, salted
waited, dusted, rented, seated

Reading. Read and discuss the maxim for the Lesson.

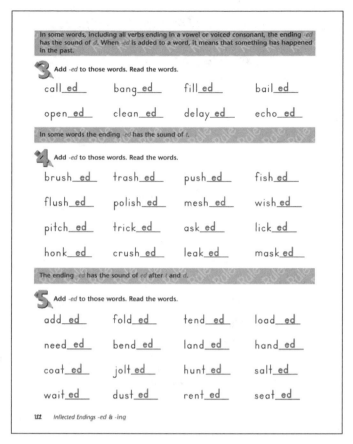

In some words, including all verbs ending in a vowel or voiced consonant, the ending *-ed* has the sound of *d*. When *-ed* is added to a word, it means that something has happened in the past.

3 Add *-ed* to those words. Read the words.

call_ed_   bang_ed_   fill_ed_   bail_ed_
open_ed_   clean_ed_   delay_ed_   echo_ed_

In some words the ending *-ed* has the sound of *t*.

4 Add *-ed* to those words. Read the words.

brush_ed_   trash_ed_   push_ed_   fish_ed_
flush_ed_   polish_ed_   mesh_ed_   wish_ed_
pitch_ed_   trick_ed_   ask_ed_   lick_ed_
honk_ed_   crush_ed_   leak_ed_   mask_ed_

The ending *-ed* has the sound of *ed* after *t* and *d*.

5 Add *-ed* to those words. Read the words.

add_ed_   fold_ed_   tend_ed_   load_ed_
need_ed_   bend_ed_   land_ed_   hand_ed_
coat_ed_   jolt_ed_   hunt_ed_   salt_ed_
wait_ed_   dust_ed_   rent_ed_   seat_ed_

122   *Inflected Endings –ed & -ing*

Read the story *I Teach Friday Many Things (continued)*. This is another chapter of the *Robinson Crusoe* story. Preview the story and explain words or sentence structures that are not familiar to the student. With every story ask questions: who are the characters, what are they doing, what are they saying, where does the action take place, what is the order of events, what words are being used, what new information is given, what lesson can be learned?

Comprehension questions:

What did Friday tell Robinson about his home?
What was Robinson's new goal?
Why was Friday unhappy about the prospect of leaving the island?
Why did Friday want Robinson with him when he returned to his country?
How badly did Friday want to stay will Robinson?

Assign. Lesson activities or reading that are to be completed as homework.

Lesson 57: Review Inflected Endings -s & -es

Overview:

- Apply the correct rule to add plural endings to base words
- Add suffixes to base words
- Read words with plural endings
- Apply the rules to add suffix **-s** or **-es** to words
- Complete sentences with the correct plural form of words
- Answer questions with words that are plurals
- Correctly pronounce words with **-s** and **-es** endings

Materials and Supplies:

- Teacher's Guide & Student Workbook 1
- White board or chalkboard
- Word cards (as necessary)
- Phonics rules flashcards
- Reader: *Robinson Crusoe & Other Classic Stories*

Teaching Tips:

Review for Mastery. Discuss and review any work from the previous lesson that was assigned as homework. Check for completion of the activities and orally quiz the student for comprehension. Review any reading that was assigned, discussing the characters, setting, plot, theme, language, sequence, etc.

Strengthen fluency and phonemic awareness by reviewing words and sentences from previous lessons. Build vocabulary skills by using some of the words in sentences.

Review plurals with Lesson 56, Activity 1. Write some of the base words on the board. Have the student come to the board and make the words plural. Check for the correct spelling and read the plurals that are formed.

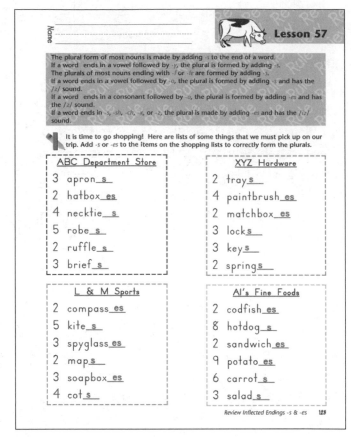

Activity 1. Have the student read the words aloud. Review all of the rules. The student will use the rules to write new words by adding **-s** or **-es** to the end of each base word. The student can underline the word ending that is the clue for the rule to use in adding **-s** or **-es**.

Words:

aprons	**trays**
hatboxes	**paintbrushes**
neckties	**matchboxes**
robes	**locks**
ruffles	**keys**
briefs	**springs**
compasses	**codfishes**
kites	**hotdogs**
spyglasses	**sandwiches**
maps	**potatoes**
soapboxes	**carrots**
cots	**salads**

Activity 2. Help the student read the words in the sentences, forming verbal plurals as they read. Instruct the student to use the rules to correctly write the words as a plural in the sentence.

Sentences:

1. We picked up two <u>goldfishes</u> at the pet shop.
2. Three <u>churches</u> played two <u>games</u> of softball.
3. She saw five <u>planes</u> in the sky.
4. The two <u>buses</u> crossed three <u>bridges</u> on the trip.
5. The football team had four <u>plays</u> to run in the game.
6. I went up six <u>jumpoffs</u> with my bike.
7. The man had two <u>tattoos</u> on his <u>legs</u>.
8. She got two <u>kisses</u> from the baby.
9. The three <u>badgers</u> ran ten <u>inches</u> to the crate.
10. See the seven <u>jays</u> resting on the <u>fences</u>.

Activity 3. Have the student read all the words in the box aloud. Read the questions. Help the students with any word meanings they don't understand. The student will find the word in the box and make it plural to answer the question.

Words:

  carrots
  takeoffs
  toothbrushes
  taxes
  tomatoes

Reading. Read and discuss the maxim for the Lesson.

Read the story *I Make a New Boat*. This is another chapter of the *Robinson Crusoe* story. Preview the story and explain words or sentence structures that are not familiar to the student. With every story ask questions: who are the characters, what are they doing, what

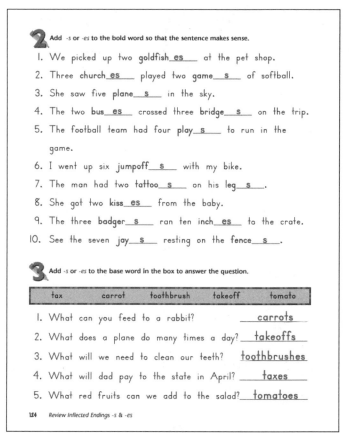

are they saying, where does the action take place, what is the order of events, what words are being used, what new information is given, what lesson can be learned?

Comprehension questions:

  Where did Robinson search for a tree?
  What was Robinson's next goal?
  How long did it take to build the canoe and to get it into the water?
  Who made the mast for the boat?
  What did Robinson use to make the sail?
  How did Friday want to make the boat move?
  Did Friday learn how to sail the boat?
  Was Robinson ready to sail to the mainland?

Assign. Lesson activities or reading that are to be completed as homework.

Lesson 58: Review Inflected Endings -ed & -ing

Overview:

- Add suffixes **-ed** and **-ing** to base words
- Sentence completion
- Add suffix **-ing** to a base word for things that are happening now
- Correctly pronounce words with **-ed** endings

Materials and Supplies:

- Teacher's Guide & Student Workbook 1
- White board or chalkboard
- Alphabet flashcards
- Word cards (as necessary)
- Reader: *Robinson Crusoe & Other Classic Stories*

Teaching Tips:

Review for Mastery. Discuss and review any work from the previous lesson that was assigned as homework. Check for completion of the activities and orally quiz the student for comprehension. Review any reading that was assigned, discussing the characters, setting, plot, theme, language, sequence, etc.

Strengthen fluency and phonemic awareness by reviewing words and sentences from previous lessons. Build vocabulary skills by using some of the words in sentences.

Review the rules for adding suffixes **-ing** and **-ed** to words. Do several examples on the white board or chalkboard. Have the student think of other examples.

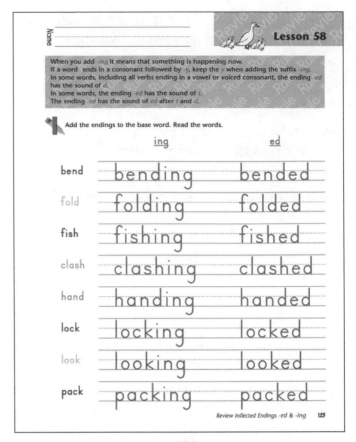

Activity 1. Have the student read the base words aloud. The student will write new words by adding **-ing** and **-ed** to the end of each base word. Read the new words.

Words:

bending	bended
folding	folded
fishing	fished
clashing	clashed
handing	handed
locking	locked
looking	looked
packing	packed

Activity 2. Read the base words. Help the student read the sentences and the base word. Instruct the student to add **-ing** or **-ed** to the base word to compete the sentence. Have the student write the word on the line.

Sentences:

1. The big backpack was <u>crushing</u> my shoulder.
2. I <u>crushed</u> the sandwich with my hand.
3. Mom <u>mended</u> the broken cup for my dad.
4. She is <u>mending</u> the zipper in the jeans.
5. The roast is <u>cooking</u> on the stove.
6. When the potatoes are <u>cooked</u> we will have lunch.
7. The bride was <u>dressing</u> at home for the wedding.
8. The groom had <u>dressed</u> at the tux shop.
9. I had <u>fixed</u> the gate last weeks.
10. Today I am <u>fixing</u> a hole in the fence.
11. She had letters <u>etched</u> on the dog tags.
12. The flow of water was <u>etching</u> the concrete.
13. The baby was <u>licking</u> the candy.
14. My sister <u>licked</u> the ice cream to get a taste.
15. We <u>munched</u> on the carrots that were on the plate.
16. Dad is <u>munching</u> on the chips.

Reading. Read and discuss the maxim for the Lesson.

Read the story *I Make a New Boat (continued).* This is another chapter of the *Robinson Crusoe* story. Preview the story and explain words or sentence structures that are not familiar to the student. With every story ask questions: who are the characters, what are they doing, what are they saying, where does the action take place, what is the order of events, what words are being used, what new information is given, what lesson can be learned?

2 Add *-ed* or *-ing* to the base word so that the sentences makes sense.

crush
1. The big backpack was _____ crushing _____ my shoulder.
2. I _____ crushed _____ the sandwich with my hand.

mend
3. Mom _____ mended _____ the broken cup for my dad.
4. She is _____ mending _____ the zipper in the jeans.

cook
5. The roast is _____ cooking _____ on the stove.
6. When the potatoes are _____ cooked _____ we will have lunch.

dress
7. The bride was _____ dressing _____ at home for the wedding.
8. The groom had _____ dressed _____ at the tux shop.

fix
9. I had _____ fixed _____ the gate last week.
10. Today I am _____ fixing _____ a hole in the fence.

etch
11. She had letters _____ etched _____ on the dog tags.
12. The flow of water was _____ etching _____ the concrete.

lick
13. The baby was _____ licking _____ the candy.
14. My sister _____ licked _____ the ice cream to get a taste.

munch
15. We _____ munched _____ on the carrots that were on the plate.
16. Dad is _____ munching _____ on the chips.

126   *Review Inflected Endings -ed & -ing*

Comprehension questions:
 How long had Robinson and Friday been together on the island?
 Although Robinson wanted to leave the island what did he continue to do?
 Where was the new boat stored?
 What things did Robinson teach to Friday?
 What things did Friday teach to Robinson?
 Who did Friday say had made all things?

Assign. Lesson activities or reading that are to be completed as homework.

Lesson 59: Long Vowel a Spelled ea, eigh, ei, and ey

Overview:

- Auditory recognition of long **a** sound
- Read words with long **a** sound spelled **ei**, **ey**, & **ea**
- Read words with vowels that are spelled the same but have different sounds
- Match words with a long **a** sound to the picture
- Define a vowel digraph
- Apply the rule to read vowel digraphs
- Complete a crossword with long **a** digraph words
- Sentence completion with long **a** digraph words

Materials and Supplies:

- Teacher's Guide & Student Workbook 1
- White board or chalkboard
- Alphabet flashcards
- Word cards (as necessary)
- Phonics rules flashcards
- Reader: *Robinson Crusoe & Other Classic Stories*

Teaching Tips:

Review for Mastery. Discuss and review any work from the previous lesson that was assigned as homework. Check for completion of the activities and orally quiz the student for comprehension. Review any reading that was assigned, discussing the characters, setting, plot, theme, language, sequence, etc.

Strengthen fluency and phonemic awareness by reviewing words and sentences from previous lessons. Build vocabulary skills by using some of the words in sentences.

Review inflected endings with Lesson 58, Activity 1. Have the student make up sentences using the words from the activity.

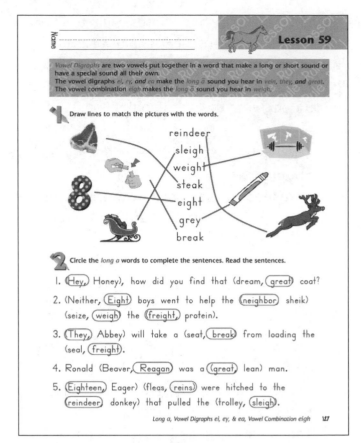

Activity 1. Review the long **a** vowel digraphs rules. *Words to teach the concept:* eighty, freight, neighbor, lei, reign, veil, vein, hey, they, great, yea. Have the student read the words aloud. Discuss the pictures and make sure the student can identify them. The student will draw a line to match the picture to the word.

Pictures:

steak	weight
break	grey
eight	reindeer
sleigh	

Note: *Gray* and *grey* are two spellings for the color.

Activity 2. Help the student read the words in the sentences and all of the word choices. Watch the detractors in this exercise because they are spelled with the same digraphs as covered in this lesson but have a different sound. Instruct the student to circle the words that complete the sentence. Read the sentences after the words have been circled.

Activity 2 continued:

Sentences:

1. <u>Hey</u>, how did you find that <u>great</u> coat?
   Note the long **e** in *honey* and *dream*; the
   long **o** in *coat*.

2. <u>Eight</u> boys went to help the <u>neighbor</u>
   <u>weigh</u> the <u>freight</u>. Note the long **o** in
   boys; the long **e** in *neither*, *sheik*, *seize*, and
   protein.

3. <u>They</u> will take a <u>break</u> from loading the
   <u>freight</u>. Note the long **e** in *Abbey*, *seat*,
   and *seal*; the long **o** in *loading*.

4. Ronald <u>Reagan</u> was a <u>great</u> man. Note
   the long **e** in *Beaver* and *lean*.

5. <u>Eighteen</u> <u>reins</u> were hitched to the <u>rein-
   deer</u> that pulled the <u>sleigh</u>. Note the
   long **e** in *eager*, *fleas*, *donkey*, and *trolley*.

Activity 3. Review the words in the list. Help
the student read the crossword puzzle clues.
Assist the student as necessary with the crossword puzzle.

Across:	Down:
2. neighbor	1. veil
4. steak	2. break
6. vein	5. mein

Activity 4. Help the student read words in the
list and the sentences. Instruct the student to
select the word that will correctly complete
each sentence, and write the word on the line.

Sentences:

1. It would be silly if <u>reindeer</u> rode in a
   <u>sleigh</u>.
2. It would be silly if <u>eight</u> came after nine.
3. It would be silly if a stop sign was <u>grey</u>.
4. It would be silly if <u>freight</u> trains had
   wings.

Reading. Read and discuss the maxim for the
Lesson.

Read the story *I See a Strange Sail*. This is
another chapter of the *Robinson Crusoe* story.
Preview the story and explain words or

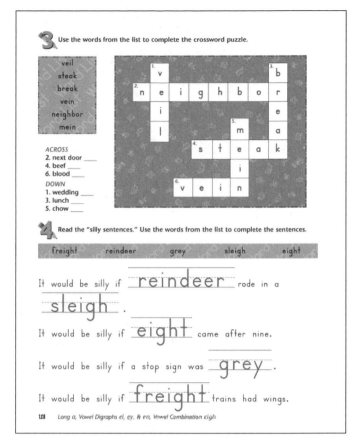

sentence structures that are not familiar to the
student. With every story ask questions: who
are the characters, what are they doing, what
are they saying, where does the action take
place, what is the order of events, what words
are being used, what new information is given,
what lesson can be learned?

Comprehension questions:
   What did Friday see one morning?
   How did Robinson react to the news of a
   boat?
   What kind of ship did Robinson see?
   Why was Robinson worried?

Assign. Lesson activities or reading that are to
be completed as homework.

Lesson 60: Long Vowel oo Spelled oo & ou

Overview:

- Auditory recognition of long **oo** sound
- Read words with long **oo** sound spelled **oo** & **ou**
- Match words with a long **oo** sound to the picture
- Define a vowel digraph
- Apply the rule to read vowel digraphs
- Sentence completion with long **oo** digraph words

Materials and Supplies:

- Teacher's Guide & Student Workbook 1
- White board or chalkboard
- Word cards (as necessary)
- Phonics rules flashcards
- Reader: *Robinson Crusoe & Other Classic Stories*

Teaching Tips:

Review for Mastery. Discuss and review any work from the previous lesson that was assigned as homework. Check for completion of the activities and orally quiz the student for comprehension. Review any reading that was assigned, discussing the characters, setting, plot, theme, language, sequence, etc.

Strengthen fluency and phonemic awareness by reviewing words and sentences from previous lessons. Build vocabulary skills by using some of the words in sentences.

Review long **a** digraphs with Lesson 59, Activity 2. Have the student sort the words by the spelling of the long **a** sound.

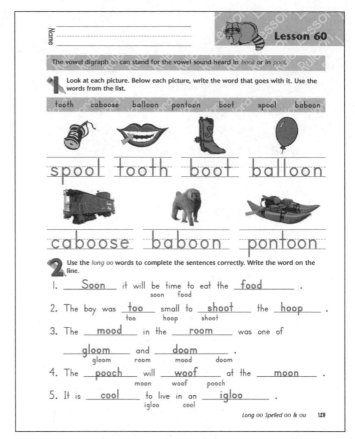

Activity 1. Review the rule and the examples with the student. This activity will cover the long **oo** digraph sound. *Words to teach the concept:* bamboo, bloom, boom, boost, broom, coot, goof, groom, hoot, loop, roost, scoop, shampoo, smooth, snooze, spoon, stool, tool, zoo. Identify the pictures with the student. Have the student listen as you say the name of each picture. Instruct the student to write the correct word underneath each picture.

Words:
  spool, tooth, boot, balloon
  caboose, baboon, pontoon

Activity 2. Help the student read the sentences and the word choices. Instruct the student to write the correct word on the line to complete the sentence.

Sentences:
1. **Soon** it will be time to eat the **food**.
2. The boy was **too** small to **shoot** the **hoop**.
3. The **mood** in the **room** was one of **gloom** and **doom**.
4. The **pooch** will **woof** at the **moon**.
5. It is **cool** to live in an **igloo**.

Activity 3. Review the rule and the example with the student. *Words to teach the concept:* caribou, cougar, coulee, joule, routine, souvenir, troupe. Identify the pictures with the student. Have the student listen as you say the name of each picture. Instruct the student to write the correct word underneath each picture.

Words:

wound, soup, group, youth
coupon, toucan, croutons

Activity 4. Help the student read the sentences and review the word choices from Activity 3. Instruct the student to write the correct word on the line to complete the sentence.

Sentences:
1. His <u>toucan</u> has a yellow beak. Note the long **o** in *yellow* and the long **e** in *beak*.
2. The <u>coupon</u> will save us some money. Note the long **e** in *money*.
3. Do you like to eat <u>croutons</u> in <u>soup</u>? Note the long **e** in *eat*.
4. We will meet the <u>group</u> at the beach. Note the long **e** in *beach*.
5. His <u>wound</u> will not heal soon. Note the long **e** in *heal* and the long **oo** in *soon*.
6. The <u>youth</u> in the band plays the drums. Note the long **a** in *plays*.

Review for Test. The instructor should plan to use some time at the end of the class to review and prepare for the test that follows this lesson. Review the objectives for the test and then look over the lessons that it will cover. If the student has struggled with any of the concepts that will be included in the test, some additional drill, practice, or review may be needed to adequately prepare him for the test.

Reading. Read and discuss the maxim for the Lesson.

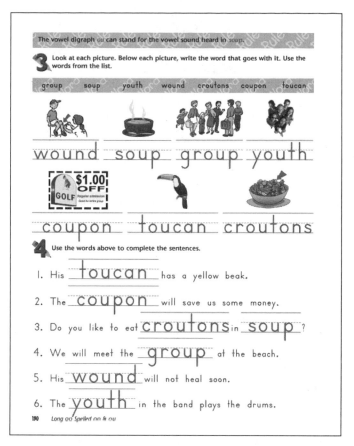

Read the story *I See a Strange Sail (continued)*. This is another chapter of the *Robinson Crusoe* story. Preview the story and explain words or sentence structures that are not familiar to the student. With every story ask questions: who are the characters, what are they doing, what are they saying, where does the action take place, what is the order of events, what words are being used, what new information is given, what lesson can be learned?

Comprehension questions:
What kind of men were in the boat?
What groups of men were in the boat?
What did the men do with the prisoners?
Why were the men from the ship stuck on the shore?
What did the men decide to do?

Assign. Lesson activities or reading that are to be completed as homework.

Test 6
Lessons 45-54

Overview:

- Auditory discrimination of long vowel sounds
- Match long vowel words to pictures
- Code long vowels
- Auditory discrimination of long vowels in words with open syllables and vowel digraphs
- Sort words by their long vowel sound
- Apply spelling rules to make words plural

Materials and Supplies:

- Teacher's Guide & Student Workbook 1

Instructions:

Assessment Start-up. Read through the test with the student. Help the student with any words that he is still unsure of. The teacher should be available to answer any questions that the student may have during the test.

Activity 1. Read the instruction with the student. Review the pictures, making sure the student can correctly identify them. Instruct the student to match the picture to the word.

Pictures:

necktie	goalpost
spacesuit	doughnut
loaf	tissue
scroll	type
fishbowl	music

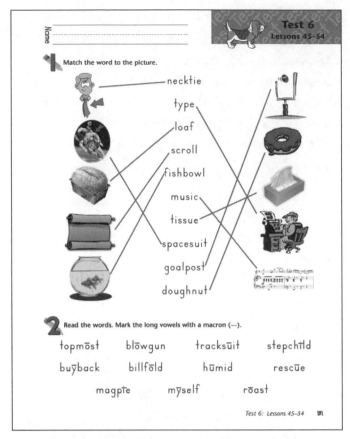

Activity 2. Read the instruction with the student. Instruct the student to read the words with long vowels. The student is to mark the long vowels in each word with a macron.

Words:

topm_o_st, bl_o_wgun, tracks_ui_t, stepch_i_ld
b_u_yback, billf_o_ld, h_u_mid, resc_ue_
magp_ie_, m_y_self, r_oa_st

Activity 3. Read the instruction with the student. Make sure the student can read the words. Instruct the student to sort the words by the long vowel sound.

Words:

long i	long o	long u
tried	soak	user
child	doe	glue
eyelid	bold	flute
right	most	fruit
buy	roll	unit
sigh	fellow	tuna
dry	shoulder	suit

Activity 4. Read the instruction with the student. Make sure the student can read the words. Instruct the student to make the words plural.

Words:

peanuts, pickles, videos, zebras
driveways, cafes, handcuffs, igloos

Assessment Follow-up. Every test is an important assessment of both the student's comprehension of the concepts and the instructional process. This makes follow-up after each test essential to the learning process. Review all of the errors made on the test with the student. Check for understanding of the concepts and of the problem instructions. Compare the errors made on the test to the test objectives to identify specific areas of weakness. If weak areas of understanding are detected it might be necessary to go back to those lessons to devise some enrichment activities for the concept.

The test results can be used to determine what concepts are reviewed during the daily time of classroom instruction. Devise enrichment activities that will provide development in those areas.

If time permits, choose a selection and have the student read it again. This can also be used as a catch-up time to complete unfinished selections.

Lesson 61: Short Vowel oo Spelled u and oo

Overview:

- Auditory recognition of short **oo** sound
- Read words with short **oo** sound spelled **oo** & **u**
- Match words with a short **oo** sound spelled **oo** to the picture
- Answer questions with short **oo** spelled **oo** words
- Match words with a short **oo** sound spelled **u** to the picture
- Define a vowel digraph
- Apply the rule to read vowel digraphs
- Sentence completion with short **oo** spelled **u** words

Materials and Supplies:

- Teacher's Guide & Student Workbook 1
- White board or chalkboard
- Alphabet flashcards
- Word cards (as necessary)
- Phonics rules flashcards
- Reader: *Robinson Crusoe & Other Classic Stories*

Teaching Tips:

Review for Mastery. Discuss and review any work from the previous lesson that was assigned as homework. Check for completion of the activities and orally quiz the student for comprehension. Review any reading that was assigned, discussing the characters, setting, plot, theme, language, sequence, etc.

Strengthen fluency and phonemic awareness by reviewing words and sentences from previous lessons. Build vocabulary skills by using some of the words in sentences.

Review the long **oo** digraph with Lesson 60, Activities 1 & 2. Have the student code the **oo** digraph with a macron drawn over both vowels.

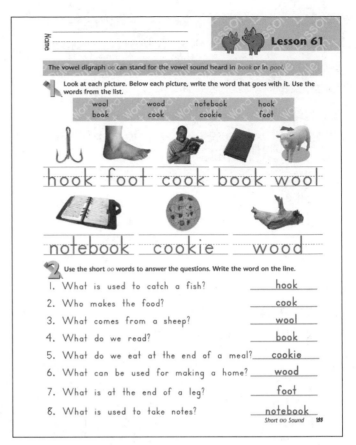

Review the long **oo** digraph spelled **ou** with Lesson 60, Activities 3 & 4. Have the student write the words with a phonetic spelling on a sheet of paper. The **ou** digraph should be written **oo** with a macron over both vowels.

Activity 1. Review the rule and the examples with the student. This activity will cover the short **oo** digraph sound. *Words to teach the concept:* brook, crook, good, hood, look, nook, rook, room, shook, stood, took. Identify the pictures with the student. Have the student listen as you say the name of each picture. Instruct the student to write the correct word underneath each picture.

Words:
  hook, foot, cook, book, wool
  notebook, cookie, wood

Activity 2. Help the student read the questions and review the word choices from Activity 1. Instruct the student to write the correct word on the line to answer the question.

Answers:
  hook, cook, wool, book, cookie, wood, foot, notebook

Horizons Phonics & Reading Grade 2 Teacher's Guide

Activity 3. Review the rule and the examples with the student. This activity will cover the short **oo** sound spelled as **u** in some words. *Words to teach the concept:* put, cushion, pulled, pushing. Identify the pictures with the student. Have the student listen as you say the name of each picture. Instruct the student to write the correct word underneath each picture.

Words:

full, bull, push, bush, pull
butcher, pudding, bullet

Activity 4. Help the student read the words in the sentences and the word choices. Instruct the student to underline the word that completes the sentence. Read the sentences after the words have been underlined.

Sentences:

1. **We had <u>pudding</u> today at lunch.**
   Note the long **a** in *today* and the short **oo** in the detractor *pushing*.
2. **The glass was <u>full</u> of milk.**
3. **The gun shot a <u>bullet</u> at the bullseye.**
   Note the short **oo** sound in *bullseye* and the detractor *poor*.
4. **It will take a <u>push</u> to open the door.**
   Note the long **oo** in the detractor *soup*.
5. **A big <u>bull</u> was standing behind the gate.**
6. **Give the <u>bush</u> some water with the hose.**
   Note the long **oo** in the detractor *tissue*.
7. **<u>Pull</u> the handle to open the package.**
   Note the long **oo** in the detractor *Fool*.
8. **We went to the <u>butcher</u> to get some fresh meat for dinner.**
   Note the long **e** in *meat* and the long **oo** in the detractor *cruise*.

Reading. Read and discuss the maxim for the Lesson.

Read the story *I Make a Bold Rescue*. This is another chapter of the *Robinson Crusoe* story. Preview the story and explain words or sentence structures that are not familiar to the student.

Comprehension questions:
How did Robinson prepare to meet the strangers?
What was the weather like?
When did Robinson decide to leave the castle?
How did Robinson and Friday surprise the men from the boat?
What story did the three men tell to Robinson and Friday?
Where were the other men from the boat?
What was said about the ringleaders?

Read the poem *There Was a Crooked Man*. Preview the poem and explain words or sentence structures that are not familiar to the student.

Comprehension questions:
What short vowel digraph is found in the poem?
What words rhyme in the poem?

Assign. Lesson activities or reading that are to be completed as homework.

Lesson 62: Short Vowel oo Spelled oul, Long Vowel oo Spelled ough, Review Long & Short oo

Overview:

- Auditory recognition of short **oo** sound
- Auditory recognition of long **oo** sound
- Read words with short **oo** sound spelled **oul** & **oo**
- Read words with long **oo** sound spelled **ough** & **oo**
- Write sentences with a short **oo** spelled **oul** words
- Identify words with long **oo** spelled **ough** sound
- Auditory discrimination of the short and long **oo** sound

Materials and Supplies:

- Teacher's Guide & Student Workbook 1
- White board or chalkboard
- Word cards (as necessary)
- Reader: *Robinson Crusoe & Other Classic Stories*

Teaching Tips:

Review for Mastery. Discuss and review any work from the previous lesson that was assigned as homework. Check for completion of the activities and orally quiz the student for comprehension. Review any reading that was assigned, discussing the characters, setting, plot, theme, language, sequence, etc.

Strengthen fluency and phonemic awareness by reviewing words and sentences from previous lessons. Build vocabulary skills by using some of the words in sentences.

Review short and long **oo** with Lessons 60 and 61. Write the two categories on the board. Call out a word from one of the lessons and have a student write the word under the correct category.

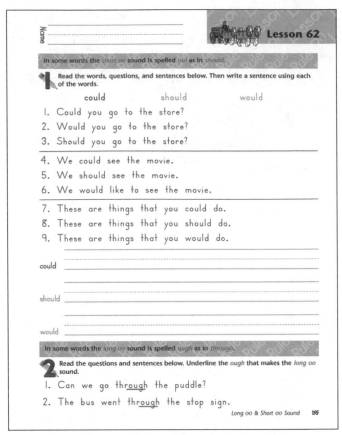

Activity 1. Review the rule and the example with the student. This activity will cover the short **oo** digraph sound with the **oul** spelling. Help the student as is needed to read the questions and sentences that use the words. The student will write a sentence that uses each of the words.

Activity 2. Help the student as is needed to read the questions and sentences that use the word *through* with the long **oo** sound. Have the student underline the **ough** in the word *through* in each sentence.

Note: Look for other long **oo** words in the sentences like *groom*, *caboose*, and *hoop*.

Activity 3. Have the student read the words aloud with a long **oo** sound. The other words in each row have the long **oo** sound that is to be a sound pattern applied to the words *hoof, roof,* and *root.* Try to use the words in sentences.

Activity 4. Have the student read the words aloud with a short **oo** sound. The other words in each row have the short **oo** sound that is to be a sound pattern applied to the words *hoof, roof,* and *root.* Try to use the words in sentences.

Note: The common pronunciation of the words in Activities 3 and 4 varies. Both are given here and in many dictionaries.

Reading. Read and discuss the maxim for the Lesson.

Read the story *I Have an Anxious Day.* This is another chapter of the *Robinson Crusoe* story. Preview the story and explain words or sentence structures that are not familiar to the student. With every story ask questions: who are the characters, what are they doing, what are they saying, where does the action take place, what is the order of events, what words are being used, what new information is given, what lesson can be learned?

Comprehension questions:
   What promises did the captain make?
   How did Robinson prepare the captain and his men to get control of the ship?
   What woke the seamen up who were in the grove?
   Did the fight last a long time?
   What was the result of the fight?
   Who guarded the captives?
   Why had the men seized the ship from the captain?

Assign. Lesson activities or reading that are to be completed as homework.

---

3. Go **through** the doorway to reach the restroom.
4. Should the groom run **through** the caboose?
5. The kids ran **through** the sprinklers.
6. Sue will jump **through** the hoop.

Some words are pronounced with either the *short oo* or the *long oo* sound.

3 Read these words with a *long oo* sound.

hoof	roof	root
hoop	hoot	hoof
proof	roost	roof
room	shoot	root
too	goof	hoof
soon	moo	roof
coot	hoot	root
hoof	roof	root

4 Read these words with a *short oo* sound.

hoof	roof	root
hook	hood	hoof
look	rook	roof
foot	soot	root
wood	shook	hoof
brook	rookie	roof
took	crook	root
hoof	roof	root

196   *Long oo & Short oo Sound*

Lesson 63: Review Long & Short oo Sound

Overview:

- Auditory recognition of long and short **oo** sound
- Read words with long and short **oo** sound
- Auditory discrimination of the short and long **oo** sound
- Identify spellings of the long **oo** sound
- Define a vowel digraph
- Apply the rule to read vowel digraphs
- Sentence reading
- Sentence writing

Materials and Supplies:

- Teacher's Guide & Student Workbook 1
- White board or chalkboard
- Word cards (as necessary)
- Reader: *Robinson Crusoe & Other Classic Stories*

Teaching Tips:

Review for Mastery. Discuss and review any work from the previous lesson that was assigned as homework. Check for completion of the activities and orally quiz the student for comprehension. Review any reading that was assigned, discussing the characters, setting, plot, theme, language, sequence, etc.

Strengthen fluency and phonemic awareness by reviewing words and sentences from previous lessons. Build vocabulary skills by using some of the words in sentences.

Review long **oo** with Lesson 62, Activity 2. Read the sentences again. Ask the student to find the words in the sentences that have the long **oo** vowel (restroom, groom, caboose, hoop).

Review previous lessons and the rules for the long and short **oo** sound.

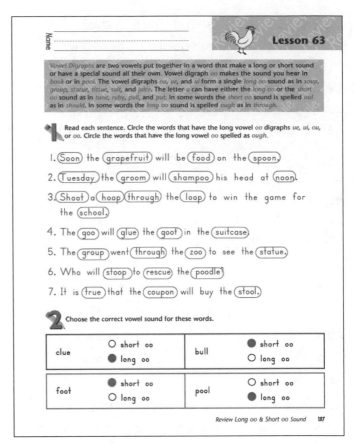

Activity 1. Review the rules given in the lesson. Ask the student for other words that fit the rules. Help the student read the sentences. Instruct the student to listen for the long **oo** sound and use the rules to circle the long **oo** words.

Words:

1. **Soon, grapefruit, food, spoon**
2. **Tuesday, groom, shampoo, noon**
3. **Shoot, hoop, through, loop, school**
4. **goo, glue, goof, suitcase**
5. **group, through, zoo, statue**
6. **stoop, rescue, poodle**
7. **true, coupon, stool**

Activity 2. Have the student read the words aloud. The student will select the vowel sound for each word.

Words:

clue	long oo
bull	short oo
foot	short oo
pool	long oo

Horizons Phonics & Reading Grade 2 Teacher's Guide

Activity 3. Help the student read the sentences. Instruct the student to listen for the long **oo** sound and use the rules to circle the long **oo** spelled **u** words.

Words:

1. June, July

   Note: *two* also has the long **oo** sound.
2. tuna
3. flu
4. ruby
5. crude, ruin

   Note: *fruit* also has the long **oo** sound.
6. rude, rules
7. flute, lute, yule, tune

Activity 4. Have the student write two sentences using at least three of the words in Activity 3. Help with ideas as needed, and remind the student about correct punctuation, capitalization, and penmanship.

Reading. Read and discuss the maxim for the Lesson.

Read the story *I Have an Anxious Day (continued)*. This is another chapter of the *Robinson Crusoe* story. Preview the story and explain words or sentence structures that are not familiar to the student. With every story ask questions: who are the characters, what are they doing, what are they saying, where does the action take place, what is the order of events, what words are being used, what new information is given, what lesson can be learned?

---

3 Read each sentence. Circle the words that have the long vowel *oo* sound spelled as *u*.

1. (June) and (July) are two summer months.
2. We had a (tuna) sandwich for lunch.
3. My brother is sick in bed with the (flu.)
4. The ring had a red (ruby) in the center.
5. The (crude) blade will (ruin) the fruit.
6. The (rude) lad did not obey the (rules.)
7. A (flute) and a (lute) will play the (yule) (tune.)

4 Write two sentences. Use at least *three* of the words used in this lesson in each sentence.

_____

_____

_____

_____

_____

_____

_____

_____

_____

_____

_____

198   *Review Long oo & Short oo Sound*

Comprehension questions:

What was in the boat that Robinson had not tasted for many years?

When did they hear a gun fired from the ship?

How did Robinson and the captain respond to the signals from the ship?

How many men were in Robinson's group and how many were coming from the ship?

What did the men from the ship do after they saw the hole in the boat that was on the shore?

How many men from the boat explored the country?

Why did the men return to their boat on the shore?

Assign. Lesson activities or reading that are to be completed as homework.

Lesson 64: Review Long & Short oo Sound

Overview:

- Auditory recognition of long and short **oo** sound
- Read words with long and short **oo** sound
- Auditory discrimination of the short and long **oo** sound
- Identify spellings of the long **oo** sound
- Define a vowel digraph
- Apply the rule to read vowel digraphs
- Sentence reading
- Classify words by the vowel sound

Materials and Supplies:

- Teacher's Guide & Student Workbook 1
- White board or chalkboard
- Word cards (as necessary)
- Reader: *Robinson Crusoe & Other Classic Stories*

Teaching Tips:

Review for Mastery. Discuss and review any work from the previous lesson that was assigned as homework. Check for completion of the activities and orally quiz the student for comprehension. Review any reading that was assigned, discussing the characters, setting, plot, theme, language, sequence, etc.

Strengthen fluency and phonemic awareness by reviewing words and sentences from previous lessons. Build vocabulary skills by using some of the words in sentences.

Review previous lessons and the rules for the long and short **oo** sound.

Build vocabulary skills by using some of the words from Lesson 63 in sentences.

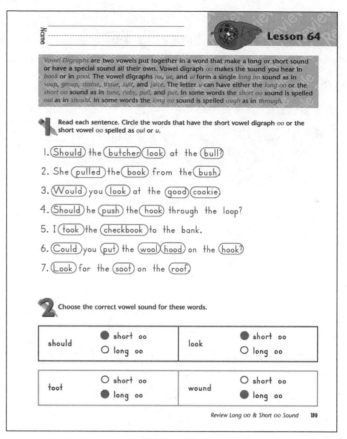

Activity 1. Review the rules given in the lesson. Ask the student for other words that fit the rules. Help the student read the sentences. Instruct the student to listen for the short **oo** sound and use the rules to circle the short **oo** words.

Words:
1. Should, butcher, look, bull
2. pulled, book, bush
3. Would, look, good, cookie
4. Should, push, hook
5. took, checkbook
6. Could, put, wool, hood, hook
7. Look, soot, roof

Activity 2. Have the student read the words aloud. The student will select the vowel sound for each word.

Words:

should	short oo
look	short oo
toot	long oo
wound	long oo

174

Activity 3. Help the student read the words. Instruct the student to listen for the long or short **oo** sound in each word. Have the student write the word under the correct category for the vowel sound.

Long oo	Short oo
food	football
too	brook
room	handbook
soon	goodbye
voodoo	wood

Long oo	Short oo
blueprint	pudding
true	could
fruitcake	would
wetsuit	pulling
toucan	put

Reading. Read and discuss the maxim for the Lesson.

Read the story *I Am Called Governor*. This is another chapter of the *Robinson Crusoe* story. Preview the story and explain words or sentence structures that are not familiar to the student. With every story ask questions: who are the characters, what are they doing, what are they saying, where does the action take place, what is the order of events, what words are being used, what new information is given, what lesson can be learned?

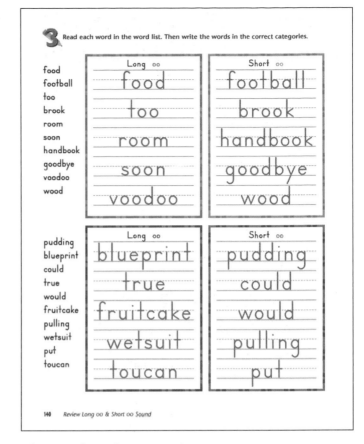

Comprehension questions:
  What did Friday and the captain's mate do to distract the men who were from the boat?
  What did Robinson seize first?
  What were the men from the boat saying as they went through the bushes?
  Who called out to the men and what did he tell them to do?
  Why was Will Atkins not willing to surrender?
  How did the matter end?

Assign. Lesson activities or reading that are to be completed as homework.

Lesson 65: Initial Triple Consonant Blends sch and chr

Overview:

- Auditory recognition of the **sk** sound of **sch**
- Match words to pictures
- Auditory recognition of the **kr** sound of **chr**
- Sentence completion
- Sentence reading
- Identify words by the consonant sound

Materials and Supplies:

- Teacher's Guide & Student Workbook 1
- White board or chalkboard
- Word cards (as necessary)
- Reader: *Robinson Crusoe & Other Classic Stories*

Teaching Tips:

Review for Mastery. Discuss and review any work from the previous lesson that was assigned as homework. Check for completion of the activities and orally quiz the student for comprehension. Review any reading that was assigned, discussing the characters, setting, plot, theme, language, sequence, etc.

Strengthen fluency and phonemic awareness by reviewing words and sentences from previous lessons. Build vocabulary skills by using some of the words in sentences.

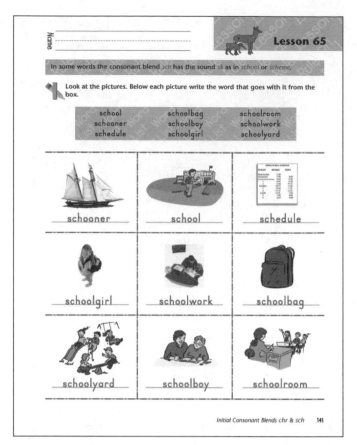

Initial Consonant Blends chr & sch 141

Activity 1. Review the rule for the **sk** sound of **sch**. In some words **sch** makes the **sh** sound as in *schwa, Schilling, schlock, schmo,* etc. *Words to teach the concept:* scholastic, scheme, scholar. Identify the pictures with the student. Have the student listen as you say the name of each picture. Instruct the student to write the correct word underneath each picture.

Words:

   schooner, school, schedule
   schoolgirl, schoolwork, schoolbag
   schoolyard, schoolboy, schoolroom

Note the R-controlled vowels in *girl*, *work*, and *yard*.

Note the **j** sound of **d** in *schedule*.

Activity 2. Review the rule for the **kr** sound of **chr**. Discuss some words with **chr** as a medial sound. *Words to teach the concept:* synchro, synchronize, polychrome, bichromate, chronic, Chris, chromosome. Help the student read the words aloud. Read the sentences. Have the students select the correct word to complete the sentence and write it on the line.

Sentences:
1. Many feel the birth of <u>Christ</u> took place on <u>Christmas</u> Day.
2. My friend <u>Christy</u> has a bike with <u>chrome</u> fenders.
3. <u>Christmas</u> Day is in December.
4. The new car has a <u>chrome</u> bumper that is a bright silver color.

Activity 3. Have the student read the paragraph aloud. The student will circle all of the words with the **sch-** or **chr-** initial consonants.

Words:
Christy, scholar, schedule, school, schoolgirl, schoolbag, chrome, school, Chris, schoolyard, Chris, schoolboy, Christmas, schoolwork, Christmas, Chris, schoolroom

Reading. Read and discuss the maxim for the Lesson.

Read the story *I Am Called Governor (continued).* This is another chapter of the *Robinson Crusoe* story. Preview the story and explain words or sentence structures that are not familiar to the student. With every story ask questions: who are the characters, what are they doing, what are they saying, where does the action take place, what is the order of events, what words are being used, what new information is given, what lesson can be learned?

In words the consonant blend *chr* has the sound *kr*: Chris, chrome

2 Read the words with the *chr-* initial blend. Use the words to complete the sentences.

Christ   chrome   Christmas   Christy

Many feel the birth of _____Christ_____ took place on _____Christmas_____ Day.

My friend _____Christy_____ has a bike with _____chrome_____ fenders.

_____Christmas_____ Day is in December.

The new car has a _____chrome_____ bumper that is a bright silver color.

3 Read the paragraph. Circle all of the words with the *sch-* or *chr-* initial consonant blend.

(Christy) is a (scholar) who just got her new (schedule) for (school). As a (schoolgirl) she will need a (schoolbag) with a (chrome) clasp. Before (school) she will play with her friend (Chris) in the (schoolyard). (Chris) is a (schoolboy) who looks forward to the days off at (Christmas). To finish all of his (schoolwork) before (Christmas), (Chris) must stay in the (schoolroom) at recess.

142 Initial Consonant Blends chr & sch

Comprehension questions:
What was done with the prisoners?
Why were the prisoners separated?
Why were the men so afraid?
How did they plan to retake the ship?
What would happen to the five men if they helped retake the ship?
Who was in charge of all the affairs of the island?
How many boats and men returned to the ship?
What time was it when they left for the ship?
How did the men get back onto the ship?
What were the events of the battle?
How did the men surrender?

Assign. Lesson activities or reading that are to be completed as homework.

Lesson 66: Vowel Diphthongs ou & ow

Overview:

- Auditory recognition of the **ou** & **ow** diphthong sound
- Match words to pictures
- Code words with **ou** & **ow** diphthongs
- Sentence reading
- Identify words by the diphthong sound

Materials and Supplies:

- Teacher's Guide & Student Workbook 1
- White board or chalkboard
- Word cards (as necessary)
- Reader: *Robinson Crusoe & Other Classic Stories*

Teaching Tips:

Review for Mastery. Discuss and review any work from the previous lesson that was assigned as homework. Check for completion of the activities and orally quiz the student for comprehension. Review any reading that was assigned, discussing the characters, setting, plot, theme, language, sequence, etc.

Strengthen fluency and phonemic awareness by reviewing words and sentences from previous lessons. Build vocabulary skills by using some of the words in sentences.

Review the rule for the diphthong sound of **ou** and **ow**. The phrase, "How now brown cow" can be used to illustrate the diphthong sound and word spelling. This phrase used to be used in elocution teaching to demonstrate rounded vowel sounds. A natural and spontaneous way of providing children with exposure to phonemes is to focus on literature that deals playfully with speech sounds through rhymes.

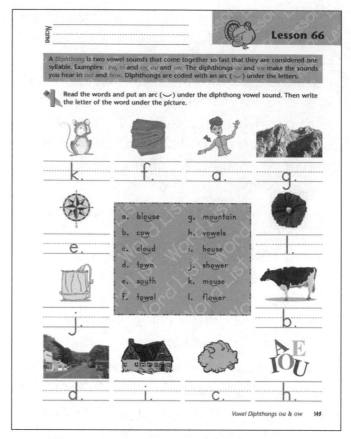

Activity 1. In Lesson 50 the long /o/ sound of the **ow** and the **ou** digraphs was covered (snow plow, slow cow, through cloud, boulder round). In this lesson the /ou/ sound of diphthongs **ow** and **ou** will be covered. Review the rule and the examples. *Words to teach the concept:* out, aloud, count, couch, doubt, found, grouch, ground, grouse, hound, sound, down, crown, crowd, power, powder, tower, plow, vow. Have the student read the words in the list aloud. After reading the words, have the student code the diphthong with an arc under the vowels. Review the pictures to make sure the student can correctly identify them. Instruct the student to write the correct letter for the word from the list underneath the pictures.

Pictures:

m<u>ou</u>se, t<u>ow</u>el, bl<u>ou</u>se, m<u>ou</u>ntain
s<u>ou</u>th, fl<u>ow</u>er
sh<u>ow</u>er, c<u>ow</u>
t<u>ow</u>n, h<u>ou</u>se, cl<u>ou</u>d, v<u>ow</u>els

Horizons Phonics & Reading Grade 2 Teacher's Guide

Activity 2. Have the student read the sentences aloud. The student will circle all of the words with the **ou** or **ow** diphthong.

Words:

clouds, towel, flowers, house, blouse, cow, brown, crowd, playground, found, Mayflower

Reading. Read and discuss the maxim for the Lesson.

Read the story *I Have a New Suit of Clothes*. This is another chapter of the *Robinson Crusoe* story. Preview the story and explain words or sentence structures that are not familiar to the student. With every story ask questions: who are the characters, what are they doing, what are they saying, where does the action take place, what is the order of events, what words are being used, what new information is given, what lesson can be learned?

Comprehension questions:

Why did Robinson sleep late the next morning?

What did Robinson hear when he woke up? Where was the ship?

Who did the captain say was the owner of the ship?

What plans were made?

Why were some of the men left on the island?

What things were told to the men who were saying on the island?

Read the poem *The Stars*. Preview the poem and explain words or sentence structures that are not familiar to the student.

How do we look at the stars?

What words in the poem have R-controlled vowels?

What is counting the stars compared to?

How large are the stars?

Assign. Lesson activities or reading that are to be completed as homework.

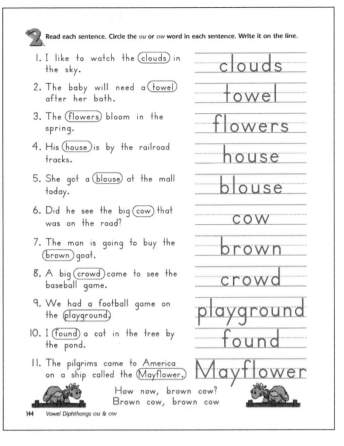

2 Read each sentence. Circle the *ou* or *ow* word in each sentence. Write it on the line.

1. I like to watch the (clouds) in the sky.
2. The baby will need a (towel) after her bath.
3. The (flowers) bloom in the spring.
4. His (house) is by the railroad tracks.
5. She got a (blouse) at the mall today.
6. Did he see the big (cow) that was on the road?
7. The man is going to buy the (brown) goat.
8. A big (crowd) came to see the baseball game.
9. We had a football game on the (playground).
10. I (found) a cat in the tree by the pond.
11. The pilgrims came to America on a ship called the (Mayflower.)

clouds
towel
flowers
house
blouse
cow
brown
crowd
playground
found
Mayflower

How now, brown cow?
Brown cow, brown cow

144   *Vowel Diphthongs ou & ow*

Lesson 67: Vowel Diphthongs oi & oy

Overview:

- Auditory recognition of the **oi** & **oy** diphthong sound
- Match words to pictures
- Code words with **oi** & **oy** diphthongs
- Sentence reading
- Identify words by the diphthong sound

Materials and Supplies:

- Teacher's Guide & Student Workbook 1
- White board or chalkboard
- Word cards (as necessary)
- Reader: *Robinson Crusoe & Other Classic Stories*

Teaching Tips:

Review for Mastery. Discuss and review any work from the previous lesson that was assigned as homework. Check for completion of the activities and orally quiz the student for comprehension. Review any reading that was assigned, discussing the characters, setting, plot, theme, language, sequence, etc.

Strengthen fluency and phonemic awareness by reviewing words and sentences from previous lessons. Build vocabulary skills by using some of the words in sentences.

Review digraphs **ow** and **ou** with Lesson 50, Activities 1-3 and diphthongs **ow** and **ou** with Lesson 66, Activities 1 & 2. Write long /o/ sound and long /ou/ sound categories on the board and have the student sort random words from both lessons into the correct category.

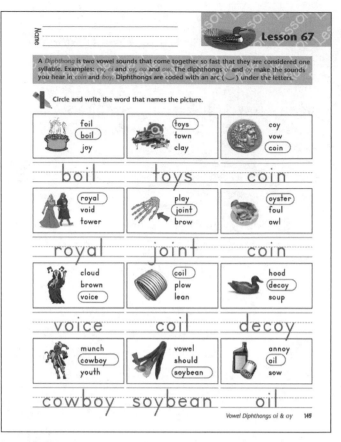

Activity 1. Review the rule and the examples. *Words to teach the concept:* choice, noise, broil, spoil, poison, moisture, soil, rejoice, steroid, tabloid, void, loyal, employer, joyful, employ, enjoy, annoy, destroy, boy. These words all have the long /oi/ sound. Have the student read the words in each box aloud. Review the pictures to make sure the student can correctly identify them. Instruct the student to select the correct word in the box for the picture and write it on the blank.

Pictures:
   boil, toys, coin
   royal, joint, oyster
   voice, coil, decoy
   cowboy, soybean, oil

Activity 2. Have the student read the sentences aloud. The student will draw an arc under all of the words with the **oi** or **oy** diphthong.

Words:

1. p<u>oi</u>nt
2. s<u>oi</u>l
3. j<u>oi</u>n
4. f<u>oi</u>l
5. av<u>oi</u>d
6. n<u>oi</u>se
7. sp<u>oi</u>l
8. <u>oi</u>nk
9. rej<u>oi</u>ce
10. ch<u>oi</u>ce
11. t<u>oi</u>l
12. b<u>oy</u>
13. enj<u>oy</u>
14. l<u>oy</u>al
15. t<u>oy</u>
16. dec<u>oy</u>
17. paperb<u>oy</u>
18. batb<u>oy</u>
19. bellb<u>oy</u>
20. cowb<u>oy</u>
21. b<u>oy</u>hood

Reading. Read and discuss the maxim for the Lesson.

Read the story *I Bring My Tale to a Close*. This is the final chapter of the *Robinson Crusoe* story. Preview the story and explain words or sentence structures that are not familiar to the student. With every story ask questions: who are the characters, what are they doing, what are they saying, where does the action take place, what is the order of events, what words are being used, what new information is given, what lesson can be learned?

2 Read each sentence. Put an arc (⌣) under the *oi* or *oy* diphthongs.

1. The needle has a point on one end.
2. He will plant the flower in some soil.
3. Can he join us for the game?
4. Mom will bake the potatoes in some foil.
5. Do your best to avoid the snake by the trail.
6. The fans made a lot of noise at the game.
7. We must keep the meat cold so it does not spoil.
8. The big pig made a loud oink.
9. The team will rejoice if they win the game.
10. They made a choice to buy the puppy.
11. The man will toil to paint the fence.
12. A boy will ride the bike.
13. He will enjoy going fast.
14. His loyal little puppy will run along.
15. The puppy likes to play with a toy.
16. The puppy can fetch an old decoy.
17. Some day he will be a paperboy.
18. As a batboy he can help the team.
19. Then he can find a job in a hotel as a bellboy.
20. Later he wants to be a cowboy.
21. His boyhood will end when he becomes a man.

146   *Vowel Diphthongs oi & oy*

Comprehension questions:
  On what date did Robinson leave the island?
  What did Robinson take with him?
  On what date did Robinson get back to England?
  What had happened to Robinson's parents while he was gone?
  What did Robinson find out about his plantations in Brazil?
  Did Robinson live the rest of his life in one place?
  Why did Robinson end his story?

Assign. Lesson activities or reading that are to be completed as homework.

Lesson 68: Vowel Diphthong ew

Overview:

- Auditory recognition of the **ew** diphthong sound
- Match words to pictures
- Code words with **ew** diphthongs
- Sentence reading
- Complete a crossword with **ew** diphthong words
- Identify words by the diphthong sound

Materials and Supplies:

- Teacher's Guide & Student Workbook 1
- White board or chalkboard
- Word cards (as necessary)
- Reader: *Robinson Crusoe & Other Classic Stories*

Teaching Tips:

Review for Mastery. Discuss and review any work from the previous lesson that was assigned as homework. Check for completion of the activities and orally quiz the student for comprehension. Review any reading that was assigned, discussing the characters, setting, plot, theme, language, sequence, etc.

Strengthen fluency and phonemic awareness by reviewing words and sentences from previous lessons. Build vocabulary skills by using some of the words in sentences.

Review /oi/ diphthongs **oi** and **oy** with Lesson 67, Activity 1. Have the student code the diphthong in each word with an arc under the letters. Include the detractors listed for each picture in this activity. Read all of the words.

Review digraphs **ow** and **ou** with Lesson 50, Activities 1-3 and diphthongs **ow** and **ou** with Lesson 66, Activities 1 & 2. Write long /o/ sound and /ou/ sound categories on the board and have the student sort random words from both lessons into the correct category.

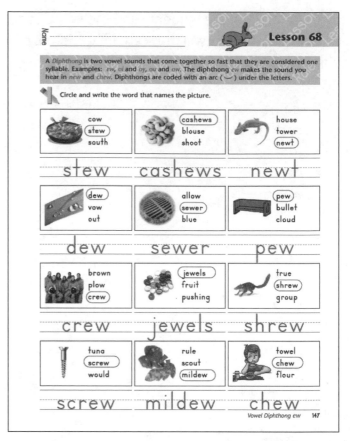

Activity 1. Review the rule and the examples. *Words to teach the concept:* blew, brew, drew, few, Hebrew, hew, interview, Jew, Matthew, nephew, new, preview, renew, slew, stewardess, threw, view. These words all have the long /**oo**/ sound. Have the student read the words in each box aloud. Review the pictures to make sure the student can correctly identify them. Instruct the student to select the correct word in the box for the picture and write it on the blank.

Pictures:
stew, cashews, newt
dew, sewer, pew
crew, jewels, shrew
screw, mildew, chew

Horizons Phonics & Reading Grade 2 Teacher's Guide

Activity 2. Have the student read the sentences aloud. The student will draw an arc under all of the words with the **ew** diphthong.

Words:

n<u>ew</u>, cr<u>ew</u>, fl<u>ew</u>

kn<u>ew</u>, ch<u>ew</u>, st<u>ew</u>

f<u>ew</u>, scr<u>ew</u>s, fl<u>ew</u>, p<u>ew</u>

dr<u>ew</u>, shr<u>ew</u>

Matth<u>ew</u>, vi<u>ew</u>, n<u>ew</u>s

n<u>ew</u>t, s<u>ew</u>er

bl<u>ew</u>, d<u>ew</u>, n<u>ew</u>

mild<u>ew</u>, gr<u>ew</u>

shr<u>ew</u>, ch<u>ew</u>, cash<u>ew</u>

thr<u>ew</u>, j<u>ew</u>el, cr<u>ew</u>cut

Activity 3. Review the words in the list. Help the student read the crossword puzzle clues. Assist the student as necessary with the crossword puzzle.

Across:
1. knew
3. drew
4. flew

Down:
2. new
3. dew
4. few

Reading. Read and discuss the maxim for the Lesson.

Read the poem *The Boy to the Schoolmaster*. Preview the poem and explain words or sentence structures that are not familiar to the student. With every story ask questions: who are the characters, what are they doing, what are they saying, where does the action take place, what is the order of events, what words are being used, what new information is given, what lesson can be learned?

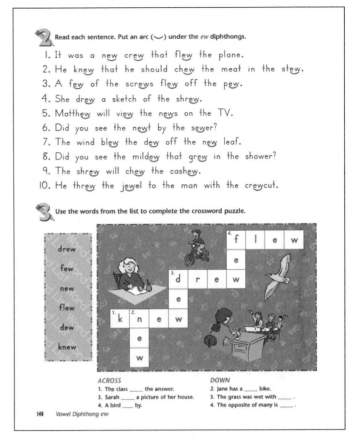

Comprehension questions:

What are some of the old English words in the poem?

Who is speaking in the poem?

Why is the student asking the teacher questions?

What kind of things is the student asking the teacher about?

Did the teacher look comfortable while the student was asking the questions?

Who had been called a dunce at the beginning of the poem?

At the end of the poem, who admitted he was the dunce?

Assign. Lesson activities or reading that are to be completed as homework.

Lesson 69: Review Diphthongs

Overview:

- Auditory recognition of diphthong sound
- Sentence completion
- Sort words by the diphthong sound
- Identify words by the diphthong sound

Materials and Supplies:

- Teacher's Guide & Student Workbook 1
- White board or chalkboard
- Word cards (as necessary)
- Reader: *Robinson Crusoe & Other Classic Stories*

Teaching Tips:

Review for Mastery. Discuss and review any work from the previous lesson that was assigned as homework. Check for completion of the activities and orally quiz the student for comprehension. Review any reading that was assigned, discussing the characters, setting, plot, theme, language, sequence, etc.

Strengthen fluency and phonemic awareness by reviewing words and sentences from previous lessons. Build vocabulary skills by using some of the words in sentences.

Review /ou/ diphthongs **ou** and **ow** with Lesson 68, Activity 1. Have the student find these diphthongs that were used as detractors for some of the pictures. Code the diphthong in each word with an arc under the letters. Read all of the words.

Review /ou/ diphthongs **ow** and **ou**, long /oo/ diphthong **ew**, and /oi/ diphthongs **oi** and **oy** with Lessons 66-68. Write the sound categories on the board and have the student sort random words from the lessons into the correct category.

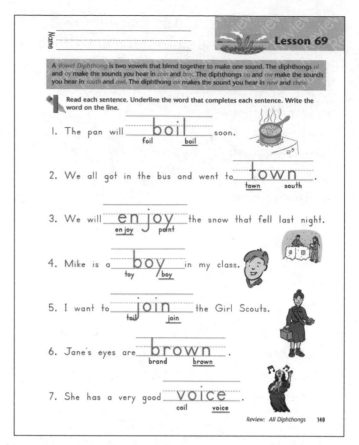

Activity 1. Review the diphthong rules and the example words. Help the student read the words in the sentences and the word choices. Instruct the student to underline the word that completes the sentence. Read the sentences after the words have been underlined.

Sentences:

1. The pan will <u>boil</u> soon.
2. We all got in the bus and went to <u>town</u>.
3. We will <u>enjoy</u> the snow that fell last night.
   Note the **ow** diphthong in *snow*.
4. Mike is a <u>boy</u> in my class.
5. I want to <u>join</u> the Girl Scouts.
6. Jane's eyes are <u>brown</u>.
7. She has a very good <u>voice</u>.

Activity 2. Help the student read the words. Instruct the student to listen for the digraph or diphthong sound in each word. Have the student write the wood under the correct category for the vowel sound.

Long o Digraph	Diphthongs
grow	around
below	house
low	ground
know	found
follow	south
court	sound
boulder	brown
poultry	town
shoulder	flower
show	vowel

Reading. Read and discuss the maxim for the Lesson.

Read the story *The Owl*. Preview the story and explain words or sentence structures that are not familiar to the student. With every story ask questions: who are the characters, what are they doing, what are they saying, where does the action take place, what is the order of events, what words are being used, what new information is given, what lesson can be learned?

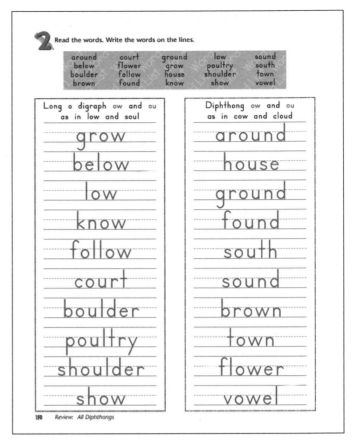

Comprehension questions:
Where had the boys found an owl?
How was the owl captured?
Why did the boy plan to let the owl go?
What did the father say was good about the owl?
What did the boys find interesting about the owl?
What vowel digraphs are used in the story?
How can the owl easily surprise his prey?
How does an owl eat his food?

Assign. Lesson activities or reading that are to be completed as homework.

Lesson 70: Review Diphthongs

Overview:

- Auditory recognition of diphthong sound
- Sentence completion
- Sort words by the diphthong sound
- Identify words by the diphthong sound

Materials and Supplies:

- Teacher's Guide & Student Workbook 1
- White board or chalkboard
- Word cards (as necessary)
- Reader: *Robinson Crusoe & Other Classic Stories*

Teaching Tips:

Review for Mastery. Discuss and review any work from the previous lesson that was assigned as homework. Check for completion of the activities and orally quiz the student for comprehension. Review any reading that was assigned, discussing the characters, setting, plot, theme, language, sequence, etc.

Strengthen fluency and phonemic awareness by reviewing words and sentences from previous lessons. Build vocabulary skills by using some of the words in sentences.

Review /ou/ diphthongs **ow** and **ou**, long /oo/ diphthong **ew**, and /oi/ diphthongs **oi** and **oy** with Lessons 66-69. Write the sound categories on the board and have the student sort random words from the lessons into the correct category.

Build vocabulary skills by using some of the words from Lesson 69 in sentences. Form sentences with the detractors used in Activity 1.

Activity 1. Review the diphthong rules and the example words. Review the pictures to make sure the student can correctly identify them. Have the student circle the diphthong sound for each picture.

Pictures:
toy, oil, boy, boil
joy, towel, crown, mouth
flower, clown, vowels, mouse
cowboy, coin, house, foil
south, decoy, cloud, voice

Activity 2. Help the student read the words. Instruct the student to listen for the digraph or diphthong sound in each word. Have the student write the word under the correct category for the vowel sound.

Long oo Digraph	Diphthongs
youth	count
coupon	mouth
crouton	blouse
toucan	noun
routine	mouse
soup	shout

Activity 3. Help the student read the sentences and review the word choices from Activity 2. Instruct the student to write the correct word on the line to complete the sentence.

Sentences:
1. We will have hot <u>soup</u> for lunch.
2. John found a <u>mouse</u> in the box.
3. John is a good name for a <u>youth</u>.
4. We will <u>shout</u> when the team wins.

Review for Test. The instructor should plan to use some time at the end of the class to review and prepare for the test that follows this lesson. Review the objectives for the test and then look over the lessons that it will cover. If the student has struggled with any of the concepts that will be included in the test, some additional drill, practice, or review may be needed to adequately prepare him for the test.

Reading. Read and discuss the maxim for the Lesson.

Read the story *Willie and Bounce*. Preview the story and explain words or sentence structures that are not familiar to the student. With every story ask questions: who are the characters, what are they doing, what are they saying, where does the action take place, what is the order of events, what words are being used, what new information is given, what lesson can be learned?

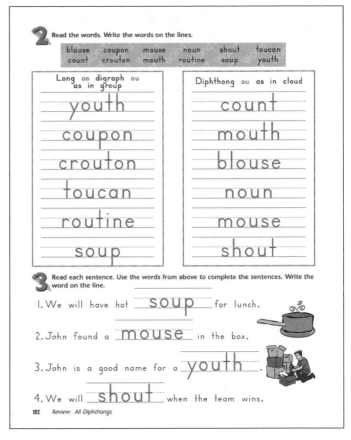

Comprehension questions:
  Who was Bounce?
  What was the day like?
  Where did Willie and Bounce go?
  What was Willie doing at the river?
  What made Willie fall into the water?
  What did Bounce do when he saw that Willie was in trouble?
  How did Bounce get Mr. Brown's attention?
  What vowel digraphs are used in the story?
  Who was happiest about the outcome of this story?

Read the poem *The Clouds*. Preview the poem and explain words or sentence structures that are not familiar to the student.

Comprehension questions:
  When are the clouds in the sky?
  How do the clouds help the earth?
  What vowel digraphs are used in the poem?
  What is the spelling of the rhyming words?

Assign. Lesson activities or reading that are to be completed as homework.

Test 7
Lessons 55-64

Overview:

- Make nouns plural by adding **-es** without spelling changes
- Add **-ing** ending to verbs without spelling changes to show that something is happening now
- Add **-ed** ending to verbs without spelling changes to show that something has happened already
- Auditory discrimination of long **a** in words with vowel digraphs
- Auditory discrimination of short **oo** in words
- Auditory discrimination of long **oo** in words
- Sort words by their long vowel spelling
- Apply spelling rules to make words plural

Materials and Supplies:

- Teacher's Guide & Student Workbook 1

Instructions:

Assessment Start-up. Read through the test with the student. Help the student with any words that he is still unsure of. The teacher should be available to answer any questions that the student may have during the test.

Activity 1. Read the instruction with the student. Make sure the student can read the words. Instruct the student to make the words plural.

Words:
   pushes, flushes, glasses, buzzes
   riches, pitches, buses, potatoes
   zeroes, foxes, taxes

Activity 2. Help the student read the words. Instruct the student to listen for the vowel sound in each word. Have the student write the word under the correct category for the vowel sound.

Long a	Short oo
rein	hook
great	good
weigh	look
hey	stood

Activity 3. Review the instruction with the student. Make sure the student can read the words. Instruct the student to add **-ing** to make the words say that something is happening now.

Words:
   honking, flying, crying, brushing
   ticking, cleaning, folding, rolling

Activity 4. Review the instruction with the student. Make sure the student can read the words. Instruct the student to add **-ed** to make the words say that something has happened already.

Words:

landed	loaded	added	pushed
filled	tricked	opened	rented

Activity 5. Help the student read the words. Instruct the student to listen for the vowel sound in each word. Have the student write the word under the correct category for the vowel spelling.

Long o spelled oo	Long o spelled ou
tooth	soup
balloon	group
igloo	coupon

Activity 6. Help the student read the words. Instruct the student to listen for the vowel sound in each word. Have the student circle the words with a short **oo** sound.

Short oo	Detractors
push	tune, /oo/
pull	soon, /oo/
would	
could	

Activity 7. Help the student read the words. Instruct the student to listen for the vowel sound in each word. Have the student circle the words with a long **oo** sound.

Long oo	Detractors
Tuesday	bush, short /oo/
true	build, short /i/
suitcase	
through	

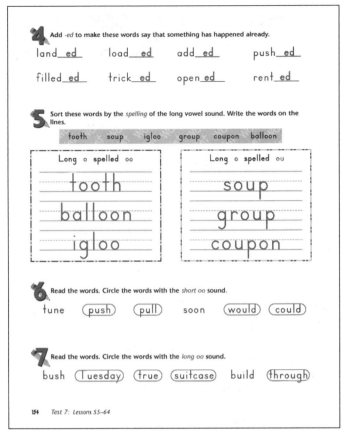

Assessment Follow-up. Every test is an important assessment of both the student's comprehension of the concepts and the instructional process. This makes follow-up after each test essential to the learning process. Review all of the errors made on the test with the student. Check for understanding of the concepts and of the problem instructions. Compare the errors made on the test to the test objectives to identify specific areas of weakness. If weak areas of understanding are detected it might be necessary to go back to those lessons to devise some enrichment activities for the concept.

The test results can be used to determine what concepts are reviewed during the daily time of classroom instruction. Devise enrichment activities that will provide development in those areas.

If time permits, choose a selection and have the student read it again. This can also be used as a catch-up time to complete unfinished selections.

Lesson 71: R-controlled ar with /ar/ Sound

Overview:

- Auditory recognition of R-controlled **ar** with /**ar**/ sound
- Picture/word match
- Word completion
- Sentence completion
- Read words with R-controlled **ar**

Materials and Supplies:

- Teacher's Guide & Student Workbook 1
- White board or chalkboard
- Word cards (as necessary)
- Poems: *What do the Stars Do?* and *I See You, Little Star*
- Story: *One Way to be Brave*

Teaching Tips:

Review for Mastery. Discuss and review any work from the previous lesson that was assigned as homework. Check for completion of the activities and orally quiz the student for comprehension. Review any reading that was assigned, discussing the characters, setting, plot, theme, language, sequence, etc.

Strengthen fluency and phonemic awareness by reviewing words and sentences from previous lessons. Build vocabulary skills by using some of the words in sentences.

Review /ou/ diphthongs **ow** and **ou**, long /oo/ diphthong **ew**, and /oi/ diphthongs **oi** and **oy** with Lessons 66-70. Write the sound categories on the board and have the student sort random words from the lessons into the correct category.

Review the sounds of the diphthong words in Lesson 70, Activity 1. Review the sorted words in Lesson 70, Activity 2. Have the student use each word in a sentence.

Review the rule given for this lesson. Begin the lesson by introducing the letter **r** as a bully! Explain that any vowel in front of the letter **r** loses its sound. The vowel and the letter **r** make a single sound. The vowel and letter **r** combine to make

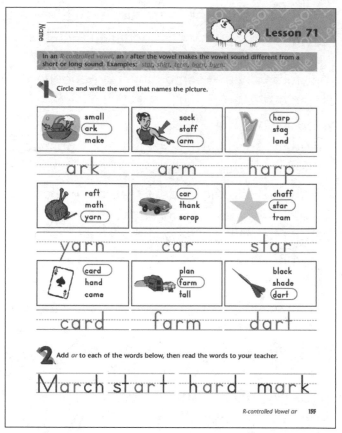

what is known as a R-controlled vowel. Explain that there are five vowels, but there are only three different R-controlled vowels. The three different sounds are the /**ar**/ sound, "Start the warm car!"; the /**or**/ sound, "Four forks!"; and the /**er**/ sound (or /**ur**/ in some dictionaries), "Her first nurse works early!"

Write the word *are* on the board. Have the student write examples of other words that begin with **ar_** on the board. Write the word *art* on the board. Have the student write examples of other words that end with **_art** on the board. Do the same activity with other ar words and have them change the beginning or ending sound to make more words.

Write several short **a** words on the board and have the student compare the short **a** sound to the R-controlled sound of **a** in the **ar** words that have been written on the board.

ar Words to teach the concept: alarm, apart, apartment, arbor, arc, arch, arctic, are, ark, arm, armor, art, artist, bar, Barb, barb, barber, bark, barn, Bart, car, card, Carl, Carmen, carpenter, carpet, cart, charm, chart, collar, dark, darn, dart, dollar, far, farm, farmer, garden, garlic, hard, hark, harm, harp, harsh, harvest, jar, lard, large, lark, mar, marble, March, march, mark, Mark, market, marsh, par, parch, park, part, partner, party, radar, scar, scarf, shark, sharp, similar, smart, spark, sparkle, standard, star, starch, start, startle, tar, tarnish, tarp, tart, yard, yarn

Activity 1. Assist the student as needed in identifying the pictures in the boxes. Have the student read the three words in each box aloud. The student will circle the correct word for the picture and write it on the line.

Pictures:
    ark, arm, harp
    yarn, car, star
    card, farm, dart

Activity 2. Have the student add **ar** to each of the words. Ask the student to read the words aloud.

Words:
    March, start, hard, mark

Activity 3. Help the student read the words in the list and the sentences. Instruct the student to select the word that will correctly complete each sentence and write the word on the line. Note the other **ar** words used in the sentences.

Sentences:
1. (Marcy) is a <u>smart</u> student.
2. We have a <u>large</u> snake for a pet.
3. The (farmer) was busy weeding in his <u>garden</u>.
4. (Carl) used <u>tar</u> to fix a hole in the roof.
5. How (far) is it to the <u>park</u>?
6. We saw a <u>lark</u> in the (marsh).

Activity 4. Have the student read the sentences. Read both of the words for each choice. Have the student circle the correct words to complete each sentence.

Sentences:
1. <u>Carmen</u> will clean the dishes until they <u>start</u> to <u>sparkle</u>.
2. The <u>charm</u> will cost a <u>dollar</u>.
3. <u>Are</u> <u>Bart</u> and <u>Mark</u> <u>part</u> of the <u>artist</u> group?
4. It will be <u>dark</u> when the <u>car</u> gets to the <u>market</u>.
5. <u>Barb</u> will keep the <u>tart</u> fruit in a <u>jar</u>.
6. The <u>radar</u> <u>alarm</u> on the planes will keep them <u>apart</u>.

Reading. Read and discuss the maxim for the Lesson.

Read the poem *What Do the Stars Do*. Preview the poem and explain words or sentence structures that are not familiar to the student.

Horizons Phonics & Reading Grade 2 Teacher's Guide

3 Read each sentence. Use the words from the list to complete each sentence. Write the word on the line.

| park | large | garden | tar | smart | lark |

1. Marcy is a <u>smart</u> student.
2. We have a <u>large</u> snake for a pet.
3. The farmer was busy weeding in his <u>garden</u>.
4. Carl used <u>tar</u> to fix a hole in the roof.
5. How far is it to the <u>park</u>?
6. We saw a <u>lark</u> in the marsh.

4 Read each sentence. Circle the correct words to complete each sentence.

1. (Hard, (Carmen)) will clean the dishes until they ((start), ark) to (harp, (sparkle)).
2. The ((charm), scar) will cost a (lard, (dollar)).
3. (Arm, (Are)) ((Bart), cart) and (chart, (Mark)) ((part), shark) of the (tarp, (artist)) group?
4. It will be ((dark), tarp) when the (startle, (car)) gets to the ((market), hard).
5. (Start, (Barb)) will keep the ((tart), harp) fruit in a (shark, (jar)).
6. The ((radar), starch) (far, (alarm)) on the planes will keep them ((apart), party).

156   *R-controlled Vowel ar*

Comprehension questions:
    What are the words with R-controlled vowels in the poem?
    What sounds do the R-controlled vowels make?
    What are the rhyming words in the poem?

Read the poem *I See You, Little Star*. Preview the poem and explain words or sentence structures that are not familiar to the student.

Comprehension questions:
    What are the words with R-controlled vowels in the poem?
    What sounds do the R-controlled vowels make?
    What are the rhyming words in the poem?

Read the poem *March*. Preview the poem and explain words or sentence structures that are not familiar to the student.

Comprehension questions:
    What are the words with R-controlled vowels in the poem?
    What sounds do the R-controlled vowels make?
    What are the rhyming words in the poem?

Extension Activity. Have the student play marble games at recess. Hold a marble tournament.

Assign. Lesson activities or reading that are to be completed as homework.

Lesson 72: R-controlled er with /er/ Sound

Overview:

- Auditory recognition of R-controlled **er** with /**er**/ sound
- Picture/word match
- Word completion
- Sentence completion
- Read words with R-controlled **er**

Materials and Supplies:

- Teacher's Guide & Student Workbook 1
- White board or chalkboard
- Word cards (as necessary)
- Reader: *Robinson Crusoe & Other Classic Stories*

Teaching Tips:

Review for Mastery. Discuss and review any work from the previous lesson that was assigned as homework. Check for completion of the activities and orally quiz the student for comprehension. Review any reading that was assigned, discussing the characters, setting, plot, theme, language, sequence, etc.

Strengthen fluency and phonemic awareness by reviewing words and sentences from previous lessons. Build vocabulary skills by using some of the words in sentences.

Review the R-controlled vowel **ar** with Lesson 71, Activity 4. Have the student make up sentences that use the detractor words.

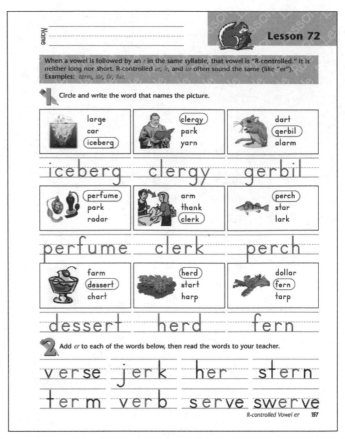

Activity 1. Review the rule for the **er** spelling of the R-controlled /**er**/ vowel sound: "Her first nurse works early!" *Words to teach the concept:* berg, berth, concern, desert, diverse, kern, nervous, perk, perm, servant, vertical. Have the student read the words in each box aloud. Review the pictures to make sure the student can correctly identify them. Instruct the student to select the correct word in the box for the picture and write it on the blank.

Pictures:
  iceberg, clergy, gerbil
  perfume, clerk, perch
  dessert, herd, fern

Activity 2. Review the rule for R-controlled vowel **er**. Have the student complete the words. Read the words.

Words:
  verse, jerk, her, stern
  term, verb, serve, swerve

Activity 3. Help the student read the word choices and the sentences. Instruct the student to underline the word that will correctly complete each sentence and write the word on the line.

Sentences:

1. **The bell will <u>alert</u> us that lunch is over.**
   Note that the **er** in *over* is a schwa.
2. **Bert is a <u>person</u> that we all like.**
   Note the **er** in *Bert*.
3. **I hit a <u>nerve</u> that made my arm jerk.**
   Note the **er** in *jerk* and the **ar** in *arm*.
4. **The <u>clergy</u> will read a proverb at the service.**
   Note the **er** in *proverb* and *service* and the long **e** digraph in *read*.
5. **Please <u>serve</u> her the large dessert.**
   Note the **er** in *dessert* and the **ar** in *large*.

Activity 4. Review the rule for the schwa sound of **er**. This has a similar sound to the /er/ words covered in this lesson. Have the student complete the words. Read the words.

Words:
**under, better, never
offer, river, summer
brisker, letter, sister
winter, liberty, camera**

Reading. Read and discuss the maxim for the Lesson.

Read the story *The Shepherd Boy*. Preview the story and explain words or sentence structures that are not familiar to the student. With every story ask questions: who are the characters, what are they doing, what are they saying, where does the action take place, what is the order of events, what words are being used, what new information is given, what lesson can be learned?

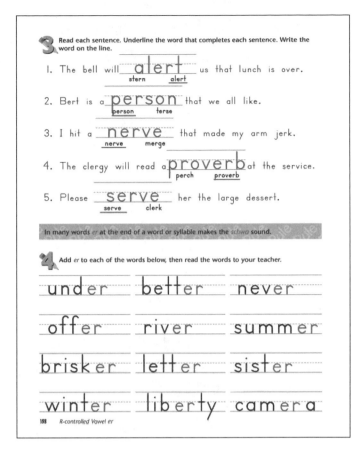

Comprehension questions:
What is unusual about the cows?
What is unusual about the grass?
Who made the bleat of the sheep?
How did the cows move?
Where was the pasture?
What were the sheep?
What vowel digraphs are used in the story?
What R-controlled vowels are used in the story?
What happened to the cows and sheep while the shepherd was sleeping?

Assign. Lesson activities or reading that are to be completed as homework.

Lesson 73: R-controlled ur and er with /er/ Sound

Overview:

- Auditory recognition of R-controlled **ur** and **er** with /**er**/ sound
- Auditory discrimination of R-controlled /**er**/ sound
- Word completion
- Sort words by the spelling of the R-controlled vowel
- Sentence completion
- Read words with R-controlled **ur** and **er** with /**er**/ sound

Materials and Supplies:

- Teacher's Guide & Student Workbook 1
- White board or chalkboard
- Word cards (as necessary)
- Reader: *Robinson Crusoe & Other Classic Stories*

Teaching Tips:

Review for Mastery. Discuss and review any work from the previous lesson that was assigned as homework. Check for completion of the activities and orally quiz the student for comprehension. Review any reading that was assigned, discussing the characters, setting, plot, theme, language, sequence, etc.

Strengthen fluency and phonemic awareness by reviewing words and sentences from previous lessons. Build vocabulary skills by using some of the words in sentences.

Review the R-controlled vowel **er** with Lesson 72, Activity 3. Have the student make up sentences that use the detractor words.

Activity 1. Review the rule for the R-controlled **ur** vowel with the /**er**/ sound. "Her first nurse works early!" *Words to teach the concept:* urn, burn, curl, Thursday, curb, surface, further, spur, burst, furnish, burden, occur, hurt, lurch, purple, spurt, sure, surprise, turn, urge. Have the student complete the words. Read the words.

When a vowel is followed by an *r* in the same syllable, that vowel is "R-controlled." It is neither long nor short. R-controlled *er, ir,* and *ur* often sound the same (like "er").
Examples: *term, sir, fir, fur.*

Add **ur** to each of the words below, then read the words to your teacher.

p u r ple	n ur se	t ur tle
h ur ry	t ur key	church
s ur plus	p ur se	t ur nip

2 Write a word from above to complete the sentences.

1. The lady lost her _____purse_____ at the mall.
2. A _____nurse_____ can help when you are sick.
3. Sunday we have a service at the _____church_____ .
4. A _____turtle_____ was on a log near the pond.
5. We will have _____turkey_____ for dinner.
6. Tie a _____purple_____ ribbon around the gift.
7. The batter must _____hurry_____ to run the bases.
8. There was a _____surplus_____ of cake for the party.
9. She will add a _____turnip_____ to the soup.

R-controlled Vowels er, ir, ur **199**

Words:
purple, nurse, turtle
hurry, turkey, church
surplus, purse, turnip

Activity 2. Help the student read the sentences and review the word choices from Activity 1. Instruct the student to write the correct word on the line to complete the sentence.

Sentences:

1. **The lady lost her** <u>purse</u> **at the mall.**
   Note the **er** in *her*.
2. **A** <u>nurse</u> **can help when you are sick.**
   Note the **ar** in *are*.
3. **Sunday we have a service at the** <u>church</u>.
   Note the **er** in *service*.
4. **A** <u>turtle</u> **was on a log near the pond.**
   Note the **ear** in *near*.
5. **We will have** <u>turkey</u> **for dinner.**
   Note the **er** in *dinner* is a schwa.
6. **Tie a** <u>purple</u> **ribbon around the gift.**
   Note the **ou** diphthong in *around*.
7. **The batter must** <u>hurry</u> **to run the bases.**
   Note the **er** in *batter* is a schwa.
8. **There was a** <u>surplus</u> **of cake for the party.**
   Note the **ar** in *party*.
9. **She will add a** <u>turnip</u> **to the soup.**
   Note the **ou** long **oo** in *soup*.

Horizons Phonics & Reading Grade 2 Teacher's Guide

Activity 3. Help the student read the words. Instruct the student to listen for the R-controlled vowel sound in each word. Have the student write the word under the correct category for the spelling of the vowel sound.

er spelling	ur spelling
swerve	sure
invert	burst
service	slurp
stern	burn
merge	curb

Activity 4. Help the student read the sentences and review the word choices from Activity 3. Instruct the student to write the correct word on the line to complete the sentence.

Sentences:
1. **Are you <u>sure</u> you can do the task?**
   Note the **ar** in *are*.
2. **It is bad manners to <u>slurp</u> when you eat soup.**
   Note the **ou** long **oo** in *soup*.
3. **Curt hit the <u>curb</u> when he parked the car.**
   Note the **ur** in *Curt* and the **ar** in *parked* and *car*.
4. **The balloon <u>burst</u> when it hit the sharp needle.**
   Note the **ar** in *sharp*.
5. **The <u>burn</u> from the sun made his skin hurt.**
   Note the **ur** in *hurt*.
6. **The cars must <u>merge</u> to get on the freeway.**
   Note the **ar** in *cars*.
7. **His mom spoke with a <u>stern</u> voice when the lamp broke.**
   Note the **oi** diphthong and the ending **s** sound in *voice*.
8. **The wind made the car <u>swerve</u> on the road.**
   Note the **ar** in *car*.
9. **<u>Invert</u> the bottle to get the last drop out.**
   Note the **ou** diphthong in *out*.
10. **The host gave us good <u>service</u> for the meal.**

Reading. Read and discuss the maxim for the Lesson.

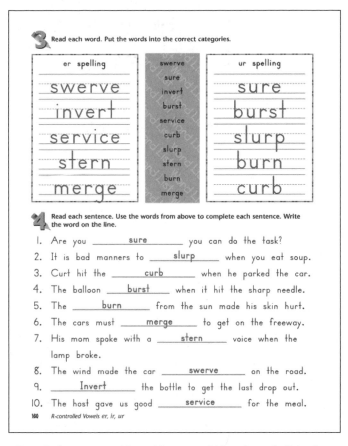

Read the story *How Margery Wondered*. Preview the story and explain words or sentence structures that are not familiar to the student.
Comprehension questions:
  What is the time of year?
  Where is Margery walking?
  What was the weather like?
  What questions is Margery asking?
  What did Margery hear?
  What vowel digraphs are used in the story?
  What are the bird and the sea saying to each other?

Read the poem *The Caterpillar*. Preview the poem and explain words or sentence structures that are not familiar to the student.
Comprehension questions:
  Who are the caterpillar's enemies?
  Where is the caterpillar going?
  What R-controlled vowels are used in the poem?
  What happens to the caterpillar?

Assign. Lesson activities or reading that are to be completed as homework.

Lesson 74: R-controlled ir with /er/ Sound

Overview:

- Auditory recognition of R-controlled **ir** with /**er**/ sound
- Word completion
- Sentence completion
- Form compound words with R-controlled **ar** vowels
- Read words with R-controlled **ar** and **ir** with /**ar**/ and /**er**/ sounds

Materials and Supplies:

- Teacher's Guide & Student Workbook 1
- White board or chalkboard
- Word cards (as necessary)
- Reader: *Robinson Crusoe & Other Classic Stories*

Teaching Tips:

Review for Mastery. Discuss and review any work from the previous lesson that was assigned as homework. Check for completion of the activities and orally quiz the student for comprehension. Review any reading that was assigned, discussing the characters, setting, plot, theme, language, sequence, etc.

Strengthen fluency and phonemic awareness by reviewing words and sentences from previous lessons. Build vocabulary skills by using some of the words in sentences.

Review the **er** and **ur** spellings of the /**er**/ sound with Lessons 72 & 73. Ask the student for words that use the different spellings.

Activity 1. Review the rule for R-controlled **ir** with the /**er**/ vowel sound: "Her first nurse works early!" *Words to teach the concept:* first, third, shirt, dirt, skirt, birthday, thirsty, circle, birth, confirm, birthplace, circus, stirrup, thirst. Have the student complete the words. Read the words.

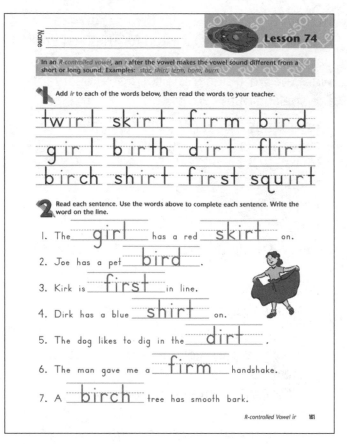

Activity 1 continued:

Words:

  twirl, skirt, firm, bird
  girl, birth, dirt, flirt
  birch, shirt, first, squirt

Activity 2. Help the student read the sentences and review the word choices from Activity 1. Instruct the student to write the correct word on the line to complete the sentence.

Sentences:

1. The <u>girl</u> has a red <u>skirt</u> on.
2. Joe has a pet <u>bird</u>.
3. Kirk is <u>first</u> in line.
   Note the **ir** in *Kirk*.
4. Dirk has a blue <u>shirt</u> on.
   Note the **ir** in *Dirk*.
5. The dog likes to dig in the <u>dirt</u>.
6. The man gave me a <u>firm</u> handshake.
7. A <u>birch</u> tree has smooth bark.
   Note the **ar** in *bark*.

196

Horizons Phonics & Reading Grade 2 Teacher's Guide

Activity 3. Have the student read all the words in the box aloud. Read the riddles. Help the students with any word meanings they don't understand. The student is to find a word in the box that fits the riddle.

Words:
1. first
2. girl
3. dirt
4. shirt
5. third
6. thirteen
7. thirty
8. sir
9. stir
10. chirp

Activity 4. Review the rule for compound words. Have the student read the words in each word list. The student will match a word from the first list to one in the second to form a compound word. Read the compound words that are formed.

Words:
yardbird
birthmark
birdfarm
firstborn

Reading. Read and discuss the maxim for the Lesson.

Read the story *How Margery Wondered (continued).* Preview the story and explain words or sentence structures that are not familiar to the student. With every story ask questions: who are the characters, what are they doing, what are they saying, where does the action take place, what is the order of events, what words are being used, what new information is given, what lesson can be learned?

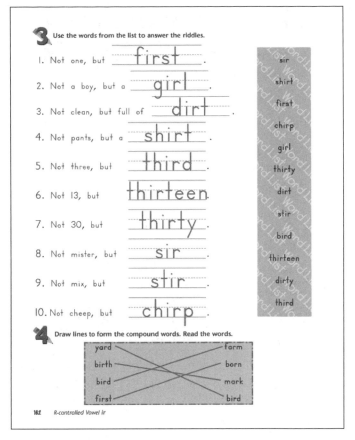

Comprehension questions:
What is Margery looking at?
What questions is Margery asking about the flowers?
Who called for Margery to come home?
What questions does Margery ask her mother?
Where does Margery continue to sit and wonder?
What R-controlled vowels are used in the story?
How does Margery end her day?

Assign. Lesson activities or reading that are to be completed as homework.

Lesson 75: R-controlled wor, ear, yr, and our with /er/ Sound

Overview:

- Auditory recognition of R-controlled **ear**, **wor**, **our**, and **yr** with **/er/** sound
- Picture/word match
- Form compound words with R-controlled **wor** words
- Read words with R-controlled **ear**, **wor**, **our**, and **yr** with **/er/** sound

Materials and Supplies:

- Teacher's Guide & Student Workbook 1
- White board or chalkboard
- Word cards (as necessary)
- Reader: *Robinson Crusoe & Other Classic Stories*

Teaching Tips:

Review for Mastery. Discuss and review any work from the previous lesson that was assigned as homework. Check for completion of the activities and orally quiz the student for comprehension. Review any reading that was assigned, discussing the characters, setting, plot, theme, language, sequence, etc.

Strengthen fluency and phonemic awareness by reviewing words and sentences from previous lessons. Build vocabulary skills by using some of the words in sentences.

Review the **er**, **ur**, and **ir** spellings of the **/er/** sound with Lessons 72-74. Ask the student for words that use the different spellings to list on the board.

Review the rule. Begin the lesson by introducing the letter **r** as a bully! Explain that any vowel in front of the letter **r** loses its sound. The vowel and the letter **r** make a single sound. The vowel and letter **r** combine to make what is known as an R-controlled vowel. Explain that there are five vowels, but there are only three different R-controlled vowels.

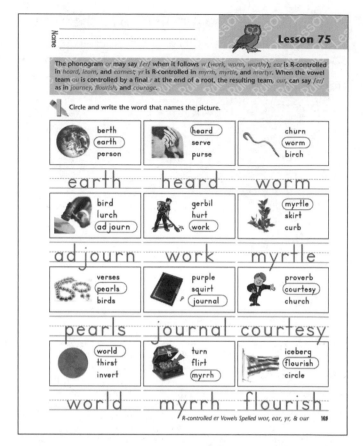

The three different sounds are the **/ar/** sound, the **/or/** sound, and the **/er/** sound (or **/ur/** in some dictionaries).

This lesson covers other ways the R-controlled **/er/** sound is spelled in some words: "Her first nurse works early!"

Activity 1. Review the rules and the example words. *Words to teach the concept:* worthy, beadwork, crossword, housework, workshop, worldwide, early, earnest, learn, search, martyr, journey, courage, encourage. Have the student read the words in each box aloud. Review the pictures to make sure the student can correctly identify them. Instruct the student to select and circle the correct word in the box for the picture and write it on the blank.

Pictures:

earth, heard, worm
adjourn, work, myrtle
pearls, journal, courtesy
world, myrrh, flourish

Horizons Phonics & Reading Grade 2 Teacher's Guide

Activity 2. Review the rule for compound words. Have the student read the words in each word list. The student will write the compound words formed from the base words in each list. Read the compound words that are formed.

Words:

<u>work</u>	<u>work</u>
artwork	workbag
earthwork	workbench
farmwork	workbook
roadwork	workday
steelwork	workhorse
yardwork	workman
<u>worm</u>	<u>worm</u>
bookworm	wormhole
earthworm	wormwood
inchworm	wormlike
roundworm	wormroot
tapeworm	wormseed
silkworm	

Reading. Read and discuss the maxim for the Lesson.

Read the poem *Evening Hymn*. Preview the poem and explain words or sentence structures that are not familiar to the student. With every story ask questions: who are the characters, what are they doing, what are they saying, where does the action take place, what is the order of events, what words are being used, what new information is given, what lesson can be learned?

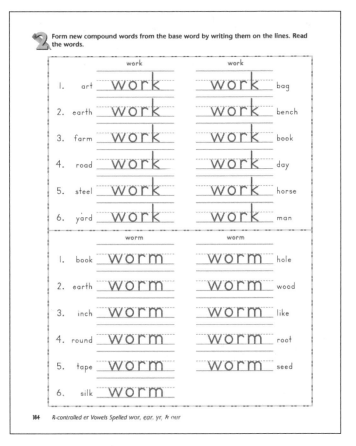

Comprehension questions:
 What is the time of day?
 What has ended?
 What is there to look forward to?
 What are the rhyming words used in the poem?
 What is not in the world beyond the grave?
 What R-controlled vowels are used in the poem?
 What does the word Sabbath mean?

Assign. Lesson activities or reading that are to be completed as homework.

Lesson 76: R-controlled eer, ere, ear, ier, and eir with /ir/ Sound

Overview:

- Auditory recognition of R-controlled **eer**, **ere**, **ear**, and **ier** with **/ir/** sound
- Picture/word match
- Form compound words with R-controlled **eer** and **ear**
- Read words with R-controlled **eer**, **ere**, **ear**, and **ier** with **/ir/** sound
- Riddle completion

Materials and Supplies:

- Teacher's Guide & Student Workbook 1
- White board or chalkboard
- Word cards (as necessary)
- Reader: *Robinson Crusoe & Other Classic Stories*

Teaching Tips:

Review for Mastery. Discuss and review any work from the previous lesson that was assigned as homework. Check for completion of the activities and orally quiz the student for comprehension. Review any reading that was assigned, discussing the characters, setting, plot, theme, language, sequence, etc.

Strengthen fluency and phonemic awareness by reviewing words and sentences from previous lessons. Build vocabulary skills by using some of the words in sentences.

Review R-controlled vowels with Lesson 75, Activity 1. Have the student circle the **ear**, **wor**, **our**, **myr**, or **our** that forms the R-controlled vowel in the words for the pictures. The R-controlled vowels in the detractor words can also be reviewed by drawing a square around them.

Activity 1. Review the rule for the R-controlled /er/ sound: "Her first nurse works early!" Review the rule for Lesson 76 and the examples. Compare the sounds in heard–hear, bird–beard, dirt–deer,

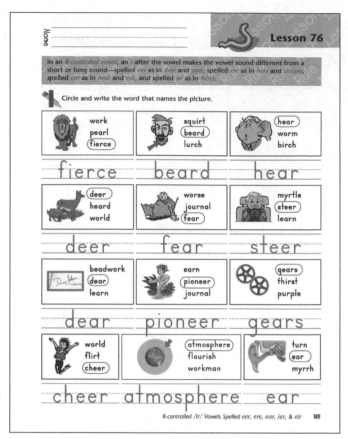

hurt–here to illustrate the contrast between the **/er/** and **/ir/** sound. *Words to teach the concept:* beer, domineer, engineer, leer, peer, queer, rocketeer, sheer, interfere, mere, bleary, clear, dearly, drear, rear, yearly, chocolatier, fiercely, tier. Have the student read the words in each box aloud. Review the pictures to make sure the student can correctly identify them. Instruct the student to select and circle the correct word in the box for the picture and write it on the blank.

Pictures:
   fierce, beard, hear
   deer, fear, steer
   dear, pioneer, gears
   cheer, atmosphere, ear

Activity 2. Have the student read the words aloud. Discuss the pictures and make sure the student can identify them. The student will draw a line to match the picture to the word.

Pictures:
veer	**jeer**
tear	**sear**
	year

Horizons Phonics & Reading Grade 2 Teacher's Guide

Activity 3. Help the student read the questions. Instruct the student to circle **yes** or **no** to correctly answer the question.

Answers:

1. **yes**
2. **yes**
3. **yes**
4. **no**
5. **no**
6. **yes**
7. **no**

Activity 4. Help the student read the riddles. Instruct the student to look at the words in the riddle for clues to the correct answer. Write the answer on the line. Read the completed riddles.

Answers:

1. **earwax**
2. **headgear**
3. **eyedrop**
4. **veer**
5. **year**
6. **earache**
7. **deerskin**

Reading. Read and discuss the maxim for the Lesson.

Read the poem *The Child's World*. Preview the poem and explain words or sentence structures that are not familiar to the student. With every story ask questions: who are the characters, what are they doing, what are they saying, where does the action take place, what is the order of events, what words are being used, what new information is given, what lesson can be learned?

Comprehension questions:

What is the child talking about?
What things does the child see?
How does the child compare himself to the word?
What are the rhyming words used in the poem?

What are the R-controlled vowels used in the poem?
What does the child seem to hear?
What difference does the child recognize between himself and the earth?

Read the story *Sheep Shearing*. Preview the story and explain words or sentence structures that are not familiar to the student.

Comprehension questions:

What is the time of the year?
Who has a fun time during this time of the year?
Why does the wool need to be taken off from the sheep?
What is the wool used for?
What R-controlled vowels are used in the story?
How are the sheep ready for winter?

Assign. Lesson activities or reading that are to be completed as homework.

Lesson 77: R-controlled air, ear, ar, are, eir, and ere with /air/ Sound

Overview:

- Auditory recognition of R-controlled **ar**, **are**, **air**, **eir**, **ear**, and **ere** with /**air**/ sound
- Picture/word match
- Write sentences with R-controlled **ar**, **are**, **air**, **eir**, **ear**, and **ere** words
- Read words with R-controlled **ar**, **are**, **air**, **eir**, **ear**, and **ere** with /**air**/ sound
- Auditory discrimination of R-controlled **ar**, **are**, **air**, **eir**, **ear**, and **ere** with /**air**/ sound
- Riddle completion

Materials and Supplies:

- Teacher's Guide & Student Workbook 1
- White board or chalkboard
- Word cards (as necessary)
- Reader: *Robinson Crusoe & Other Classic Stories*

Teaching Tips:

Review for Mastery. Discuss and review any work from the previous lesson that was assigned as homework. Check for completion of the activities and orally quiz the student for comprehension. Review any reading that was assigned, discussing the characters, setting, plot, theme, language, sequence, etc.

Strengthen fluency and phonemic awareness by reviewing words and sentences from previous lessons. Build vocabulary skills by using some of the words in sentences.

Review R-controlled vowels with Lesson 76, Activity 1. Have the student circle the **ier**, **ear**, **eer**, or **ere** that forms the R-controlled vowel in the words for the pictures. The R-controlled vowels in the detractor words can also be reviewed by drawing a square around them.

Activity 1. Review the rule and the examples. Compare the /**ar**/ sound to the /**air**/ sound with the words bar–bare, mar–Mary, star–stair, are–their, tar–tear (to rip), jar–where. *Words to teach the concept:* daring, January, February, dictionary, scarcely, aware, beware, declare, affair, airline, unfair, heiress, bear, pear, there, where. Have the student read the words in each box aloud. Review the pictures to make sure the student can correctly identify them. Instruct the student to select and circle the correct word in the box for the picture and write it on the blank.

Pictures:
  bear, where, flare
  heir, parent, chair
  mare, there, canary
  pair, pear, bareback

Activity 2. Have the student read the riddles. Instruct the student to circle the words with the **air** R-controlled sound. There are two words in each riddle.

Words:
1. pair, pears
2. Where, chair
3. There, hare
4. Repair, tear
5. heir, heirloom
6. Stare, bear
7. Dare, airboat
8. Wear, care
9. Beware, bear
10. Share, glassware
11. Glare, rare
12. their, hair
13. Careful, flare
14. Farewell, airline
15. Aware, affair
16. Parents, heir
17. area, airstrike
18. dairy, mare
19. Mary, swear

Activity 3. Have the student write two sentences using two or three of the words in Activity 2. Help with ideas as needed, and remind the student about correct punctuation and capitalization.

Reading. Read and discuss the maxim for the Lesson.

Read the poem *If Stars Dropped Out of Heaven*. Preview the poem and explain words or sentence structures that are not familiar to the student. With every story ask questions: who are the characters, what are they doing, what are they saying, where does the action take place, what is the order of events, what words are being used, what new information is given, what lesson can be learned?

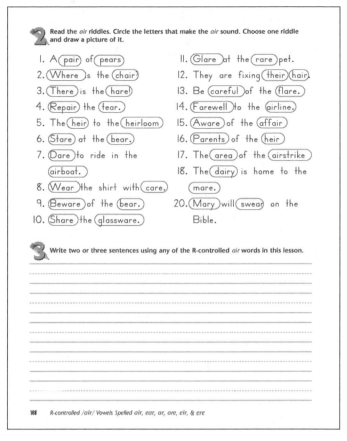

Comprehension questions:
What places is the poem talking about?
What things are trading places in the poem?
What are the rhyming words used in the poem?
What R-controlled vowels are used in the poem?
What would the child long for if the flowers were no longer on the earth?

Read the story *Sam and Harry*. Preview the story and explain words or sentence structures that are not familiar to the student.

Comprehension questions:
What had Sam bought with his money?
Where is Sam going?
Who does Sam meet?
What did Harry do with the money?
How did Sam help the blind man?
What R-controlled vowels are used in the story?
Who was the better boy?

Assign. Lesson activities or reading that are to be completed as homework.

Lesson 78: R-controlled or with /or/ Sound

Overview:

- Auditory recognition of R-controlled **or** with /**or**/ sound
- Picture/word match
- Sentence completion with R-controlled **or**
- Read words with R-controlled **or** with /**or**/ sound
- Riddle completion

Materials and Supplies:

- Teacher's Guide & Student Workbook 1
- White board or chalkboard
- Word cards (as necessary)
- Reader: *Robinson Crusoe & Other Classic Stories*

Teaching Tips:

Review for Mastery. Discuss and review any work from the previous lesson that was assigned as homework. Check for completion of the activities and orally quiz the student for comprehension. Review any reading that was assigned, discussing the characters, setting, plot, theme, language, sequence, etc.

Strengthen fluency and phonemic awareness by reviewing words and sentences from previous lessons. Build vocabulary skills by using some of the words in sentences.

Review R-controlled vowels with Lesson 77, Activity 1. Have the student circle the **ar**, **are**, **air**, **eir**, **ear**, or **ere** that forms the R-controlled vowel in the words for the pictures. The R-controlled vowels in the detractor words can also be reviewed by drawing a square around them.

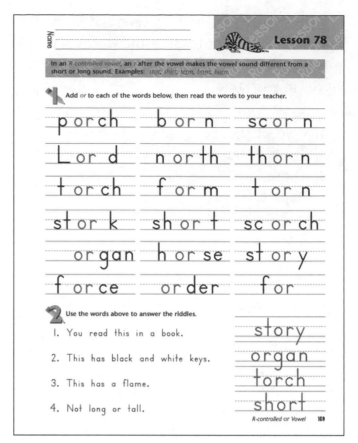

Activity 1. Review the rule for the R-controlled **or** vowel sound: "Her first nurse works early!" *Words to teach the concept:* or, Oregon, oral, absorb, distort, escort, for, format, lord, morn, orphan, port, sort, sport, storm worn. Have the student complete the words. Read the words.

Words:

porch, born, scorn
Lord, north, thorn
torch, form, torn
stork, short, scorch
organ, horse, story
force, order, for

Activity 2. Help the student read the riddles. Instruct the student to select the word from Activity 1 that will correctly answer each riddle and write the word on the line.

Answers:
1. story
2. organ
3. torch
4. short

Horizons Phonics & Reading Grade 2 Teacher's Guide

Activity 3. Review the pictures to make sure the student can correctly identify them. Have the student read the words under each picture aloud. Instruct the student to circle the correct word for the picture.

Pictures:

orbit, horn, fork, thorn, north

acorn, organ, orchid, corner, hornet

Activity 4. Help the student read the sentences and review the word choices from Activity 3. Instruct the student to write the correct word on the line to complete the sentence.

Sentences:

1. **Tie the bundle with a strong <u>cord</u>.**
2. **From the garden we had ears of yellow <u>corn</u>.**
   Note the **ar** in *garden* and the **ear** in *ears*.
3. **We went to ride the <u>horse</u> at the farm.**
   Note the **ar** in *farm*.
4. **We can sit on the front <u>porch</u> of the house.**
5. **We went to a <u>resort</u> at the lake.**
6. **After dark we will park the car in the <u>carport</u>.**
   Note the **ar** in *dark*, *park*, and *car*.
7. **On what day were you <u>born</u>?**
   Note the **ere** in *were*.
8. **Go <u>forth</u> into the center of the room.**

Reading. Read and discuss the maxim for the Lesson.

Read the poem *Hush, Little Baby*. Preview the poem and explain words or sentence structures that are not familiar to the student. With every story ask questions: who are the characters, what are they doing, what are they saying, where does the action take place, what is the order of events, what words are being used, what new information is given, what lesson can be learned?

Comprehension questions:

Who are the characters in the poem?

What is taking place in the poem?

What are the rhyming words used in the poem?

What R-controlled vowels are used in the poem?

Read the poem *There Was a Little Girl*. Preview the poem and explain words or sentence structures that are not familiar to the student.

Comprehension questions:

Who is the character in the poem?

What is taking place in the poem?

What are the rhyming words used in the poem?

What R-controlled vowels are used in the poem?

Read the story *The Torn Doll*. Preview the story and explain words or sentence structures that are not familiar to the student.

What bad habit does Mary have?

What happened because Mary was not careful with her doll?

Who fixed the doll?

Who is Dash?

What R-controlled vowels are used in the story?

What lesson did Mary learn?

Assign. Lesson activities or reading that are to be completed as homework.

Lesson 79: R-controlled wore, war, ore, oar, oor, and our with /or/ Sound

Overview:

- Auditory recognition of R-controlled **wor**, **war**, **ore**, **oar**, **our**, and **oor** with /or/ sound
- Picture/word match
- Form compound words with R-controlled **wor**, **war**, **ore**, **oar**, **our**, and **oor**
- Read words with R-controlled /or/ sound

Materials and Supplies:

- Teacher's Guide & Student Workbook 1
- White board or chalkboard
- Word cards (as necessary)
- Reader: *Robinson Crusoe & Other Classic Stories*

Teaching Tips:

Review for Mastery. Discuss and review any work from the previous lesson that was assigned as homework. Check for completion of the activities and orally quiz the student for comprehension. Review any reading that was assigned, discussing the characters, setting, plot, theme, language, sequence, etc.

Strengthen fluency and phonemic awareness by reviewing words and sentences from previous lessons. Build vocabulary skills by using some of the words in sentences.

Review R-controlled or words with the detractors from Lesson 78, Activity 3. Make up sentences for the words or draw illustrations to picture the word.

Activity 1. Review the rule for the R-controlled **or** with the /or/ sound. "Pour out your soup" is a phrase that illustrates the **r**-control of the **ou** sound. *Words to teach the concept:* worn, sworn, warn, war, warden, warp, adore, ashore, before, onshore, outscore, forecast, foresee, boar, board, keyboard, backcourt, fourplex, fourth, doorbell, subfloor. Have the student read the words in each box aloud. Review the pictures to make sure the student can correctly identify them. Instruct the student to select and circle the correct word in the box for the picture and write it on the blank.

Pictures:
   door, oar, sworn
   court, snore, warn
   pour, floor, worn
   chore, soar, swarm

Activity 2. Help the student read the words in each box as necessary. The student will write a compound word from the words on the line. Read the compound words that are formed.

Words:
warhorse
seashore
forewarn
doorpost
forecourt
hardboard
courtyard
trapdoor
fourscore
floorboard
foresworn
storyboard

Reading. Read and discuss the maxim for the Lesson.

Read the story *The Four Children*. Preview the story and explain words or sentence structures that are not familiar to the student. With every story ask questions: who are the characters, what are they doing, what are they saying, where does the action take place, what is the order of events, what words are being used, what new information is given, what lesson can be learned?

Comprehension questions:
Who are the characters in the story?
What is taking place in the story?
What are the children watching?
What can the children do to the moon that they can't to the sun?
What R-controlled vowels are used in the story?

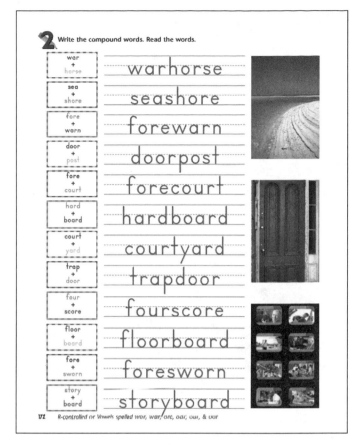

Read the story *Little Robin Redbreast*. Preview the story and explain words or sentence structures that are not familiar to the student.

Comprehension questions:
Who is in the garden?
What are some things that the robin is doing?
Who would like to catch the robin?
What would happen to the robin if the cat were to catch him?
What R-controlled vowels are used in the story?

Assign. Lesson activities or reading that are to be completed as homework.

Lesson 80: Review R-controlled Vowels

Overview:

- Auditory recognition of the R-controlled vowel sound
- Sort words with the R-controlled vowel sound
- Complete R-controlled words
- Solve a puzzle with words that have R-controlled vowels
- Read words with R-controlled vowels

Materials and Supplies:

- Teacher's Guide & Student Workbook 1
- White board or chalkboard
- Word cards (as necessary)
- Reader: *Robinson Crusoe & Other Classic Stories*

Teaching Tips:

Review for Mastery. Discuss and review any work from the previous lesson that was assigned as homework. Check for completion of the activities and orally quiz the student for comprehension. Review any reading that was assigned, discussing the characters, setting, plot, theme, language, sequence, etc.

Strengthen fluency and phonemic awareness by reviewing words and sentences from previous lessons. Build vocabulary skills by using some of the words in sentences.

Review R-controlled or words with the detractors from Lesson 79, Activity 1. Circle the **wor**, **war**, **oer**, **our**, or **oor** that spells the /or/ sound in each word. Make up sentences for the words or draw illustrations to picture the word.

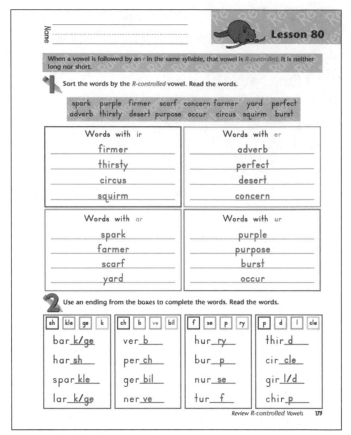

Activity 1. Help the student read the words. Instruct the student to listen for the R-controlled vowel sound in each word. Have the student write the word under the correct category for the vowel sound.

words with ir	words with er
firmer	adverb
thirsty	perfect
circus	desert
squirm	concern

words with ar	words with ur
spark	purple
farmer	purpose
scarf	burst
yard	occur

Activity 2. Review the sounds of the word endings in the boxes. Have the student add an ending to complete the words by writing the letter(s) on the blank. Read the completed words.

Words: **bark(barge), verb, hurry, third harsh, perch, burp, circle sparkle, gerbil, nurse, girl(gird) large(lark), nerve, turf, chirp**

Activity 3. Help the student read the words in puzzle. The student will draw a line to connect all of the R-controlled words to find the way through the puzzle. Read the R-controlled words that have been found.

Words:

start, pork, turn, perk, fort, burn, skirt, card, first, cork, serve, third, glory, smart, servant, sure, plural, were, girl, farm

Review for Test. The instructor should plan to use some time at the end of the class to review and prepare for the test that follows this lesson. Review the objectives for the test and then look over the lessons that it will cover. If the student has struggled with any of the concepts that will be included in the test, some additional drill, practice, or review may be needed to adequately prepare him for the test.

Reading. Read and discuss the maxim for the Lesson.

Read the story *Planting Corn*. Preview the story and explain words or sentence structures that are not familiar to the student. With every story ask questions: who are the characters, what are they doing, what are they saying, where does the action take place, what is the order of events, what words are being used, what new information is given, what lesson can be learned?

Comprehension questions:
Who are the characters in the story?
What is taking place in the story?
What has Henry been doing all day?
What does Henry want to do?
What does Henry expect from his father?
Why can't Henry help his father plant the corn?
What R-controlled vowels are used in the story?

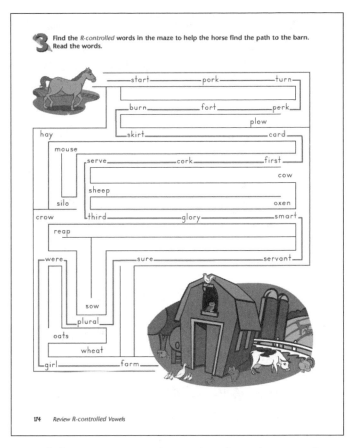

174   *Review R-controlled Vowels*

Read the story *Poor Davy*. Preview the story and explain words or sentence structures that are not familiar to the student.

Comprehension questions:
What time is it in the story?
Why was Davy the last to go out for recess?
How did Davy feel?
What route was Davy taking to get home?
Who spoke to Davy in the woods?
How did the teacher volunteer to help Davy?
What made Davy feel better?
What R-controlled vowels are used in the story?

Assign. Lesson activities or reading that are to be completed as homework.

Extension Activity. View a movie of Robinson Crusoe or another adventure such as Swiss Family Robinson.

Test 8
Lessons 65-74

Overview:

- Auditory recognition of the **sk** sound of **sch**
- Match words to pictures
- Auditory recognition of the **kr** sound of **chr**
- Auditory recognition of the **ou** & **ow** diphthong sound
- Code words with **ou**, **oi**, **oy**, **ew**, & **ow** diphthongs
- Auditory recognition of R-controlled **ar** with /**ar**/ sound
- Auditory recognition of R-controlled **ur**, **er**, and **ir** with /**er**/ sound

Materials and Supplies:

- Teacher's Guide & Student Workbook 1

Instructions:

Assessment Start-up. Read through the test with the student. Help the student with any words that he is still unsure of. The teacher should be available to answer any questions that the student may have during the test.

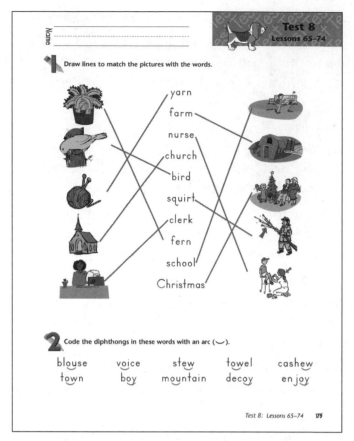

Activity 1. Make sure the student can correctly identify the pictures and read the words. Instruct the student to match the picture to the word.

Pictures:

fern	**school**
bird	**farm**
yarn	**Christmas**
church	**squirt**
clerk	**nurse**

Activity 2. Have the student read the words aloud. The student will draw an arc under the diphthong that they find in each word.

Words:

blo**ou**se, v**oi**ce, st**ew**, t**ow**el, cash**ew**
t**ow**n, b**oy**, m**ou**ntain, dec**oy**, enj**oy**

Activity 3. Review the words in the list with the student. The student will match the words with the same R-controlled vowels.

Words:

> **garden, sparkle**
> **gerbil, clergy**
> **thirteen, dirty**
> **hurry, turtle**

Activity 4. Review the instruction with the student. Review the R-controlled vowels that can be used to complete the words. Instruct the student to complete the words. Some of the unfinished words can be used several times. The student may need a sheet of scratch paper for this activity. Read the completed words.

Words:

<u>words with ar</u>	<u>words with er</u>
star	herd
farm	person
dart	perk
hard	
parson	<u>words with ir</u>
barn	stir
park	firm
harry	dirt
carb	
	<u>words with ur</u>
	burn
	hurry

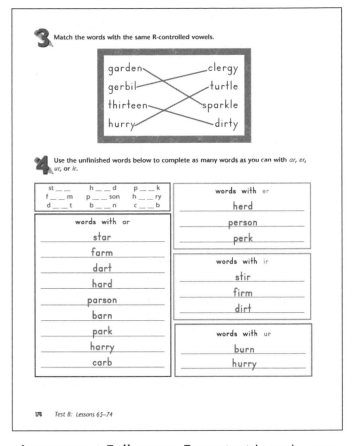

Assessment Follow-up. Every test is an important assessment of both the student's comprehension of the concepts and the instructional process. This makes follow-up after each test essential to the learning process. Review all of the errors made on the test with the student. Check for understanding of the concepts and of the problem instructions. Compare the errors made on the test to the test objectives to identify specific areas of weakness. If weak areas of understanding are detected it might be necessary to go back to those lessons to devise some enrichment activities for the concept.

The test results can be used to determine what concepts are reviewed during the daily time of classroom instruction. Devise enrichment activities that will provide development in those areas.

If time permits, choose a selection and have the student read it again. This can also be used as a catch-up time to complete unfinished selections.

Lesson 81: Medial Double Consonants

Overview:

- Identify medial double consonants in words
- Divide words with medial double consonant into syllables
- Read words with medial double consonants
- Complete words with medial double consonant

Materials and Supplies:

- Teacher's Guide & Student Workbook 2
- White board or chalkboard
- Word cards (as necessary)
- Dictionary
- Reader: *A Little Princess & Other Classic Stories*

Teaching Tips:

Review for Mastery. Discuss and review any work from the previous lesson that was assigned as homework. Check for completion of the activities and orally quiz the student for comprehension. Review any reading that was assigned, discussing the characters, setting, plot, theme, language, sequence, etc.

Strengthen fluency and phonemic awareness by reviewing words and sentences from previous lessons. Build vocabulary skills by using some of the words in sentences.

Review R-controlled vowels with words from Lessons 71-80. Random words can be selected from the lessons for word sorts by either sound or spelling. The words can also be used in sentences.

Activity 1. Review the rule for consonant letters that double in two-syllable words. Have the student write examples of the rule on the chalkboard or white board. Mark the vowels in the words and the consonants between them. Review final stable syllables and how to code the final syllable with a bracket. *Words to teach the concept:* abbey, blubber, crabby, broccoli, yucca, addition, bladder, Buddha, buffalo, caffeine, difference, effective, offense, baggy, buggy, trigger, allergy, balloon, ballot, Billy, collect, jelly, pillow, drummer, glimmer, announce, bunny, cinnamon, dinner, appeal, applause, support, array, barrel berry, cherry, hurry, stirrup, assume, bassoon, essay, passage, batter, bottle, flutter, letter, little, fizzle, muzzle, nozzle. Have the student mark the vowels in the words. A few words have final stable syllables, which should be coded with a bracket. Then have the student divide each word into syllables by drawing a slash between the double consonants. Have the student read the words aloud. This is a lengthy activity and can be worked by columns with the incomplete work assigned as homework.

Activity 1 continued:

Words:

cab/bage, rab/bi, rub/ber, Bob/by, blab/ber
oc/cur, ac/count, ac/cord, hic/cup, rac/coon
ad/dress, dad/dy, shud/der, mud/dy, lad/der
cof/fee, dif/fer, af/ford, of/fice, of/fer
big/ger, fog/gy, sug/gest, Peg/gy, jug/gler
al/low, hel/lo, val/ley, fol/low, Sal/ly
com/mon, ham/mer, Jim/my, sum/mer, bum/mer
ban/ner, Don/ny, con/nect, pen/ny, an/noy
dip/per, sup/per, flop/py, sup/pose, ap/point
ar/rive, cur/rent, car/ry, sor/row, sur/round
as/sign, scis/sor, is/sue, blos/som, mes/sy
bet/ter, rat[tle, Bet/ty, but/ton, at/tend
sav/vy, div/vy, fliv/ver, skiv/vies, chiv/vy
driz[zle, diz/zy, puz[zle, buz/zard, bliz/zard

Activity 2. Have the student write the missing double consonants for each word. Read the words that are formed.

Words:

**attain, ballad, arrow
bottom, pollute, borrow
attract, wallet, error
oppose, mission, connect
supply, message, manner
approach, classic, skinny**

Reading. Read and discuss the maxim for the Lesson.

Read the poem *The Wolf and the Goslings*. Preview the poem and explain words or sentence structures that are not familiar to the student. With every story ask questions: who are the characters, what are they doing, what are they saying, where does the action take place, what is the order of events, what words are being used, what new information is given, what lesson can be learned?

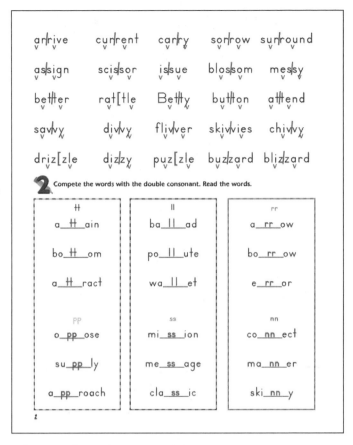

Comprehension questions:

Who are the characters in the poem?
What is taking place in the poem?
Who warned the goose about the wolf?
What warning did the goose give to her goslings?
What did the goslings promise to do?
What happened when the wolf first came to the door?
What did the wolf do to change his voice?
What happened the second time the wolf came to the door?

Assign. Lesson activities or reading that are to be completed as homework.

Lesson 82: Consonant Digraphs kn, wr, wh, ng, tch

Overview:

- Recognize consonant digraphs **kn**, **wr**, **wh**, **ng**, and **tch**
- Apply the rules to pronounce consonant digraphs **kn**, **wr**, **wh**, **ng**, and **tch**
- Auditory discrimination of words with silent letters
- Identify the silent letter in consonant digraphs **kn** and **wr**
- Identify consonant digraphs **kn**, **wr**, **wh**, **ng**, and **tch**
- Word/picture match

Materials and Supplies:

- Teacher's Guide & Student Workbook 2
- White board or chalkboard
- Word cards (as necessary)
- Dictionary
- Reader: *A Little Princess & Other Classic Stories*

Teaching Tips:

Review for Mastery. Discuss and review any work from the previous lesson that was assigned as homework. Check for completion of the activities and orally quiz the student for comprehension. Review any reading that was assigned, discussing the characters, setting, plot, theme, language, sequence, etc.

Strengthen fluency and phonemic awareness by reviewing words and sentences from previous lessons. Build vocabulary skills by using some of the words in sentences.

Review R-controlled vowels with words from Lessons 71-80. Random words can be selected from the lessons for word scrambles or spelling bees. The words can also be used in sentences.

Review medial double consonants with Lesson 81, Activities 1 & 2. Read through the words. Select random words to use in sentences.

Activity 1. Review the rules. Have the student write examples of the rule on the chalkboard or white board. *Words to teach the concept:* knit, knock, kneel, knowledge, knuckle, written, wring, wrapper, wreckage, rewrite, unwrap. Have the student read the words in each box aloud. Review the pictures to make sure the student can correctly identify them. The student will write the word for the picture on the line.

Pictures:

   knee, wrist, knuckle
   wren, knight, wreath
   knapsack, penknife, wrap
   knickknack, typewriter

An optional activity would be to have the student draw a slash through the silent letter of the consonant digraph found in each of the words.

Activity 2. Review the rules. Have the student write examples of the rule on the chalkboard or white board. *Words to teach the concept:* while, wheat, whisper, wheeze, whimper, somewhat, cartwheel, thing, king, fling, hung, string, wrong, ditch, hatch, itch, latch, snatch, pitcher, watchman. A problem sound is the **wh** consonant team, which when properly enunciated says /**hw**/. This is sometimes called the hard sound of **wh**, or the stressed **wh**. In modern English many times we pronounce this team the same as a single **w**. It is hard for a child to hear the difference between *which* and *witch* when they are both pronounced as "**w**-short **i-ch**." When pronounced properly, the difference is clear, and the children's spelling will reflect that difference. Assist the student as needed in reading the words in the activity. Have the student read the sentences aloud. The student will underline the **wh**, **ng**, and **tch** digraphs.

Sentences:

1. <u>Wh</u>en will the songbirds ha<u>tch</u>?
2. <u>Wh</u>y is the pa<u>tch</u> so lo<u>ng</u>?
3. <u>Wh</u>at can we hi<u>tch</u> to the spri<u>ng</u>?
4. <u>Wh</u>ich of the si<u>ng</u>ers can stay on pi<u>tch</u>?
5. <u>Wh</u>ere is the ske<u>tch</u> of the ki<u>ng</u>?
6. Some<u>wh</u>ere the ri<u>ng</u> has a scra<u>tch</u>.
7. The you<u>ng</u> bu<u>tch</u>er was no<u>wh</u>ere to be found.
8. Wa<u>tch</u> the rope on the swi<u>ng</u> while it le<u>ng</u>thens.
9. Bri<u>ng</u> a <u>wh</u>istle to the soccer ma<u>tch</u>.
10. There was a blo<u>tch</u> on the wi<u>ng</u> of the bob<u>wh</u>ite.
11. The men will stre<u>tch</u> the ga<u>ng</u>plank from the ship to the <u>wh</u>arf.
12. Bu<u>tch</u> will ha<u>ng</u> the <u>wh</u>ip near the light swi<u>tch</u>.
13. It will be hard to ca<u>tch</u> the stro<u>ng</u> <u>wh</u>ale.
14. It would be wro<u>ng</u> to <u>wh</u>ack the man with a cru<u>tch</u>.
15. The wa<u>tch</u>man followed the ga<u>ng</u> every<u>wh</u>ere they went.

Reading. Read and discuss the maxim for the Lesson.

Read the poem *The Wolf and the Goslings (continued)*. Preview the poem and explain words or sentence structures that are not familiar to the student. With every story ask questions: who are the characters, what are they doing, what are they saying, where does the action take place, what is the order of events,

---

In consonant digraph *wh*, the *wh* makes the *hw* sound as in *what* and *when*.
In consonant digraph *ng*, the *ng* makes a blend of the *ng* sound as in *sing* and *rung*.
In consonant digraph *tch*, the *tch* makes the *ch* sound as in *itch* and *pitcher*. It always follows a short vowel.

 Read each sentence. Underline the *wh*, *ng*, and *tch* digraphs.

1. <u>Wh</u>en will the songbirds ha<u>tch</u>?
2. <u>Wh</u>y is the pa<u>tch</u> so lo<u>ng</u>?
3. <u>Wh</u>at can we hi<u>tch</u> to the spring?
4. <u>Wh</u>ich of the singers can stay on pi<u>tch</u>?
5. <u>Wh</u>ere is the ske<u>tch</u> of the king?
6. Some<u>wh</u>ere the ring has a scra<u>tch</u>.
7. The young bu<u>tch</u>er was no<u>wh</u>ere to be found.
8. Wa<u>tch</u> the rope on the swing <u>wh</u>ile it le<u>ng</u>thens.
9. Bring a <u>wh</u>istle to the soccer ma<u>tch</u>.
10. There was a blo<u>tch</u> on the wing of the bob<u>wh</u>ite.
11. The men will stre<u>tch</u> the ga<u>ng</u>plank from the ship to the <u>wh</u>arf.
12. Bu<u>tch</u> will hang the <u>wh</u>ip near the light swi<u>tch</u>.
13. It will be hard to ca<u>tch</u> the strong <u>wh</u>ale.
14. It would be wro<u>ng</u> to <u>wh</u>ack the man with a cru<u>tch</u>.
15. The wa<u>tch</u>man followed the gang every<u>wh</u>ere they went.

4   *Consonant Digraphs kn, wr, wh, ng, & tch*

---

what words are being used, what new information is given, what lesson can be learned?

Comprehension questions:
Where did the wolf go for help in disguising himself?
How did the wolf trick the man at the mill?
What was different about the wolf the third time that he went to the house?
What did the goslings want to see?
What happened to the goslings after they let the wolf in the house?
What did the mother goose see when she came home?
Who told the mother goose the story about what had happened.?
What did the mother goose do?

Read the poems *Wrens and Robins* & *The Old Woman in a Basket*. Preview the poems and explain words or sentence structures that are not familiar to the student.
What consonant digraphs are used in the poems?

Assign. Lesson activities or reading that are to be completed as homework.

Lesson 83: Digraph qu

Overview:

- Auditory recognition of the /kw/ sound of **qu**
- Spell words with phonetic and picture clues
- Apply the spelling rule for **qu**
- Complete sentences
- Match words with meanings

Materials and Supplies:

- Teacher's Guide & Student Workbook 2
- White board or chalkboard
- Word cards (as necessary)
- Dictionary
- Reader: *A Little Princess & Other Classic Stories*

Teaching Tips:

Review for Mastery. Discuss and review any work from the previous lesson that was assigned as homework. Check for completion of the activities and orally quiz the student for comprehension. Review any reading that was assigned, discussing the characters, setting, plot, theme, language, sequence, etc.

Strengthen fluency and phonemic awareness by reviewing words and sentences from previous lessons. Build vocabulary skills by using some of the words in sentences.

Review R-controlled vowels with words from Lessons 71-80. Random words can be selected from the lessons and ask the student to call out or write on the board other words with the same vowel spelling. The words can also be used in sentences.

Review medial double consonants with Lesson 81, Activities 1 & 2. Pick random words from the lesson and ask the student to apply the spelling rule to the medial double consonant. Use some detractor words with a medial **h, j, k, qu, w, x,** or **y.**

Review silent letter consonant digraphs with Lesson 82, Activity 1. Read the words in the boxes and code the silent letter with a slash.

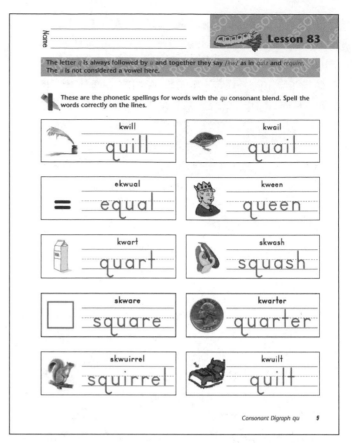

Review **wh**, **ng**, and **tch** digraphs with Lesson 82, Activity 2. Continue to read the sentences for fluency. Ask comprehension questions about the sentences.

Activity 1. Review the rules and the examples. Have the student write examples of the rule on the chalkboard or white board. *Words to teach the concept:* quite, queer, quake, quiz, liquid, squire, banquet, acquire, frequent, require. Review the pictures to make sure the student can correctly identify them. Have the student rewrite the phonetic spelling of the word with the actual spelling.

Pictures:
  quill, quail
  equal, queen
  quart, squash
  square, quarter
  squirrel, quilt

Activity 2. Help the student read the sentences and the word choices. Instruct the student to circle the word that will correctly complete the sentence. Unknown words can be looked up in a dictionary.

Sentences:
1. We saw a <u>quail</u> in the tall grass.
2. Put the milk in a <u>quart</u> jar.
3. Mom bought a new <u>quilt</u> for the bed.
4. The toys will fit in the <u>square</u> box.
5. There was a grey <u>squirrel</u> in the oak tree.
6. A large <u>squash</u> was growing in the garden.

Activity 3. Have the student read the words and the meanings aloud. The student will write the words on the line after the meanings. Unknown words can be looked up in a dictionary.

Words:
1. quack
2. squirt
3. squeak
4. quiz
5. quake
6. squint
7. quiet
8. question
9. squish
10. quick
11. quit

Reading. Read and discuss the maxim for the Lesson.

Read the poem *The Wolf and the Goslings (continued)*. Preview the poem and explain words or sentence structures that are not familiar to the student. With every story ask questions: who are the characters, what are they doing, what are they saying, where does the action take place, what is the order of events, what words are being used, what new information is given, what lesson can be learned?

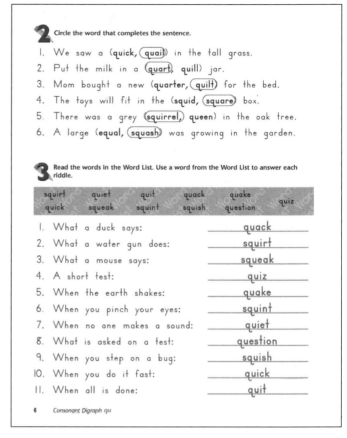

Comprehension questions:
Where did the goose's neighbors go?
What did they find down by the river?
What plan did the goose have?
What was found inside the wolf?
What did the mother goose put back inside the wolf?
What happened to the wolf when he woke up?
How did the goose feel about her goslings?

Assign. Lesson activities or reading that are to be completed as homework.

Lesson 84: Final Adjacent Clusters with r

Overview:

- Complete words with a final adjacent consonant cluster **rk**, **rm**, **rn**, **rt**
- Read words with R-controlled vowels
- Add an initial consonant or consonant blend to complete words with R-controlled vowels
- Sentence completion

Materials and Supplies:

- Teacher's Guide & Student Workbook 2
- White board or chalkboard
- Word cards (as necessary)
- Dictionary
- Reader: *A Little Princess & Other Classic Stories*

Teaching Tips:

Review for Mastery. Discuss and review any work from the previous lesson that was assigned as homework. Check for completion of the activities and orally quiz the student for comprehension. Review any reading that was assigned, discussing the characters, setting, plot, theme, language, sequence, etc.

Strengthen fluency and phonemic awareness by reviewing words and sentences from previous lessons. Build vocabulary skills by using some of the words in sentences.

Review R-controlled vowels with words from Lessons 71-80. Random words can be selected from the lessons for word sorts by either sound or spelling. The words can also be used in sentences.

Review medial double consonants with Lesson 81, Activities 1 & 2. Read through the words. Use the words in sentences or for a spelling bee.

Review silent letter consonant digraphs with Lesson 82, Activity 1. Read the words in the boxes and use them in sentences.

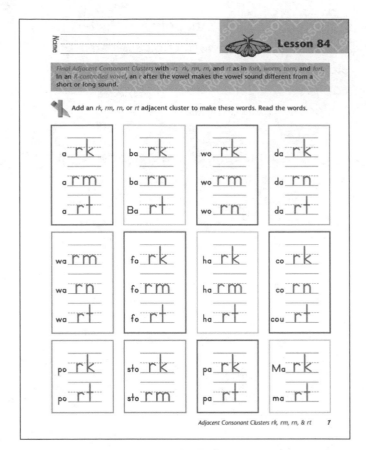

Review the **qu** consonant blend with Lesson 83, Activity 2. Use the detractors in sentences.

Activity 1. Review the rule. Have the student write examples of the rule on the chalkboard or white board. *Words to teach the concept:* irk, jerk, lark, mark, germ, term, fern, yarn, hurt, tort, sort, tart. Have the student complete the words using the adjacent clusters listed in the instructions. They should be real words. Read the words.

Words: (Answers will vary)

ark	bark	work	dark
arm	barn	worm	darn
art	Bart	worn	dart
warm	fork	hark	cork
warn	form	harm	corn
wart	fort	hart	court
pork	stork	park	Mark
port	storm	part	mart

Activity 2. Have the student complete the words using an initial consonant or consonant blend. *Words to teach the concept:* clerk, shark, spark, charm, squirm, storm, churn, scorn, shorn, sworn, stern, blurt, smart, sport, squirt, start. Read the words.

Words: (Answers will vary)

Activity 3. Help the student read the sentences and the word choices. Instruct the student to circle the word that completes the sentence. Explain the **A(n)** that is used in the second sentence. Unknown words can be looked up in a dictionary.

Sentences:
1. Read the words from the <u>chart</u> on the wall.
2. A(n) <u>acorn</u> fell from the oak tree.
3. The game will <u>start</u> when the team is ready.
4. To read a book you must <u>turn</u> the pages.
5. A cactus <u>thorn</u> is very sharp.
6. The girl wore a <u>charm</u> on her wrist.
7. Curt will drive the car down the <u>parkway</u>.
8. After the <u>storm</u> is over we will play in the yard.
9. Sit still in your chair and do not <u>squirm</u>.
10. Bert saw a large <u>shark</u> at the beach.
11. Today we have a <u>short</u> time for lunch.
12. Mark went to the <u>market</u> for some fruit.

Reading. Read and discuss the maxim for the Lesson.

Read the poem *The Bishop's Visit*. Preview the poem and explain words or sentence structures that are not familiar to the student. With every story ask questions: who are the characters, what are they doing, what are they saying, where does the action take place, what is the order of events, what words are being used, what new information is given, what lesson can be learned?

2. Add an initial consonant or consonant blend to each phonogram to make a word.
Answers will vary.

____orn	____ark	____erm	____art
____orn	____ark	____erm	____art
____orn	____ark	____erm	____art
____orn	____ark	____erm	____art
____arm	____orm	____arn	____ork
____arm	____orm	____arn	____ork
____arm	____orm	____arn	____ork
____arm	____orm	____arn	____ork

3. Circle the word that completes the sentence.
1. Read the words from the (**chart,** dirt) on the wall.
2. A(n) (burn, **acorn**) fell from the oak tree.
3. The game will (cart, **start**) when the team is ready.
4. To read a book you must (**turn,** stern) the pages.
5. A cactus (**thorn,** morn) is very sharp.
6. The girl wore a (**charm,** farm) on her wrist.
7. Curt will drive the car down the (clerk, **parkway**).
8. After the (**storm,** firm) is over we will play in the yard.
9. Sit still in your chair and do not (**squirm,** form).
10. Bert saw a large (lurk, **shark**) at the beach.
11. Today we have a (flirt, **short**) time for lunch.
12. Mark went to the (**market,** spark) for some fruit.

Comprehension questions:
  Why wasn't the boy looking forward to the bishop's visit?
  How did the boy prepare for the bishop's visit?
  What did Bridget do to prepare for the bishop's visit?
  What did the bishop say to the boy?
  Did the bishop like the cake?
  What did the boy and the bishop do?
  What word did the bishop need help to spell?

Assign. Lesson activities or reading that are to be completed as homework.

Lesson 85: Medial Double cc with Both a Hard and Soft c

Overview:

- Auditory recognition of the **k** and **s** sound
- Spell words from phonetic clues
- Apply the spelling rule for the **k** sound of **c**
- Apply the spelling rule for the **s** sound of **c**
- Complete sentences
- Match words with pictures

Materials and Supplies:

- Teacher's Guide & Student Workbook 2
- White board or chalkboard
- Word cards (as necessary)
- Dictionary
- Reader: *A Little Princess & Other Classic Stories*

Teaching Tips:

Review for Mastery. Discuss and review any work from the previous lesson that was assigned as homework. Check for completion of the activities and orally quiz the student for comprehension. Review any reading that was assigned, discussing the characters, setting, plot, theme, language, sequence, etc.

Strengthen fluency and phonemic awareness by reviewing words and sentences from previous lessons. Build vocabulary skills by using some of the words in sentences.

Review final adjacent consonant cluster with **r** with Lesson 84, Activity 3. Use the detractor words in sentences.

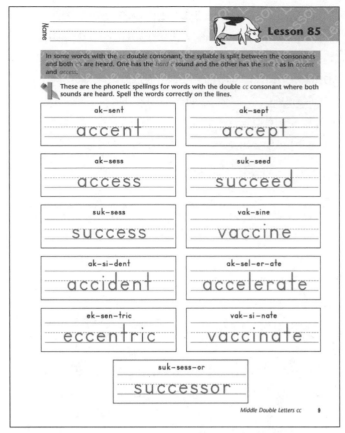

Activity 1. Review the rule. Have the student write examples of the rule on the chalkboard or white board. *Words to teach the concept:* acceptance, accessory, succession, successive, succinct. Have the student read the phonetically spelled words aloud. The student will spell the words from the phonetic spellings. Write the word on the line. Read the words again.

Words:
  accent, accept
  access, succeed
  success, vaccine
  accident, accelerate
  eccentric, vaccinate
  successor

Activity 2. Assist the student in identifying the pictures. The student will use the words from Activity 1 to write the word for each picture.

Words:

accent, success or succeed

accident, accept

vaccine, successor

eccentric, vaccinate

accelerate

Activity 3. Help the student read the sentences and the word choices. Instruct the student to circle the word that will correctly complete each sentence. Unknown words can be looked up in a dictionary.

Sentences:

1. Mark the first syllable with an <u>accent</u> mark.
2. He will be happy to <u>accept</u> the prize.
3. The man wearing the broken sunglasses is a little <u>eccentric</u>.
4. Watch the car <u>accelerate</u> when the light turns green.
5. The yard sale was a huge <u>success</u>.
6. My doctor gave me a shot of <u>vaccine</u>.
7. The queen will crown her next <u>successor</u>.
8. My friend had an <u>accident</u> on the playground.
9. The vet will <u>vaccinate</u> the cat.

Reading. Read and discuss the maxim for the Lesson.

Read the poem *The Little Lion-Charmer*. Preview the poem and explain words or sentence structures that are not familiar to the student. With every story ask questions: who are the characters, what are they doing, what are they saying, where does the action take place, what is the order of events, what words are being used, what new information is given, what lesson can be learned?

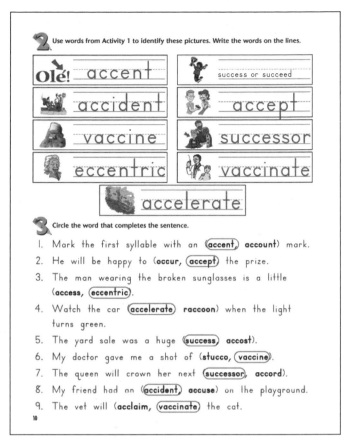

Comprehension questions:

Where does the story in the poem take place?

What emergency took place?

What could be heard during the fire?

Who came to save the lion from being shot?

Who did the keeper's wife ask for?

What did the boy play to soothe the lion?

Where did the boy lead the lion?

Who made the boy feel the best for being a hero?

Assign. Lesson activities or reading that are to be completed as homework.

Lesson 86: Review Consonants

Overview:

- Identify double consonants in words
- Read words with double consonants
- Recognize consonant digraphs **kn**, **wr**, **wh**, **ng**, and **tch**
- Apply the rules to pronounce consonant digraphs **kn**, **wr**, **wh**, **ng**, and **tch**
- Identify consonant digraphs with silent letters **kn** and **wr**
- Auditory recognition of the /**kw**/ sound of **qu**
- Sort words by digraph or consonant cluster
- Read words with R-controlled vowels
- Auditory recognition of the hard and soft **c**

Materials and Supplies:

- Teacher's Guide & Student Workbook 2
- White board or chalkboard
- Word cards (as necessary)
- Dictionary
- Reader: *A Little Princess & Other Classic Stories*

Teaching Tips:

Review for Mastery. Discuss and review any work from the previous lesson that was assigned as homework. Check for completion of the activities and orally quiz the student for comprehension. Review any reading that was assigned, discussing the characters, setting, plot, theme, language, sequence, etc.

Strengthen fluency and phonemic awareness by reviewing words and sentences from previous lessons. Build vocabulary skills by using some of the words in sentences.

Review hard and soft **c** with Lesson 85, Activity 3. Use the detractor words in sentences. Identify the sound of **c** in each word.

Activity 1. Review the rule. Have the student write examples of the rule on the board. This activity reviews the double consonants that were studied in Lesson 81. Assist the student in reading the words in the box. Help the student identify the pictures. Instruct the student to print the correct word underneath each picture.

Pictures:

> bully, winner, addition, bobbin
> coffee, kitty, buggy, cherry
> stucco, toffee, copper, butter
> drummer, belly, dresser, bunny

Activity 2. Review the consonant digraphs that were studied in Lesson 82. Have the student read the words in the box. The student will sort the words by the special sound and write them in the correct box.

Words:

n sound kn	hw sound wh	kw sound qu
knock	white	quite
kneel	wheat	squeal
doorknob	whisper	squirm

r sound wr	ch sound tch	ng sound
wring	watch	bring
wrapper	snatch	string
wrote	ditch	thing

Activity 3. This activity reviews the consonant blends with **r** that were studied in Lesson 84 and the hard and soft sound of **c** studied in Lesson 85. Have the student write examples of the rule on the chalkboard or white board. Have the student read the words in the box. The student will sort the words by the consonant cluster and write them in the correct box.

Words:

rk cluster	rm cluster	double cc
jerk	former	success
murky	germ	vaccine
work	army	accent
rt cluster	rn cluster	access
smart	scorn	accept
sport	churn	
hurt	cornmeal	

Reading. Read and discuss the maxim for the Lesson.

Read the story *Sara*. This is the first chapter of the *A Little Princess* story. Preview the story and explain words or sentence structures that are not familiar to the student. With every story ask questions: who are the characters, what are they doing, what are they saying, where does the action take place, what is the order of events, what words are being used, what new information is given, what lesson can be learned?

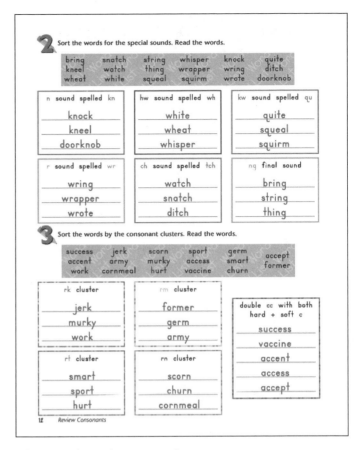

Comprehension questions:

Where is the story taking place?

What is the weather like?

Who is riding in the cab?

What is happening as they ride through the streets?

What things are they talking about?

Was Sara's father really happy?

What were the first impressions that Sara had of the school?

Assign. Lesson activities or reading that are to be completed as homework.

Lesson 87: Short e Vowel Digraph ea

Overview:

• Auditory recognition of short vowel **e** sound
• Match pictures to words
• Read words with the **ea** short **e** digraph
• Apply the Short **e** Digraph Rule to words
• Complete sentences

Materials and Supplies:

• Teacher's Guide & Student Workbook 2
• White board or chalkboard
• Word cards (as necessary)
• Dictionary
• Reader: *A Little Princess & Other Classic Stories*

Teaching Tips:

Review for Mastery. Discuss and review any work from the previous lesson that was assigned as homework. Check for completion of the activities and orally quiz the student for comprehension. Review any reading that was assigned, discussing the characters, setting, plot, theme, language, sequence, etc.

Strengthen fluency and phonemic awareness by reviewing words and sentences from previous lessons. Build vocabulary skills by using some of the words in sentences.

Review previous concepts with Lesson 86, Activities 1-3. Read the words, sort the words, spell the words, use the words in sentences, or whatever review is appropriate for the student.

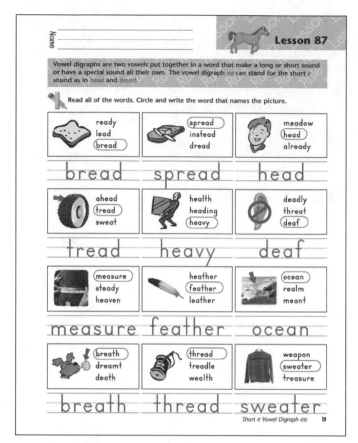

Activity 1. Review the Digraph Rule. This lesson begins a study of the short vowel digraphs. *Words to teach the concept:* ready, ahead, breakfast, already, instead, pleasant, pageant, steadfast, wealthy. Have the student read the words in each box aloud. Review the pictures to make sure the student can correctly identify them. The student will write the word for the picture on the line.

Pictures:
  bread, spread, head
  tread, heavy, deaf
  measure, feather, ocean
  breath, thread, sweater

An optional activity would be to have the student draw a slash through the silent letter of the vowel digraph found in each of the words given in the boxes.

Activity 2. Help the student read the sentences and the word choices. Instruct the student to write the word that will correctly complete each sentence on the line. Unknown words can be looked up in a dictionary.

Sentences:
1. The robin ate the <u>bread</u> on the sidewalk.
2. He ran <u>ahead</u> of me.
3. She is wearing a <u>heavy</u> sweater today.
   Note the **ear** in *wear* and the short **ea** in *sweater*.
4. I will <u>spread</u> butter and jam on my bread.
   Note the short **ea** in *bread*.
5. He has a <u>sweatband</u> on his head.
   Note the short **ea** in *head*.
6. Patch the hole with a needle and <u>thread</u>.
7. There is rain in the <u>weather</u> forecast.
8. Use a cup to the <u>measure</u> flour.
   Note the **our** in *flour*.
9. We found a <u>treasure</u> chest in the back-yard.
10. When will lunch be <u>ready</u>?

Reading. Read and discuss the maxim for the Lesson.

Read the story *Sara (continued)*. This is another chapter of the *A Little Princess* story. Preview the story and explain words or sentence structures that are not familiar to the student. With every story ask questions: who are the characters, what are they doing, what are they saying, where does the action take place, what is the order of events, what words are being used, what new information is given, what lesson can be learned?

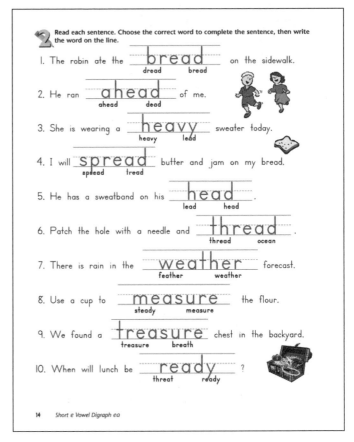

Comprehension questions:
   What was Sara's first reaction to Miss Minchin?
   How did Miss Minchin react to Sara?
   What did Sara later learn about the things that were said during the first meeting?
   Who is Emily?
   What final instruction did Captain Crewe give to Miss Minchin?

Assign. Lesson activities or reading that are to be completed as homework.

Lesson 88: Short i Vowel Digraphs ai & ui, Digraph gu

Overview:

- Auditory recognition of hard **g** sound
- Auditory discrimination of long and short vowels
- Sort words by the vowel sound
- Read words with **gu** digraph
- Form compound words to answer riddles
- Auditory recognition of short **i** sound
- Apply Short **i**, **ui** Digraph Rule to words
- Match pictures to words
- Auditory recognition of short **i** sound
- Apply Short **i**, **ai** Digraph Rule to words

Materials and Supplies:

- Teacher's Guide & Student Workbook 2
- White board or chalkboard
- Word cards (as necessary)
- Dictionary
- Reader: *A Little Princess & Other Classic Stories*

Teaching Tips:

Review for Mastery. Discuss and review any work from the previous lesson that was assigned as homework. Check for completion of the activities and orally quiz the student for comprehension. Review any reading that was assigned, discussing the characters, setting, plot, theme, language, sequence, etc.

Strengthen fluency and phonemic awareness by reviewing words and sentences from previous lessons. Build vocabulary skills by using some of the words in sentences.

Review the short **e**, **ea** digraph with Lesson 87, Activity 1. Code the vowel digraphs in all of the words.

Review silent letters with Lesson 86, Activity 2. Draw a slash through the silent letters found in the words.

Activity 1. Review the rule for the **gu** hard **g** silent **u** digraph. Help the student read the words in the box. Instruct the student to sort the words by the vowel sound and write them in the correct box.

Words:

Long Vowel Words	Short Vowel Words
plague	guess
vague	guest
guide	guilt
guile	guitar
league	guild

Activity 2. Have the student read the sentences. In each sentence the student is to find words to form a compound word that will fit the riddle. Write the compound word on the line. Unknown words can be looked up in a dictionary.

Words:

guestroom
guideline
guesswork
guesthouse

Activity 3. Review the rule for the **ui** short **i** digraph. Have the student read the words in each box aloud. Review the pictures to make sure the student can correctly identify them. The student will write the word for the picture on the line.

Pictures:
  build, circuit, biscuit

Activity 4. Have the student read the sentences. In each sentence the student is to find words to form a compound word that will fit the riddle. Write the compound word on the line. Unknown words can be looked up in a dictionary.

Words:
  boatbuilder
  homebuilder
  shipbuilder
  bodybuilder

Activity 5. Review the rule for the **ai** short **i** vowel digraph. Discuss each of the pictures so that the student can correctly identify them. Read the words and have the student listen for the vowel sound. The student will write the word for each picture on the line.

Pictures:
  captain, mountain
  curtain, chieftain
  certain, fountain

Reading. Read and discuss the maxim for the Lesson.

Read the story *Sara (continued)*. This is another chapter of the *A Little Princess* story. Preview the story and explain words or sentence structures that are not familiar to the student. With every story ask questions: who are the characters, what are they doing, what are they saying, where does the action take place, what is the order of events, what words are being used, what new information is given, what lesson can be learned?

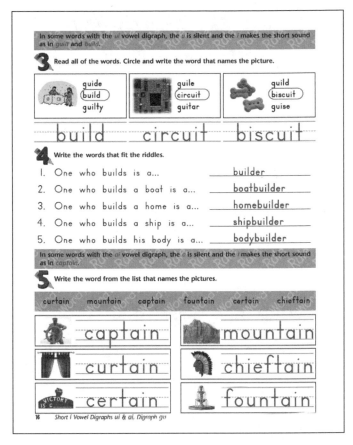

Comprehension questions:
  Where were Sara and her father staying?
  What were Sara and her father doing?
  What was hard for them to find?
  Who had charge of Captain Crewe's affairs in England?
  What was Sara's reaction to her father's leaving?
  What was Miss Minchin's reaction to Sara's clothing and toys?
  What was Sara's final sight of her father?

Assign. Lesson activities or reading that are to be completed as homework.

Lesson 89: Digraph /aw/ Spelled qua & wa

Overview:

- Auditory recognition of digraph /aw/ or /ô/ sound
- Auditory discrimination of long and short vowels
- Read words with **wa** digraph
- Read words with **qua** digraph
- Form compound words to answer riddles
- Match pictures to words

Materials and Supplies:

- Teacher's Guide & Student Workbook 2
- White board or chalkboard
- Word cards (as necessary)
- Dictionary
- Reader: *A Little Princess & Other Classic Stories*

Teaching Tips:

Review for Mastery. Discuss and review any work from the previous lesson that was assigned as homework. Check for completion of the activities and orally quiz the student for comprehension. Review any reading that was assigned, discussing the characters, setting, plot, theme, language, sequence, etc.

Strengthen fluency and phonemic awareness by reviewing words and sentences from previous lessons. Build vocabulary skills by using some of the words in sentences.

Review previous lessons. Have the student code some of the short digraph words in Lesson 88.

Review the short **e**, **ea** digraph with Lesson 87, Activity 2. Use the detractor words in sentences.

Review the **gu** digraph with Lesson 88, Activity 1. Code the silent **u** in each word.

Review the short **i**, **ui** digraph with Lesson 88, Activity 3. Code the silent **u** and the short **i** in each word.

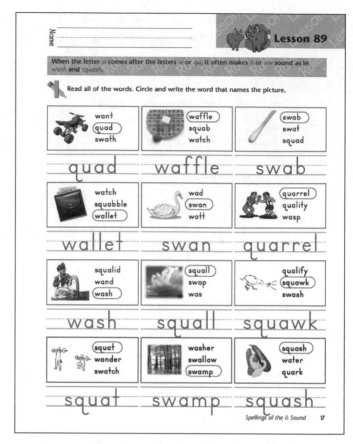

Review the short **i**, **ai** digraph with Lesson 88, Activity 1. Code the silent **a** and the short **i** in each word.

Activity 1. Review the rule and the examples. The digraph /aw/ sound of **a** in these words is coded with a breve (⌣) in some dictionaries, in others with a circumflex (ô), and some give both codings. *Words to teach the concept:* qualify, quality, qualm quark, swallow, swap, wand, wander, was, washer, watt. Have the student read the words in each box aloud. Review the pictures to make sure the student can correctly identify them. The student will write the word for the picture on the line.

Pictures:
  quad, waffle, swab
  wallet, swan, quarrel
  wash, squall, squawk
  squat, swamp, squash

An optional activity would be to have the student draw a slash through the silent **u** of the **qua** digraph found in the words given in the boxes.

Activity 2. Read the words in the Word List. Have the student read the sentences. In each sentence the student is to find words to form a compound word that will fit the riddle. The words are also listed in the Word List. Write the compound word on the line. Unknown words can be looked up in a dictionary.

Words:

1. carwash
2. watchdog
3. washroom
4. mouthwash
5. waterline
6. washtub
7. watercooler
8. watchband
9. watercraft
10. washday
11. washcloth
12. eyewash
13. waterfall
14. backwash
15. watercolor
16. washbowl
17. watchman
18. washstand
19. watchtower
20. watchcase
21. dishwash

Reading. Read and discuss the maxim for the Lesson.

Read the story *A French Lesson*. This is another chapter of the *A Little Princess* story. Preview the story and explain words or sentence structures that are not familiar to the student. With every story ask questions: who are the characters, what are they doing, what are they saying, where does the action take place, what is the order of events, what words are being used, what new information is given, what lesson can be learned?

Use the words from the Word List to write a compound word that fits the riddles.

carwash	eyewash	washcloth	washstand	watchcase	watchtower	watercraft
backwash	mouthwash	washday	washtub	watchdog	watercolor	waterfall
dishwash	washbowl	washroom	watchband	watchman	watercooler	waterline

1. To wash a car — carwash
2. A dog that will watch — watchdog
3. A room to wash in — washroom
4. A wash for the mouth — mouthwash
5. A line of water — waterline
6. A tub to wash in — washtub
7. A cooler for water — watercooler
8. A band for a watch — watchband
9. A craft to ride on the water — watercraft
10. A day to wash the clothes — washday
11. A cloth to wash with — washcloth
12. A wash for the eye — eyewash
13. A fall of water — waterfall
14. To wash a back — backwash
15. A color put on with water — watercolor
16. A bowl to wash in — washbowl
17. A man who has the watch — watchman
18. A stand on which to wash — washstand
19. Tower from which to watch — watchtower
20. A case for a watch — watchcase
21. To wash a dish — dishwash

18   *Spellings of the ô Sound*

Comprehension questions:
  Where is Sara going?
  What position was Sara to have in the school?
  What things did the other students notice about Sara?
  What did Sara do in her schoolroom seat?
  Where was Captain Crewe at this time?
  What had Sara told Emily to do while she was in the schoolroom?
  Why had Miss Minchin chosen to get Sara lessons in French?

Read the poem *Sun-Loving Swallow*. Preview the poem and explain words or sentence structures that are not familiar to the student.

Comprehension questions:
  How is the /ô/ digraph spelled in this poem?
  What does the swallow bring?

Assign. Lesson activities or reading that are to be completed as homework.

Lesson 90: Digraph /aw/ Spelled o, all, alt, & alk

Overview:

- Auditory recognition of digraph /aw/ or /ô/ sound
- Auditory discrimination of /aw/ or ô digraph sound
- Read words with several spellings of the /aw/ or ô digraph sound
- Sort words by the spelling of the /aw/ ô digraph sound
- Select words to answer riddles
- Read sentences

Materials and Supplies:

- Teacher's Guide & Student Workbook 2
- White board or chalkboard
- Word cards (as necessary)
- Dictionary
- Reader: *A Little Princess & Other Classic Stories*

Teaching Tips:

Review for Mastery. Discuss and review any work from the previous lesson that was assigned as homework. Check for completion of the activities and orally quiz the student for comprehension. Review any reading that was assigned, discussing the characters, setting, plot, theme, language, sequence, etc.

Strengthen fluency and phonemic awareness by reviewing words and sentences from previous lessons. Build vocabulary skills by using some of the words in sentences.

Review the digraph /aw/ sound with Lesson 89, Activity 1. Read the detractor words and use them in sentences.

Review the digraph /aw/ sound with Lesson 89, Activity 2. Orally read the riddles and ask the student to answer with the correct compound word.

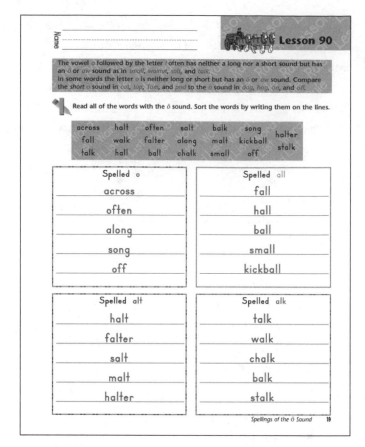

Activity 1. Review the rule for the spellings of the /aw/ or /ô/ sound. Have the student write examples of the rule on the chalkboard or white board. *Words to teach the concept:* gone, office, onto, onward, soft, long, cloth, toss, call, stall, tall, wall, catwalk, shoptalk, alter, although, exalt, Walt. Help the student read the words in the box. Instruct the student to sort the words by the spelling of the vowel sound and write them in the correct box. Read the words after they have been sorted.

Words:

Spelled o	Spelled all
across	fall
often	hall
along	ball
song	small
off	kickball

Spelled alt	Spelled alk
halt	talk
falter	walk
salt	chalk
malt	balk
halter	stalk

Horizons Phonics & Reading Grade 2 Teacher's Guide

Activity 2. Have the student read the sentences. In each sentence the student is to find the word that completes the either/or statement. Circle the word that completes the sentence. Unknown words can be looked up in a dictionary.

Words:
1. on
2. tall
3. long
4. fall
5. wrong
6. soft
7. all
8. often
9. across
10. moth

Activity 3. Have the student read the sentences. Then the student is to circle all of the words in each sentence that have the /aw/ sound. The spelling rules for the sound can be used to help find the words. Unknown words can be looked up in a dictionary.

Sentences:
1. Toss, cloth, halter
2. rainfall, on, crosswalk, dog, halt
3. Talk, officer, frost, on, skywalk
4. Strong, coffee, often, sleepwalk
5. nightfall, baseball, football, softball, tetherball, volleyball
6. Walt, install, small, waterfall, mall
7. baseball, call, fastball
8. Along, sidewalk, soft, puffball, tall
9. All, shoptalk, frost, on, beanstalk
10. cost, walk, on, wall

Review for Test. The instructor should plan to use some time at the end of the class to review and prepare for the test that follows this lesson. Review the objectives for the test and then look over the lessons that it will cover. If the student has struggled with any of the concepts that will be included in the test, some additional drill, practice, or review may be needed to adequately prepare him for the test.

Reading. Read and discuss the maxim for the Lesson.

Read the story *A French Lesson (continued)*. This is another chapter of the *A Little Princess* story.

Horizons Phonics & Reading Grade 2 Teacher's Guide

2 Circle the correct ô word to complete the either/or statements.

1. A switch is either off or _____. fog (on) cross
2. A wall is either small or _____. (tall) moth log
3. A sidewalk is either short or _____. talk salt (long)
4. The rain will either stall or _____. song (fall) chalk
5. The answer is either right or _____. (wrong) halt toss
6. The ball is either hard or _____. stalk dog (soft)
7. The count is either none or _____. (all) cloth walk
8. The event is either never or _____. fog (often) mall
9. We will either walk along or _____. malt frost (across)
10. The insect is either a fly or a _____. (moth) offer spitball

3 Read the sentences that have words with the ô sound. Circle the words with the ô sound.

1. (Toss) me the (cloth) for the (halter).
2. The (rainfall) (on) the (crosswalk) made the (dog) (halt).
3. (Talk) to the (officer) about the (frost) (on) the (skywalk).
4. (Strong) (coffee) (often) causes me to (sleepwalk).
5. Before (nightfall) the boys played (baseball), (football), (softball), (tetherball), and (volleyball).
6. (Walt) will (install) the (small) (waterfall) at the new (mall).
7. The (baseball) ump will (call) the (fastball) a strike.
8. (Along) the (sidewalk) a (soft) (puffball) grew (tall).
9. (All) the (shoptalk) was about the (frost) (on) the (beanstalk).
10. There is no (cost) to (walk) (on) the stone (wall).

10 *Spellings of the ô Sound*

Preview the story and explain words or sentence structures that are not familiar to the student. With every story ask questions: who are the characters, what are they doing, what are they saying, where does the action take place, what is the order of events, what words are being used, what new information is given, what lesson can be learned?

Comprehension questions:
Why was Sara unable to explain herself about knowing French?
Who was to teach Sara French?
What instruction did Miss Minchin give to Sara?
What kind of a man was Monsieur Dufarge?
How was Monsieur Dufarge made aware of Sara's ability to speak French?

Note the words: *Madame* – used as a form of polite address for a woman in a French-speaking area.

Monsieur – used as a form of polite address for a man in a French-speaking area.

Assign. Lesson activities or reading that are to be completed as homework.

Test 9
Lessons 75-84

Overview:

- Auditory recognition of R-controlled vowels
- Match R-controlled words to pictures
- Identify the R-controlled vowels in words
- Syllabication of double consonant words
- Read words with silent letters
- Spell words with R-controlled vowels
- Read words with consonant digraphs
- Read words with final adjacent consonant clusters

Materials and Supplies:

- Teacher's Guide & Student Workbook 2

Instructions:

Assessment Start-up. Read through the test with the student. Help the student with any words that he is still unsure of. The teacher should be available to answer any questions that the student may have during the test.

Activity 1. Make sure the student can correctly identify the pictures and read the words. Instruct the student to match the picture to the word.

Pictures:

pearls	**cheer**
gear	**fierce**
earth	**work**
adjourn	**adhere**

Activity 2. Make sure the student can correctly read the words. Instruct the student to circle the two R-controlled vowels in each of the words.

Words:

w<u>ar</u>h<u>or</u>se, f<u>l</u>oo<u>r</u>b<u>oar</u>d, c<u>ar</u>p<u>or</u>t, f<u>ore</u>w<u>ar</u>n, c<u>our</u>ty<u>ar</u>d

Activity 3. Make sure the student can correctly read the words. Instruct the student to divide each word into syllables by drawing a slash or a bracket for the words with stable syllables.

Words:

crab/by, stuc/co, bud/dy, siz[zle, bag/gy
Bil/ly, drum/mer, win/ner, sup/port, wor/ry
tis/sue, bot[tle, tof/fee, bar/rel, nut/ty

Activity 4. Instruct the student to add either a single consonant or a consonant blend to each phoneme to complete each word.

Words: (Answers will vary.)
b<u>orn</u>, sp<u>ark</u>, g<u>erm</u>, ch<u>art</u>
w<u>arm</u>, st<u>orm</u>, b<u>arn</u>, st<u>ork</u>

Activity 5. Make sure the student can correctly identify the pictures and read the words. Instruct the student to match the picture to the word.

Pictures:

c. heir	**e.** oar	**a.** worn	**b.** bear
d. snore	**h.** flare	**k.** pear	**l.** court
j. there	**f.** pair	**g.** door	**i.** warn

Activity 6. Make sure the student can correctly identify the pictures and read the words. Instruct the student to match the picture to the word.

Pictures:

knuckle	wrist
ring	wren
whistle	queen
squirrel	butcher

Assessment Follow-up. Every test is an important assessment of both the student's comprehension of the concepts and the instructional process. This makes follow-up after each test essential to the learning process. Review all of the errors made on the test with the student. Check for understanding of the concepts and of the problem instructions. Compare the errors made on the test to the test objectives to identify specific areas of weakness. If weak areas of understanding are detected it might be necessary to go back to those lessons to devise some enrichment activities for the concept.

The test results can be used to determine what concepts are reviewed during the daily time of classroom instruction. Devise enrichment activities that will provide development in those areas.

If time permits, choose a selection and have the student read it again. This can also be used as a catch-up time to complete unfinished selections.

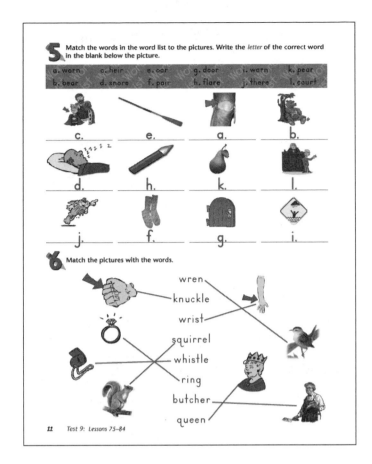

Lesson 91: Digraph /aw/ Spelled au, ough, aw, & augh

Overview:

- Recognition of spellings for the /aw/ or ô digraph sound
- Auditory discrimination of /aw/ or ô digraph sound
- Read words with several spellings of the /aw/ or ô digraph sound
- Sentence completion
- Write words to match pictures
- Select words to answer riddles
- Read sentences

Materials and Supplies:

- Teacher's Guide & Student Workbook 2
- White board or chalkboard
- Phonics rules flashcards
- Word cards (as necessary)
- Dictionary
- Reader: *A Little Princess & Other Classic Stories*

Teaching Tips:

Review for Mastery. Discuss and review any work from the previous lesson that was assigned as homework. Check for completion of the activities and orally quiz the student for comprehension. Review any reading that was assigned, discussing the characters, setting, plot, theme, language, sequence, etc.

Strengthen fluency and phonemic awareness by reviewing words and sentences from previous lessons. Build vocabulary skills by using some of the words in sentences.

Review the digraph /aw/ or ô sound of **a** and **o** with Lesson 90, Activities1-3. Code the **o** vowels in the words with a circumflex (ˆ), and write an ô over the **a** vowels to show that they have the same /aw/ sound as vowel **o**.

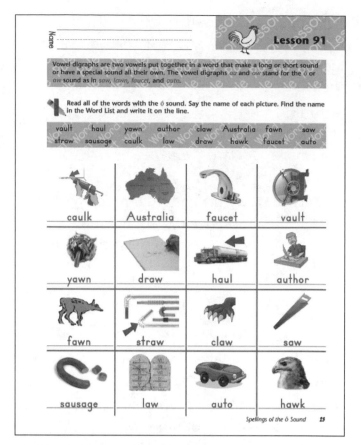

Activity 1. Review the rule. Have the student write examples of the rule on the chalkboard or white board. *Words to teach the concept:* autumn, cause, fault, audio, sauce, awful, brawn, flaw, lawn, raw, hacksaw. Assist the student in reading the words in the box. Help the student identify the pictures and print the correct word underneath each picture.

Pictures:
caulk, Australia, faucet, vault
yawn, draw, haul, author
yawn, straw, claw, saw
sausage, law, auto, hawk

Activity 2. Help the student read the sentences and the word choices. Instruct the student to circle the word that will correctly complete each sentence and write the word on the line. Unknown words can be looked up in a dictionary.

Sentences:
1. My aunt from <u>Australia</u> has auburn hair.
2. In August they will <u>haul</u> the new autos to the stores.

Activity 2 continued:

3. Paul will <u>caulk</u> the leak by the faucet.
4. It is not my <u>fault</u> that the laundry is closed.
5. At the <u>launch</u> the audience choose to applaud.
6. Laura saw the <u>hawk</u> on the lawn.
7. A <u>yawn</u> made his jaw drop.
8. The claw of the crawdad was a help to <u>crawl</u>.
9. The lawsuit was over a <u>flaw</u> in the law.
10. It is awkward to <u>draw</u> the fawn with a straw.

Activity 3. Review the rule. Have the student write examples of the rule on the chalkboard or white board. *Words to teach the concept:* brought, thought, wrought, sought, taught, caught, haughty, slaughter. Help the student read the sentences and the word choices. Instruct the student to write the word on the line that will correctly complete each sentence. This would be a good time to review verb tenses with the student. Unknown words can be looked up in a dictionary.

Words:
1. caught
2. taught
3. naughty
4. fought
5. brought
6. bought
7. thought

Reading. Read and discuss the maxim for the Lesson.

Read the story *Erma*. This is another chapter of the *A Little Princess* story. Preview the story and explain words or sentence structures that are not familiar to the student. With every story ask questions: who are the characters, what are they doing, what are they saying, where does the action take place, what is the order of events, what words are being used, what new information is given, what lesson can be learned?

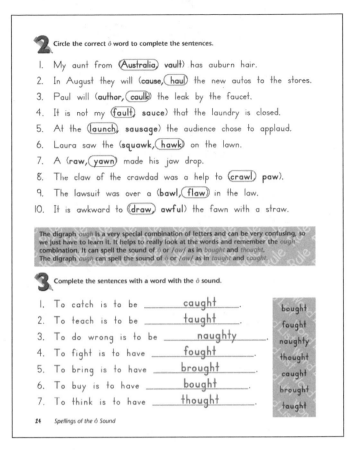

Comprehension questions:
What things did Sara notice about Erma?
What was Erma's reaction to Sara's French?
How was Erma scolded?
How did Erma's French lesson go?
Who looked for Erma after the lessons were over?
What did Sara say to Erma about her name?

Read the story *Frank and Rose*. Preview the story and explain words or sentence structures that are not familiar to the student.

Comprehension questions:
What had Frank made?
Who did Frank and Rose ask for permission to go to the river?
What was Frank going to do with the boat if it worked well?
What words in the poem have the ô sound?

Assign. Lesson activities or reading that are to be completed as homework.

Lesson 92: Short u Spelled o, o_e, oo, & ou

Overview:

- Auditory recognition of short **u** sound
- Auditory discrimination of short **u** sound
- Read words with several spellings of the short **u** sound
- Sentence completion
- Write words to match pictures
- Select words with the short **u** sound
- Read sentences

Materials and Supplies:

- Teacher's Guide & Student Workbook 2
- White board or chalkboard
- Word cards (as necessary)
- Dictionary
- Reader: *A Little Princess & Other Classic Stories*

Teaching Tips:

Review for Mastery. Discuss and review any work from the previous lesson that was assigned as homework. Check for completion of the activities and orally quiz the student for comprehension. Review any reading that was assigned, discussing the characters, setting, plot, theme, language, sequence, etc.

Strengthen fluency and phonemic awareness by reviewing words and sentences from previous lessons. Build vocabulary skills by using some of the words in sentences.

Review the /aw/ or ô digraph sound with Lesson 91, Activity 2. There are a number of words with the /aw/ or ô sound. Have the student read the sentences again and circle words with the ô sound. Words: <u>au</u>nt, <u>au</u>burn, <u>Au</u>gust, <u>au</u>tos, P<u>au</u>l, f<u>au</u>cet, l<u>au</u>ndry, <u>au</u>dience, appl<u>au</u>d, L<u>au</u>ra, s<u>aw</u>, l<u>aw</u>n, j<u>aw</u>, cl<u>aw</u>, cr<u>aw</u>dad, l<u>aw</u>suit, l<u>aw</u>, <u>aw</u>kward, f<u>aw</u>n, str<u>aw</u>.

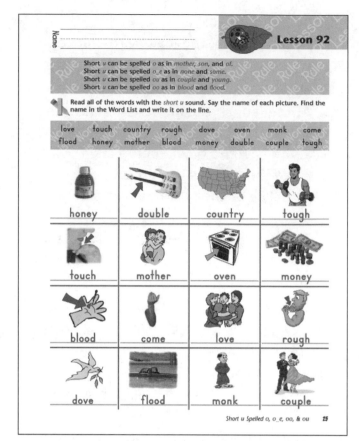

Activity 1. Review the rule and the examples. Have the student write examples of the rule on the chalkboard or white board. Assist the student in reading the words in the box. Help the student identify the pictures and print the correct word underneath each picture.

Pictures:
 honey, double, country, tough
 touch, mother, oven, money
 blood, come, love, rough
 dove, flood, monk, couple

Activity 2. Help the student read the sentences and the word choices. Instruct the student to choose the word from the Word List that will correctly complete each sentence and write the word on the line. Unknown words can be looked up in a dictionary.

Sentences:

1. Do you <u>wonder</u> what went wrong?
2. What <u>month</u> is your birthday?
3. <u>Does</u> Megan have any gum?
4. When will the <u>young</u> child go to bed?
5. Is the cake in the oven <u>done</u>?
6. Can <u>some</u> of the milk be saved?
7. Is there <u>another</u> person who can help?
8. Where is the <u>front</u> of the line?
9. How can <u>none</u> of the shoes fit?
10. When did the <u>trouble</u> start?

Activity 3. Review the spellings of the short **u** sound. Read the words in each row and have the student circle the short **u** words in each row.

Words:

of, money, flood
done, brother, young
son, cousin, monk
oven, some, couple
blood, ton, does
another, love, touch
wonder, somebody, honey
double, none, trouble
mother, month, front

Reading. Read and discuss the maxim for the Lesson.

Read the story *Erma (continued)*. This is another chapter of the *A Little Princess* story. Preview the story and explain words or sentence structures that are not familiar to the student. With every story ask questions: who are the characters, what are they doing, what are they saying, where does the action take place, what is the order of events, what words are being used, what new information is given, what lesson can be learned?

2 Complete the questions with a word with the *short u* sound.

| another | young | some | month | wonder |
| none | does | trouble | done | front |

1. Do you _____wonder_____ what went wrong?
2. What _____month_____ is your birthday?
3. _____Does_____ Megan have any gum?
4. When will the _____young_____ child go to bed?
5. Is the cake in the oven _____done_____?
6. Can _____some_____ of the milk be saved?
7. Is there _____another_____ person who can help?
8. Where is the _____front_____ of the line?
9. How can _____none_____ of the shoes fit?
10. When did the _____trouble_____ start?

3 Circle all of the words the the *short u* sound.

of	box	money	flood	home
pond	done	brother	spot	young
son	shop	cousin	broke	monk
oven	slope	some	couple	moth
blood	ton	does	chop	stone
those	another	toss	love	touch
wonder	froze	somebody	honey	soul
double	boulder	none	trouble	scope
dough	mother	month	front	frog

18   Short u Spelled o, o_e, oo, & ou

Comprehension questions:

What was Erma's chief trouble in life?
What had Erma's father instructed Miss Minchin?
Why was Sara able to speak French?
Why did Sara and Erma walk quietly to Sara's room?
What story did Sara tell Erma about dolls?
Why did Sara and Erma sit down?

Assign. Lesson activities or reading that are to be completed as homework.

Lesson 93: Review Short Vowel Digraphs

Overview:

• Auditory recognition of short vowel sounds
• Auditory discrimination of short and long vowel sounds
• Auditory discrimination of the /aw/ or ô digraph sound

Materials and Supplies:

• Teacher's Guide & Student Workbook 2
• White board or chalkboard
• Word cards (as necessary)
• Dictionary
• Reader: *A Little Princess & Other Classic Stories*

Teaching Tips:

Review for Mastery. Discuss and review any work from the previous lesson that was assigned as homework. Check for completion of the activities and orally quiz the student for comprehension. Review any reading that was assigned, discussing the characters, setting, plot, theme, language, sequence, etc.

Strengthen fluency and phonemic awareness by reviewing words and sentences from previous lessons. Build vocabulary skills by using some of the words in sentences.

Review the /**aw**/ or **ô** digraph sound with Lesson 91, Activity 1. Have the student read the words again and circle the digraphs that make the **ô** sound.

Review spellings of the short **u** sound with Lesson 92, Activity 1. Have the student circle the letters or letters in each word that make the short **u** sound.

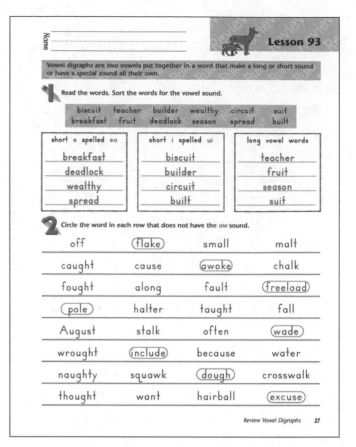

Activity 1. Review the rules for the short **ea** and **ui** vowel digraphs. Have the student read the words in the box. The student will sort the words by the special sound and write them in the correct box.

Words:

e spelled ea	i spelled ui	long vowel
breakfast	biscuit	teacher
deadlock	builder	fruit
wealthy	circuit	season
spread	built	suit

Activity 2. Review the rules and spellings of the /**aw**/ **ô** sound. Read the words in each row and have the student circle the word in each row that does not have the /**aw**/ **ô** sound.

Words:
  flake
  awoke
  freeload
  pole
  wade
  include
  dough
  excuse

Horizons Phonics & Reading Grade 2 Teacher's Guide

Activity 3. Review the spellings of the short **u** sound. Have the student read the word in each box. The student will fill in the circle for the vowel sound he hears in the word.

Answers:
  long o, short u, short u
  short u, short o, long o
  long o, short u, short u
  short u, long o, short u
  long o, short o, long o
  short u, long o, short u
  short u, short u, short u

Reading. Read and discuss the maxim for the Lesson.

Read the story *Erma (continued)*. This is another chapter of the *A Little Princess* story. Preview the story and explain words or sentence structures that are not familiar to the student. With every story ask questions: who are the characters, what are they doing, what are they saying, where does the action take place, what is the order of events, what words are being used, what new information is given, what lesson can be learned?

Comprehension questions:
  What ended Sara's story?
  What stories did Sara tell Erma?
  What was Sara's pain?
  Did Erma love her father like Sara loved hers?
  What does the word bear mean in the story? (endure, suffer, put up with, etc.)
  Who planned to be friends?

Assign. Lesson activities or reading that are to be completed as homework.

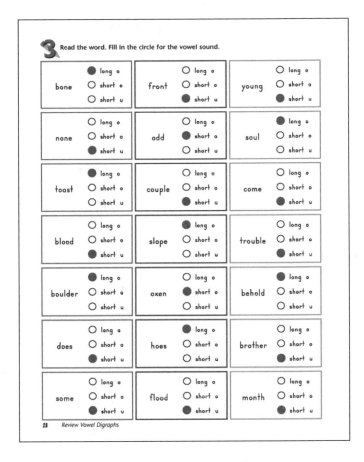

Lesson 94: Hard & Soft c, Spellings of the s, h, and r Sounds

Overview:

- Auditory discrimination of the **k** and **c** sound
- Sort words by the sound of letter **c**
- Apply the spelling rule for the **k** sound of **c**
- Apply the spelling rule for the **s** sound of **c**
- Identify silent letters
- Identify the sound of consonant digraphs with silent letters
- Auditory discrimination of the **s**, **h**, and **r** sound

Materials and Supplies:

- Teacher's Guide & Student Workbook 2
- White board or chalkboard
- Word cards (as necessary)
- Dictionary
- Reader: *A Little Princess & Other Classic Stories*

Teaching Tips:

Review for Mastery. Discuss and review any work from the previous lesson that was assigned as homework. Check for completion of the activities and orally quiz the student for comprehension. Review any reading that was assigned, discussing the characters, setting, plot, theme, language, sequence, etc.

Strengthen fluency and phonemic awareness by reviewing words and sentences from previous lessons. Build vocabulary skills by using some of the words in sentences.

Review the /**aw**/ or **ô** digraph sound with Lesson 91, Activities 2 & 3 and Lesson 93, Activity 2. Have the student read the words again and circle the digraphs that make the **ô** sound.

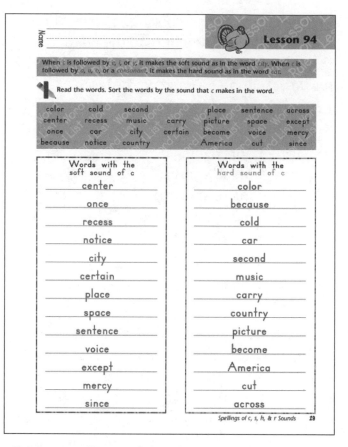

Review spellings of the short **u** sound with Lesson 92, Activity 3. Have the student read the circled words that make the short **u** sound.

Review spellings of the long **o**, short **o**, and short **u** with Lesson 93, Activity 3. Have the student read the words again and sort them by the vowel sound on the board or a sheet of paper.

Activity 1. Review the rule for the spellings of the sounds of **c**. *Words to teach the concept:* cement, ceiling, cinch, circus, excite, face, ice, justice, peace, rice, spicy, camp, copter, cousin, call, come, could. Ask the student for other examples. Help the student read the words in the box. Instruct the student to sort the words by the sound that **c** makes and write them in the correct box. Read the words after they have been sorted.

Activity 1 continued:

Words:

Soft c	Hard c
center	color
once	because
recess	cold
notice	car
city	second
certain	music
place	carry
space	country
sentence	picture
voice	become
except	America
mercy	cut
since	across

Activity 2. Review the rules and the examples. *Words to teach the concept:* scenic, sceptic (skeptic), scenario, psychic, psycho, psychology, psychiatrist, swordsman, wholesale, whooping cough, wrap, wreak, wrestle, written, wrote, rhubarb, rhythm, rheumatic fever. Have the student name the pictures and read the words in the boxes. The student will fill in the circle for the consonant sound that is heard for the underlined letters.

Consonants:

r	s	r	s
r	h	r	s
r	h	s	r
h	r	r	h
r	h	s	s
s	s	r	r

Reading. Read and discuss the maxim for the Lesson.

Read the story *Lottie*. This is another chapter of the *A Little Princess* story. Preview the story and explain words or sentence structures that are not familiar to the student. With every story ask questions: who are the characters, what are they doing, what are they saying, where does the action take place, what is the

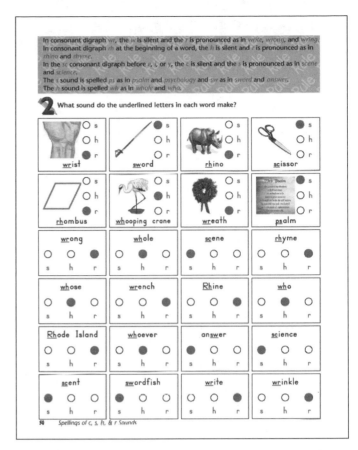

order of events, what words are being used, what new information is given, what lesson can be learned?

Comprehension questions:

How was Sara treated at the school?

Why did Miss Minchin treat Sara so well?

What reason did Miss Minchin give for Lavvy being so bad?

What was Sara asked to do when parents came to visit the school?

What treats did Sara share with the younger girls?

What made Lottie worship Sara?

What "weapon" did Lottie use to get her way?

Assign. Lesson activities or reading that are to be completed as homework.

Lesson 95: Spellings of the Final k Sound

Overview:

- Auditory discrimination of the **k** sound
- Auditory discrimination of long and short vowels
- Apply rules to read the long or short vowel sound
- Apply the spelling rule for the **k** sound after a short vowel
- Apply the spelling rule for the **k** sound after a long vowel

Materials and Supplies:

- Teacher's Guide & Student Workbook 2
- White board or chalkboard
- Word cards (as necessary)
- Dictionary
- Reader: *A Little Princess & Other Classic Stories*

Teaching Tips:

Review for Mastery. Discuss and review any work from the previous lesson that was assigned as homework. Check for completion of the activities and orally quiz the student for comprehension. Review any reading that was assigned, discussing the characters, setting, plot, theme, language, sequence, etc.

Strengthen fluency and phonemic awareness by reviewing words and sentences from previous lessons. Build vocabulary skills by using some of the words in sentences.

Review soft **c** with Lesson 94, Activity 1. Review the rule for soft **c** and the vowels that come after it. Have the student circle the soft **c** and the vowel that follows it in the words that were sorted.

Review consonant digraphs with silent letters with Lesson 94, Activity 2. Have the student read the words again and sort them on the board or a sheet of paper by the consonant sound.

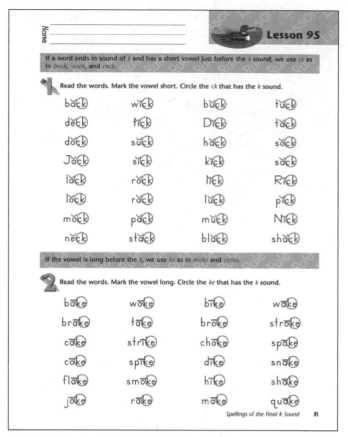

Activity 1. Discuss the rule for the **ck** spelling of the **k** sound. *Words to teach the concept:* block, chick, duck, flock, rack, speck, stick, stock, struck, thick, track, wreck. Ask the student for other examples. Have the student read the words in each row. The student will code the short vowel and circle the letters that make the **k** sound.

Words:
  ba<u>ck</u>, wi<u>ck</u>, bu<u>ck</u>, tu<u>ck</u>
  de<u>ck</u>, ti<u>ck</u>, Di<u>ck</u>, ta<u>ck</u>
  do<u>ck</u>, su<u>ck</u>, ha<u>ck</u>, so<u>ck</u>
  Ja<u>ck</u>, si<u>ck</u>, ki<u>ck</u>, sa<u>ck</u>
  la<u>ck</u>, ro<u>ck</u>, li<u>ck</u>, Ri<u>ck</u>
  lo<u>ck</u>, ra<u>ck</u>, lu<u>ck</u>, pi<u>ck</u>
  mo<u>ck</u>, pa<u>ck</u>, mu<u>ck</u>, Ni<u>ck</u>
  ne<u>ck</u>, sta<u>ck</u>, bla<u>ck</u>, sha<u>ck</u>

Activity 2. Discuss the rule for the **ke** spelling of the **k** sound. *Words to teach the concept:* cuke, drake, Mike, nuke, poke, stoke, yoke. Have the student read the words in each row. The student will code the long vowel and circle the letters that make the **k** sound.

Activity 2 continued:

Words:

ba**ke**, wo**ke**, bi**ke**, wa**ke**
bra**ke**, ta**ke**, bro**ke**, stro**ke**
ca**ke**, stri**ke**, cho**ke**, spo**ke**
co**ke**, spi**ke**, di**ke**, sna**ke**
fla**ke**, smo**ke**, hi**ke**, sha**ke**
jo**ke**, ra**ke**, ma**ke**, qua**ke**

Activity 3. Review the spelling rules for **k** following the long and short vowel sound. The student will write words with the final **k** sound from the words beginnings that are given. Read the words, paying special attention to the sound of the vowels.

Words:

ck	ke	ck	ke
back	bake	duck	duke
Jack	Jake	jock	joke
lick	like	lack	lake
luck	Luke	Mack	make
rack	rake	Mick	Mike
sack	sake	pick	pike
tack	take	quack	quake
chock	choke	shack	shake
block	bloke	smock	smoke
Dick	dike	snack	snake

Reading. Read and discuss the maxim for the Lesson.

Read the story *Lottie (continued)*. This is another chapter of the *A Little Princess* story. Preview the story and explain words or sentence structures that are not familiar to the student. With every story ask questions: who are the characters, what are they doing, what are they saying, where does the action take place, what is the order of events, what words are being used, what new information is given, what lesson can be learned?

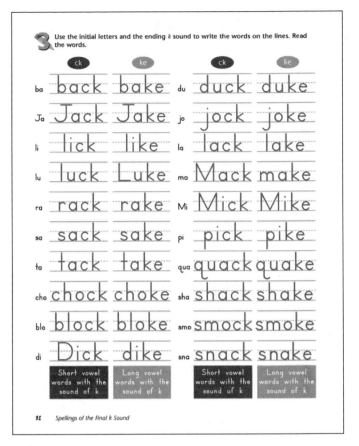

Comprehension questions:
  What happened that caused Sara to take charge of Lottie?
  Who gave Sara permission to help Lottie?
  Who was trying to quiet Lottie?
  How did Sara ask Amy to leave the room?

Assign. Lesson activities or reading that are to be completed as homework.

Lesson 96: Spellings of the Final k Sound

Overview:

- Auditory discrimination of the **k** sound
- Auditory discrimination of long and short vowels
- Apply rules to read the long or short vowel sound
- Apply the spelling rule for the **k** sound after a consonant or double vowel
- Apply the spelling rule for the **k** sound after a consonant or double vowel

Materials and Supplies:

- Teacher's Guide & Student Workbook 2
- White board or chalkboard
- Word cards (as necessary)
- Dictionary
- Reader: *A Little Princess & Other Classic Stories*

Teaching Tips:

Review for Mastery. Discuss and review any work from the previous lesson that was assigned as homework. Check for completion of the activities and orally quiz the student for comprehension. Review any reading that was assigned, discussing the characters, setting, plot, theme, language, sequence, etc.

Strengthen fluency and phonemic awareness by reviewing words and sentences from previous lessons. Build vocabulary skills by using some of the words in sentences.

Review hard **c** with Lesson 94, Activity 1. Review the rule for hard **c** and the vowels or consonants that come after it. Have the student circle the hard **c** and the vowel or consonant that follows it in the words that were sorted.

Review spellings of the **k** sound with Lesson 95, Activities 1 & 2. Have the student read the words again and sort them on the board or a sheet of paper by the vowel sound.

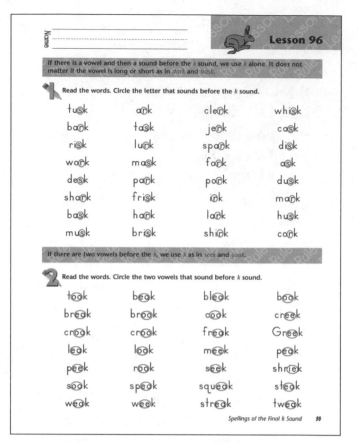

Spellings of the Final k Sound **33**

Activity 1. Discuss the rule for the spelling of the **k** sound after another consonant sound. Review the rules for the R-controlled vowels. *Words to teach the concept:* perk, quirk, schoolwork, smirk, stork, flask, chunk, drink, dunk, honk. Have the student read the words in each row. The student will circle the letter that makes the consonant sound before the **k** sound.

Words:
   tu<u>s</u>k, a<u>r</u>k, cle<u>r</u>k, whi<u>s</u>k
   ba<u>r</u>k, ta<u>s</u>k, je<u>r</u>k, ca<u>s</u>k
   ri<u>s</u>k, lu<u>r</u>k, spa<u>r</u>k, di<u>s</u>k
   wo<u>r</u>k, ma<u>s</u>k, fo<u>r</u>k, a<u>s</u>k
   de<u>s</u>k, pa<u>r</u>k, po<u>r</u>k, du<u>s</u>k
   sha<u>r</u>k, fri<u>s</u>k, i<u>r</u>k, ma<u>r</u>k
   ba<u>s</u>k, ha<u>r</u>k, la<u>r</u>k, hu<u>s</u>k
   mu<u>s</u>k, bri<u>s</u>k, shi<u>r</u>k, co<u>r</u>k

Activity 2. Discuss the rule for the spelling of the **k** sound after a double vowel. *Words to teach the concept:* cheek, cloak, creak, leek, nook, oak, reek, sleek, rookie, sneak, shook, spook, teak. Have the student read the words in each row. The student will circle the double vowel before the **k** sound.

Activity 2 continued:

Words:

t<u>oo</u>k, b<u>ea</u>k, bl<u>ea</u>k, b<u>oo</u>k
br<u>ea</u>k, br<u>oo</u>k, c<u>oo</u>k, cr<u>ee</u>k
cr<u>oa</u>k, cr<u>oo</u>k, fr<u>ea</u>k, Gr<u>ee</u>k
l<u>ea</u>k, l<u>oo</u>k, m<u>ee</u>k, p<u>ea</u>k
p<u>ee</u>k, r<u>oo</u>k, s<u>ee</u>k, shr<u>ie</u>k
s<u>oa</u>k, sp<u>ea</u>k, squ<u>ea</u>k, st<u>ea</u>k
w<u>ea</u>k, w<u>ee</u>k, str<u>ea</u>k, tw<u>ea</u>k

Activity 3. Review the spelling rules for the **k** sound following long and short vowels, and consonant sounds. The student will write words with the final **k** sound from the words beginnings that are given. Read the words.

Words:

<u>ck</u>	<u>rk</u>	<u>sk</u>	<u>ke</u>
back	bark	bask	bake
Mack	mark	mask	make
Dick	Dirk	disk	dike
luck	lurk	<u>nk</u>	Luke
shack	shark	shank	shake
quack	quark		quake

Activity 4. Review the spelling rules for the **k** sound following double vowels. The student will write words with the final **k** sound from the word beginnings and endings that are given. Read the words.

Words:

speak, break, sneak, bleak
freak, beak, streak, peak
steak, squeak, weak, speak
spook, brook, took, book
look, crook, nook, hook
cloak, soak, croak, oak

Reading. Read and discuss the maxim for the Lesson.

Read the story *Lottie (continued)*. This is another chapter of the *A Little Princess* story. Preview the story and explain words or sentence structures that are not familiar to the student. With every story ask questions: who are the characters, what are they doing, what are they saying, where does the action take

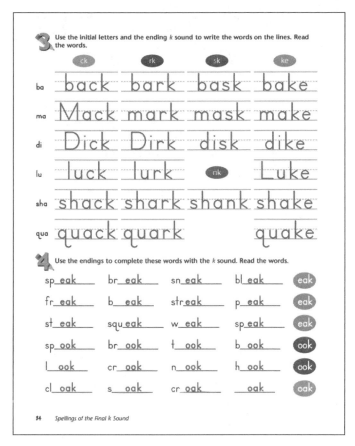

place, what is the order of events, what words are being used, what new information is given, what lesson can be learned?

Comprehension questions:

What did Sara do when she came into the room where Lottie was crying?
Why did Lottie say she was crying?
How was Sara able to make Lottie stop crying?
Where did Sara say her mother was?
What did Sara say heaven was like?
How did Lottie respond to Sara's stories about heaven?
What did Sara offer to be for Lottie?

Assign. Lesson activities or reading that are to be completed as homework.

Lesson 97: Spellings of the Final k Sound

Overview:

- Auditory discrimination of the **k** sound
- Apply rule to read the final **k** sound of a two or more syllable word
- Match pictures to words
- Sentence completion
- Comprehension of questions

Materials and Supplies:

- Teacher's Guide & Student Workbook 2
- White board or chalkboard
- Word cards (as necessary)
- Dictionary
- Reader: *A Little Princess & Other Classic Stories*

Teaching Tips:

Review for Mastery. Discuss and review any work from the previous lesson that was assigned as homework. Check for completion of the activities and orally quiz the student for comprehension. Review any reading that was assigned, discussing the characters, setting, plot, theme, language, sequence, etc.

Strengthen fluency and phonemic awareness by reviewing words and sentences from previous lessons. Build vocabulary skills by using some of the words in sentences.

Review spellings of the **k** sound with Lesson 95, Activity 3. Have the student read the words again, paying special attention to the change in sound between the short and long vowel words. Code the vowels in the words.

Review R-controlled vowels with Lesson 96, Activity 1. Have the student read the words again, paying special attention to the vowel sounds. Sort the words on the board or a sheet of paper as either short or R-controlled vowel words.

Review vowel digraphs with Lesson 96, Activity 2. Have the student read the words again,

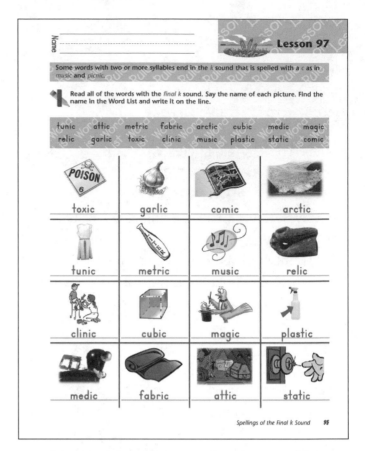

paying special attention to the short and long vowel words. Sort the words on the board or a sheet of paper.

Activity 1. Review the rule for the spelling of the final **k** sound in words of two or more syllables. *Words to teach the concept:* acrylic, antic, athletic, atomic, autistic, automatic, catholic, caustic, chronic, colic, cynic, domestic, dramatic, dynamic, electric, elastic, ethic, fanatic, frantic, generic, genetic, historic, hydraulic, kinetic, lunatic, magnetic, mechanic, mosaic, mystic, narcotic, optic, Pacific, poetic, republic, skeptic, synthetic, tragic. Assist the student in reading the words in the box. Help the student identify the pictures and print the correct word underneath each picture.

Pictures:

> **toxic, garlic, comic, arctic**
> **tunic, metric, music, relic**
> **clinic, cubic, magic, plastic**
> **medic, fabric, attic, static**

Activity 2. Help the student read the sentences and the word choices. Instruct the student to circle the word that will correctly complete each sentence. Unknown words can be looked up in a dictionary.

Sentences:

1. Alec will store the box in the <u>attic</u>.
2. My sister has a cold and must go to the <u>clinic</u>.
3. I read the <u>comic</u> in the newspaper.
4. The <u>music</u> will soon begin to play.
5. Mac did a <u>magic</u> trick for the class.
6. The <u>static</u> made her hair stand up.
7. I have some <u>fabric</u> to make the tunic.
8. The soda came in a <u>metric</u> bottle.
9. A <u>plastic</u> wrap was over the food.
10. We must find a safe place to put this <u>toxic</u> waste.

Activity 3. Help the student read the words in the questions. Instruct the student to select either **yes** or **no** as the answer to the question. Unknown words can be looked up in a dictionary.

Answers:

1. no
2. yes
3. no
4. no
5. no
6. no
7. yes
8. yes
9. yes
10. yes

Reading. Read and discuss the maxim for the Lesson.

Read the story *Becky*. This is another chapter of the *A Little Princess* story. Preview the story and explain words or sentence structures that are not familiar to the student. With every story ask questions: who are the characters, what are they doing, what are they saying,

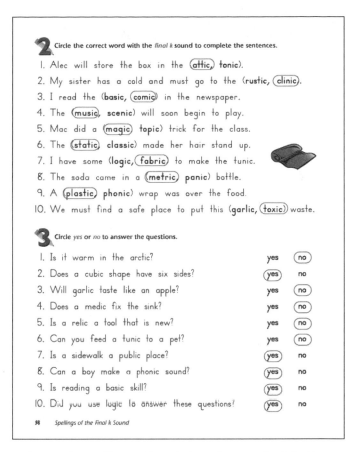

where does the action take place, what is the order of events, what words are being used, what new information is given, what lesson can be learned?

Comprehension questions:
What power did Sara have that the other students were most jealous of?
What did Sara see between the railings?
When did Sara see the little girl again?
What was the little girl doing while Sara told her story?
What stopped the story?
Too whom did Sara say stories belonged?
What was Sara's response to criticism for telling stories about heaven?

Assign. Lesson activities or reading that are to be completed as homework.

Lesson 98: Review Spellings of Consonant Sounds

Overview:

- Auditory discrimination of the **k** and **s** sound
- Auditory discrimination of long and short vowels
- Apply rules to correctly spell the **k** sound
- Identify the spellings of words with silent letters
- Auditory discrimination of consonant sounds

Materials and Supplies:

- Teacher's Guide & Student Workbook 2
- White board or chalkboard
- Word cards (as necessary)
- Dictionary
- Reader: *A Little Princess & Other Classic Stories*

Teaching Tips:

Review for Mastery. Discuss and review any work from the previous lesson that was assigned as homework. Check for completion of the activities and orally quiz the student for comprehension. Review any reading that was assigned, discussing the characters, setting, plot, theme, language, sequence, etc.

Strengthen fluency and phonemic awareness by reviewing words and sentences from previous lessons. Build vocabulary skills by using some of the words in sentences.

Review the final **k** sound with Lesson 97, Activity 2. Have the student use the detractor words in sentences.

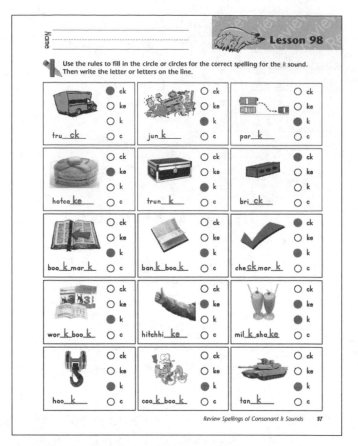

Activity 1. Review the rules from previous lessons. Have the student write examples of the rule on the chalkboard or white board. Have the student name the pictures. The student will fill in the circle for the spelling of the final **k** sound heard and write it on the line to complete the spelling of the word for the picture.

Pictures:
  truck, junk, park
  hotcake, trunk, brick
  bookmark, bankbook, checkmark
  workbook, hitchhike, milkshake
  hook, cookbook, tank

Activity 2. Have the student name the pictures. The student will fill in the circle for the spelling of the final **k** sound heard and write it on the line to complete the spelling of the word for the picture.

Pictures:
   vac, croc, cleric
   pac boot, conic, italic
   lilac, tropic, tic tac toe

Activity 3. Review the rule for the spellings of the sounds of **c**. Help the student read the words in each row. Instruct the student to circle the words with the soft **c** sound.

Words:
   advice, Cindy
   icy, twice, fancy

Activity 4. Review the rules for consonant digraphs with silent letters. Have the student read the words in the box. The student will sort the words by the beginning sound and write them in the correct box.

Words:

sound of s	sound of h	sound of r
scenic	wholesale	wrestle
sword	whose	rhythmic
psychic	who	rhubarb

Reading. Read and discuss the maxim for the Lesson.

Read the story *Becky (continued)*. This is another chapter of the *A Little Princess* story. Preview the story and explain words or sentence structures that are not familiar to the student. With every story ask questions: who are the characters, what are they doing, what are they saying, where does the action take place, what is the order of events, what words are being used, what new information is given, what lesson can be learned?

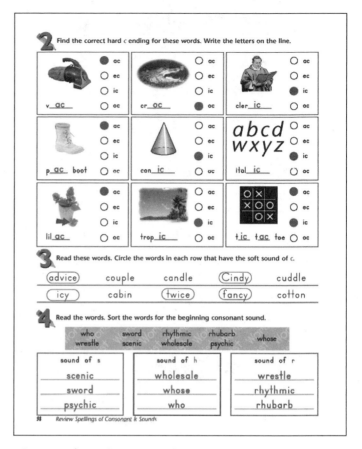

Comprehension questions:
   What were some of Becky's jobs?
   Who told Sara what Becky's name was?
   Why had Becky sat down in Sara's room?
   What did Sara find one afternoon in her room?
   What did Sara think as she looked at Becky sleeping?

Assign. Lesson activities or reading that are to be completed as homework.

Lesson 99: Silent Letter Digraphs mb, gm, mn, & lm Spellings of the z Sound of s, Silent Vowels before Letter l

Overview:

- Apply the rules to pronounce words with silent letters
- Recognition of **mb**, **gm**, **mn**, **lm** silent letter digraphs
- Recognition of silent vowels before letter **l**
- Code words with silent letters
- Auditory discrimination of the **s** and **z** sound
- Sort words by the spelling of the **z** sound

Materials and Supplies:

- Teacher's Guide & Student Workbook 2
- White board or chalkboard
- Word cards (as necessary)
- Dictionary
- Reader: *A Little Princess & Other Classic Stories*

Teaching Tips:

Review for Mastery. Discuss and review any work from the previous lesson that was assigned as homework. Check for completion of the activities and orally quiz the student for comprehension. Review any reading that was assigned, discussing the characters, setting, plot, theme, language, sequence, etc.

Strengthen fluency and phonemic awareness by reviewing words and sentences from previous lessons. Build vocabulary skills by using some of the words in sentences.

Review the spelling of the final **k** sound with Lesson 98, Activity 1. Have the student read each word and give the rule for how it is spelled.

Review the consonant digraphs with silent letters with Lesson 98, Activity 4. Have the student code the silent letters in the words.

Activity 1. Review the rule for silent **b** in the consonant digraph **mb**. *Words to teach the concept:* bomb, breadcrumb, divebomb, door-

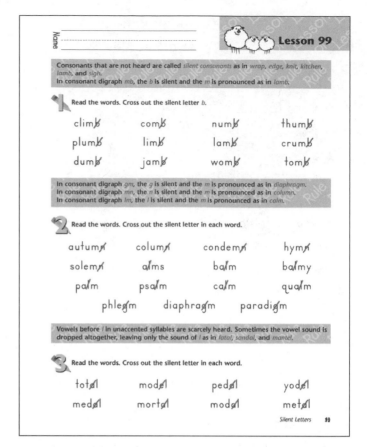

jamb, plumber. Help the student read the words in the activity. The student will cross out the silent letter in each word.

Words:
  clim**b**, com**b**, num**b**, thum**b**
  plum**b**, lim**b**, lam**b**, crum**b**
  dum**b**, jam**b**, wom**b**, tom**b**

Activity 2. Review the rule for silent **n** in the consonant digraph **mn**. Review the rule for silent **g** in the consonant digraph **gm**. Review the rule for silent **l** in the consonant digraph **lm**. There are not many words in these categories. *Words to teach the concept:* damn, hymnbook, balmy, becalm, calmly, Holm, napalm, overwhelm, apothegm. Help the student read the words in the activity. The student will cross out the silent letter in each word.

Words:
  autum**n**, colum**n**, condem**n**, hym**n**
  solem**n**, a**l**ms, ba**l**m, ba**l**my
  pa**l**m, psa**l**m, ca**l**m, qua**l**m
  phleg**m**, diaphrag**m**, paradig**m**

Note the silent **p** in *psalm*.

Horizons Phonics & Reading Grade 2 Teacher's Guide

Activity 3. Review the rule for silent vowel in the unaccented syllables that end in letter **l**. Other words to use as examples: credal (creedal), feudal, nodal, sandal, scandal, suicidal, tidal, vandal, dreidel, remodel, strudel, lintel, mantel, brutal, capital, dental, departmental, digital, fatal, fetal, frontal, fundamental, genital, gunmetal, horizontal, hospital, immortal, marital, mental, natal, orbital, oriental, ornamental, parental, petal, pivotal, portal, recital, skeletal, subtotal, vital. Help the student read the words in the activity. The student will cross out the silent letter in each word.

Words:

tot**a**l, mod**e**l, ped**a**l, yod**e**l
med**a**l, mort**a**l, mod**a**l, met**a**l

Activity 4. Review the rule for the spellings of the sounds of **z**. *Words to teach the concept:* present, season, poison, as, is, was, yours, days, choose, fuse, hose, noise, pleased, raise, rose, daisy, easy, noisy, pansy, rosy. Help the student read the words in the box. Instruct the student to sort the words by the sound that s makes and write them in the correct box. Read the words after they have been sorted.

Words:

Spelled se	Spelled s
tease	as
praise	music
close	odds
suppose	easy
please	news
those	busy
because	says
excuse	hers
rise	does
reserve	suds
berserk	eyes
cheese	result
wise	has
these	ours

Reading. Read and discuss the maxim for the Lesson.

Read the story *Becky (continued)*. This is another chapter of the *A Little Princess* story. Preview the story and explain words or sentence structures that are not familiar to the student. With every

story ask questions: who are the characters, what are they doing, what are they saying, where does the action take place, what is the order of events, what words are being used, what new information is given, what lesson can be learned?

Comprehension questions:
 What woke Becky up?
 What was Becky's reaction when she woke up?
 What surprised Becky the most about Sara's reaction?
 Why was Becky's stay in Sara's room like a dream?
 Was Sara able to complete her story for Becky?
 Why was Becky a different person when she went back downstairs?

Read the poems *A Frisky Lamb*, *The Lambkins* and *Ring Around the Rosy*. Preview the poems and explain words or sentence structures that are not familiar to the student.
 What are the rhyming words in the poems?
 What silent letter digraphs are used in the poems?

Assign. Lesson activities or reading that are to be completed as homework.

Lesson 100: Spellings of the j Sound

Overview:

- Auditory discrimination of the **j** and **g** sound
- Apply the rules to read words with hard and soft **g**
- Match words to pictures
- Identify the spelling of the **j** sound
- Sentence completion
- Read words with a **j** sound spelled with a **d**

Materials and Supplies:

- Teacher's Guide & Student Workbook 2
- White board or chalkboard
- Word cards (as necessary)
- Dictionary
- Reader: *A Little Princess & Other Classic Stories*

Teaching Tips:

Review for Mastery. Discuss and review any work from the previous lesson that was assigned as homework. Check for completion of the activities and orally quiz the student for comprehension. Review any reading that was assigned, discussing the characters, setting, plot, theme, language, sequence, etc.

Strengthen fluency and phonemic awareness by reviewing words and sentences from previous lessons. Build vocabulary skills by using some of the words in sentences.

Review the silent letters with Lesson 99, Activities 1-3. Have the student use the words in sentences.

Review the **z** sound of **s** with Lesson 99, Activity 4. Have the student use the words in sentences.

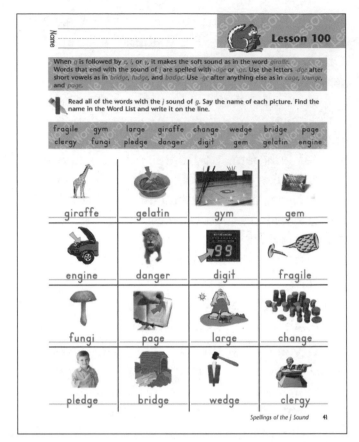

Activity 1. Review the rules for the spelling of the **g** sound in words. *Words to teach the concept:* gently, gypsy, germ, general, gesture, genius, region, original, oxygen, village, gingerly, hygiene, legion, religion, ecology, cage, cabbage, damage, fringe, hinge, page, stage, wage, budge, fudge, hedge, ledge, nudge, ridge. Assist the student in reading the words in the box. Help the student identify the pictures and print the correct word underneath each picture.

Pictures:
  **giraffe, gelatin, gym, gem
  engine, danger, digit, fragile
  fungi, page, large, change
  pledge, bridge, wedge, clergy**

Activity 2. Review the spelling rules for the **j** sound. Have the student read the words and circle the letter or letters that spell the **j** sound in each word. Then, for the words to which it applies, have the student write the vowel that follows the **g** and gives it the **j** sound.

Words:

gentle, e, huge, margin, i
package, logic, i, ginger, i & e
edge, giant, i, gyp, y
strange, stingy, y, badge
orange, dodge, energy, y

Activity 3. Help the student read the sentences and the base word. Instruct the student to select the correct word from Activity 2 that completes the sentence and write the word on the line. Unknown words can be looked up in a dictionary.

Sentences:

1. The huge horse was <u>gentle</u> to ride.
2. There was an orange in the <u>package</u>.
3. Some people eat <u>ginger</u> to give them energy.
4. The <u>margin</u> of the page is near the edge.
5. The thief ran to dodge the man with the <u>badge</u>.

Activity 4. Review the rule for the **j** sound that **d** has in some words and the example word. Have the student read the words using the pictures as clues.

Words:

deciduous, educate, gradual
individual, pendulum, procedure
schedule, graduate

Review for Test. The instructor should plan to use some time at the end of the class to review and prepare for the test that follows this lesson. Review the objectives for the test and then look over the lessons that it will cover. If the student has struggled with any of the concepts that will be included in the test, some additional drill, practice, or review may be needed to adequately prepare him for the test.

---

2 Read the words. Circle the letter or letters that spell the *j* sound. For some of the words, write the vowel on the line that follows the *g* and gives it the *j* sound.

gentle ___e___	huge _____	margin ___i___
package_____	logic ___i___	ginger ___i___ ___e___
edge _____	giant ___i___	gyp ___y___
strange_____	stingy ___y___	badge _____
orange _____	dodge _____	energy ___y___

3 Use the words above to complete the following sentences.

1. The huge horse was _____gentle_____ to ride.
2. There was an orange in the _____package_____ .
3. Some people eat _____ginger_____ to give them energy.
4. The _____margin_____ of the page is near the edge.
5. The thief ran to dodge the man with the _____badge_____ .

When *d* is followed by *u* in some words, it has the sound of *j* as in *education*.

4 Read these words with your teacher that have the *j* sound spelled as *d*.

deciduous   educate   gradual

individual   pendulum   procedure

schedule   graduate

41   *Spellings of the j Sound*

Reading. Read and discuss the maxim for the Lesson.

Read the story *The Diamond Mines*. This is another chapter of the *A Little Princess* story. Preview the story and explain words or sentence structures that are not familiar to the student. With every story ask questions: who are the characters, what are they doing, what are they saying, where does the action take place, what is the order of events, what words are being used, what new information is given, what lesson can be learned?

Comprehension questions:
What story was in Captain Crewe's letter?
What fortune did Captain Crewe seem to have?
What was one of Sara's "pretends?"
What usually took place after the day's lessons?

Assign. Lesson activities or reading that are to be completed as homework.

Test 10
Lessons 85-94

Overview:

- Auditory recognition of **k** and **s** sounds
- Spell words phonetically with both hard and soft **c** sounds
- Auditory recognition of short **e**, **o**, and **u** sounds with several spellings
- Read words with silent letters
- Identify silent letter digraphs
- Syllabication of double consonant words
- Select vowel spellings for words
- Read words with /**aw**/ digraph sound
- Match words with similar vowel sounds

Materials and Supplies:

- Teacher's Guide & Student Workbook 2

Instructions:

Assessment Start-up. Read through the test with the student. Help the student with any words that he may still be unsure of. The teacher should be available to answer any questions that the student may have during the test.

Activity 1. Review the instructions and the words in the list with the student. The student is to fill in the circle beside the correct phonetic spelling of each word.

Words:

accept	ak-sept
because	be-kause
success	suk-sess
vaccine	vak-sine
notice	no-tis
recess	re-sess
mercy	mer-se
certain	ser-tain

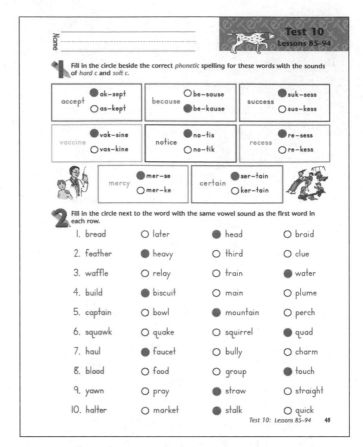

Activity 2. Review the words and the instructions with the student. The student is to fill in the circle beside the word with the sample vowel sound as the sample word.

Words:

1. bread	head
2. feather	heavy
3. waffle	water
4. build	biscuit
5. captain	mountain
6. squawk	quad
7. haul	faucet
8. blood	touch
9. yawn	straw
10. halter	stalk

Activity 3. Review the instruction with the student. Make sure the student can recognize the pictures and can read the words. The student is to underline the silent letter(s) in each word.

Words:

w̲rist, r̲hino, s̲c̲issor

p̲sal̲m, s̲word, w̲hooping crane

Activity 4. Review the instructions with the student. Make sure the student can identify the pictures. The student is to fill in the circle beside the vowel(s) that will correctly complete the word and write the letters on the line.

Words:

c̲aught, wh̲eat, th̲ought, wr̲apper

m̲easure, w̲allet, m̲oth, f̲awn

Assessment Follow-up. Every test is an important assessment of both the student's comprehension of the concepts and the instructional process. This makes follow-up after each test essential to the learning process. Review all of the errors made on the test with the student. Check for understanding of the concepts and of the problem instructions. Compare the errors made on the test to the test objectives to identify specific areas of weakness. If weak areas of understanding are detected it might be necessary to go back to those lessons to devise some enrichment activities for the concept.

The test results can be used to determine what concepts are reviewed during the daily time of classroom instruction. Devise enrichment activities that will provide development in those areas.

If time permits, choose a selection and have the student read it again. This can also be used as a catch-up time to complete unfinished selections.

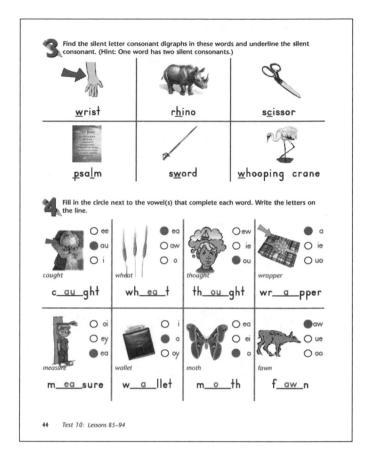

Lesson 101: Spellings of the f Sound

Overview:

- Auditory discrimination of the **f** sound
- Apply the rules to read words with consonant digraphs
- Match words to pictures
- Identify the spelling of the **f** sound
- Sentence completion
- Read words with a **f** sound spelled with **ph**, **gh**, or **lf**

Materials and Supplies:

- Teacher's Guide & Student Workbook 2
- White board or chalkboard
- Word cards (as necessary)
- Dictionary
- Reader: *A Little Princess & Other Classic Stories*

Teaching Tips:

Review for Mastery. Discuss and review any work from the previous lesson that was assigned as homework. Check for completion of the activities and orally quiz the student for comprehension. Review any reading that was assigned, discussing the characters, setting, plot, theme, language, sequence, etc.

Strengthen fluency and phonemic awareness by reviewing words and sentences from previous lessons. Build vocabulary skills by using some of the words in sentences.

Review the rules for the spelling of the **j** sound with Lesson 100, Activity 1. Have the student circle the letters of the words in Activity 1 that spell the **j** sound. Another activity would be to sort the words into lists by the spelling category and write them on the board or a sheet of paper.

Review spellings of the **j** sound with Lesson 100, Activity 3. Have the student circle the other words in the sentences with the **j** sound.

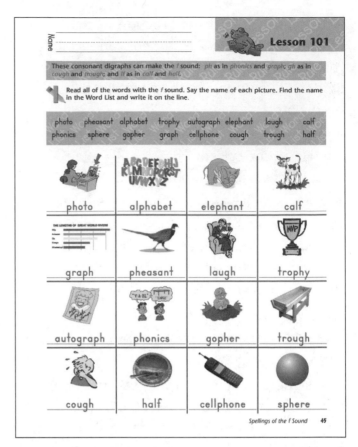

Activity 1. Review the rules for the spellings of the **f** sound. *Words to teach the concept:* physical, phase, phantom, phonetic, phoenix, orphan, sulphur, graphic, telephone, telegraph, triumph, laughter, roughhouse, toughen, calfskin, halfbaked. Assist the student in reading the words in the box. Help the student identify the pictures and print the correct word underneath each picture.

Pictures:
  **photo, alphabet, elephant, calf
  graph, pheasant, laugh, trophy
  autograph, phonics, gopher, trough
  cough, half, cellphone, sphere**

Activity 2. Assist the student as necessary in reading the words. Instruct the student to identify the consonant digraph in each word that makes the **f** sound. The student will write the digraph on the line.

Digraphs:

ph, ph, ph

gh, lf, ph

ph, ph, gh

lf, ph, ph

gh, lf, ph & ph

Activity 3. Instruct the student to select the word from Activity 2 that will correctly complete each sentence and write the word on the line. Unknown words can be looked up in a dictionary.

Sentences:

1. A road that is not smooth is <u>rough</u>
2. A man that is not weak is <u>tough</u>.
3. To run out of food is to not have <u>enough</u>.
4. A child with parents is not an <u>orphan</u>.
5. A concrete street is not made out of <u>asphalt</u>.

Activity 4. Help the student read the sentences. Instruct the student to identify and circle the digraphs in the words that make the **f** sound.

Sentences:

1. <u>Ph</u>ony <u>Ph</u>il can outlau<u>gh</u> his ne<u>ph</u>ew.
2. Ha<u>lf</u>back Mur<u>ph</u>y got a tro<u>ph</u>y at ha<u>lf</u>-time.
3. Rou<u>gh</u>neck Ral<u>ph</u> wrote a <u>ph</u>rase in a paragra<u>ph</u> with a hy<u>ph</u>en.
4. Tough Tony <u>ph</u>oned an or<u>ph</u>an in <u>Ph</u>oenix with a cell<u>ph</u>one.
5. Ha<u>lf</u>hearted <u>Ph</u>yllis has enou<u>gh</u> <u>ph</u>oto-gra<u>ph</u>s to fill the pam<u>ph</u>let.

Reading. Read and discuss the maxim for the Lesson.

Read the story *The Diamond Mines (continued)*. This is another chapter of the *A Little Princess*

story. Preview the story and explain words or sentence structures that are not familiar to the student. With every story ask questions: who are the characters, what are they doing, what are they saying, where does the action take place, what is the order of events, what words are being used, what new information is given, what lesson can be learned?

Comprehension questions:

What story was Sara reading?

Who started howling?

Who called Lottie a cry-baby?

What promise did Sara remind Lottie about?

Assign. Lesson activities or reading that are to be completed as homework.

Lesson 102: Silent Letters gh

Overview:

- Auditory discrimination of silent letters
- Apply the rules to read words with silent consonant digraphs
- Match words to pictures
- Identify the spelling of the silent letters
- Sort words by the silent letter spelling
- Read words with silent letters spelled **gh**

Materials and Supplies:

- Teacher's Guide & Student Workbook 2
- White board or chalkboard
- Word cards (as necessary)
- Dictionary
- Reader: *A Little Princess & Other Classic Stories*

Teaching Tips:

Review for Mastery. Discuss and review any work from the previous lesson that was assigned as homework. Check for completion of the activities and orally quiz the student for comprehension. Review any reading that was assigned, discussing the characters, setting, plot, theme, language, sequence, etc.

Strengthen fluency and phonemic awareness by reviewing words and sentences from previous lessons. Build vocabulary skills by using some of the words in sentences.

Review spellings of the **f** sound with Lesson 101, Activity 1. Sort the words by the spelling of the **f** sound, either **ph**, **lf**, or **gh**, on the board or a sheet of paper.

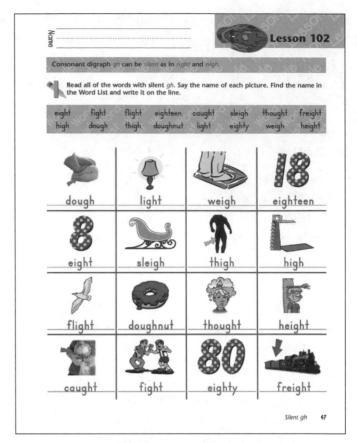

Activity 1. Review the rules for the silent letter spelling of **gh**. *Words to teach the concept:* aweigh, borough, neighborhood, nigh, slaughter, thorough, though, ought. Assist the student in reading the words in the box. Help the student identify the pictures and print the correct word underneath each picture.

Pictures:
  dough, light, weigh, eighteen
  eight, sleigh, thigh, high
  flight, doughnut, thought, height
  caught, fight, eighty, freight

Activity 2. Help the student read the sentences. Instruct the student to underline the silent **gh** consonant digraphs that they find in the words.

Sentences:
  1. That ni<u>gh</u>t the hi<u>gh</u> and mi<u>gh</u>ty were not in si<u>gh</u>t.
  2. Ei<u>gh</u>t dou<u>gh</u>nuts can be bou<u>gh</u>t for ei<u>gh</u>ty cents.
  3. I sou<u>gh</u>t for some li<u>gh</u>t to bri<u>gh</u>ten the ni<u>gh</u>t.

Horizons Phonics & Reading Grade 2 Teacher's Guide

Activity 2 continued:

4. The freighter brought the freight straight through the tight channel.
5. They caught the haughty and naughty neighbor who sought to fight.
6. My slight height and weight might change before I turn eighteen.
7. The sight of the high flight brought a sigh through the crowd.
8. Although the bright lightning crashed through the clouds, it also brought rain for the drought.
9. His right thigh might get tight from the fight.
10. She taught the bright daughter to read by sight.

Activity 3. Review the rule for the spellings of silent consonant digraph **gh**. Instruct the student to find words with the different spellings in Activity 2 and write them in the correct box. Read the words after they have been sorted.

Words: (Answers will vary.)

Silent gh	Silent gh with t
high	night
doughnuts	mighty

Reading. Read and discuss the maxim for the Lesson.

Read the story *The Diamond Mines (continued)*. This is another chapter of the *A Little Princess* story. Preview the story and explain words or sentence structures that are not familiar to the student. With every story ask questions: who are the characters, what are they doing, what are they saying, where does the action take place, what is the order of events, what words are being used, what new information is given, what lesson can be learned?

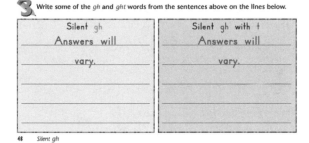

Comprehension questions:
  Who did Sara want to slap?
  Why didn't Sara slap anyone?
  What did Lavvy say that showed how she felt about Sara?
  What two meanings did the girls have when they called Sara a princess?
  Who told Sara about the rats in the attic?
  How was Sara helping Becky not to be so hungry?

Read the poem *Teddy and the Echo*. Preview the poem and explain words or sentence structures that are not familiar to the student.
  What is Teddy doing?
  What silent letter digraphs are used in the poem?
  What can Teddy never see?

Assign. Lesson activities or reading that are to be completed as homework.

Lesson 103: Review Silent Letters & Consonant Sounds

Overview:

- Auditory discrimination of silent letters
- Auditory discrimination of the **j** sound
- Auditory discrimination of the **f** sound
- Auditory discrimination of the **z** sound
- Apply the rules to read words with silent consonant digraphs
- Apply the rules to read words with the **ph** spelling of the **f** sound
- Apply the rules to read words with the different spellings of the **j** sound
- Identify spellings of the **j** sound
- Identify spellings of the **z** sound
- Identify silent letter spellings
- Identify spellings of the **f** sound
- Sort words by the silent letter spelling
- Read words with silent letters spelled **gh**

Materials and Supplies:

- Teacher's Guide & Student Workbook 2
- White board or chalkboard
- Word cards (as necessary)
- Dictionary
- Reader: *A Little Princess & Other Classic Stories*

Teaching Tips:

Review for Mastery. Discuss and review any work from the previous lesson that was assigned as homework. Check for completion of the activities and orally quiz the student for comprehension. Review any reading that was assigned, discussing the characters, setting, plot, theme, language, sequence, etc.

Strengthen fluency and phonemic awareness by reviewing words and sentences from previous lessons. Build vocabulary skills by using some of the words in sentences.

Review silent **gh** with Lesson 102, Activity 2. Ask the student to continue sorting the **gh** and

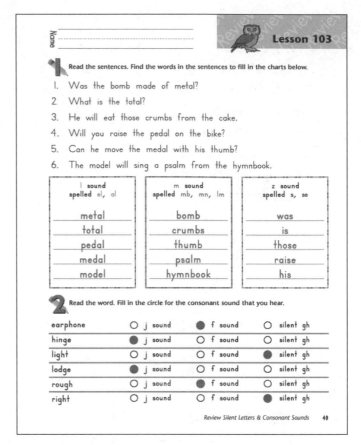

ght words from the activity as they did in Activity 3 on the board or a sheet of paper.

Review the silent letter and other rules from Lessons 99, 100, 101, and 102. Have the student write examples of the rules on the chalkboard or white board. Assist the student as needed in identifying the pictures or reading the words in the lesson.

Activity 1. Have the student read the sentences aloud. The student will find words in the sentences that fit the categories in the boxes and write them on the lines. It may help the student to go through the sentences and circle all words that have silent letters and words with the **z** sound before they do the sort.

Words:

l sound	m sound	z sound
metal	bomb	was
total	crumbs	is
pedal	thumb	those
medal	psalm	raise
model	hymnbook	his

Horizons Phonics & Reading Grade 2 Teacher's Guide

Activity 2. Review the words in the list. Help the student read any difficult words. The student is to determine if he hears a **j** or **f** sound in the word or if the word has silent letters. Instruct them to fill in the circle of their choice for each word.

Word	Sound
earphone	f sound
hinge	j sound
light	silent gh
lodge	j sound
rough	f sound
right	silent gh
fudge	j sound
germ	j sound
calfskin	f sound
schedule	j sound
through	silent gh
damage	j sound
enough	f sound
tough	f sound
ought	silent gh
halfbake	f sound
thought	silent gh
oxygen	j sound
nigh	silent gh
graphic	f sound
night	silent gh
pledge	j sound
cage	j sound
region	j sound
orphan	f sound
though	silent gh
high	silent gh
fought	silent gh
laughter	f sound
prophet	f sound

Reading. Read and discuss the maxim for the Lesson.

Read the story *The Diamond Mines (continued)*. This is another chapter of the *A Little Princess* story. Preview the story and explain words or sentence structures that are not familiar to the student. With every story ask questions: who are the characters, what are they doing, what

fudge	● j sound	○ f sound	○ silent gh
germ	● j sound	○ f sound	○ silent gh
calfskin	○ j sound	● f sound	○ silent gh
schedule	● j sound	○ f sound	○ silent gh
through	○ j sound	○ f sound	● silent gh
damage	● j sound	○ f sound	○ silent gh
enough	○ j sound	● f sound	○ silent gh
tough	○ j sound	● f sound	○ silent gh
ought	○ j sound	○ f sound	● silent gh
halfboke	○ j sound	● f sound	○ silent gh
thought	○ j sound	○ f sound	● silent gh
oxygen	● j sound	○ f sound	○ silent gh
nigh	○ j sound	○ f sound	● silent gh
graphic	○ j sound	● f sound	○ silent gh
night	○ j sound	○ f sound	● silent gh
pledge	● j sound	○ f sound	○ silent gh
cage	● j sound	○ f sound	○ silent gh
region	● j sound	○ f sound	○ silent gh
orphan	○ j sound	● f sound	○ silent gh
though	○ j sound	○ f sound	● silent gh
high	○ j sound	○ f sound	● silent gh
fought	○ j sound	○ f sound	● silent gh
laughter	○ j sound	● f sound	○ silent gh
prophet	○ j sound	● f sound	○ silent gh

50   *Review Silent Letters & Consonant Sounds*

are they saying, where does the action take place, what is the order of events, what words are being used, what new information is given, what lesson can be learned?

Comprehension questions:
  Who did Becky look forward to seeing every day?
  What had nature given to Sara?
  What did Sara's dad say was wrong with him in his letter?
  Why did Sara want the "last" doll?
  What in Sara's letter had cheered up Captain Crewe?
  Who left a package for Sara?
  Where had the card that Becky gave to Sara came from?

Assign. Lesson activities or reading that are to be completed as homework.

Lesson 104: Spellings of the sh Sound

Overview:

- Auditory discrimination of the **s** sound
- Auditory discrimination of the **sh** sound
- Apply the rules to read words with spellings of the **s** sound
- Apply the rules to read words with spellings of the **sh** sound
- Sort words by the **s** or **sh** sound

Materials and Supplies:

- Teacher's Guide & Student Workbook 2
- White board or chalkboard
- Word cards (as necessary)
- Dictionary
- Reader: *A Little Princess & Other Classic Stories*

Teaching Tips:

Review for Mastery. Discuss and review any work from the previous lesson that was assigned as homework. Check for completion of the activities and orally quiz the student for comprehension. Review any reading that was assigned, discussing the characters, setting, plot, theme, language, sequence, etc.

Strengthen fluency and phonemic awareness by reviewing words and sentences from previous lessons. Build vocabulary skills by using some of the words in sentences.

Review silent letters with Lesson 103, Activities 1-3. Read the lists of words again. It is important that the student recognize the spelling of the silent letters and pronounce the words correctly.

Activity 1. Review the rule for the spellings of the **sh** sound and the examples. Have the student write examples of the rule on the chalkboard or white board. *Words to teach the concept:* artificial, delicious, judicial, optician, politician, technician,

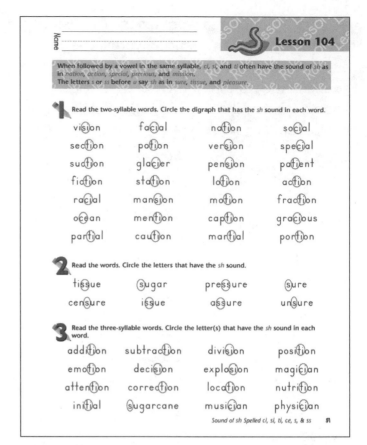

Sound of sh Spelled ci, si, ti, ce, s, & ss **51**

abrasion, discussion, erosion, illusion, occasion, percussion, television, cautious, convention, creation, devotion, digestion, direction, donation, eviction, inflation, petition, reception, relation, rotation, salvation, sensation, situation, taxation, vacation, ocean, essential, initials, potential, spatial. Have the student read the words aloud. The student will circle the digraph in each word that makes the **sh** sound.

Words:

vi**si**on, fa**ci**al, na**ti**on, so**ci**al
sec**ti**on, po**ti**on, ver**si**on, spe**ci**al
suc**ti**on, gla**ci**er, pen**si**on, pa**ti**ent
fic**ti**on, sta**ti**on, lo**ti**on, ac**ti**on
ra**ci**al, man**si**on, mo**ti**on, frac**ti**on
o**ce**an, men**ti**on, cap**ti**on, gra**ci**ous
par**ti**al, cau**ti**on, mar**ti**al, por**ti**on

Note that some of the **si** words have a **/zh/** sound but they are commonly placed into this category.

Activity 2. Review the rule for the **s** or **ss** spelling of the **sh** sound and the examples. Have the student read the words aloud. The

Horizons Phonics & Reading Grade 2 Teacher's Guide

student will circle the letter or letters in each word that makes the **sh** sound.

Words:

ti<u>ss</u>ue, <u>s</u>ugar, pre<u>ss</u>ure, <u>s</u>ure
cen<u>s</u>ure, i<u>ss</u>ue, a<u>ss</u>ure, un<u>s</u>ure

Activity 3. Have the student read the words aloud. The student will circle the digraph or letter in each word that makes the **sh** sound.

Words:

addi<u>ti</u>on, subtrac<u>ti</u>on, divi<u>si</u>on, posi<u>ti</u>on
emo<u>ti</u>on, deci<u>si</u>on, explo<u>si</u>on, magi<u>ci</u>an
atten<u>ti</u>on, correc<u>ti</u>on, loca<u>ti</u>on, nutri<u>ti</u>on
ini<u>ti</u>al, <u>s</u>ugarcane, musi<u>ci</u>an, physi<u>ci</u>an

Note that some of the **si** words have a **/zh/** sound but they are commonly placed into this category.

Activity 4. Review the rules for the spellings of the **s** sound and the **sh** sound. Instruct the student to sort the words and write them in the correct box. Read the words after they have been sorted.

Words:

Sound of s	Sound of sh
secret	special
certain	ocean
sentence	mission
city	pressure
sound	social
once	station
seesaw	partial
since	action
sample	sugar
pencil	tissue
single	motion
voice	nation
summer	vision
address	passion
across	session

Reading. Read and discuss the maxim for the Lesson.

Read the story *A Change of Fortune*. This is another chapter of the *A Little Princess* story.

4 Read the words. Sort the words by the *s* sound in each word. Some have both sounds, so put them in the *sh* group.

secret	mission	once	action	single	address
special	city	station	sample	motion	vision
certain	pressure	seesaw	sugar	voice	across
ocean	sound	partial	pencil	summer	passion
sentence	social	since	tissue	nation	session

Sound of s	Sound of sh
secret	special
certain	ocean
sentence	mission
city	pressure
sound	social
once	station
seesaw	partial
since	action
sample	sugar
pencil	tissue
single	motion
voice	nation
summer	vision
address	passion
across	session

51   Sound of sh Spelled ci, si, ti, ce, s, & ss

Preview the story and explain words or sentence structures that are not familiar to the student. With every story ask questions: who are the characters, what are they doing, what are they saying, where does the action take place, what is the order of events, what words are being used, what new information is given, what lesson can be learned?

Comprehension questions:

Who led the parade into the classroom?
Who forgot herself in the excitement of the parade?
Who was asked to stay in the room while the presents were opened?
What excuse did Miss Minchin give for why Becky should not be allowed to remain in the room?
Where was Becky asked to stand?
How did Miss Minchin treat Sara like she was a princess?

Assign. Lesson activities or reading that are to be completed as homework.

Lesson 105: Spellings of the n Sound

Overview:

- Auditory discrimination of the n sound
- Apply the rules to read words with Ghost Letter digraphs
- Read words using picture clues
- Code silent letters
- Complete sentences
- Sort words by the **s** or **sh** sound

Materials and Supplies:

- Teacher's Guide & Student Workbook 2
- White board or chalkboard
- Word cards (as necessary)
- Dictionary
- Reader: *A Little Princess & Other Classic Stories*

Teaching Tips:

Review for Mastery. Discuss and review any work from the previous lesson that was assigned as homework. Check for completion of the activities and orally quiz the student for comprehension. Review any reading that was assigned, discussing the characters, setting, plot, theme, language, sequence, etc.

Strengthen fluency and phonemic awareness by reviewing words and sentences from previous lessons. Build vocabulary skills by using some of the words in sentences.

Review the **sh** digraphs with Lesson 104, Activity 1. Underline the vowel that follows the digraph in each word.

Review the **sh** digraphs with Lesson 104, Activity 2. Underline the **u** that follows the letters **s** and **ss**.

Review the silent letter and other rules from Lessons 99, 100, 101, and 102. Have the student write examples of the rules on the chalkboard or white board. Assist the student as needed in identifying the pictures or reading the words in the lesson.

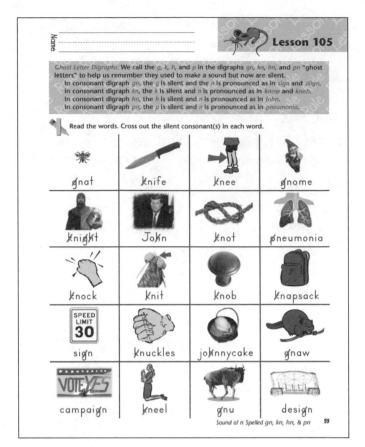

Review sounds of **s** with Lesson 104, Activities 1-3. Read the lists of words again. It is important that the student recognize the spelling of the **s** or **sh** sound and pronounce the words correctly. Use the words in sentences.

Activity 1. Review the rules for the silent letter spelling of **n** and the examples. *Words to teach the concept:* knack, knave, knelt, knitting, knoll, knowledge, known, arraign, foreign, gnarled, lasagna, malign, johnboat, Rohn, pneumonia. Help the student identify the pictures and read the word underneath each picture. Have the student cross out the silent letter(s) in each words.

Pictures:
  gnat, k̲nife, k̲nee, gnome
  k̲nig̲ht, John, k̲not, p̲neumonia
  k̲nock, k̲nit, k̲nob, k̲napsack
  sign, k̲nuckles, johnnycake, gnaw
  campaign, k̲neel, gnu, design

Horizons Phonics & Reading Grade 2 Teacher's Guide

Activity 2. Read the words in the box. Read each sentence. Instruct the student to select the word that will correctly complete each sentence and write the word on the line. Unknown words can be looked up in a dictionary.

Sentences:

Tie a <u>knot</u> in the rope.
I <u>know</u> how to fix the toy.
The king had a long <u>reign</u>.
The man was from a <u>foreign</u> country.
Our teacher will <u>assign</u> homework.
He will <u>kneel</u> to pet the cat.
The boy <u>knew</u> who broke the window.
She will <u>align</u> the tops of the pictures.
You can ask <u>John</u> to carry the bag.
He has <u>knowledge</u> about many things.
A <u>gnat</u> is a small insect.
The price of the dress is on the <u>sign</u>.

Activity 3. Review the spelling rules for the **kn** Ghost Letter digraph. The student will write words with the initial **n** sound from the words endings that are given. Read the words.

Words:

knew, knight, know, knot
knit, knock, knap, knob

Activity 4. Review the spelling rules for the **gn** Ghost Letter digraph. The student will write words with the **gn** digraph from the words endings that are given. Read the words in the first row. Read the words written by the student. Compare the sound and the spelling of the words.

Words:

sign, arraign, campaign, reign

Reading. Read and discuss the maxim for the Lesson.

Read the story *A Change of Fortune (continued)*. This is another chapter of the *A Little Princess* story. Preview the story and explain words or sentence structures that are not familiar to the student. With every story ask questions: who are the characters, what are they doing, what are they saying, where does the action take place, what is the order of events, what words are being used, what new information is given, what lesson can be learned?

Comprehension questions:

What happened when Miss Minchin left the room?
How was the Last Doll dressed?
What extra things did the Last Doll have?
Why did the girls leave the room?
What delayed Becky's leaving from the room?
Who had came to see Miss Minchin?
What had the lawyer come to tell Miss Minchin?

Assign. Lesson activities or reading that are to be completed as homework.

2 Complete the sentences with a *silent* letter word.

Tie a ____knot____ in the rope.
I ____know____ how to fix the toy.
The king had a long ____reign____.

[box: know, knot, reign]

The man was from a ____foreign____ country.
Our teacher will ____assign____ homework.
He will ____kneel____ to pet the cat.

[box: kneel, assign, foreign]

The boy ____knew____ who broke the window.
She will ____align____ the tops of the pictures.
You can ask ____John____ to carry the bag.

[box: knew, John, align]

He has ____knowledge____ about many things.
A ____gnat____ is a small insect.
The price of the dress is on the ____sign____.

[box: sign, knowledge, gnat]

3 Read these words. Add a silent *k* to these words to make new words and read them.

_k_new   _k_night   _k_now   _k_not
_k_nit   _k_nock   _k_nap   _k_nob

4 Read these words. Write a silent *g* on the blanks to make new words and read them.

sine   rain   pain   rein
si_g_n   arrai_g_n   campai_g_n   rei_g_n

54   *Sound of n Spelled gn, kn, hn, & pn*

Lesson 106: Spellings of the t Sound

Overview:

- Auditory discrimination of the **t** sound
- Apply the rules to read words with Ghost Letter digraphs
- Match words to pictures
- Identify words with silent letters
- Sort words by the spelling of the **t** sound

Materials and Supplies:

- Teacher's Guide & Student Workbook 2
- White board or chalkboard
- Word cards (as necessary)
- Phonics rules flashcards
- Dictionary
- Reader: *A Little Princess & Other Classic Stories*

Teaching Tips:

Review for Mastery. Discuss and review any work from the previous lesson that was assigned as homework. Check for completion of the activities and orally quiz the student for comprehension. Review any reading that was assigned, discussing the characters, setting, plot, theme, language, sequence, etc.

Strengthen fluency and phonemic awareness by reviewing words and sentences from previous lessons. Build vocabulary skills by using some of the words in sentences.

Review silent letter digraphs with Lesson 105, Activity 1. Sort the words by the spelling of the silent letter digraph on the board or a sheet of paper.

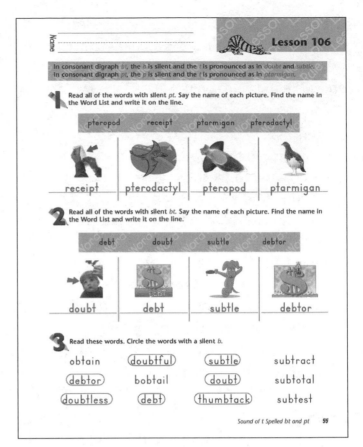

Activity 1. Review the rule for the silent letter spelling of t and the examples. Assist the student in reading the words in the box. Help the student identify the pictures and print the correct word underneath each picture.

Pictures:

receipt, pterodactyl, pteropod, ptarmigan

Activity 2. Review the rule for the silent letter spelling of **t** and the examples. Assist the student in reading the words in the box. Help the student identify the pictures and print the correct word underneath each picture.

Pictures:

doubt, debt, subtle, debtor

Activity 3. Have the student read the words in each row aloud. The student will circle the words with a silent **b**.

Words:
doub**tful, su**b**tle
de**b**tor, dou**b**t
dou**b**tless, de**b**t, thum**b**tack**

Note: The word *thumbtack* is a review of digraph **mb** from Lesson 99.

Activity 4. Have the student read the words in each row aloud. The student will circle the words with a silent **p**.

Words:
  p̲teropod, recei̲p̲ts
  p̲terodactyl, p̲tarmigan
  recei̲p̲t, p̲teropods

Activity 5. Review the rules for the spellings of the **t** sound. Instruct the student to sort the words and write them in the correct box. Read the words after they have been sorted.

Words:

Sound of t	t after a silent letter
water	debt
sentence	doubt
after	receipt
until	ptarmigan
city	debtor
into	subtle
today	pterodactyl
table	doubter
later	pteropod

Reading. Read and discuss the maxim for the Lesson.

Read the story *A Change of Fortune (continued)*. This is another chapter of the *A Little Princess* story. Preview the story and explain words or sentence structures that are not familiar to the student. With every story ask questions: who are the characters, what are they doing, what are they saying, where does the action take place, what is the order of events, what words are being used, what new information is given, what lesson can be learned?

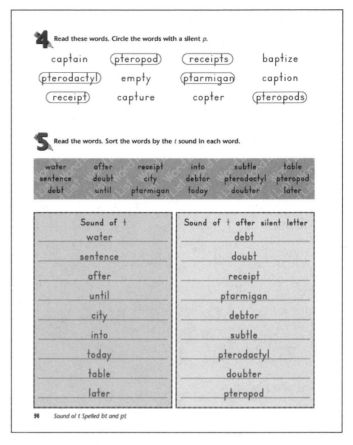

4 Read these words. Circle the words with a silent *p*.

captain (pteropod) (receipts) baptize
(pterodactyl) empty (ptarmigan) caption
(receipt) capture copter (pteropods)

5 Read the words. Sort the words by the *t* sound in each word.

water after receipt into subtle table
sentence doubt city debtor pterodactyl pteropod
debt until ptarmigan today doubter later

Sound of t	Sound of t after silent letter
water	debt
sentence	doubt
after	receipt
until	ptarmigan
city	debtor
into	subtle
today	pterodactyl
table	doubter
later	pteropod

98 *Sound of t Spelled bt and pt*

Comprehension questions:
  What had happened to Captain Crewe's fortune?
  How much money had Captain Crewe left for Sara?
  Who was going to have to bear the expense for the party?
  What did the lawyer recommend that Miss Minchin do with Sara?
  What did Miss Minchin do right after the lawyer left?

Assign. Lesson activities or reading that are to be completed as homework.

Lesson 107: Sounds of ex-

Overview:

- Auditory discrimination of the **ek**, **ek-s**, **ek-z**, **eg-z**, and **eks** sound
- Apply the rules to read words with **ex** spelling
- Match words to pictures
- Auditory discrimination of the **z** and **s** sound
- Auditory discrimination of the **g** and **k** sound

Materials and Supplies:

- Teacher's Guide & Student Workbook 2
- White board or chalkboard
- Word cards (as necessary)
- Phonics rules flashcards
- Dictionary
- Reader: *A Little Princess & Other Classic Stories*

Teaching Tips:

Review for Mastery. Discuss and review any work from the previous lesson that was assigned as homework. Check for completion of the activities and orally quiz the student for comprehension. Review any reading that was assigned, discussing the characters, setting, plot, theme, language, sequence, etc.

Strengthen fluency and phonemic awareness by reviewing words and sentences from previous lessons. Build vocabulary skills by using some of the words in sentences.

Review silent letter digraphs with Lesson 106, Activities 1 & 2. Read the words again and use them in sentences.

Activity 1. Review the rule for the **ex** spelling with an **s** sound and the examples. The **ex** in these words has an **ek** sound that is followed by either an **s** or **z** sound. *Words to teach the concept:* excavate, excellent, exception, excess, execute, exodus, exorcism, expedition, expiration, expanse, experience, experiment, explorer, export, expression, expresso

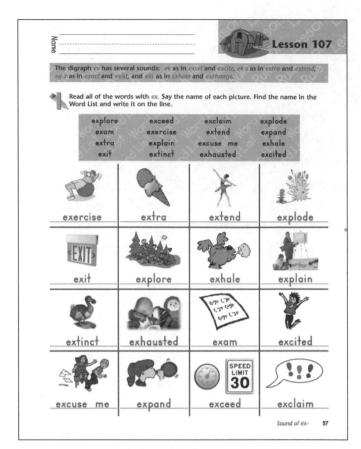

(espresso), extension, exterior, exactly, exaggerate, exalt, executive, exempt, existence, exile, exchange. There are several sounds heard in these words that will not be covered at this time. The next activity will practice the auditory discrimination of some of these sounds. Assist the student in reading the words in the box. Help the student identify the pictures and print the correct word underneath each picture.

Pictures:

    exercise, extra, extend, explode
    exit, explore, exhale, explain
    extinct, exhausted, exam, excited
    excuse me , expand, exceed, exclaim

Note: Help the student with the words of more than two syllables used in this activity (*exercise, exhausted, excited*).

Activity 2. Review the **ex** sound as heard in the word *deck* (sound it out as **d-eck**). Focus on the /ek/ sound which is the sound heard at the beginning of the words in this group. Review the sound of a soft **c**. Read the words in the first group with the **ek-s** sound. Review the **ex** sound as heard at the end of the word *beg* (sound it out as **b-eg**). Focus on the /**eg**/ sound which is the sound heard at the beginning of the words in this group. Review the **z** sound. Read the words in the second group with the **eg-z** sound. Review the **ex** sound as heard at the end of the word *neck* (sound it out as **n-eck**). Focus on the /**ek**/ sound which is the sound heard at the beginning of the words in this group. Review the **s** sound. Read the words in the third group with the **ek-s** sound.

Note: Help the student with the words of more than two syllables used in this activity (*excited, example, examine, exercise*).

Activity 3. Have the student read the word in each box aloud. The student will choose whether he hears the **s**, **z**, **g**, or **k** sound in each word and fill in the circle. This is a review of Activity 2 which can be used for reference in selecting the sounds for this activity.

Words:

Sound of s	Sound of z
extra	exam
expert	exist
expect	exact
extend	exert

Sound of g	Sound of k
exist	explore
examine	explain
exact	extreme
example	expand

Note: The student can refer back to the other activities in this lesson for help in determining the sound heard in each word.

Reading. Read and discuss the maxim for the Lesson.

Read the story *A Change of Fortune (continued)*. This is another chapter of the *A Little Princess* story. Preview the story and explain words or sentence structures that are not familiar to the student. With every story ask questions: who

are the characters, what are they doing, what are they saying, where does the action take place, what is the order of events, what words are being used, what new information is given, what lesson can be learned?

Comprehension questions:

What clothing did Miss Minchin ask Miss Amy about to see if it was in Sara's wardrobe?

What was wrong with the dress?

Who was sent to tell Sara that her father was dead?

Who had heard the conversation with the lawyer?

How did Becky make Miss Minchin feel?

Read the poem *The Man in the Tub*. Preview the poem and explain words or sentence structures that are not familiar to the student.

Comprehension questions:

What did the man in the tub tell the king?

What **ex** word is used in the poem?

Assign. Lesson activities or reading that are to be completed as homework.

Lesson 108: Review Letters & Sounds

Overview:

- Auditory discrimination of the **sh** sound
- Auditory discrimination of the **ek** and **eg** sound
- Apply the rules to read words with **ci**, **si**, and **ti** spelling of the **sh** sound
- Read sentences
- Identify words with the **sh** sound
- Apply the rules to read words with Ghost Letter digraphs
- Identify words with silent letters
- Sort words by letter sound

Materials and Supplies:

- Teacher's Guide & Student Workbook 2
- White board or chalkboard
- Word cards (as necessary)
- Phonics rules flashcards
- Dictionary
- Reader: *A Little Princess & Other Classic Stories*

Teaching Tips:

Review for Mastery. Discuss and review any work from the previous lesson that was assigned as homework. Check for completion of the activities and orally quiz the student for comprehension. Review any reading that was assigned, discussing the characters, setting, plot, theme, language, sequence, etc.

Strengthen fluency and phonemic awareness by reviewing words and sentences from previous lessons. Build vocabulary skills by using some of the words in sentences.

Review the **ex** digraph with Lesson 107, Activities 1-3. Read these words several more times with a focus on the consonant sounds made by the **ex** digraph. This requires a very high level of phonics skill to properly pronounce the words.

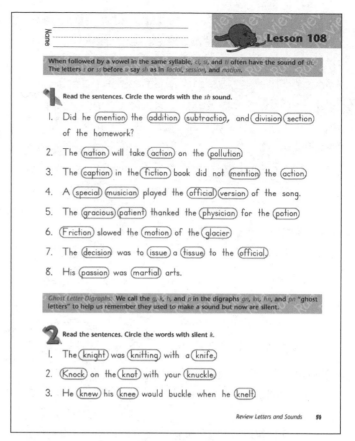

Activity 1. Review the rules for the spellings of the **sh** sound. Ask the student for examples to write on the board. Have the student read the sentences aloud. The student will circle the words with the **sh** sound.

Sentences:
1. Did he <u>mention</u> the <u>addition</u>, <u>subtraction</u>, and <u>division</u> <u>section</u> of the homework?
2. The <u>nation</u> will take <u>action</u> on the <u>pollution</u>.
3. The <u>caption</u> in the <u>fiction</u> book did not <u>mention</u> the <u>action</u>.
4. A <u>special</u> <u>musician</u> played the <u>official</u> <u>version</u> of the song.
5. The <u>gracious</u> <u>patient</u> thanked the <u>physician</u> for the <u>potion</u>.
6. <u>Friction</u> slowed the <u>motion</u> of the <u>glacier</u>.
7. The <u>decision</u> was to <u>issue</u> a <u>tissue</u> to the <u>official</u>.
8. His <u>passion</u> was <u>martial</u> arts.

Note that some of the **si** words have a /zh/ sound but they are commonly placed into this category.

Activity 2. Review the rule for the Ghost Letter digraphs. Have the student read the sentences aloud. The student will circle the words with silent **k**.

Sentences:
1. The <u>knight</u> was <u>knitting</u> with a <u>knife</u>.
2. <u>Knock</u> on the <u>knot</u> with your <u>knuckle</u>.
3. He <u>knew</u> his <u>knee</u> would buckle when he <u>knelt</u>.

Activity 3. Review the rules for silent letters and the spellings of the **ek** and **eg** sound. Ask the student for examples to write on the board. Instruct the student to sort the words and write them in the correct box. Read the words after they have been sorted.

Words:

Silent Letters	ek or eg Sound
gnash	exit
design	exist
know	exhale
known	expert
assign	example
knock	except
John	explode
sign	explain
gnaw	expel
knuckle	extra
doubt	exceed

Reading. Read and discuss the maxim for the Lesson.

Read the story *A Change of Fortune (continued)*. This is another chapter of the *A Little Princess* story. Preview the story and explain words or sentence structures that are not familiar to the student. With every story ask questions: who are the characters, what are they doing, what are they saying, where does the action take place, what is the order of events, what words are being used, what new information is given, what lesson can be learned?

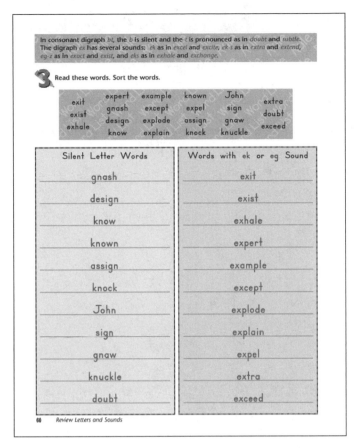

Comprehension questions:
What had happened to the party decorations and food?
How did Sara react when she was told that her father was dead?
Who had helped Sara put on the black dress?
What was Sara going to have to do?
What did Miss Minchin say Sara was when she said she was an orphan?
Who got the Last Doll?

Assign. Lesson activities or reading that are to be completed as homework.

Lesson 109: Alphabetical Order 2nd Letter

Overview:

- Recall the order of the letters in the alphabet
- Write words in alphabetical order
- Determine if words have been written in alphabetical order
- Write words in alphabetical order by the 2nd letter

Materials and Supplies:

- Teacher's Guide & Student Workbook 2
- White board or chalkboard
- Word cards (as necessary)
- Dictionary
- Reader: *A Little Princess & Other Classic Stories*

Teaching Tips:

Review for Mastery. Discuss and review any work from the previous lesson that was assigned as homework. Check for completion of the activities and orally quiz the student for comprehension. Review any reading that was assigned, discussing the characters, setting, plot, theme, language, sequence, etc.

Strengthen fluency and phonemic awareness by reviewing words and sentences from previous lessons. Build vocabulary skills by using some of the words in sentences.

Review spellings for the **sh** sound with Lesson 108, Activity 1. Have the student identify the spelling of the **sh** sound heard in each word. Sort the words into lists on the board or a sheet of paper.

Review the Ghost Letter digraphs with Lesson 108, Activity 2. Have the student code the silent letters.

Review silent letter digraphs and the **ex** digraph with Lesson 108, Activity 3. Have the student code the silent letters in the first list. Have the student determine whether the words in the second list say the **ek** or **eg-z** sound. They can sort the words on the board or a sheet of paper.

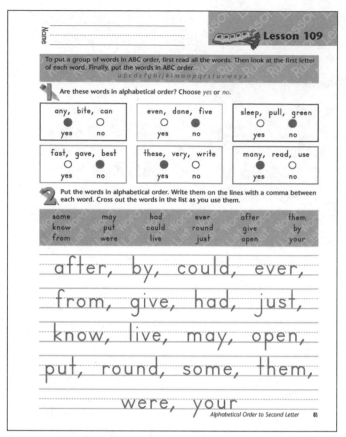

Go over the rule for alphabetical order. Write some practice lists on the board. Help the student number the words in alphabetical order by asking "Which word is first?" Ask the student why that word is first (because it starts with the letter that is closest to the beginning of the alphabet). Proceed in this manner through all the words in the list until the student has correctly alphabetized them all. Make word cards as necessary.

Review the letters of the alphabet. Have the student give you some words at random to write on the board. Have the student write the words in alphabetical order.

Activity 1. Help the student read the word choices. Instruct the student fill in the circle to answer whether the words are in alphabetical order or not.

Answers:
 yes, no, no
 no, yes, yes

Activity 2. Have the student read the words from the list aloud. The student will write the words in alphabetic order on the lines. Instruct the student to look for words that start with letter **a** first, then **b**, then **c**, etc.

Alphabetical Order:

> **after, by, could, ever, from, give, had, just, know, live, may, open, put, round, some, them, were, your**

Activity 3. Have the student read the words in each list aloud. The student will write the words in alphabetic order on the lines. Instruct the student to look at the second letter of the words because all of the words in each list have the same first letter. Look at the second letter for **a** first, then **b**, then **c**, etc.

Alphabetical Order:

about	call
again	check
always	clean
any	could
around	crack
ask	cut
walk	gave
were	give
when	gleam
wish	going
work	green
write	guard

> **take, tell, thank, tight, today, try**
> **dark, desk, dime, does, draw, dunk**

Reading. Read and discuss the maxim for the Lesson.

Read the story *A Change of Fortune (continued)*. This is another chapter of the *A Little Princess* story. Preview the story and explain words or sentence structures that are not familiar to the student. With every story ask questions: who

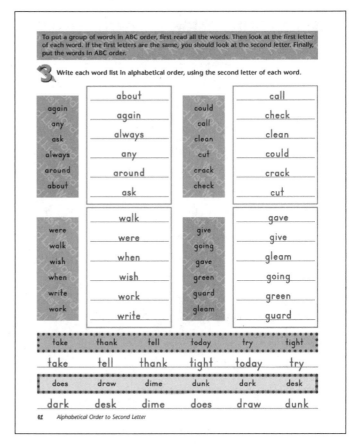

are the characters, what are they doing, what are they saying, where does the action take place, what is the order of events, what words are being used, what new information is given, what lesson can be learned?

Comprehension questions:
   What would Miss Minchin have liked to see Sara do?
   What brought a gleam to Sara's eye?
   Why did Miss Minchin say she needed to be thanked?
   Where was Sara's new room?
   What did Sara's new room look like?
   Who was the first person that came to see Sara in her attic room?

Assign. Lesson activities or reading that are to be completed as homework.

Lesson 110: Alphabetical Order 3rd Letter

Overview:

- Recall the order of the letters in the alphabet
- Write words in alphabetical order
- Determine if words have been written in alphabetical order
- Write words in alphabetical order by the 2nd letter
- Write words in alphabetical order by the 3rd letter

Materials and Supplies:

- Teacher's Guide & Student Workbook 2
- White board or chalkboard
- Word cards (as necessary)
- Dictionary
- Reader: *A Little Princess & Other Classic Stories*

Teaching Tips:

Review for Mastery. Discuss and review any work from the previous lesson that was assigned as homework. Check for completion of the activities and orally quiz the student for comprehension. Review any reading that was assigned, discussing the characters, setting, plot, theme, language, sequence, etc.

Strengthen fluency and phonemic awareness by reviewing words and sentences from previous lessons. Build vocabulary skills by using some of the words in sentences.

Review the letters of the alphabet. Have the student give you some words that start with the same letter to write on the board. Have the student write the words in alphabetical order.

Go over the rule. Write some practice lists on the chalkboard or white board. Help the student number the words in alphabetical order by asking "Which word is first?" Ask the student why that word is first (because it starts with the letter that is closest to the beginning

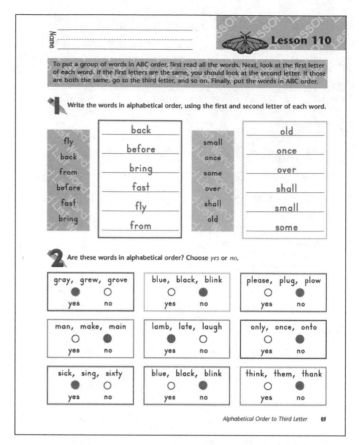

of the alphabet). Proceed in this manner through all the words in the list until the student has correctly alphabetized them all. Make word cards as necessary.

Activity 1. Have the student read the words in each list aloud. The student will write the words in alphabetic order on the lines. Instruct the student to look at the first letters and find the words that have the same first letter. Then look at the second letters and write them in alphabetical order on the lines.

Alphabetical Order:

back	old
before	once
bring	over
fast	shall
fly	small
from	some

Activity 2. Help the student read the word choices. In these words the first 2 letters in each group are the same. The student must look at the 3rd letter to determine if the words are in alphabetical order. Instruct the student fill in the circle to answer whether the words are in alphabetical order or not.

Answers:

yes, no, no
no, yes, no
yes, no, no

Activity 3. Have the student read the words in each list aloud. The student will write the words from each list in alphabetic order on the lines. Instruct the student to look at the second letter of the words and then the third letters. Look at the third letter for **a** first, then **b**, then **c**, etc. The student can use scratch paper to work with the words.

Alphabetical Order:

very	fall
which	far
why	fast
work	first
would	five
write	full
shall	grape
show	green
sing	money
sit	moose
small	ribbon
their	right

pick, pray, pride, prove, pull, put
brake, crash, dream, frame, grape, train

Review for Test. The instructor should plan to use some time at the end of the class to review and prepare for the test that follows this lesson. Review the objectives for the test and then look over the lessons that it will cover. If the student has struggled with any of the concepts that will be included in the test, some additional drill, practice, or review may be needed to adequately prepare him for the test.

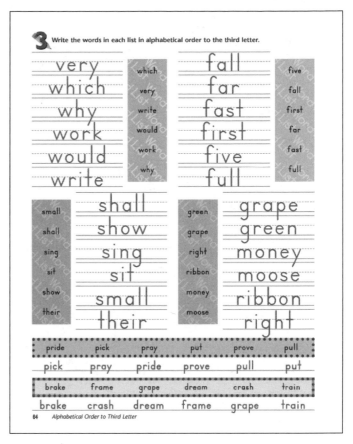

Reading. Read and discuss the maxim for the Lesson.

Read the story *In the Attic*. This is another chapter of the *A Little Princess* story. Preview the story and explain words or sentence structures that are not familiar to the student. With every story ask questions: who are the characters, what are they doing, what are they saying, where does the action take place, what is the order of events, what words are being used, what new information is given, what lesson can be learned?

Comprehension questions:
What did Sara keep thinking about as she tried to sleep her first night in the attic?
What sounds were heard in the attic room during the night?
How soon did Sara's new life begin?
Why did Sara try to be silent when corrected?
What teaching responsibilities did Sara have?
How did the other students begin to treat Sara?

Assign. Lesson activities or reading that are to be completed as homework.

Test 11
Lessons 95-104

Overview:

- Auditory recognition of **k**, **s**, **j**, and **g** sounds
- Identify spellings of the **k**, **s**, **j**, and **g** sounds
- Identify silent letter digraphs
- Auditory recognition of silent letters
- Read words with silent letters
- Auditory recognition of the **f** sound
- Identify spellings of the **f** sound
- Auditory recognition of the **sh** sound
- Recognize spellings of the **sh** sound

Materials and Supplies:

- Teacher's Guide & Student Workbook 2

Instructions:

Assessment Start-up. Read through the test with the student. Help the student with any words that he is still unsure of. The teacher should be available to answer any questions that the student may have during the test.

Activity 1. Review the instructions, the pictures, and the words with the student. Instruct the student to fill in the circle for the sound that the underlined letters make in each word.

Words:

sa<u>ck</u> – k	e<u>d</u>ucate – j	<u>g</u>uard – g	in<u>s</u>ide – s
hus<u>k</u> – k	<u>g</u>entle – j	croo<u>k</u> – k	gara<u>g</u>e – g
see<u>s</u>aw – s	musi<u>c</u> – k	we<u>dg</u>e – j	<u>g</u>iant – j
cler<u>g</u>y – j	stri<u>ke</u> – k	pa<u>g</u>e – j	sta<u>ck</u> – k

Activity 2. Make sure the students understand the instructions and can read the words. The student will draw a slash though the silent letter in each word.

Words:
> thumb, palm, comb, calm
> autumn, dough, hymn, light
> total, paradigm, model, high

Activity 3. Make sure the students understand the instructions and can read the words. The student will underline the letters in the words that make the **f** sound.

Words:
> gopher, calf, cellphone, trough
> cough, photo, half, phonics

Activity 4. Make sure the students understand the instructions and can read the words. The student will circle the words where he hears the **sh** sound.

Words:
> tissue, mission
> special, sugar
> action, sure, ocean
> nation, social, addition

Assessment Follow-up. Every test is an important assessment of both the student's comprehension of the concepts and the instructional process. This makes follow-up after each test essential to the learning process. Review all of the errors made on the test with the student. Check for understanding of the concepts and of the problem instructions. Compare the errors made on the test to the test objectives to identify specific areas of weakness. If weak areas of understanding are detected it might be necessary to go back to those lessons to devise some enrichment activities for the concept.

The test results can be used to determine what concepts are reviewed during the daily time of classroom instruction. Devise enrichment activities that will provide development in those areas.

If time permits, choose a selection and have the student read it again. This can also be used as a catch-up time to complete unfinished selections.

Lesson 111: Inflected Ending -es, Change y to i

Overview:

- Write singular words as plurals
- Apply the Sibilant Rule to read plural words
- Apply the Vowel Followed by **y** Rule to make singular words plural
- Apply the Consonant Followed by **y** Rule to make singular words plural
- Complete sentences

Materials and Supplies:

- Teacher's Guide & Student Workbook 2
- White board or chalkboard
- Word cards (as necessary)
- Dictionary
- Reader: *A Little Princess & Other Classic Stories*

Teaching Tips:

Review for Mastery. Discuss and review any work from the previous lesson that was assigned as homework. Check for completion of the activities and orally quiz the student for comprehension. Review any reading that was assigned, discussing the characters, setting, plot, theme, language, sequence, etc.

Strengthen fluency and phonemic awareness by reviewing words and sentences from previous lessons. Build vocabulary skills by using some of the words in sentences.

Review alphabetical order to the 3rd letter with Lesson 110, Activities 1-3. Select words at random from the lesson for the student to alphabetize on the board or sheet of paper. Words can also be selected from previous lessons.

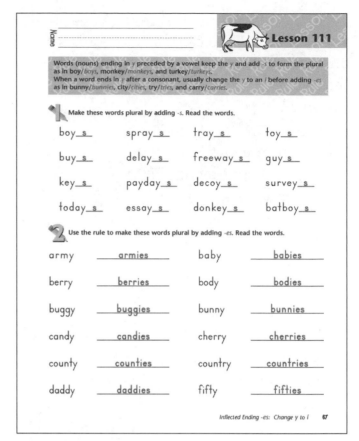

Activity 1. Review the rule and the examples with the student. *Words to teach the concept:* day, decay, display, driveway, jay, raceway, subway, workday, alley, galley, jockey, valley, enjoy, paperboy, wiseguy. Have the student read the base words aloud and add **s** to each word to make it plural. Read the plural words.

Words:

boys, sprays, trays, toys
buys, delays, freeways, guys
keys, paydays, decoys, surveys
todays, essays, donkeys, batboys

Note: The words chosen for this activity review a vowel followed by **y** digraphs and diphthongs from previous lessons.

Activity 2. Review the rule and the examples. *Words to teach the concept:* city/cities, fly/flies, diary/diaries, mystery/mysteries, fairy/fairies, twenty/twenties. Have the student read the base words aloud. Have the student change the **y** to **i** and add **es** to each word to make it plural. Read the plural words. Pay special attention to the ending /**is**/ sound.

Activity 2 continued:

Words:

armies, babies
berries, bodies
buggies, bunnies
candies, cherries
counties, countries
daddies, fifties
forties, funnies
jellies, juries
ladies, parties
pennies, ponies
puppies, stories

Activity 3. Help the student read the base word choices and the sentences aloud. Review the rules for making words plural that end in **y**. Have the student complete the sentence by writing the plural form of each word on the line.

Sentences:

There are airports in many <u>cities</u>.
A group of <u>flies</u> covered the food.
Three <u>ladies</u> were shopping at the store.
A herd of <u>ponies</u> was at the barn.
All of his <u>buddies</u> were at the game.
They had two <u>nannies</u> to care for the child.
One of his <u>duties</u> was to empty the trash.
The <u>kitties</u> could not find their mother.
The baby <u>cries</u> when it is hungry.
The girls took three <u>tries</u> to fill the sack.

Reading. Read and discuss the maxim for the Lesson.

Read the story *In the Attic (continued)*. This is another chapter of the *A Little Princess* story. Preview the story and explain words or sentence structures that are not familiar to the student. With every story ask questions: who are the characters, what are they doing, what are they saying, where does the action take place, what is the order of events, what words are being used, what new information is given, what lesson can be learned?

Comprehension questions:

forty	forties	funny	funnies
jelly	jellies	jury	juries
lady	ladies	party	parties
penny	pennies	pony	ponies
puppy	puppies	story	stories

3 Make the word in the box plural. Write it on the line to complete the sentence.

There are airports in many _____cities_____. `city`
A group of _____flies_____ covered the food. `fly`
Three _____ladies_____ were shopping at the store. `lady`
A herd of _____ponies_____ was at the barn. `pony`
All of his _____buddies_____ were at the game. `buddy`
They had two _____nannies_____ to care for the child. `nanny`
One of his _____duties_____ was to empty the trash. `duty`
The _____kitties_____ could not find their mother. `kitty`
The baby _____cries_____ when it is hungry. `cry`
The girls took three _____tries_____ to fill the sack. `try`

68   *Inflected Ending -es: Change y to i*

What were some of the things that Sara was asked to do?
Why didn't Sara complain?
How was Becky a help to Sara?
How was Erma a comfort to Sara?
How did Sara greet Erma when they met in the hallway?

Assign. Lesson activities or reading that are to be completed as homework.

Lesson 112: Inflected Endings -ed, -s, -es, & -ing, by Doubling the Final Consonant

Overview:

- Write singular words as plurals
- Apply the rule to add inflected endings **-ed** and **-ing** to short vowel words
- Read words with inflected endings
- Complete sentences

Materials and Supplies:

- Teacher's Guide & Student Workbook 2
- White board or chalkboard
- Word cards (as necessary)
- Dictionary
- Reader: *A Little Princess & Other Classic Stories*

Teaching Tips:

Review for Mastery. Discuss and review any work from the previous lesson that was assigned as homework. Check for completion of the activities and orally quiz the student for comprehension. Review any reading that was assigned, discussing the characters, setting, plot, theme, language, sequence, etc.

Strengthen fluency and phonemic awareness by reviewing words and sentences from previous lessons. Build vocabulary skills by using some of the words in sentences.

Review plurals with Lesson 111, Activities 1 & 2. Write random words from the two activities on the board and ask the student to change them to plurals. Ask the student for the rule that tells him how to make the word plural. Have the student use the word in a sentence.

Activity 1. Review the rules and the examples with the student. *Words to teach the concept:* cut, dig, dip, fit, nag, quit, rob, rub, sit, spin, stir, stop, trip. Help the student read the base word choices and the sentences aloud. Review

the rule for adding **-ing** endings to short vowel words that end in a single consonant. Have the student complete the sentence by writing the inflected form of each word on the line.

Sentences:

> The cat was <u>napping</u> in the shade.
> She was <u>skipping</u> through the park.
> The baby was <u>sobbing</u> from the pain.
> He was <u>clipping</u> the hedge by the road.
> They were <u>jabbing</u> at the target.
> She was <u>bragging</u> about her success.
> Mom is <u>scrubbing</u> the floor.
> A sock was <u>clogging</u> the drain on the sink.
> There was <u>clapping</u> after the music.
> We went <u>jogging</u> at the park.

Activity 2. Write some simple short vowel words that end in a single consonant on the chalkboard or white board. Make them plural and add inflected endings **-ed** and **-ing** to these words. Have the student read the given base words in the activity. The student will make the word plural and add endings **-ed** and **-ing** to each word and write the words on the lines.

Activity 2 continued:

Words:

add s	add ed	add ing
cans	canned	canning
plans	planned	planning
grabs	grabbed	grabbing

Activity 3. Help the student read the base word choices and the sentences aloud. Review the rule for adding **-ed** endings to short vowel words that end in a single consonant. Have the student complete the sentence by writing the inflected form of each word on the line.

Sentences:

The cat <u>napped</u> in the shade.
She <u>skipped</u> through the park.
The baby <u>sobbed</u> from the pain.
He <u>clipped</u> the hedge by the road.
They <u>jabbed</u> at the target.
She <u>bragged</u> about her success.
Mom <u>scrubbed</u> the floor.
A sock <u>clogged</u> the drain on the sink.
They <u>clapped</u> after the music.
We <u>jogged</u> at the park.

Activity 4. Have the student read the given base words. The student will make the word plural and add endings **-ed** and **-ing** to each word and write the words on the lines.

Words:

add s	add ed	add ing
hugs	hugged	hugging
slips	slipped	slipping
snaps	snapped	snapping
steps	stepped	stepping
traps	trapped	trapping
whips	whipped	whipping

Reading. Read and discuss the maxim for the Lesson.

Read the story *In the Attic (continued)*. This is another chapter of the *A Little Princess* story. Preview the story and explain words or sentence structures that are not familiar to the student. With every story ask questions: who

---

3 Use the rule to add *-ed* to the base word. Write the new word on the line to complete the sentence.

The cat ____napped____ in the shade.   nap
She ____skipped____ through the park.   skip
The baby ____sobbed____ from the pain.   sob
He ____clipped____ the hedge by the road.   clip
They ____jabbed____ at the target.   jab
She ____bragged____ about her success.   brag
Mom ____scrubbed____ the floor.   scrub
A sock ____clogged____ the drain on the sink.   clog
They ____clapped____ after the music.   clap
We ____jogged____ at the park.   jog

4 Use the rules to make new words. Read the words.

	add s	add ed	add ing
hug	hugs	hugged	hugging
slip	slips	slipped	slipping
snap	snaps	snapped	snapping
step	steps	stepped	stepping
trap	traps	trapped	trapping
whip	whips	whipped	whipping

70   *Inflected Endings: Doubling the Final Consonant*

are the characters, what are they doing, what are they saying, where does the action take place, what is the order of events, what words are being used, what new information is given, what lesson can be learned?

Comprehension questions:
Why was there a barrier between Sara and Erma?
Who made the first move in breaking down the barrier between Sara and Erma?
Why had Erma came to Sara?
Who did Sara say was the better person?
What famous place did Sara compare her life in the attic to?

Assign. Lesson activities or reading that are to be completed as homework.

Lesson 113: Inflected Endings -ed & -ing by Dropping the Final e

Overview:

• Alphabetize words to first and second letters
• Sentence completion
• Story completion

Materials and Supplies:

• Teacher's Guide & Student Workbook 2
• White board or chalkboard
• Word cards (as necessary)
• Dictionary
• Reader: *A Little Princess & Other Classic Stories*

Teaching Tips:

Review for Mastery. Discuss and review any work from the previous lesson that was assigned as homework. Check for completion of the activities and orally quiz the student for comprehension. Review any reading that was assigned, discussing the characters, setting, plot, theme, language, sequence, etc.

Strengthen fluency and phonemic awareness by reviewing words and sentences from previous lessons. Build vocabulary skills by using some of the words in sentences.

Review inflected ending with Lesson 112, Activities 2 & 4. Use each form of the word in a sentence. "Here is a can. I have three cans. The factory canned the beans. The factory is canning the peas."

Activity 1. Review the Drop **e** Rule and the examples with the student. Write some silent **e** words on the board. Use the rule to add inflected endings **-ed** and **-ing** to these words. *Words to teach the concept:* drive, fade, file, give, glance, glide, grate, like, mine, name, ride, slide, tape. Help the student read the base word choices and the sentences aloud for the

activity. Review the rule for adding **-ing** endings to silent **e** words. Have the student complete the sentence by writing the inflected form of each word on the line.

Sentences:

The cat was <u>chasing</u> the ball.
She was <u>prancing</u> through the park.
The lady was <u>filing</u> the papers.
He was <u>pruning</u> the hedge by the road.
They were <u>firing</u> at the target.
She was <u>smiling</u> about her success.
Mom is <u>wiping</u> the floor.
A sock was <u>lining</u> the drain on the sink.
There was <u>raving</u> after the music.
We went <u>biking</u> at the park.

Activity 2. The student will make the base words in Activity 1 to mean something that has already happened by adding **-ed**. Write the words on the line.

Words:

chased, pranced, filed, pruned, fired, smiled, wiped, lined, raved, biked

---

Lesson 113

Drop e Rule: If a word ends in *silent e*, drop the *e* before adding a suffix that begins with a vowel such as *-ing* or *-ed* as in bake/*baking*/*baked* and slice/*slicing*/*sliced*.
When you add *-ing* it means something is happening now!
When you add *-ed* it means something happened in the past.

1 Use the rule to add *-ing* to the base word. Write the new word on the line to complete the sentence.

The cat was ____chasing____ the ball. chase
She was ____prancing____ through the park. prance
The lady was ____filing____ the papers. file
He was ____pruning____ the hedge by the road. prune
They were ____firing____ at the target. fire
She was ____smiling____ about her success. smile
Mom is ____wiping____ the floor. wipe
A sock was ____lining____ the drain on the sink. line
There was ____raving____ after the music. rave
We went ____biking____ at the park. bike

2 Use the rule to change the base words above into something that has already happened by adding *-ed*. Read the words.

chased, pranced, filed,
pruned, fired, smiled,
wiped, lined, raved, biked

Inflected Endings: Dropping the Final e   71

Activity 3. Help the student read the base word choices and the sentences aloud. Review the rule for adding **-ed** endings to silent **e** words. Have the student complete the sentence by writing the inflected form of each word on the line.

Sentences:

The man <u>changed</u> the tire.

Our family <u>dined</u> at the cafe.

The mom <u>cared</u> for her sick son.

He <u>shared</u> the bowl of fruit.

She <u>solved</u> the addition problem.

They <u>saved</u> for a new car.

The girl <u>phoned</u> her friend.

The boy <u>gazed</u> into her eyes.

A paper <u>framed</u> the picture.

His pencil <u>traced</u> the lines.

Activity 4. The student will make the base words in Activity 1 to mean something that is happening now by adding **-ing**. Write the words on the line.

Words:

changing, dining, caring, sharing, solving, saving, phoning, gazing, framing, tracing

Reading. Read and discuss the maxim for the Lesson.

Read the story *Zedek*. This is another chapter of the *A Little Princess* story. Preview the story and explain words or sentence structures that are not familiar to the student. With every story ask questions: who are the characters, what are they doing, what are they saying, where does the action take place, what is the order of events, what words are being used, what new information is given, what lesson can be learned?

---

3 Use the rule to add *-ed* to the base word. Write the new word on the line to complete the sentence.

The man _____changed_____ the tire. `change`

Our family _____dined_____ at the cafe. `dine`

The mom _____cared_____ for her sick son. `care`

He _____shared_____ the bowl of fruit. `share`

She _____solved_____ the addition problem. `solve`

They _____saved_____ for a new car. `save`

The girl _____phoned_____ her friend. `phone`

The boy _____gazed_____ into her eyes. `gaze`

A paper _____framed_____ the picture. `frame`

His pencil _____traced_____ the lines. `trace`

4 Use the rule to change the base words above into something that is happening now by adding *-ing*. Read the words.

changing, dining, caring,
sharing, solving, saving,
phoning, gazing, framing,
tracing

71   *Inflected Endings: Dropping the Final e*

Comprehension questions:

Who was the third person who comforted Sara?

Why did Sara say she was better off than a beggar?

Did Lottie understand where Sara had to live?

How was Lottie able to keep herself from crying?

What things could be seen from the attic window?

Assign. Lesson activities or reading that are to be completed as homework.

Lesson 114: Inflected Ending -es by Changing f to v

Overview:

- Write singular words as plurals
- Apply the Sibilant Rule to read plural words
- Apply the Final **f** or **fe** Rule to make singular words plural
- Apply the Final **f** or **fe** Rule to write the base word from the plural
- Apply the Final **f** or **fe** Rule to words that may or may not change their spelling to become plural

Materials and Supplies:

- Teacher's Guide & Student Workbook 2
- White board or chalkboard
- Word cards (as necessary)
- Dictionary
- Reader: *A Little Princess & Other Classic Stories*

Teaching Tips:

Review for Mastery. Discuss and review any work from the previous lesson that was assigned as homework. Check for completion of the activities and orally quiz the student for comprehension. Review any reading that was assigned, discussing the characters, setting, plot, theme, language, sequence, etc.

Strengthen fluency and phonemic awareness by reviewing words and sentences from previous lessons. Build vocabulary skills by using some of the words in sentences.

Review inflected ending **-ed** and **-ing** with Lesson 113, Activities 2 & 4. Have the student make up sentences that use the words.

Activity 1. Review the rule and the examples with the student. *Words to teach the concept:* leaf, self, sheaf, thief. Have the student read the base words aloud and have them change the **f** to **v** before adding **es** to make it plural. Read the plural words.

Activity 1 continued:

Words:
  knives, lives
  loaves, shelves
  jackknives, elves
  halflives, wives
  ourselves, themselves

Note the word change for *myself* and *himself*.

Activity 2. Have the student read the plural aloud. Review the rule with the student. Have the student write the base word for each plural. Remind him of the long vowel silent **e** rule to help decide if the base word ends in **f** or in **fe**. Read the base words.

Words:
  wolf, thief
  leaf, sheaf
  farmwife, half
  penknife, life
  midwife, elf

Activity 3. Review the rule that there are exceptions to the Change **f** to **i** and Add **es** Rule. Have the student read the base words aloud and have them make it plural by adding **s**. Read the plural words.

Words:
   beliefs, chiefs, cliffs, muffs
   oafs, proofs, safes, giraffes
   fifes, roofs, griefs, gulfs
   turfs, mischiefs, photographs

Activity 4. Have the student read the base words aloud. Review the rule with the student. These words can do either; add **s** or change **f** to **v** and add **es**. Read the plurals.

Words:
   calfs, calves
   dwarfs, dwarves
   scarfs, scarves
   hoofs, hooves
   wharfs, wharves
   handkerchiefs, handkerchieves

Note the pronunciation changes for the plurals with **-ves**.

Reading. Read and discuss the maxim for the Lesson.

Read the story *Zedek (continued)*. This is another chapter of the *A Little Princess* story. Preview the story and explain words or sentence structures that are not familiar to the student. With every story ask questions: who are the characters, what are they doing, what are they saying, where does the action take place, what is the order of events, what words are being used, what new information is given, what lesson can be learned?

Some nouns ending in *f* or *fe* do not change their endings to *-ves* to make the word plural as in cliff/*cliffs* and safe/*safes*.

3 Read these words. Add *s* to make these words plural and read them.

belief_s_	chief_s_	cliff_s_	muff_s_
oaf_s_	proof_s_	safe_s_	giraffe_s_
fife_s_	roof_s_	grief_s_	gulf_s_
turf_s_	mischief_s_	photograph_s_	

Some nouns ending in *f* or *fe* may or may not change their endings to *-ves* to make the word plural as in dwarf/*dwarfs*/*dwarves*.

4 Read these words. Follow the rule to make the plurals of the words.

	add *s*	add *ves*
calf	calfs	calves
dwarf	dwarfs	dwarves
scarf	scarfs	scarves
hoof	hoofs	hooves
wharf	wharfs	wharves
handkerchief	handkerchiefs	handkerchieves

74   *Inflected Endings: Changing f to v*

Comprehension questions:
   Who lived in the house next door?
   What did Sara want to feed to the sparrows?
   Who had some bread in their pocket?
   What convinced the sparrow to get the bread?
   What things did Sara imagine would make the attic room comfortable?

Assign. Lesson activities or reading that are to be completed as homework.

Lesson 115: Irregular Plurals

Overview:

- Define an irregular plural
- Give examples of irregular plurals
- Use irregular plurals correctly to complete sentences
- Read irregular plurals correctly

Materials and Supplies:

- Teacher's Guide & Student Workbook 2
- White board or chalkboard
- Word cards (as necessary)
- Dictionary
- Reader: *A Little Princess & Other Classic Stories*

Teaching Tips:

Review plurals with Lesson 114, Activities 1-4. Review the rules for changing the words to plurals. Put random words on the board and ask a student to come up and make it plural. Since these words are inconsistent in how the plural form is made it will take memorization to recall the spelling for the different words.

Activity 1. Review the rule and the examples with the student. Ask the student if they can think of any other examples. Have the student identify the pictures and read the word for each picture. Pay special attention to the spelling of the plural. Note the spelling changes.

Pictures:

**man/men, woman/women, child/children
fireman/firemen, foot/feet, tooth/teeth
mouse/mice, louse/lice, goose/geese
policewoman/policewomen, ox/oxen,
policeman/policemen**

Activity 2. Have the student read the word choices for the sentences. The student will write the words on the lines in the sentences.

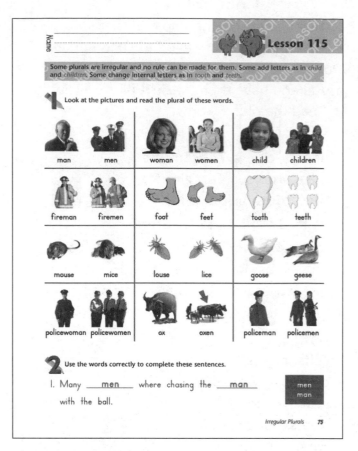

Activity 2 continued:

Sentences:

Many <u>men</u> where chasing the <u>man</u> with the ball.

All of the <u>women</u> came to help the <u>woman</u> who was crying.

The lost <u>child</u> was found playing with some other <u>children</u>.

My sore <u>tooth</u> makes all of my <u>teeth</u> hurt.

The <u>policeman</u> shared his reward with the other <u>policemen</u>.

Activity 3. Help the student read the irregular plurals in each group. There are no spelling changes for these plurals. Have the student make up sentences for the singular and plural forms of each word.

Activity 4. Help the student read the irregular plurals in each group. There are two spellings for each of these plurals.

Reading. Read and discuss the maxim for the Lesson.

Read the story *Zedek (continued)*. This is another chapter of the *A Little Princess* story. Preview the story and explain words or sentence structures that are not familiar to the student. With every story ask questions: who are the characters, what are they doing, what are they saying, where does the action take place, what is the order of events, what words are being used, what new information is given, what lesson can be learned?

Comprehension questions:
   What did Sara see in the attic after the good feeling went away?
   What came into the attic to get some of the crumbs?
   What convinced the rat to get the bread?
   Where did the rat take the large crumb?

Read the poem *Annabel Lee*. Preview the poem and explain words or sentence structures that are not familiar to the student.

Comprehension questions:
   Who was Annabel Lee?
   Where was the kingdom?

Consonant Digraph Practice:
   Paragraphs 1 and 2 contain many **th** digraphs. Find the words that contain **sh** and **ch** digraphs. Look up the word/s that contains the **ch** digraph in your dictionary. What is the sound of the **ch** digraph?

   Paragraph 3 and 4 contain two **ch** digraphs. Look the words up in your dictionary. What is the sound of the **ch** digraph?

   Paragraphs 3 and 6 contain several words that have the **gh** consonant combinations. Are these words examples of the **gh** digraph?

---

2. All of the _____women_____ came to help the
   _____woman_____ who was crying.

3. The lost ___child___ was found playing with some
   other _____children_____.

4. My sore _____tooth_____ makes all of my
   _____teeth_____ hurt.

5. The _____policeman_____ shared his reward with
   the other _____policemen_____.

Some plurals are irregular and no rule can be made for them. Some do not change as in sheep/sheep, moose/moose, deer/deer.

3 Read these words that do not change the spelling to form the plural.

one moose, two moose   one sheep, two sheep
one deer, two deer   one fish, two fish
one trout, two trout   one swine, two swine

4 Read these words that have two forms of the plural.

one person, two persons, two people
one brother, two brothers, two brethren
one cow, two cows, two cattle
one policeman, two policemen, two police

76   *Irregular Plurals*

Read the poem *There Was an Old Person of Nice*. Preview the poem and explain words or sentence structures that are not familiar to the student.

Comprehension questions:
   What benefit was it for the old man to have friends who were geese?
   What irregular plural is used in the poem?

Assign. Lesson activities or reading that are to be completed as homework.

Lesson 116: Review Inflections

Overview:

- Identify the rule that has been used to make a word plural
- Read plurals
- Identify irregular plurals

Materials and Supplies:

- Teacher's Guide & Student Workbook 2
- White board or chalkboard
- Word cards (as necessary)
- Dictionary
- Reader: *A Little Princess & Other Classic Stories*

Teaching Tips:

Review for Mastery. Discuss and review any work from the previous lesson that was assigned as homework. Check for completion of the activities and orally quiz the student for comprehension. Review any reading that was assigned, discussing the characters, setting, plot, theme, language, sequence, etc.

Strengthen fluency and phonemic awareness by reviewing words and sentences from previous lessons. Build vocabulary skills by using some of the words in sentences.

Review irregular plurals with Lesson 115, Activities 1-4. Choosing random words, write a form of the word on the board and ask the student to write the singular or plural form of the word.

Review irregular plurals with Lesson 115, Activities 3 & 4. Review the words and the spelling changes. Use both forms of the words in sentences.

Activity 1. Review the rules with the student. Point out how they are labeled. Read the base word and the plural. Note the spelling change to make the word plural. Have the student identify the rule that has been used to change the base word to a plural by filing in the circle.

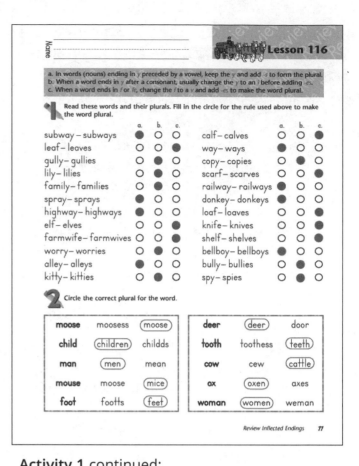

Activity 1 continued:

Plural	add s	y to i	f to ves
subways	X		
leaves			X
gullies		X	
lilies		X	
families		X	
sprays	X		
highways	X		
elves			X
farmwives			X
worries		X	
alleys	X		
kitties		X	
calves			X
ways	X		
copies		X	
scarves			X
railways	X		
donkeys	X		
loaves			X
knives			X
shelves			X
bellboys	X		
bullies		X	
spies		X	

Horizons Phonics & Reading Grade 2 Teacher's Guide

Activity 2. Have the student read the base word and review the spellings for the irregular plural. The student will circle the correct spelling for the irregular plural.

Plurals:

moose	deer
children	teeth
men	cattle
mice	oxen
feet	women

Note: Read these words similar to Activities 3 & 4 in Lesson 115 (*one foot*, *four feet*).

Activity 3. Review the rules for adding suffixes **-ed** and **-ing**. Instruct the student to read the base word and the word with the added suffix. Then the student will sort the words and write them in the correct box.

Words:

Double Consonant	Drop Final e
sitting	rated
letting	driving
tripped	taped
quitting	faded
trimmed	giving
cutting	naming

Activity 4. Review the **f** to **v** Rule and the exceptions. Instruct the student to read the base word and the plural. Then the student will sort the words and write them in the correct box.

Words:

Keep f	Change f to v
gulfs	penknives
proofs	thieves
cliffs	halves

Reading. Read and discuss the maxim for the Lesson.

Read the story *Zedek (continued)*. This is another chapter of the *A Little Princess* story. Preview the story and explain words or sentence structures that are not familiar to the

student. With every story ask questions: who are the characters, what are they doing, what are they saying, where does the action take place, what is the order of events, what words are being used, what new information is given, what lesson can be learned?

Comprehension questions:
When Erma came to the attic, who had Sara been talking to?
How did Erma feel about the rat?
What convinced the rat to come out of the wall?
What kind of a rat was Zedek?
What noise surprised Erma?

Assign. Lesson activities or reading that are to be completed as homework.

Lesson 117: Comparative Endings -er & -est

Overview:

- Define comparative endings
- Add comparative endings to base words
- Apply the correct rule to add suffixes to a base word
- Use suffix **-er** to compare two things
- Use suffix **-est** to compare more than two things
- Read and complete sentences

Materials and Supplies:

- Teacher's Guide & Student Workbook 2
- White board or chalkboard
- Word cards (as necessary)
- Phonics rules flashcards
- Dictionary
- Reader: *A Little Princess & Other Classic Stories*

Teaching Tips:

Review for Mastery. Discuss and review any work from the previous lesson that was assigned as homework. Check for completion of the activities and orally quiz the student for comprehension. Review any reading that was assigned, discussing the characters, setting, plot, theme, language, sequence, etc.

Strengthen fluency and phonemic awareness by reviewing words and sentences from previous lessons. Build vocabulary skills by using some of the words in sentences.

Review regular and irregular plurals with Lesson 116, Activities 1, 2, & 4. Choosing random words, write a form of the word on the board and ask the student to write the singular or plural form of the word.

Review inflected endings **-ed** and **-ing** with Lesson 116, Activity 3. Choosing random words, write a form of the word on the board and ask the student to either add the suffix or write the base word.

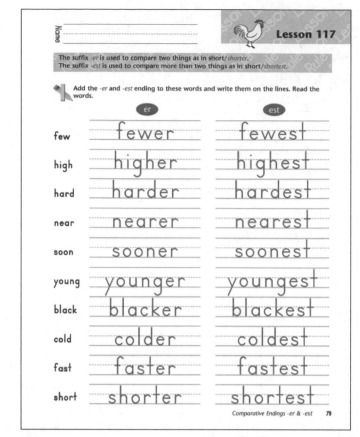

Activity 1. Review the rules for comparative endings with the student. *Words to teach the concept:* bright, clever, faint, grey, kind, narrow, old, quiet, rich, rough, shallow, slow, soft, solid, strong, stupid, warm. Have the student read the base word. The student will use the rule to add the **-er** and **-est** ending to each word and write it on the line.

Words:

Base	add er	add est
few	fewer	fewest
high	higher	highest
hard	harder	hardest
near	nearer	nearest
soon	sooner	soonest
young	younger	youngest
black	blacker	blackest
cold	colder	coldest
fast	faster	fastest
short	shorter	shortest

Activity 2. Help the student read the sentences and the base word. Instruct the student to add **-er** or **-est** to the base word to complete the sentence. Write the word on the line.

Sentences:

The blue car is <u>newer</u> than the red car.

She is the <u>smallest</u> girl in the class.

The tower is <u>taller</u> than the trees in the yard.

This speaker is the <u>loudest</u> one that we have heard at the store.

Since the moon will not shine tonight, it will be <u>darker</u> than last night.

This store has the <u>freshest</u> fruit in the whole town.

I found the <u>cheapest</u> pair of shoes at the mall.

It is <u>calmer</u> on the lake today than what it was last week.

My room is <u>neater</u> than the room where my sister sleeps.

Which is <u>tougher</u>, the phonics lesson or the math worksheet?

Reading. Read and discuss the maxim for the Lesson.

Read the story *The Indian Gentleman*. This is another chapter of the *A Little Princess* story. Preview the story and explain words or sentence structures that are not familiar to the student. With every story ask questions: who are the characters, what are they doing, what are they saying, where does the action take place, what is the order of events, what words are being used, what new information is given, what lesson can be learned?

2️⃣ Add *-er* or *-est* to the base word to finish the sentence. Use *-er* to compare two things and *-est* to compare more than two things.

new The blue car is _____ newer _____ than the red car.

small She is the _____ smallest _____ girl in the class.

tall The tower is _____ taller _____ than the trees in the yard.

loud This speaker is the _____ loudest _____ one that we have heard at the store.

dark Since the moon will not shine tonight, it will be _____ darker _____ than last night

fresh This store has the _____ freshest _____ fruit in the whole town.

cheap I found the _____ cheapest _____ pair of shoes at the mall.

calm It is _____ calmer _____ on the lake today than what it was last week.

neat My room is _____ neater _____ than the room where my sister sleeps.

laugh Which is _____ tougher _____ , the phonics lesson or the math worksheet?

10   *Comparative Endings -er & -est*

Comprehension questions:

Why was it not safe for Erma and Lottie to visit the attic?

Why didn't anyone look at Sara as she ran her errands?

Why did Sara like to walk by the houses in the evenings?

What family did Sara like to watch the best?

Why were the Richmonds out of their home?

Assign. Lesson activities or reading that are to be completed as homework.

Lesson 118: Comparative Endings -er & -est by Dropping the Final e

Overview:

- Define comparative endings
- Apply the correct rule to add suffixes to a base word
- Use suffix **-er** to compare two things
- Use suffix **-est** to compare more than two things
- Read and complete sentences

Materials and Supplies:

- Teacher's Guide & Student Workbook 2
- White board or chalkboard
- Word cards (as necessary)
- Dictionary
- Reader: *A Little Princess & Other Classic Stories*

Teaching Tips:

Review for Mastery. Discuss and review any work from the previous lesson that was assigned as homework. Check for completion of the activities and orally quiz the student for comprehension. Review any reading that was assigned, discussing the characters, setting, plot, theme, language, sequence, etc.

Strengthen fluency and phonemic awareness by reviewing words and sentences from previous lessons. Build vocabulary skills by using some of the words in sentences.

Review comparative endings **-er** and **-est** with Lesson 117, Activity 2. Have the student make up sentences to use the other form of the comparatives used in the activity.

Review comparative endings **-er** and **-est** with Lesson 117, Activity 1. Choosing random words, write a form of the word on the board and ask the student to either add the suffix or write the base word.

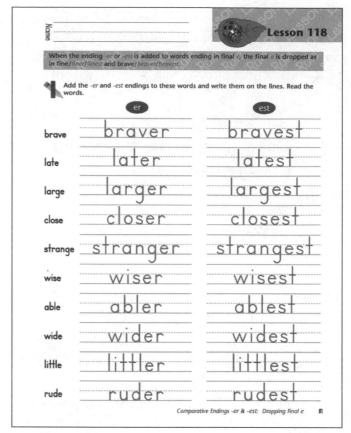

Activity 1. Review the rule and the examples with the student. *Words to teach the concept:* bare, blue, coarse, gentle, idle, nice, pale, rare, ripe, safe, simple, sore, square, sure. Have the student read the base word. The student will use the rule to add the **-er** and **-est** ending to each word and write it on the line.

Words:

Base	add er	add est
brave	braver	bravest
late	later	latest
large	larger	largest
close	closer	closest
strange	stranger	strangest
wise	wiser	wisest
able	abler	ablest
wide	wider	widest
little	littler	littlest
rude	ruder	rudest

Horizons Phonics & Reading Grade 2 Teacher's Guide

Activity 2. Help the student read the sentences and the base word. Instruct the student to add **-er** or **-est** to the base word to complete the sentence. Remind the student to look for how many things are being compared in the sentences. Write the word on the line.

Sentences:

Phonics is the <u>latest</u> class of our entire day.

She wears the <u>cutest</u> shoes in the class.

The river is <u>wider</u> under the bridge than what it is by the park.

The <u>bravest</u> boy on the team was my friend Bill.

The test will show if Megan is <u>wiser</u> than Jen.

This store is the <u>largest</u> one at the new mall.

This sheet of sandpaper is <u>finer</u> than the one we first used to sand the wood.

The <u>strangest</u> of the three stories was the one about the fish.

My room is <u>littler</u> than the room where my sister sleeps.

No one wants to be the <u>rudest</u> child in the class.

Reading. Read and discuss the maxim for the Lesson.

Read the story *The Indian Gentleman (continued)*. This is another chapter of the *A Little Princess* story. Preview the story and explain words or sentence structures that are not familiar to the student. With every story ask questions: who are the characters, what are they doing, what are they saying, where does the action take place, what is the order of events, what words are being used, what new information is given, what lesson can be learned?

---

2 Add *-er* or *-est* to the base word to finish the sentence. Use *-er* to compare two things and *-est* to compare more than two things.

late — Phonics is the _____ latest _____ class of our entire day.

cute — She wears the _____ cutest _____ shoes in the class.

wide — The river is _____ wider _____ under the bridge than what it is by the park.

brave — The _____ bravest _____ boy on the team was my friend Bill.

wise — The test will show if Megan is _____ wiser _____ than Jen.

large — This store is the _____ largest _____ one at the new mall.

fine — This sheet of sandpaper is _____ finer _____ than the one we first used to sand the wood.

strange — The _____ strangest _____ of the three stories was the one about the fish.

little — My room is _____ littler _____ than the room where my sister sleeps.

rude — No one wants to be the _____ rudest _____ child in the class.

82   Comparative Endings -er & -est: Dropping Final e

Comprehension questions:

What did the little boy give to Sara?

How did Sara react to being given the money?

What did the children notice that made Sara different from the beggar children?

What name did the children give to Sara?

Who had Zedek brought with him to the attic?

Assign. Lesson activities or reading that are to be completed as homework.

Lesson 119: Comparative Endings -er & -est by the Doubling Rule

Overview:

- Define comparative endings
- Apply the correct rule to add suffixes to a base word
- Use suffix **-er** to compare two things
- Use suffix **-est** to compare more than two things
- Read and complete sentences

Materials and Supplies:

- Teacher's Guide & Student Workbook 2
- White board or chalkboard
- Word cards (as necessary)
- Phonics rules flashcards
- Dictionary
- Reader: *A Little Princess & Other Classic Stories*

Teaching Tips:

Review for Mastery. Discuss and review any work from the previous lesson that was assigned as homework. Check for completion of the activities and orally quiz the student for comprehension. Review any reading that was assigned, discussing the characters, setting, plot, theme, language, sequence, etc.

Strengthen fluency and phonemic awareness by reviewing words and sentences from previous lessons. Build vocabulary skills by using some of the words in sentences.

Review comparative endings **-er** and **-est** with Lesson 118, Activity 2. Have the student make up sentences to use the other form of the comparatives used in the activity.

Review comparative endings **-er** and **-est** with Lesson 118, Activity 1. Choosing random words, write a form of the word on the board and ask the student to either add the suffix or write the base word.

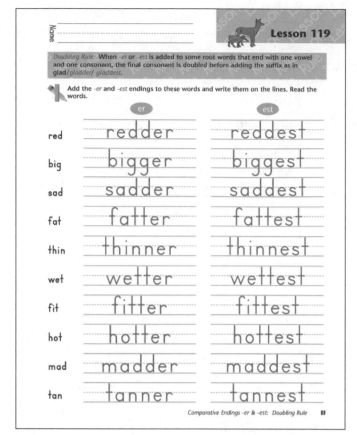

Comparative Endings -er & -est: Doubling Rule **85**

Activity 1. Review the rule and the examples with the student. *Words to teach the concept:* hip/hipper/hippest, smug/smugger/smuggest, snug/snugger/snuggest. Have the student read the base word. The student will use the rule to add the **-er** and **-est** ending to each word and write it on the line.

Words:

Base	add er	add est
red	redder	reddest
big	bigger	biggest
sad	sadder	saddest
fat	fatter	fattest
thin	thinner	thinnest
wet	wetter	wettest
fit	fitter	fittest
hot	hotter	hottest
mad	madder	maddest
tan	tanner	tannest

Activity 2. Help the student read the sentences and the base word. Instruct the student to add
-er or -est to the base word to complete the sentence. Remind the student to look for how many things are being compared in the sentences. Write the word on the line.

Sentences:

Pick the <u>reddest</u> of the six colors to paint the chair.

My arm is <u>tanner</u> than the skin is on my leg.

The floor is <u>wetter</u> by the sink than under the table.

The <u>biggest</u> boy on the team was younger than six other boys.

I am <u>madder</u> than Phil about not seeing the rocket launch.

Pick the <u>thinnest</u> of the three pickles for lunch.

She was <u>sadder</u> over breaking the dish than the glass.

It was <u>hotter</u> this morning than it is this evening.

The <u>fittest</u> runner on the team will be able to win the race.

His white pig is <u>fatter</u> than the black one.

Reading. Read and discuss the maxim for the Lesson.

Read the story *The Indian Gentleman (continued)*. This is another chapter of the *A Little Princess* story. Preview the story and explain words or sentence structures that are not familiar to the student. With every story ask questions: who are the characters, what are they doing, what are they saying, where does the action take place, what is the order of events, what words are being used, what new information is given, what lesson can be learned?

Comprehension questions:

Who was Sara beginning to feel differently about?

How did Sara defend herself from Miss Minchin's and Miss Amy's insults?

What did Sara see in Emily's eyes?

What did Sara do to Emily?

What did Sara wish about the house next door?

Assign. Lesson activities or reading that are to be completed as homework.

Lesson 120: Comparative Endings -er & -est by Dropping y and Changing to i

Overview:

- Define comparative endings
- Apply the correct rule to add suffixes to a base word
- Use suffix **-er** to compare two things
- Use suffix **-est** to compare more than two things
- Read and complete sentences

Materials and Supplies:

- Teacher's Guide & Student Workbook 2
- White board or chalkboard
- Word cards (as necessary)
- Dictionary
- Reader: *A Little Princess & Other Classic Stories*

Teaching Tips:

Review for Mastery. Discuss and review any work from the previous lesson that was assigned as homework. Check for completion of the activities and orally quiz the student for comprehension. Review any reading that was assigned, discussing the characters, setting, plot, theme, language, sequence, etc.

Strengthen fluency and phonemic awareness by reviewing words and sentences from previous lessons. Build vocabulary skills by using some of the words in sentences.

Review comparative endings **-er** and **-est** with Lesson 119, Activity 2. Have the student make up sentences to use the other form of the comparatives used in the activity.

Review comparative endings **-er** and **-est** with Lesson 119, Activity 1. Choosing random words, write a form of the word on the board and ask the student to either add the suffix or write the base word.

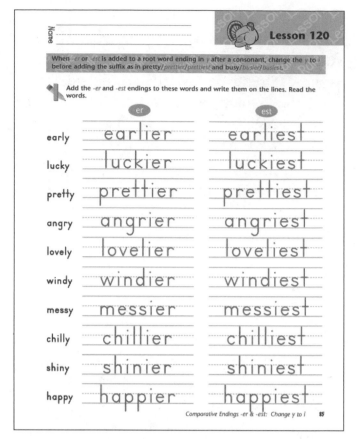

Activity 1. Review the rule and the examples with the student. *Words to teach the concept:* busy, cozy, easy, friendly, funny, fussy, muddy, roomy, silly, sleepy, snappy, sunny, thirsty, ugly. Have the student read the base word. The student will use the rule to add the **-er** and **-est** ending to each word and write it on the line.

Words:

Base	add er	add est
early	earlier	earliest
lucky	luckier	luckiest
pretty	prettier	prettiest
angry	angrier	angriest
lovely	lovelier	loveliest
windy	windier	windiest
messy	messier	messiest
chilly	chillier	chilliest
shiny	shinier	shiniest
happy	happier	happiest

Activity 2. Help the student read the sentences and the base word. Instruct the student to add **-er** or **-est** to the base word to complete the sentence. Remind the student to look for how many things are being compared in the sentences. Write the word on the line.

Sentences:

The front window looks <u>foggier</u> than the window on the side.

My mom is the <u>loveliest</u> of all the moms that I know.

Sal is <u>lazier</u> than Jose when it comes to taking out the trash.

This cod is <u>saltier</u> than the trout that we ate for lunch.

I am <u>dizzier</u> than Molly after going on the ride.

Pick the <u>driest</u> of the three shirts to iron for church.

The <u>shadiest</u> tree in the yard is the large oak.

He makes the <u>tastiest</u> chicken of the four cooks.

The <u>dirtiest</u> of the seven uniforms needs to go in the wash.

The kids said that the story was the <u>happiest</u> that they had read.

Review for Test. The instructor should plan to use some time at the end of the class to review and prepare for the test that follows this lesson. Review the objectives for the test and then look over the lessons that it will cover. If the student has struggled with any of the concepts that will be included in the test, some additional drill, practice, or review may be needed to adequately prepare him for the test.

Reading. Read and discuss the maxim for the Lesson.

Read the story *The Indian Gentleman (continued)*. This is another chapter of the *A Little Princess* story. Preview the story and explain words or sentence structures that are not familiar to the student. With every story ask

questions: who are the characters, what are they doing, what are they saying, where does the action take place, what is the order of events, what words are being used, what new information is given, what lesson can be learned?

Comprehension questions:

What did Sara see in front of the house next door?

What did Sara feel she could tell from the furniture that someone had?

What kind of furniture was being moved into the house next door?

Who was helping with the moving that was taking place next door?

Who brought Sara news about the next door neighbors?

Assign. Lesson activities or reading that are to be completed as homework.

Add -er or -est to the base word to finish the sentence. Use -er to compare two things and -est to compare more than two things.

foggy	The front window looks ___foggier___ than the window on the side.
lovely	My mom is the ___loveliest___ of all the moms that I know.
lazy	Sal is ___lazier___ than Jose when it comes to taking out the trash.
salty	This cod is ___saltier___ than the trout that we ate for lunch.
dizzy	I am ___dizzier___ than Molly after going on the ride.
dry	Pick the ___driest___ of the three shirts to iron for church.
shady	The ___shadiest___ tree in the yard is the large oak.
tasty	He makes the ___tastiest___ chicken of the four cooks.
dirty	The ___dirtiest___ of the seven uniforms needs to go in the wash.
happy	The kids said that the story was the ___happiest___ that they had read.

96   Comparative Endings -er & -est: Change y to i

Test 12
Lessons 105-114

Overview:

- Auditory recognition of **n**, **h**, and **t** sounds
- Identify spellings of the **n**, **h**, and **t** sounds
- Identify silent letter digraphs
- Auditory recognition of silent letters
- Read words with silent letters
- Auditory recognition of the **ex** sounds
- Determine if words have been written in alphabetical order to the 3rd letter
- Apply the rules to make words plural
- Apply the rules to add inflected endings **-ed** and **-ing**
- Select the correct spelling for a plural

Materials and Supplies:

- Teacher's Guide & Student Workbook 2

Instructions:

Assessment Start-up. Read through the test with the student. Help the student with any words that he is still unsure of. The teacher should be available to answer any questions that the student may have during the test.

Activity 1. Review the instruction and the words with the student. Instruct the student to fill in the circle to answer if the list is in alphabetical order.

Answers:

fall, far, full, got, grow	yes
hold, hot, if, grow, keep	no
much, myself, never, only, own	yes
cut, clean, drink, draw, done	no
seven, shall, show, six, small	yes
start, ten, today, together, warm	yes
bring, better, carry, eight, hot	no
which, why, wish, work, would	yes

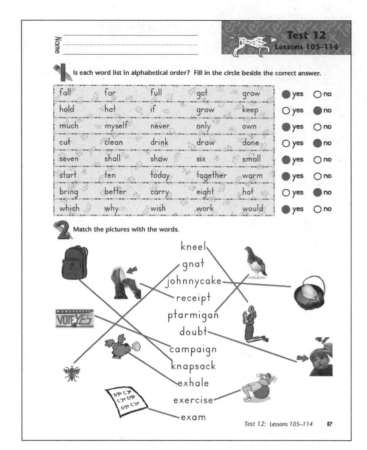

Activity 2. Review the instruction and the words with the student. Review the pictures so that the student can identify them. Instruct the student to match the picture to the word.

Pictures:

knapsack	ptarmigan
receipt	johnnycake
campaign	kneel
exhale	doubt
gnat	exercise
exam	

Activity 3. Review the instructions and the words with the student. Instruct the student to write the missing words on the lines.

Words:

Base	s or es	ing	ed
grab	grabs	grabbing	grabbed
sob	sobs	sobbing	sobbed
prune	prunes	pruning	pruned
wipe	wipes	wiping	wiped
change	changes	changing	changed
solve	solves	solving	solved
hug	hugs	hugging	hugged
clap	claps	clapping	clapped

Activity 4. Review the instructions and the words with the student. The student will write the plural form of each word on the line.

Words:

berries	ladies	shelves
countries	knives	leaves

Activity 5. Review the instructions and the words with the student. Have the student select the correct spelling of the plural form of each word.

Words:

cliffs

wolves

roofs

thieves

Assessment Follow-up. Every test is an important assessment of both the student's comprehension of the concepts and the instructional process. This makes follow-up after each test essential to the learning process. Review all of the errors made on the test with the student. Check for understanding of the concepts and of the problem instructions. Compare the errors made on the test to the test objectives to identify specific areas of weakness. If weak areas of understanding are detected it might be necessary to go back to those lessons to devise some enrichment activities for the concept.

The test results can be used to determine what concepts are reviewed during the daily time of classroom instruction. Devise enrichment activities that will provide development in those areas.

If time permits, choose a selection and have the student read it again. This can also be used as a catch-up time to complete unfinished selections.

Lesson 121: Review Comparatives

Overview:

- Define comparative endings
- Apply the correct rule to add suffixes to a base word
- Use suffix **-er** to compare two things
- Use suffix **-est** to compare more than two things
- Read and complete sentences

Materials and Supplies:

- Teacher's Guide & Student Workbook 2
- White board or chalkboard
- Word cards (as necessary)
- Dictionary
- Reader: *A Little Princess & Other Classic Stories*

Teaching Tips:

Review for Mastery. Discuss and review any work from the previous lesson that was assigned as homework. Check for completion of the activities and orally quiz the student for comprehension. Review any reading that was assigned, discussing the characters, setting, plot, theme, language, sequence, etc.

Strengthen fluency and phonemic awareness by reviewing words and sentences from previous lessons. Build vocabulary skills by using some of the words in sentences.

Review comparative endings **-er** and **-est** with Lesson 120, Activity 2. Have the student make up sentences to use the other form of the comparatives used in the activity.

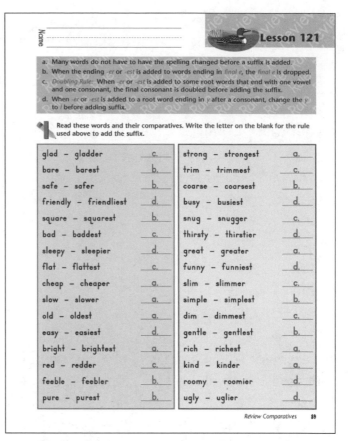

Activity 1. Review the rules with the student. Point out how they are labeled. Read the base word and the comparative. Note the spelling change to form the comparative. The student will determine which rule has been used to form the comparative and write the corresponding letter on the blank.

Words:

Base	comparative	rule
glad	gladder	c.
bare	barest	b.
safe	safer	b.
friendly	friendliest	d.
square	squarest	b.
bad	baddest	c.
sleepy	sleepier	d.
flat	flattest	c.
cheap	cheaper	a.
slow	slower	a.
old	oldest	a.
easy	easiest	d.
bright	brightest	a.

Activity 1 continued:

Base	comparative	rule
red	redder	c.
feeble	feebler	b.
pure	purest	b.
strong	strongest	a.
trim	trimmest	c.
coarse	coarsest	b.
busy	busiest	d.
snug	snugger	c.
thirsty	thirstier	d.
great	greater	a.
funny	funniest	d.
slim	slimmer	c.
simple	simplest	b.
dim	dimmest	c.
gentle	gentlest	b.
rich	richest	a.
kind	kinder	a.
roomy	roomier	d.
ugly	uglier	d.

Activity 2. Help the student read the sentences and base words. Instruct the student to add **-er** or **-est** to each base word to complete the sentence. Remind the student to look for how many things are being compared in the sentences. Write the word on the line.

Sentences:

1. **This light is <u>brighter</u> than the one on the desk.**
2. **She is the <u>nicest</u> student in the class.**
3. **Ben is <u>sillier</u> than Megan.**
4. **A blanket is <u>snugger</u> than a towel.**
5. **The large steak is the <u>rarest</u> meat on the grill.**
6. **Can you find the <u>coarsest</u> sandpaper in the box?**
7. **Some sandpaper is <u>rougher</u> than others.**
8. **He fell into the <u>muddiest</u> part of the puddle.**
9. **Which is <u>bigger</u>: a penny or a doughnut?**
10. **My coat is <u>warmer</u> than your jacket.**

Reading. Read and discuss the maxim for the Lesson.

Read the story *Ram Dass*. This is another chapter of the *A Little Princess* story. Preview the story and explain words or sentence structures that are not familiar to the student. With every story ask questions: who are the characters, what are they doing, what are they saying, where does the action take place, what is the order of events, what words are being used, what new information is given, what lesson can be learned?

Comprehension questions:

Where could all of the splendor of the sunsets be seen?

How was Sara able to see out of the skylight?

What kind of a head poked out of the skylight next door?

What escaped from the man looking out of the next door skylight?

What worries did Sara have about the monkey who had escaped?

Assign. Lesson activities or reading that are to be completed as homework.

Lesson 122: Singular & Plural Possessives

Overview:

- Define possessives
- Write possessive versions of base words
- Sentence completion
- Use singular nouns to show possession
- Use plural nouns to show possession

Materials and Supplies:

- Teacher's Guide & Student Workbook 2
- White board or chalkboard
- Word cards (as necessary)
- Dictionary
- Reader: *A Little Princess & Other Classic Stories*

Teaching Tips:

Review for Mastery. Discuss and review any work from the previous lesson that was assigned as homework. Check for completion of the activities and orally quiz the student for comprehension. Review any reading that was assigned, discussing the characters, setting, plot, theme, language, sequence, etc.

Strengthen fluency and phonemic awareness by reviewing words and sentences from previous lessons. Build vocabulary skills by using some of the words in sentences.

Review comparative endings **-er** and **-est** with Lesson 121, Activity 1. Have the student write the other comparative for the words listed in the activity.

Review comparative endings **-er** and **-est** with Lesson 121, Activity 2. Have the student make up sentences to use the other form of the comparatives used in the activity.

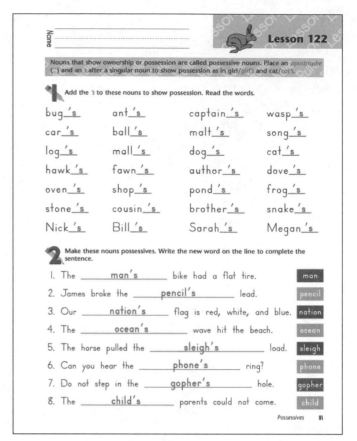

Activity 1. Review the rule for singular possessives. Have the student write examples of the rule on the board. Have the student read the base words. Then have the student add **'s** to each of the singular nouns to make them show possession. Read the plurals that show possession.

Words:

**bug's, ant's, captain's, wasp's
car's, ball's, malt's, song's
log's, mall's, dog's, cat's
hawk's, fawn's, author's, dove's
oven's, shop's, pond's, frog's
stone's, cousin's, brother's, snake's
Nick's, Bill's, Sarah's, Megan's**

Activity 2. Help the student read the sentences and the base words. Instruct the student to make the base word into a possessive and write the word on the line to complete the sentence.

Sentences:

1. The <u>man's</u> bike had a flat tire.
2. James broke the <u>pencil's</u> lead.
3. Our <u>nation's</u> flag is red, white, and blue.

Horizons Phonics & Reading Grade 2 Teacher's Guide

Activity 2 continued:

4. The <u>ocean's</u> wave hit the beach.
5. The horse pulled the <u>sleigh's</u> load.
6. Can you hear the <u>phone's</u> ring?
7. Do not step in the <u>gopher's</u> hole.
8. The <u>child's</u> parents could not come.

Activity 3. Help the student read the words in the sentences. Instruct the student to use a name of his choosing, make it possessive to complete each sentence, and write the name on the line.

Sentences: (Sample answers)

1. That is <u>John's</u> baseball.
2. Did you see <u>Mary's</u> dress?
3. Can <u>John's</u> friends come to the game?
4. I found <u>Mary's</u> book in the grass.
5. It was <u>John's</u> dog that ran the fastest in the race.
6. We would like to see <u>Mary's</u> new car.
7. Someone must carry <u>John's</u> books to the bus stop.
8. <u>Mary's</u> jacket was taken to lost and found.
9. What is the name of <u>John's</u> sister?
10. <u>Mary's</u> house is on a corner of the block.

Activity 4. Have the student read the base words. Then have the student add an apostrophe or **'s** to each of the plural nouns to make them show possession. Read the plural possessives.

Words:

girls', ladies', kings', ducks'
clocks', flies', horses', cars'
women's, oxen's, geese's, deer's
foxes', tailors', bakers', heroes'
cups', drivers', queens', hens'

Reading. Read and discuss the maxim for the Lesson.

Read the story *Ram Dass (continued)*. This is another chapter of the *A Little Princess* story.

---

3 Names are possessives when they show ownership. Write a possessive name on these blanks to make complete sentences. Answers will vary.

1. That is _____ baseball.
2. Did you see _____ dress?
3. Can _____ friends come to the game?
4. I found _____ book in the grass.
5. It was _____ dog that ran the fastest in the race.
6. We would like to see _____ new car.
7. Someone must carry _____ books to the bus stop.
8. _____ jacket was taken to lost and found.
9. What is the name of _____ sister?
10. _____ house is on a corner of the block.

Place an apostrophe after plural nouns ending in *s* to show possession as in boys/*boys'* and students/*students'*. If the plural noun does not end in *s*, add an apostrophe and *s* to show possession as in children/*children's* and men/*men's*.

4 Add an apostrophe (') or *'s* to these plural nouns to show possession. Read the words.

girls'	ladies'	kings'	ducks'
clocks'	flies'	horses'	cars'
women's	oxen's	geese's	deer's
foxes'	tailors'	bakers'	heroes'
cups'	drivers'	queens'	hens'

82   Possessives

Preview the story and explain words or sentence structures that are not familiar to the student. With every story ask questions: who are the characters, what are they doing, what are they saying, where does the action take place, what is the order of events, what words are being used, what new information is given, what lesson can be learned?

Comprehension questions:
What greatly surprised the man looking out of the next door skylight?
What did the gentleman ask of Sara?
What were some of the things that seeing Ram Dass reminded Sara of?
What was Miss Minchin planning for Sara's future?
How did Sara picture herself in order to cope with the bad treatment?

Assign. Lesson activities or reading that are to be completed as homework.

Lesson 123: Suffixes -ly & -ful

Overview:

- Add suffixes to root words
- Define the meaning of suffix **-ly**
- Define the meaning of suffix **-ful**
- Read words with suffixes
- Complete sentences using words with suffixes

Materials and Supplies:

- Teacher's Guide & Student Workbook 2
- White board or chalkboard
- Word cards (as necessary)
- Dictionary
- Reader: *A Little Princess & Other Classic Stories*

Teaching Tips:

Review for Mastery. Discuss and review any work from the previous lesson that was assigned as homework. Check for completion of the activities and orally quiz the student for comprehension. Review any reading that was assigned, discussing the characters, setting, plot, theme, language, sequence, etc.

Strengthen fluency and phonemic awareness by reviewing words and sentences from previous lessons. Build vocabulary skills by using some of the words in sentences.

Review possessives with Lesson 122, Activity 1. Use the singular possessives to make up phrases that contain the words (Examples: *The nest of the bug is the bug's nest. The bike that my cousin has is my cousin's bike.*)

Use the plural possessives from Lesson 122, Activity 4 to make up phrases that contain the words. (Examples: *The dresses of the girls are the girls' dresses. The trail that the oxen travel is the oxen's trail.*)

Activity 1. Review the definition of a suffix. Review the definition of a base or root word. Have the student write examples of words with

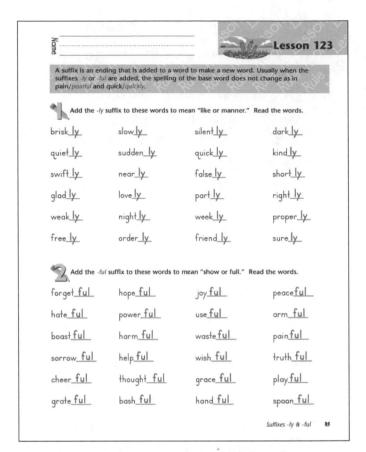

suffixes on the chalkboard or white board. Review the meaning of the **-ly** suffix. Have the student read the root words aloud. *Words to teach the concept:* bad, clear, hard, late, light, live, lone, mad, mother, recent, safe, short, slow, smell, soft, year. The student will add **-ly** to each word by writing the suffix on the line. Note that the spelling of the base word does not change to add the suffix. Read the words with the suffixes.

Words:
briskly, slowly, silently, darkly
quietly, suddenly, quickly, kindly
swiftly, nearly, falsely, shortly
gladly, lovely, partly, rightly
weakly, nightly, weekly, properly
freely, orderly, friendly, surely

Activity 2. Review the meaning of the **-ful** suffix. Have the student read the root words aloud. The student will add **-ful** to each word by writing the suffix on the line. Note that the spelling of the base word does not change to add the suffix. Read the words with the suffixes.

Activity 2 continued:

Words:

forgetful, hopeful, joyful, peaceful,
hateful, powerful, useful, armful
boastful, harmful, wasteful, painful
sorrowful, helpful, wishful, truthful
cheerful, thoughtful, graceful, playful
grateful, bashful, handful, spoonful

Activity 3. Help the student read the sentences and the base word. Instruct the student to add **-ly** or **-ful** to the base word to complete the sentence. Note that the spelling of the base word does not change to add the suffix. Write the word on the line.

Sentences:

We walk <u>quietly</u> down the hall to go to the restroom.
A broken leg can be <u>painful</u> for many days.
We must be <u>careful</u> with knives and things that are sharp.
A classroom that is neat and <u>orderly</u> is a fun place to study.
The new paint on the wall was very <u>colorful</u>.
Mother <u>kindly</u> touched the baby on the cheek.
The huge truck moved <u>slowly</u> down the highway.
A <u>helpful</u> young man helped the lady carry her bags to the car.
The store has a <u>cheerful</u> lady who greets all who come to shop.
We can see <u>clearly</u> through the new window.

Reading. Read and discuss the maxim for the Lesson.

Read the story *Ram Dass (continued)*. This is another chapter of the *A Little Princess* story. Preview the story and explain words or sentence structures that are not familiar to the student. With every story ask questions: who are the characters, what are they doing, what are they saying, where does the action take

place, what is the order of events, what words are being used, what new information is given, what lesson can be learned?

Comprehension questions:
What thoughts helped Sara cope with Miss Minchin's rudeness?
What thoughts helped Sara cope with the servants' rudeness?
What thought made Sara laugh as she sat in the schoolroom?
Where was Sara sent when she told Miss Minchin that she might be a princess?
Who said that she would not be surprised if Sara turned out to be a princess?

Assign. Lesson activities or reading that are to be completed as homework.

3 Add *-ly* or *-ful* to the base word to make a word that completes the sentence.

quiet — We walk _____quietly_____ down the hall to go to the restroom.

pain — A broken leg can be _____painful_____ for many days.

care — We must be _____careful_____ with knives and things that are sharp.

order — A classroom that is neat and _____orderly_____ is a fun place to study.

color — The new paint on the wall was very _____colorful_____.

kind — Mother _____kindly_____ touched the baby on the cheek.

slow — The huge truck moved _____slowly_____ down the highway.

help — A _____helpful_____ young man helped the lady carry her bags to the car.

cheer — The store has a _____cheerful_____ lady who greets all who come to shop.

clear — We can see _____clearly_____ through the new window.

84   Suffixes -ly & -ful

Lesson 124: Suffixes -ness & -less

Overview:

- Add suffixes to root words
- Define the meaning of suffix **-ness**
- Define the meaning of suffix **-less**
- Read words with suffixes
- Identify the base word in words with suffixes
- Write definitions for words with suffixes
- Complete sentences using words with suffixes

Materials and Supplies:

- Teacher's Guide & Student Workbook 2
- White board or chalkboard
- Word cards (as necessary)
- Dictionary
- Reader: *A Little Princess & Other Classic Stories*

Teaching Tips:

Review for Mastery. Discuss and review any work from the previous lesson that was assigned as homework. Check for completion of the activities and orally quiz the student for comprehension. Review any reading that was assigned, discussing the characters, setting, plot, theme, language, sequence, etc.

Strengthen fluency and phonemic awareness by reviewing words and sentences from previous lessons. Build vocabulary skills by using some of the words in sentences.

Review the **-ly** suffix with Lesson 123, Activity 1. Use the **-ly** words to make up phrases that contain the words. (Examples: *A brisk walk is to walk briskly down the sidewalk. To have a test every week is a weekly test.*)

Review the **-ful** suffix with Lesson 123, Activity 2. Use the **-ful** words to make up phrases that contain the words. (Examples: *A boy who forgets is a forgetful boy. The fire that can cause harm is the harmful fire.*)

Review suffixes **-ly** and **-ful** with Lesson 123, Activity 3. Have the student make up sentences to use the other form of the base word plus the suffix used in the activity.

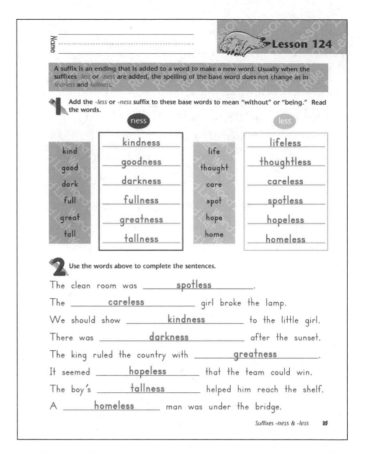

Build vocabulary skills by using some of the words from Lesson 123 in sentences.

Activity 1. Review the definition of a suffix. Review the definition of a base or root word. Have the student write examples of words with suffixes on the board. *Words to teach the concept:* bigness, calmness, coolness, deafness, dullness, fairness, freshness, illness, shortness, shyness, endless, effortless, hairless, heartless, lifeless, painless, restless, selfless, speechless, thoughtless, topless, wireless. Review the meaning of the **-ness** and **-less** suffixes. Have the student read the root words aloud. The student will add **-ness** or **-less** to each word by writing the word on the line. Note that the spelling of the base word does not change to add the suffix. Read the words with the suffixes.

Suffix -ness	Suffix -less
kindness	lifeless
goodness	thoughtless
darkness	careless
fullness	spotless
greatness	hopeless
tallness	homeless

Activity 2. Help the student read the sentences. Instruct the student to find a word from Activity 1 to complete the sentence. Write the word on the line. Unknown words can be looked up in a dictionary.

Sentences: (The answers may vary.)
The clean room was <u>spotless</u>.
The <u>careless</u> girl broke the lamp.
We should show <u>kindness</u> to the little girl.
There was <u>darkness</u> after the sunset.
The king ruled the country with <u>greatness</u>.
It seemed <u>hopeless</u> that the team could win.
The boy's <u>tallness</u> helped him reach the shelf.
A <u>homeless</u> man was under the bridge.

Activity 3. Have the student read the words with suffixes aloud. The student will circle the base or root word.

Words:
<u>end</u>less, <u>life</u>less, <u>thank</u>less, <u>aim</u>less
<u>faith</u>less, <u>fear</u>less, <u>sight</u>less, <u>worth</u>less
<u>taste</u>less, <u>help</u>less, <u>harm</u>less, <u>job</u>less
<u>tire</u>less, <u>shape</u>less, <u>doubt</u>less, <u>point</u>less
<u>dark</u>ness, <u>loud</u>ness, <u>sharp</u>ness, <u>weak</u>ness
<u>fit</u>ness, <u>sad</u>ness, <u>red</u>ness, <u>near</u>ness
<u>black</u>ness, <u>late</u>ness, <u>wide</u>ness, <u>quick</u>ness

Activity 4. The student will write the definitions for the words with suffixes on the line. Review the meanings of the suffixes **-less** and **-ness**. Review the first one which has been completed as a sample. Assist the student as needed with reading the words.

Meanings:
without life
being dark
without sight
being near
without faith
being late
without worth
being black

Reading. Read and discuss the maxim for the Lesson.

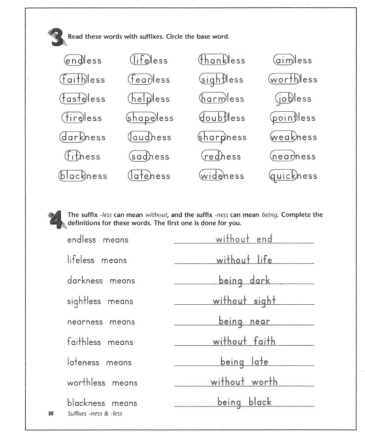

Read the story *The Other Side of the Wall*. This is another chapter of the *A Little Princess* story. Preview the story and explain words or sentence structures that are not familiar to the student. With every story ask questions: who are the characters, what are they doing, what are they saying, where does the action take place, what is the order of events, what words are being used, what new information is given, what lesson can be learned?

Comprehension questions:
Who was Sara beginning to become fond of?
What was Sara's wish for the man next door?
What had made the man next door sick?
Did Sara wonder if the man next door could feel her thoughts?
Who was able to cheer the man up who lived next door?
What possible thought did the man next door have about Sara?

Assign. Lesson activities or reading that are to be completed as homework.

Lesson 125: Suffixes -y, -en, & -able/-ible

Overview:

- Add suffixes to root words
- Define the meaning of suffix **-y**
- Define the meaning of suffix **-en**
- Define the meaning of suffix **-able/-ible**
- Read words with suffixes
- Apply spelling rules to correctly add suffixes to words
- Identify the base word in words with suffixes

Materials and Supplies:

- Teacher's Guide & Student Workbook 2
- White board or chalkboard
- Word cards (as necessary)
- Dictionary
- Reader: *A Little Princess & Other Classic Stories*

Teaching Tips:

Review for Mastery. Discuss and review any work from the previous lesson that was assigned as homework. Check for completion of the activities and orally quiz the student for comprehension. Review any reading that was assigned, discussing the characters, setting, plot, theme, language, sequence, etc.

Strengthen fluency and phonemic awareness by reviewing words and sentences from previous lessons. Build vocabulary skills by using some of the words in sentences.

Review suffixes **-ness** and **-less** with Lesson 124, Activity 1. Use the **-ness** and **-less** words to make up phrases that contain the words. (Examples: *Being kind is to show kindness. To be without life is to be lifeless.*)

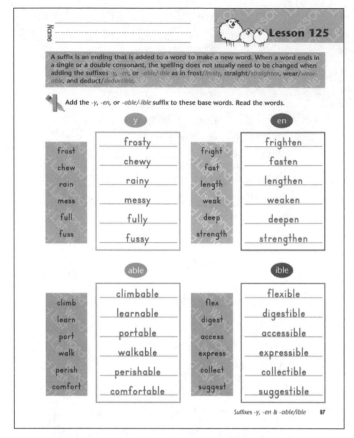

Activity 1. Review the rule for adding the suffixes **-y**, **-en**, **-able/-ible**. Review the meaning of the **-y**, **-en**, and **-able/-ible** suffixes. Suffix **-ible** is another spelling for suffix **-able**. Suffix **-y** means full of (*bumpy*), containing (*salty*), having (*cloudy*), inclined to (*sleepy*), like (*dreamy*), a small (*dolly*), dear (*daddy*). Suffix **-en** means to cause to be (*cheapen*), to become (redden), to cause to have (*hearten*), to come or have (lengthen), made of or resemble (earthen). Suffix **-able/-ible** means that can be ___**ed** (*enjoyable* = *can be enjoyed*), able, liable or likely (*breakable* = *likely to break*). Have the student read the root words aloud. The student will add the suffixes in the circles to each word by writing the word on the line. Note that the spelling of the base word does not change to add the suffix. Read the words with the suffixes.

Suffix -y	Suffix -en
frosty	frighten
chewy	fasten
rainy	lengthen
messy	weaken
fully	deepen
fussy	strengthen

Horizons Phonics & Reading Grade 2 Teacher's Guide

Activity 1 continued:

<u>Suffix -able</u>	**<u>Suffix -ible</u>**
climbable	**flexible**
learnable	**digestible**
portable	**accessible**
walkable	**expressible**
perishable	**collectible**
comfortable	**suggestible**

Activity 2. Have the student read the words with suffixes aloud. Review the 1-1-1 Rule, words of 1 syllable, having 1 vowel, followed by 1 consonant, usually double the final consonant before adding a suffix that starts with a vowel. *Words to teach the concept:* penny, witty, furry, kitty, bunny, carry. The student will circle the base or root word.

Words:

baggy, buggy, choppy, daddy
doggy, drippy, foggy, funny
knotty, nutty, piggy, puppy
skinny, sloppy, snappy, spotty
chatty, floppy, muddy, sunny

Activity 3. The student will write the root for the words with suffixes on the line. Review the Drop **e** Rule for adding a suffix to words that end in **e**. *Words to teach the concept:* driven, forgiven, forsaken, liken, ripen, risen, shapen, sharpen, spoken, stolen, taken, waken, increasable, restorable, revisable, solvable, collapsible, condensible, enforcible, fusible, producible, reducible, reversible, risible. Assist the student as needed with reading the words.

Words:

chose, adore
force, sense
use, give
broke, store
hide, prove

Reading. Read and discuss the maxim for the Lesson.

Read the story *The Other Side of the Wall (continued)*. This is another chapter of the *A*

When a word ends with a single consonant that follows a single vowel, the final consonant is usually doubled before the suffix *-y* is added as in fun/*funny* and fog/*foggy*.

2 Read these words with suffixes. Use the rule to circle the base word.

baggy	buggy	choppy	daddy
doggy	drippy	foggy	funny
knotty	nutty	piggy	puppy
skinny	sloppy	snappy	spotty
chatty	floppy	muddy	sunny

A word that ends in *e* usually drops the *e* when adding a suffix beginning with a vowel as in move/*movable*, force/*forcible*, and rise/*risen*.

3 Read these words with suffixes. Use the rule to write the base word.

chosen	chose	adorable	adore
forcible	force	sensible	sense
usable	use	given	give
broken	broke	storable	store
hidable	hide	proven	prove

98 *Suffixes -y, -en & -able/ible*

Little Princess story. Preview the story and explain words or sentence structures that are not familiar to the student. With every story ask questions: who are the characters, what are they doing, what are they saying, where does the action take place, what is the order of events, what words are being used, what new information is given, what lesson can be learned?

Comprehension questions:

Where was Mr Crawford looking for a child?
What was the name of the child who had been in Paris?
Who had put his trust in Mr. Crawford?
Why had Mr. Crawford run away?
What name for the little girl could Mr. Crawford remember?
What name that her father had called her was Sara thinking of that evening?

Assign. Lesson activities or reading that are to be completed as homework.

Lesson 126: Prefixes re- & un-

Overview:

- Add prefixes to root words
- Define the meaning of prefix **re-**
- Define the meaning of prefix **un-**
- Read words with prefixes
- Apply spelling rules to correctly add prefixes to words
- Complete sentences using words with prefixes

Materials and Supplies:

- Teacher's Guide & Student Workbook 2
- White board or chalkboard
- Word cards (as necessary)
- Dictionary
- Reader: *A Little Princess & Other Classic Stories*

Teaching Tips:

Review for Mastery. Discuss and review any work from the previous lesson that was assigned as homework. Check for completion of the activities and orally quiz the student for comprehension. Review any reading that was assigned, discussing the characters, setting, plot, theme, language, sequence, etc.

Strengthen fluency and phonemic awareness by reviewing words and sentences from previous lessons. Build vocabulary skills by using some of the words in sentences.

Review suffixes and their meanings with Lesson 125, Activities 1-3. Use the words to make up phrases that contain the words. (Examples: *A trail that can be walked is a walkable trail. A day having rain is a rainy day. Making a rope weak from wearing away is to weaken a rope.*)

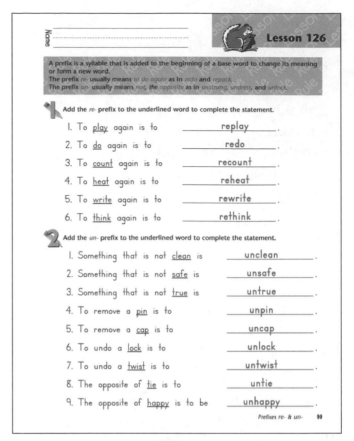

Activity 1. Review the definition for the prefix **re-**. Have the student write examples of words with the prefix on the board. *Words to teach the concept:* recap, refit, renew, rerun, reset, reborn, recall, recoil, refill, refine, reform, rejoin, relive, remark, repaid, resale, resign, retake, rewind, reword, rework, rebound, rebuild, reclaim, recline, recount, recover, recycle, refresh, recharge, recreate, rephrase. The student will add a prefix to the underlined word that will match the definition and write it on the line. Read the words.

Words:
1. replay
2. redo
3. recount
4. reheat
5. rewrite
6. rethink

Activity 2. Review the definition for the prefix **un-**. Have the student write examples of words with the prefix on the board. *Words to teach*

Horizons Phonics & Reading Grade 2 Teacher's Guide

the concept: unfit, unlit, unbolt, unborn, uncoil, uncork, undone, unfair, unjust, unlace, unload, unpack, unroll, unseen, unused, unwell, unwind, unscrew, unfasten, ungrateful. The student will add a prefix to the underlined word that will match the definition and write it on the line. Read the words.

Words:
1. unclean
2. unsafe
3. untrue
4. unpin
5. uncap
6. unlock
7. untwist
8. untie
9. unhappy

Activity 3. Help the student read the sentences and the base word. Instruct the student to add **re-** or **un-** to the base word to complete the sentence. Note that the spelling of the base word does not change to add the prefix. Write the word on the line.

Sentences:

We will <u>unplug</u> the lamp to change the light bulb.

It was hard to ride a bike on the <u>uneven</u> sidewalk.

It is almost time to <u>return</u> the books to the library.

Ask your mom to <u>remind</u> you about the party.

She will need help to <u>unzip</u> her coat.

Please <u>remove</u> your wet shoes when you come in the house.

It was <u>unkind</u> to laugh when the girl fell.

Try to <u>review</u> the seatwork before you turn it in.

<u>Unbutton</u> the shirt before you hang it on the hook.

A new broom is in the garage to <u>replace</u> the one that was broken.

---

3 Add *re-* or *un-* to the base word to make a word that completes the sentence.

plug	We will ___unplug___ the lamp to change the light bulb.
even	It was hard to ride a bike on the ___uneven___ sidewalk.
turn	It is almost time to ___return___ the books to the library.
mind	Ask your mom to ___remind___ you about the party.
zip	She will need help to ___unzip___ her coat.
move	Please ___remove___ your wet shoes when you come in the house.
kind	It was ___unkind___ to laugh when the girl fell.
view	Try to ___review___ the seatwork before you turn it in.
button	___Unbutton___ the shirt before you hang it on the hook.
place	A new broom is in the garage to ___replace___ the one that was broken.

100 *Prefixes re- & un-*

Reading. Read and discuss the maxim for the Lesson.

Read the story *One of the People*. This is another chapter of the *A Little Princess* story. Preview the story and explain words or sentence structures that are not familiar to the student. With every story ask questions: who are the characters, what are they doing, what are they saying, where does the action take place, what is the order of events, what words are being used, what new information is given, what lesson can be learned?

Comprehension questions:

What was the winter weather like?

What helped Sara and Becky cope with the poor conditions?

What "supposing" was Sara doing after several rainy days?

How did Sara "suppose" she might be able to get some hot buns?

Assign. Lesson activities or reading that are to be completed as homework.

Lesson 127: Prefixes dis- & pre-

Overview:

- Add prefixes to root words
- Define the meaning of prefix **dis-**
- Define the meaning of prefix **pre-**
- Read words with prefixes
- Apply spelling rules to correctly add prefixes to words
- Complete sentences using words with prefixes

Materials and Supplies:

- Teacher's Guide & Student Workbook 2
- White board or chalkboard
- Word cards (as necessary)
- Dictionary
- Reader: *A Little Princess & Other Classic Stories*

Teaching Tips:

Review for Mastery. Discuss and review any work from the previous lesson that was assigned as homework. Check for completion of the activities and orally quiz the student for comprehension. Review any reading that was assigned, discussing the characters, setting, plot, theme, language, sequence, etc.

Strengthen fluency and phonemic awareness by reviewing words and sentences from previous lessons. Build vocabulary skills by using some of the words in sentences.

Review prefixes **re-** and **un-** with Lesson 126, Activities 1 & 2. Use the words to make up sentences or phrases that contain the words. (Examples: *They will replay the game that was not completed. Please uncap the soda for me.*)

Activity 1. Review the definition for the prefix **dis-**. Have the student write examples of words with the prefix on the board. *Words to teach the concept:* disappoint, disapprove, disarm, disband, discharge, disclose, discord, discount, discover, disinfect, dislodge, disown, display, displace, disprove, disrobe. Have the student

read each root word aloud. The student will add the prefix **dis-** to the word and write it on the line. Read the words.

Words:

disagree, disappear, disarm, disbelief
disconnect, discard, disgrace, dishonest
dislike, disloyal, dismiss, dismount
disobey, disorder, displease, distrust

Activity 2. Help the student read the sentences and the word choices. Instruct the student to choose the word that completes the sentence and fill in the circle by the word. Write the word on the line.

Sentences:

John is unhappy so he will <u>disobey</u> his mother.
When class is over the teacher will <u>dismiss</u> the students.
Sally was <u>disloyal</u> to her team and did not practice.
The police will try to quiet the <u>disorder</u> of the angry crowd.

Activity 2 continued:

It will <u>displease</u> your dad if you do not finish your meal.
Eggplant is a food that some people <u>dislike</u>.
My friend and I <u>disagree</u> on the rules of the game.
After the sun comes out, the water on the sidewalk will <u>disappear</u>.

Activity 3. Review the definition for the prefix **pre-**. Have the student write examples of words with the prefix on the board. *Words to teach the concept:* prearm, preassign, prebake, prebill, preboil, prebook, precheck, prechill, preclean, precook, precool, precut, predate, predrill, preflight, preheat, premix, prepack, prepaid, preprice, preprint, presale, prescreen, preset, preshape, preshow, preshrink, pretape, preterm, prewarm, prewash. Help the student read the sentences and the underlined words. Instruct the student to add the prefix **pre-** to the word that completes the sentence and write the word on the line.

Sentences:

<u>Fix</u> means to place, so <u>prefix</u> means to place before.
A <u>season</u> is a period of time, so the <u>preseason</u> comes before the period of time.
<u>Pay</u> means to give money for something, so the word <u>prepay</u> means to pay beforehand.
<u>View</u> means to watch, so <u>preview</u> means to watch beforehand.
<u>School</u> is a planned time to learn, so <u>preschool</u> is a time to learn before that time.

Reading. Read and discuss the maxim for the Lesson.

Read the story *One of the People (continued)*. This is another chapter of the *A Little Princess* story. Preview the story and explain words or sentence structures that are not familiar to the student. With every story ask questions: who

are the characters, what are they doing, what are they saying, where does the action take place, what is the order of events, what words are being used, what new information is given, what lesson can be learned?

Comprehension questions:

What did Sara see in the gutter?
What was right in front of her after Sara picked up the money?
Who did Sara see before she went into the bake shop?
What did Sara ask the beggar girl?
How long had it been since the beggar girl had something to eat?
What did Sara tell the beggar girl to do?

Assign. Lesson activities or reading that are to be completed as homework.

It will _____displease_____ your dad if you do not finish your meal.
○ discolor
● displease

Eggplant is a food that some people _____dislike_____.
○ dishonest
● dislike

My friend and I _____disagree_____ on the rules of the game.
● disagree
○ disable

After the sun comes out, the water on the sidewalk will _____disappear_____.
● disappear
○ discount

3 Add the *pre-* prefix to the underlined word to complete the statement.

<u>Fix</u> means to place, so _____prefix_____ means to place before.
A <u>season</u> is a period of time, so the _____preseason_____ comes before the period of time.
<u>Pay</u> means to give money for something, so the word _____prepay_____ means to pay beforehand.
<u>View</u> means to watch, so _____preview_____ means to watch beforehand.
<u>School</u> is a planned time to learn, so _____preschool_____ is a time to learn before that time.

102   *Prefixes dis- & pre-*

Lesson 128: Prefixes mis- & non-

Overview:

- Add prefixes to root words
- Define the meaning of prefix **mis-**
- Define the meaning of prefix **non-**
- Read words with prefixes
- Apply spelling rules to correctly add prefixes to words
- Add a suffix to a word to match the definition
- Complete sentences using words with prefixes
- Identify the base word in words with suffixes

Materials and Supplies:

- Teacher's Guide & Student Workbook 2
- White board or chalkboard
- Word cards (as necessary)
- Dictionary
- Reader: *A Little Princess & Other Classic Stories*

Teaching Tips:

Review for Mastery. Discuss and review any work from the previous lesson that was assigned as homework. Check for completion of the activities and orally quiz the student for comprehension. Review any reading that was assigned, discussing the characters, setting, plot, theme, language, sequence, etc.

Strengthen fluency and phonemic awareness by reviewing words and sentences from previous lessons. Build vocabulary skills by using some of the words in sentences.

Review the prefix **dis-** with Lesson 127, Activity 2. Use the leftover words not used in the sentences to make up sentences that contain the words. (Examples: *They will disconnect our phone in the morning. I have a distaste for sour candy.*)

Activity 1. Review the definitions for the prefix **mis-**. Have the student write examples of words with the prefix on the board. *Words to*

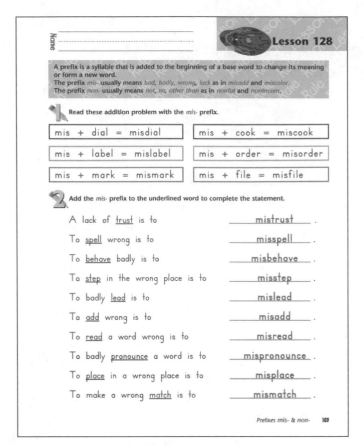

teach the concept: misaddress, misadjust, misbelieve, misbill, misbuild, miscarry, mischarge, miscolor, misconnect, miscook, miscut, misdate, misdeal, misdial, misfile, misfire, misfit, misgiving, mishandle, misjudge, miskick, mislabel, mislay, misprint, mistake, mistrial. Have the student read the "addition" problem that forms the new word with a prefix: "mis plus dial equals misdial." Use the word in a sentence or definition. "To dial a phone number wrong is to misdial it."

Activity 2. Review the definition of the prefix **mis-**. Have the student read the definition aloud. The student is to add a prefix to the underlined word that will match the definition and write it on the line. Read the words.

Words:
mistrust
misspell
misbehave
misstep
mislead

Horizons Phonics & Reading Grade 2 Teacher's Guide

Activity 2 continued:

    misadd

    misread

    mispronounce

    misplace

    mismatch

Activity 3. Review the definitions for the prefix **non-**. Have the student write examples of words with the prefix on the board. *Words to teach the concept:* nonbeliever, nonbinding, noncombat, nonconcern, nonconductor, nondelivery, nonedible, nonelastic, nonfinal, nonformal, nonhuman, nonliquid, nonreader, nonshrink, nonsmoker, nonsocial, nonverbal, nonwhite. Have the student read the words with their prefixes aloud. The student will circle the base or root word. For this exercise, ignore the fact that some of these words have suffixes.

Words:

    non<u>action</u>, non<u>answer</u>, non<u>basic</u>, non<u>belief</u>

    non<u>color</u>, non<u>conform</u>, non<u>contact</u>,
    non<u>credit</u>

    non<u>dairy</u>, non<u>decision</u>, non<u>defense</u>,
    non<u>metal</u>

    non<u>drug</u>, non<u>elect</u>, non<u>ending</u>, non<u>equal</u>

    non<u>factor</u>, non<u>graded</u>, non<u>leaded</u>, non<u>stop</u>

    non<u>zero</u>, non<u>pagan</u>, non<u>profit</u>, non<u>living</u>

Activity 4. Have the student read the phrase aloud. Review the definition of the prefix **non-**. The student will add a prefix to the key word in each phrase that will match the definition and write it on the line. Read the words.

Words:

    noncrime

    nonfood

    nonanswer

    nonadult

    nonbasic

    nonpaid

    nonequal

    nonfat

    nonstick

    nonfrozen

3 Read these words with the *non-* prefix. Circle the base in each word.

non(action)	non(answer)	non(basic)	non(belief)
non(color)	non(conform)	non(contact)	non(credit)
non(dairy)	non(decision)	non(defense)	non(metal)
non(drug)	non(elect)	non(ending)	non(equal)
non(factor)	non(graded)	non(leaded)	non(stop)
non(zero)	non(pagan)	non(profit)	non(living)

4 Find the key word in each phrase and add the *non-* prefix to complete the statement.

Not a crime is a	noncrime .
Not a food is a	nonfood .
Not an answer is a	nonanswer .
Not an adult is a	nonadult .
Not basic is	nonbasic .
Not paid is	nonpaid .
Not equal is	nonequal .
No fat is	nonfat .
No stick is	nonstick .
Not frozen	nonfrozen .

104   *Prefixes mis- & non*

Reading. Read and discuss the maxim for the Lesson.

Read the story *One of the People (continued)*. This is another chapter of the *A Little Princess* story. Preview the story and explain words or sentence structures that are not familiar to the student. With every story ask questions: who are the characters, what are they doing, what are they saying, where does the action take place, what is the order of events, what words are being used, what new information is given, what lesson can be learned?

Comprehension questions:

    What did Sara ask the lady in the bake shop?

    Why did the lady in the bake shop put two extra buns in the bag?

    What was the beggar girl doing when Sara left the store?

    How many buns did Sara give to the beggar girl?

    How many buns did Sara save for herself?

Assign. Lesson activities or reading that are to be completed as homework.

Lesson 129: Syllabication with Affixes

Overview:

- Define the term "syllable"
- Divide words with affixes into syllables
- Use the rules for adding suffixes to separate words into the root and suffix
- Read words with affixes

Materials and Supplies:

- Teacher's Guide & Student Workbook 2
- White board or chalkboard
- Word cards (as necessary)
- Dictionary
- Reader: *A Little Princess & Other Classic Stories*

Teaching Tips:

Review for Mastery. Discuss and review any work from the previous lesson that was assigned as homework. Check for completion of the activities and orally quiz the student for comprehension. Review any reading that was assigned, discussing the characters, setting, plot, theme, language, sequence, etc.

Strengthen fluency and phonemic awareness by reviewing words and sentences from previous lessons. Build vocabulary skills by using some of the words in sentences.

Review the prefix **mis-** with Lesson 128, Activity 1. Use the words in a phrase similar to the phrases found in Activity 2.

Review the prefix **mis-** with Lesson 128, Activity 2. Add the suffixes **-ed** or **-ing** to the words.

Review the prefix **non-** with Lesson 128, Activity 3. Try to find words that have both a suffix and a prefix. Make up phrases for the words similar to the phrases found in Activity 4.

Review the definition of a syllable. Review the definitions for the all the prefixes and suffixes that have been covered. Have the student write examples of words with those affixes on the chalkboard or white board.

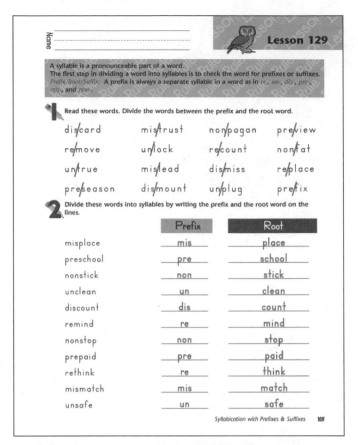

Activity 1. Have the student read the words aloud. Review the rule for dividing a word with a prefix into syllables. The student will divide each word into syllables by drawing a slash between the prefix and the root word.

Words:

  dis/card, mis/trust, non/pagan, pre/view
  re/move, un/lock, re/count, non/fat
  un/true, mis/lead, dis/miss, re/place
  pre/season, dis/mount, un/plug, pre/fix

Activity 2. Have the student read the words aloud. The student will divide each word into syllables and write the prefix and the root on the line.

Prefix	Root
mis	place
pre	school
non	stick
un	clean
dis	count
re	mind
non	stop

Activity 2 continued:

Prefix	Root
pre	paid
re	think
mis	match
un	safe

Activity 3. Review the rules for adding suffixes to root words. Read the words. Have the student divide the word into syllables by drawing a slash between the root word and the suffix.

Words:

ador/able, aim/less, clear/ly, fast/est
fit/ness, flex/ible, fuss/y length/en
life/less, neat/er, pain/ful, red/der
sight/less, slow/ly, strength/en, sun/ny
tall/est, waste/ful, weak/ness, beach/es
brush/ing, seat/ed, munch/ing, push/es

Activity 4. Have the student read the words aloud. The student will divide each word into syllables and write the root and the suffix on the line.

Root	Suffix
pitch	ing
wait	ed
deep	en
hope	less
color	ful
good	ness
suggest	ible
night	ly
glass	es
neat	est
wide	er

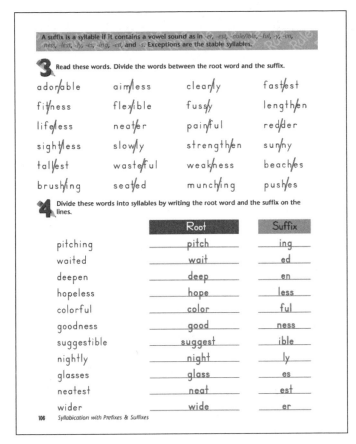

Reading. Read and discuss the maxim for the Lesson.

Read the story *One of the People (continued)*. This is another chapter of the *A Little Princess* story. Preview the story and explain words or sentence structures that are not familiar to the student. With every story ask questions: who are the characters, what are they doing, what are they saying, where does the action take place, what is the order of events, what words are being used, what new information is given, what lesson can be learned?

Comprehension questions:
Who spoke to the beggar girl after Sara left?
What did the bake shop lady do for the beggar girl?
What was Mr. Richmond preparing to do?
Where was Mr. Richmond planning to travel?
What did Janet say about how Sara looked?

Assign. Lesson activities or reading that are to be completed as homework.

Lesson 130: Syllabication with Affixes

Overview:

- Define the term "syllable"
- Divide words with affixes into syllables
- Use the rules for adding suffixes to separate words into the root and suffix
- Classify syllables as the root or type of affix
- Recognize the spellings of affixes
- Divide words with both a prefix and a suffix into syllables
- Read words with affixes

Materials and Supplies:

- Teacher's Guide & Student Workbook 2
- White board or chalkboard
- Word cards (as necessary)
- Dictionary
- Reader: *A Little Princess & Other Classic Stories*

Teaching Tips:

Review for Mastery. Discuss and review any work from the previous lesson that was assigned as homework. Check for completion of the activities and orally quiz the student for comprehension. Review any reading that was assigned, discussing the characters, setting, plot, theme, language, sequence, etc.

Strengthen fluency and phonemic awareness by reviewing words and sentences from previous lessons. Build vocabulary skills by using some of the words in sentences.

Review the meanings of prefixes with Lesson 129, Activities 1 & 2. Make up sentences or phrases using the words.

Review suffixes with Lesson 129, Activities 2 & 4. Add some of the suffixes covered so far to the root words.

Review the definition of a syllable. Review the definitions for the all the prefixes and suffixes that have been covered. Have the student write examples of words with those affixes on the chalkboard or white board.

A syllable is a pronounceable part of a word.
A prefix is always a separate syllable in a word as in *re-, un-, dis-, pre-, mis-,* and *non-*.
A suffix is a syllable if it contains a vowel sound as in *-er, -est, -able/ible, -ful, -en, -ness, -less, -ly, -es, -ing, -ed,* and *-s*. Exceptions are the stable syllables.

Read these words. Divide the words into syllables. Write a *P* over a prefix, an *R* over the root, and an *S* over a suffix.

dis/grace	arm/ful	cut/est	mis/step
drip/py	few/er	non/crime	rich/es
lock/ing	week/ly	thank/less	pre/pay
port/able	re/play	great/ness	un/kind
flush/es	help/ful	dis/like	knot/ty
loud/er	help/less	re/heat	land/ing
pinch/es	dark/est	non/food	jolt/ed
hard/est	quick/ly	short/er	weak/en
mis/mark	near/ness	un/twist	strang/est
use/ful	learn/able	inch/ing	rent/ed

Syllabication with Prefixes & Suffixes **107**

Activity 1. Review the definition of a syllable. Review the definitions for the all the prefixes and suffixes that have been covered. Have the student write examples of words with those affixes on the board. Practice dividing those words into syllables and label the prefix or suffix, and the root. Have the student read the words in the activity aloud. The student will divide each word into syllables by drawing a slash between the prefix and the root word or the root word and the suffix. Remind the student that in Final **e** words the **e** was dropped and then the suffix was added. Then the student is to label the root and the prefix or suffix.

Words:

dis/grace, arm/ful, cut/est, mis/step
drip/py, few/er, non/crime, rich/es
lock/ing, week/ly, thank/less, pre/pay
port/able, re/play, great/ness, un/kind
flush/es, help/ful, dis/like knot/ty
loud/er, help/less, re/heat, land/ing
pinch/es, dark/est, non/food, jolt/ed
hard/est, quick/ly, short/er, weak/en
mis/mark, near/ness, un/twist, strang/est
use/ful, learn/able, inch/ing, rent/ed

Activity 2. Have the student read the words aloud. These are all three-syllable words with both a prefix and a suffix. *Words to teach the concept:* discarded, disagreeable, misadded, dismounted, misreading, misspelling, redoing, reminding, reminded, removing, replaying, returning, reviewing, unlocking, unplugging, unsafely, untwisting, unclearly, unendless, unending, unfasten, unlucky, untruthful, unseated, unneeded, unfolded, undressing, unpacking. The student will divide each word into syllables by drawing a slash between the prefix the root word and the suffix. Remind the student that in Final **e** words the **e** was dropped and then the suffix was added. Then the student is to label the prefix, root, and suffix.

Words:

dis/count/ed, mis/dial/ing, non/end/ing
pre/pay/ing, re/count/ing, un/kind/ly
re/think/ing, pre/fold/ed, dis/count/er
mis/lead/ing, non/grad/ed, pre/view/ing
re/heat/ing, un/zip/ping, re/load/ed
pre/coat/ed, dis/taste/ful, mis/trust/ed
non/lead/ed, re/mind/er, un/climb/able

Activity 3. Have the student read the words aloud. These words have both a prefix and a suffix. The student will divide each word into syllables and write the prefix, root, and suffix on the line.

Prefix	Root	Suffix
re	place	ing
un	faith	ful
pre	load	ed
non	live	ing
dis	trust	ful
un	thought	ful

Review for Test. The instructor should plan to use some time at the end of the class to review and prepare for the test that follows this lesson. Review the objectives for the test and then look over the lessons that it will cover. If the student has struggled with any of the concepts that will be included in the test, some additional drill, practice, or review may be needed to adequately prepare him for the test.

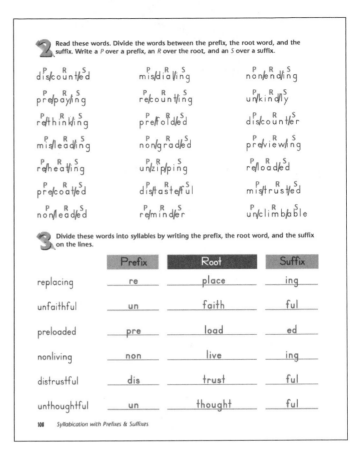

2. Read these words. Divide the words between the prefix, the root word, and the suffix. Write a *P* over a prefix, an *R* over the root, and an *S* over a suffix.

dis/count/ed   mis/dial/ing   non/end/ing
pre/pay/ing   re/count/ing   un/kind/ly
re/think/ing   pre/fold/ed   dis/count/er
mis/lead/ing   non/grad/ed   pre/view/ing
re/heat/ing   un/zip/ping   re/load/ed
pre/coat/ed   dis/taste/ful   mis/trust/ed
non/lead/ed   re/mind/er   un/climb/able

3. Divide these words into syllables by writing the prefix, the root word, and the suffix on the lines.

	Prefix	Root	Suffix
replacing	re	place	ing
unfaithful	un	faith	ful
preloaded	pre	load	ed
nonliving	non	live	ing
distrustful	dis	trust	ful
unthoughtful	un	thought	ful

108   *Syllabication with Prefixes & Suffixes*

Reading. Read and discuss the maxim for the Lesson.

Read the story *What Zedek Heard and Saw*. This is another chapter of the *A Little Princess* story. Preview the story and explain words or sentence structures that are not familiar to the student. With every story ask questions: who are the characters, what are they doing, what are they saying, where does the action take place, what is the order of events, what words are being used, what new information is given, what lesson can be learned?

Comprehension questions:
Who came to Sara's room while she was gone?
Who made the notes about the attic room?
Who had been watching what Sara did every day?
Who had made the plan to help Sara?

Assign. Lesson activities or reading that are to be completed as homework.

Test 13
Lessons 115-124

Overview:

- Define an irregular plural
- Select the correct irregular plural for a given word
- Read irregular plurals correctly
- Define comparative endings
- Apply the correct rule to add comparative endings to a base word
- Complete sentences with comparative endings
- Apply the correct rule to add affixes to a base word
- Define possessives
- Write possessive versions of base words
- Add an apostrophe plus **s** to a singular noun to show possession
- Select the correct suffix for a word

Materials and Supplies:

- Teacher's Guide & Student Workbook 2

Instructions:

Assessment Start-up. Help the student with any words that he is still unsure of. The teacher should be available to answer any questions that the student may have during the test.

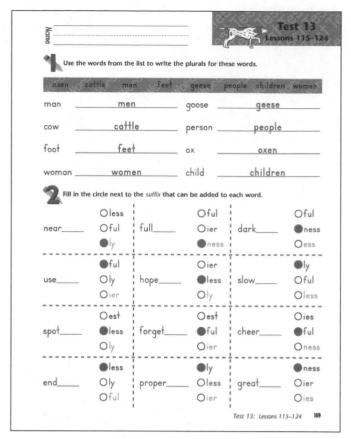

Activity 1. Review the instructions, the words in the list, and the given words with the student. Instruct the student to select the correct irregular plural for each word and write it on the line.

Words:

man/<u>men</u>	goose/<u>geese</u>
cow/<u>cattle</u>	person/<u>people</u>
foot/<u>feet</u>	ox/<u>oxen</u>
woman/<u>women</u>	child/<u>children</u>

Activity 2. Review the instructions, the words, and the suffixes with the student. Instruct the student to select a suffix for each word by filling in the circle by the suffix.

Words:

near<u>ly</u>	full<u>ness</u>	dark<u>ness</u>
use<u>ful</u>	hope<u>less</u>	slow<u>ly</u>
spot<u>less</u>	forget<u>ful</u>	cheer<u>ful</u>
end<u>less</u>	proper<u>ly</u>	great<u>ness</u>

Activity 3. Review the instructions, the base words, and the sentences. Make sure the student can correctly read everything in the activity. Instruct the student to write the correct possessive in each blank.

Sentences:

1. My shirt is <u>redder</u> than Bill's and is the <u>reddest</u> one in the class.
2. This store is the <u>largest</u> one in the mall and it is <u>larger</u> than the bank across the street.
3. Today it is <u>hotter</u> than yesterday so it is the <u>hottest</u> day of the summer.
4. I bought the <u>brightest</u> flashlight in the store, It is <u>brighter</u> than the light in the ceiling.
5. A ruby is <u>shinier</u> than a garnet but a diamond is the <u>shiniest</u> gem of all.

Activity 4. Review the instructions and the phrases with the student. Instruct the student to form the correct singular possessive for each phrase.

Words:

painter<u>'s</u> brushes	author<u>'s</u> book
nation<u>'s</u> flag	tree<u>'s</u> leaves
frog<u>'s</u> leg	cousin<u>'s</u> parents
oven<u>'s</u> door	dog<u>'s</u> leash
dad<u>'s</u> tools	Megan<u>'s</u> hair

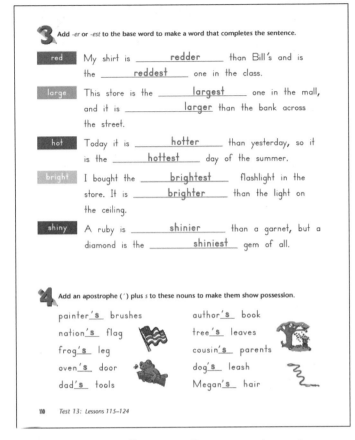

Assessment Follow-up. Every test is an important assessment of both the student's comprehension of the concepts and the instructional process. This makes follow-up after each test essential to the learning process. Review all of the errors made on the test with the student. Check for understanding of the concepts and of the problem instructions. Compare the errors made on the test to the test objectives to identify specific areas of weakness. If weak areas of understanding are detected it might be necessary to go back to those lessons to devise some enrichment activities for the concept.

The test results can be used to determine what concepts are reviewed during the daily time of classroom instruction. Devise enrichment activities that will provide development in those areas.

If time permits, choose a selection and have the student read it again. This can also be used as a catch-up time to complete unfinished selections.

Lesson 131: Syllabication with Compound Words

Overview:

- Define a compound word
- Form compound words from several choices
- Apply syllable rules to compound words
- Determine which words in a group can be used to form compound words
- Read sentences

Materials and Supplies:

- Teacher's Guide & Student Workbook 2
- White board or chalkboard
- Word cards (as necessary)
- Dictionary
- Reader: *A Little Princess & Other Classic Stories*

Teaching Tips:

Review for Mastery. Discuss and review any work from the previous lesson that was assigned as homework. Check for completion of the activities and orally quiz the student for comprehension. Review any reading that was assigned, discussing the characters, setting, plot, theme, language, sequence, etc.

Strengthen fluency and phonemic awareness by reviewing words and sentences from previous lessons. Build vocabulary skills by using some of the words in sentences.

Review the meanings of affixes with Lesson 130, Activity 1. Use the words in a phrase or sentence.

Activity 1. Review the rule for compound words and the examples. Have the student write examples of the rule on the board. *Words to teach the concept:* goldfish, lifeblood, lifeline, nightlife, wildlife, airboat, boathook, boatload, flatboat, longboat, tugboat, flatfoot, footgear, footnote, hotfoot, tenderfoot, birdhouse, coffeehouse, housefly, jailhouse, lighthouse, steakhouse, card-

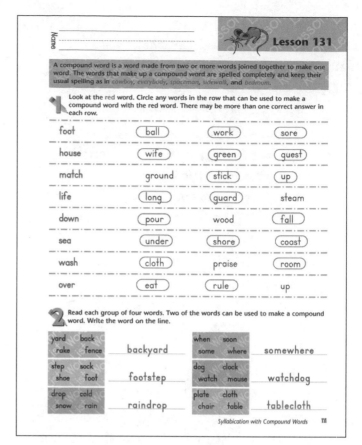

board, scorecard, timecard, matchstick, tightrope, softball, motorboat. Have the student read the red word and the other words in each row. The student will circle all words in the row that can be used to form compound words with the red word. The red word can be either the first or the last word in the compound word. Instruct the student to read them both ways to find the words that can be used (*football, footwork, footsore, ballfoot, workfoot, sorefoot,* etc.).

Words:
  ball, work, sore
  wife, green, guest
  stick, up
  long, guard
  pour, fall
  under, shore, coast
  cloth, room
  eat, rule

Activity 2. In this activity the student has four word choices from which they must use two of the words to form a compound word. Assist the student in reading the words in each box.

If the student does not quickly recognize a compound word in the group instruct him to work with one word at a time to see if it can be used to form a compound with one of the other three words. Some of the words sound good together but they are not compound words.

Words:
backyard, somewhere
footstep, watchdog
raindrop, tablecloth

Activity 3. Help the student read the sentences. Instruct the student to select the compound word from the sentence and write the word on the line. Then divide the word into syllables with a slash. Some of the words have suffixes.

Words:
house/boat
down/town
some/one
sun/light
camp/site
pan/cakes
store/keep/er
eye/glass/es
hand/ball
down/stairs

Activity 4. In this activity the student has a number of word choices from which he must use two of the words to form a compound word. Assist the student in reading the words. If the student does not quickly recognize a compound word in the group instruct him to work with one word at a time to see if it can be used to form a compound with one of the other words. Some of the words sound good together but they are not compound words. Have the student write the compound words on the lines and divide them into syllables.

Words:
type/writ/er   **over/eat**
ear/drum   **bull/frog**
head/light   **cup/cake**
sweet/heart   **scare/crow**
or **care/worn**

Horizons Phonics & Reading Grade 2 Teacher's Guide

---

3 Find the compound word in each sentence and write it on the line. Divide the word into syllables between the two words. Some of the words have suffixes.

1. Alex would like a houseboat.   house/boat
2. Let us go downtown this evening.   down/town
3. Have someone turn off the lights.   some/one
4. The sunlight is very bright.   sun/light
5. A campsite is near the stream.   camp/site
6. I ate pancakes this morning.   pan/cakes
7. The storekeeper works every day.   store/keep/er
8. Jill lost her eyeglasses.   eye/glass/es
9. Phil played handball last night.   hand/ball
10. She lives downstairs.   down/stairs

4 Put these words together to form compound words. Write them on the lines. Divide them into syllables.

writer	drum	head	sweet	light	cup	there
over	frog	type	crow	worn	eat	scare
tale	bull	cake	still	heart	care	ear

type/writ/er   over/eat
ear/drum   bull/frog
head/light   cup/cake
sweet/heart   scare/crow

112   *Syllabication with Compound Words*

Reading. Read and discuss the maxim for the Lesson.

Read the story *What Zedek Heard and Saw (continued)*. This is another chapter of the *A Little Princess* story. Preview the story and explain words or sentence structures that are not familiar to the student. With every story ask questions: who are the characters, what are they doing, what are they saying, where does the action take place, what is the order of events, what words are being used, what new information is given, what lesson can be learned?

Comprehension questions:
What notes did the secretary make?
Who first came up with the idea of helping Sara?
How was Ram Dass going to be able to make the changes to the room without Sara hearing?
Who was relieved when the men left Sara's room?

Assign. Lesson activities or reading that are to be completed as homework.

Lesson 132: Syllabication with Schwa Sound

Overview:

- Define a schwa vowel
- Read two-syllable words with schwa sounds
- Apply the rules to divide words into syllables
- Auditory discrimination of similar schwa sounds

Materials and Supplies:

- Teacher's Guide & Student Workbook 2
- White board or chalkboard
- Word cards (as necessary)
- Dictionary
- Reader: *A Little Princess & Other Classic Stories*

Teaching Tips:

Review for Mastery. Discuss and review any work from the previous lesson that was assigned as homework. Check for completion of the activities and orally quiz the student for comprehension. Review any reading that was assigned, discussing the characters, setting, plot, theme, language, sequence, etc.

Strengthen fluency and phonemic awareness by reviewing words and sentences from previous lessons. Build vocabulary skills by using some of the words in sentences.

Review compound word syllabication with Lesson 131, Activity 2. Read the words and divide each word into syllables.

Review compound words with Lesson 131. Have the student read the compound words from the activities in the lesson.

Activity 1. Review the rule for the schwa and the examples. Have the student write examples of the rule on the board. *Words to teach the concept:* ballot, blotter, carrot, chapter, cheerful, circus, hamper, luster, ponder, winter. These are VC/CV words. Read the activity instructions carefully. Have the student read the words aloud. The student will divide each word into syllables.

Lesson 132

The *schwa* is the vowel sound in many lightly pronounced unaccented syllables in words of more than one syllable. It is the most common vowel sound in the English language. In a strong syllable the vowel is strong, and in a weak syllable the vowel is weak and makes the *schwa* sound.

1 Divide these words into syllables between two consonants. Read the words and listen for the *schwa* sound of *uh*. These are VC/CV words.

or/der	slen/der	wan/der
blos/som	doc/tor	let/ter
or/gan	slip/per	bet/ter
bot/tom	fas/ter	man/ner
rib/bon	sum/mer	cac/tus
bash/ful	chil/dren	help/ful

2 Divide these words into syllables after a consonant and before a vowel. Read the words and listen for the *schwa* sound of *uh*. These are VC/V words.

drag/on	kitch/en	wag/on
lem/on	oth/er	sal/ad
moth/er	sev/en	nick/el

3 Divide these words into syllables after a vowel and before a consonant. Read the words and listen for the *schwa* sound of *uh*. Some of these are V/CVopen words.

a/bout	a/gainst	care/ful
fla/vor	a/bove	a/round
grate/ful	Pe/ter	a/cross
a/way	waste/ful	mo/tor

Syllabication with Schwa Sound 115

Activity 1 continued:

Words:

  or/der, slen/der, wan/der

  blos/som, doc/tor, let/ter

  or/gan, slip/per, bet/ter

  bot/tom, fas/ter, man/ner

  rib/bon, sum/mer, cac/tus

  bash/ful, chil/dren, help/ful

Activity 2. Read the activity instructions carefully. *Words to teach the concept:* butcher, bushel, trailer. These are VC/V words. Have the student read the words aloud. The student will divide each word into syllables.

Words:

  drag/on, kitch/en, wag/on

  lem/on, oth/er, sal/ad

  moth/er, sev/en, nick/el

Activity 3. Read the activity instructions carefully. *Words to teach the concept:* apron, bacon, freedom, pilot, tailor. Some of these are V/CVopen words. Have the student read the words aloud. The student will divide each word into syllables.

Horizons Phonics & Reading Grade 2 Teacher's Guide

Activity 3 continued:

Words:

> a/bout, a/gainst, care/ful
> fla/vor, a/bove, a/round
> grate/ful, Pe/ter, a/cross
> a/way, waste/ful, mo/tor

Activity 4. Remind the students that the schwa has more than one sound. Read the activity instructions carefully. Have the student read the first word in each row aloud, paying careful attention to the schwa sound. Have the student read the other words in the row and circle those with the same schwa sound as the first word. Point out some of the spelling clues that may help them like the **-er** endings in *letter*, *Peter*, and *faster*.

Words:

> **above, across**
> **dragon, ribbon**
> **afraid, along**
> **Peter, faster**
> **metal, novel**
> **order, manner**
> **wander, doctor**
> **better, mother**
> **careful, grateful**
> **model, nickel**
> **topic, timid**

Reading. Read and discuss the maxim for the Lesson.

Read the story *The Dream*. This is another chapter of the *A Little Princess* story. Preview the story and explain words or sentence structures that are not familiar to the student. With every story ask questions: who are the characters, what are they doing, what are they saying, where does the action take place, what is the order of events, what words are being used, what new information is given, what lesson can be learned?

4   Read the first word in each row. Find the *schwa* sound in the word. Read the other words in the row and circle those with the same *schwa* sound.

about	(above)	(across)	apron
lemon	(dragon)	photo	(ribbon)
away	agent	(afraid)	(along)
letter	(Peter)	(faster)	career
model	(metal)	(novel)	folktale
other	anywhere	(order)	(manner)
slipper	(wander)	(doctor)	ignore
flavor	(better)	indoor	(mother)
helpful	(careful)	(grateful)	blowtube
medal	(model)	baby	(nickel)
limit	(topic)	locate	(timid)

114   *Syllabication with Schwa Sound*

Comprehension questions:
> What was the man next door thinking about?
> What food did the cook offer to Sara?
> Why was there a light shining from under Sara's door when she went up the stairs?
> Who else was waiting for Sara to return to her room?
> Who was disappointed that Sara hadn't brought any food?

Assign. Lesson activities or reading that are to be completed as homework.

Lesson 133: Accents and Compound Words

Overview:

- Identify compound words
- Divide compound words into syllables
- Identify the accented syllable in a compound word
- Divide compound words that have a suffix into syllables
- Read words of three syllables
- Identify the accented syllable in a compound word that has a suffix

Materials and Supplies:

- Teacher's Guide & Student Workbook 2
- White board or chalkboard
- Word cards (as necessary)
- Dictionary
- Reader: *A Little Princess & Other Classic Stories*

Teaching Tips:

Review for Mastery. Discuss and review any work from the previous lesson that was assigned as homework. Check for completion of the activities and orally quiz the student for comprehension. Review any reading that was assigned, discussing the characters, setting, plot, theme, language, sequence, etc.

Strengthen fluency and phonemic awareness by reviewing words and sentences from previous lessons. Build vocabulary skills by using some of the words in sentences.

Review the schwa and syllabication with Lesson 132, Activity 4. Divide the words into syllables. Use a dictionary if needed.

A compound word is a word made from two or more words joined together to make one word.
A compound word is divided between the words that make up the compound word. Most compound words are accented on the first word.

Read these statements. Each statement has a compound word. Write the compound word on the line, divide it into syllables, and mark the accented syllable.

SAMPLE: an egg for breakfast	break'/fast
1. the lights at the airport	air'/port
2. on the backside of the tree	back'/side
3. a crackdown on crime	crack'/down
4. a drawbridge over the water	draw'/bridge
5. the earthquake shook the table	earth'/quake
6. the weather forecast	fore'/cast
7. the guardhouse by the gate	guard'/house
8. a headache from the noise	head'/ache
9. the inmate was set free	in'/mate
10. a jawbone of a fish	jaw'/bone
11. a keyboard for typing	key'/board
12. a landslide on the road	land'/slide
13. the bright moonlight at night	moon'/light
14. a newborn baby	new'/born
15. an offspring of the pet	off'/spring

Compound Words with Unaccented Syllables 115

Activity 1. Review the rules for compound words. Have the student write examples of the rules on the board. *Words to teach the concept:* bedrock, eyebrow, eyelid, handbag, pigtail, sandbox, thumbnail, airbrush, backhand, clockwise, dashboard, downtown, dustpan, earthworm, farmhouse, flagship, grandstand, guesswork, horseback, jigsaw, kickback, lifeguard, manhole, milestone, nightgown, nutshell, offshore, outburst, payload, peacetime, racetrack, roommate, schoolchild, shorthand, somewhat, spotlight, starfish, taillight, thumbnail, trademark, washroom, wildfire, yardstick. Have the student read the phrases aloud using expression. The student will identify the compound word in each phrase and write it on the line. Read the words again and listen for the accented syllable. Then have the student divide the word into syllables and mark the accented syllable.

Words:
  break'/fast
  air'/port
  back'/side
  crack'/down

Horizons Phonics & Reading Grade 2 Teacher's Guide

Activity 1 continued:

draw'/bridge
earth'/quake
fore'/cast
guard'/house
head'/ache
in'/mate
jaw'/bone
key'/board
land'/slide
moon'/light
new'/born
off'/spring
play'/ground
quick'/sand
road'/side
scrap'/book
tea'/spoon
up'/swing
view'/point
whole'/some
your/self'
zig'/zag

Activity 2. Help the student read the words. Instruct the student to write the word on the line, divide the word into syllables, and mark the accented syllable. Assist the student in using the word in a phrase or sentence if the student is not hearing the accented syllable. Remind the student to think of the syllable rules for suffixes.

Words:

bed'/rid/den, key/board'/ing, gate'/keep/er
hand'/writ/ing, ice'/break/er, king'/fish/er
life'/guard/ing, match'/mak/er, news'/pap/er
out/stand'/ing, peace'/mak/er, ring'/lead/er
sight'/see/ing, thanks/giv'/ing, weight'/lift/ing

16. the playground at the park	play'/ground	
17. the quicksand by the river	quick'/sand	
18. a roadside fruit stand	road'/side	
19. a scrapbook of photos	scrap'/book	
20. a teaspoon of salt	tea'/spoon	
21. the upswing of the golf club	up'/swing	
22. the viewpoint of the writer	view'/point	
23. a wholesome thing to do	whole'/some	
24. to read the book yourself	your/self'	
25. ran in a zigzag up the hill	zig'/zag	

2 Divide these compound words with suffixes into syllables. Mark the accented syllable.

bedridden	keyboarding	gatekeeper
bed'/rid/den	key/board'/ing	gate'/keep/er
handwriting	icebreaker	kingfisher
hand'/writ/ing	ice'/break/er	king'/fish/er
lifeguarding	matchmaker	newspaper
life'/guard/ing	match'/mak/er	news'/pap/er
outstanding	peacemaker	ringleader
out/stand'/ing	peace'/mak/er	ring'/lead/er
sightseeing	thanksgiving	weightlifting
sight'/see/ing	thanks/giv'/ing	weight'/lift/ing

118   *Compound Words with Unaccented Syllables*

Reading. Read and discuss the maxim for the Lesson.

Read the story *The Dream (continued)*. This is another chapter of the *A Little Princess* story. Preview the story and explain words or sentence structures that are not familiar to the student. With every story ask questions: who are the characters, what are they doing, what are they saying, where does the action take place, what is the order of events, what words are being used, what new information is given, what lesson can be learned?

Comprehension questions:

Why did Erma feel that it was safe to go to Sara's room?

What things had Erma brought with her?

Why didn't Erma want the books?

How did Sara offer to help Erma with the books?

Assign. Lesson activities or reading that are to be completed as homework.

Lesson 134: Accents and the Schwa Sound

Overview:

- Use picture clues to read words
- Define an open syllable
- Recognize open syllables
- Divide words into syllables
- Identify the accented syllable in a word
- Auditory discrimination of the schwa
- Complete sentences

Materials and Supplies:

- Teacher's Guide & Student Workbook 2
- White board or chalkboard
- Word cards (as necessary)
- Dictionary
- Reader: *A Little Princess & Other Classic Stories*

Teaching Tips:

Review for Mastery. Discuss and review any work from the previous lesson that was assigned as homework. Check for completion of the activities and orally quiz the student for comprehension. Review any reading that was assigned, discussing the characters, setting, plot, theme, language, sequence, etc.

Strengthen fluency and phonemic awareness by reviewing words and sentences from previous lessons. Build vocabulary skills by using some of the words in sentences.

Review accents and compound words with Lesson 133, Activity 1. Have the student make complete sentences from the phrases.

Activity 1. Review the rule for the schwa sound. Review the definition of an open syllable from previous lessons. Give some examples on the board. *Words to teach the concept:* about', away', balloon', fa'mous, fla'vor, free'-dom, jeal'ous, ner'vous, pen'nant. Have the student identify the pictures and read the words that match the pictures. Instruct the student to divide each word into syllables with a slash and to mark the accent. Unknown words can be looked up in a dictionary.

Pictures:

ba'/con, a/bove', car'/rot, cir'/cus
blos'/som, rib'/bon, a/fraid', sev'/en
or'/gan, li'/on, sal'/ad, can'/non
a/ward', bal'/lot, wag'/on, ketch'/up

Activity 2. Have the student identify the pictures and read the words that match the pictures. Instruct the student to circle the words where the underline vowel makes the schwa sound.

Pictures:

   pilot, candy, dragon, cactus
   against, lemon, bottom, cheese
   apron, parade, city, across
   popcorn, banana, around, machine

Answers:

   pilot, dragon, cactus
   against, lemon, bottom
   apron, parade, across
   banana, around, machine

Activity 3. Instruct the student to select the word from Activity 2 that will correctly complete each sentence and write the word on the line. Unknown words can be looked up in a dictionary.

Sentences:

   The pilot of the airplane was careful.
   Ring around the rosey, a pocket full of posies.
   Ice tea with lemon is a good drink.
   The broom was leaning against the wall.
   She has gum on the bottom of her shoe.

Reading. Read and discuss the maxim for the Lesson.

Read the story *The Dream (continued)*. This is another chapter of the *A Little Princess* story. Preview the story and explain words or sentence structures that are not familiar to the student. With every story ask questions: who are the characters, what are they doing, what are they saying, where does the action take place, what is the order of events, what words are being used, what new information is given, what lesson can be learned?

---

2 Circle the words where the underlined vowel makes the *schwa* sound.

p**i**l**o**t	c**a**ndy	dr**a**g**o**n	c**a**ct**u**s
ag**ai**nst	l**e**m**o**n	b**o**tt**o**m	ch**ee**se
apr**o**n	p**a**r**a**de	c**i**ty	**a**cross
popc**o**rn	b**a**n**a**n**a**	**a**r**o**und	m**a**ch**i**n**e**

3 Complete the sentences with a word with the *schwa* sound from the words above.

The _____pilot_____ of the airplane was careful.

Ring _____around_____ the rosy, a pocket full of posies.

Ice tea with _____lemon_____ is a good drink.

The broom was leaning _____against_____ the wall.

She has gum on the _____bottom_____ of her shoe.

118   *Accented Syllables in Words with the Schwa Sound*

Comprehension questions:

   Was Erma able to remember things well?
   How did Sara help Erma remember things?
   What had Sara helped Lottie learn?
   Did Erma recognize that Sara was hungry?
   Sara was not able to spread a feast from her "castle" but what was she able to do for those who came?

Assign. Lesson activities or reading that are to be completed as homework.

Lesson 135: Accents and Schwa Sound

Overview:

- Use picture clues to read words
- Define an open syllable
- Recognize open syllables
- Divide words into syllables
- Identify the accented syllable in a word
- Auditory discrimination of the schwa
- Complete sentences

Materials and Supplies:

- Teacher's Guide & Student Workbook 2
- White board or chalkboard
- Word cards (as necessary)
- Dictionary
- Reader: *A Little Princess & Other Classic Stories*

Teaching Tips:

Review for Mastery. Discuss and review any work from the previous lesson that was assigned as homework. Check for completion of the activities and orally quiz the student for comprehension. Review any reading that was assigned, discussing the characters, setting, plot, theme, language, sequence, etc.

Strengthen fluency and phonemic awareness by reviewing words and sentences from previous lessons. Build vocabulary skills by using some of the words in sentences.

Review the schwa and accents with Lesson 134, Activity 1. Use the words in phrases or sentences. Pay special attention to the accented syllables.

Activity 1. Review the rule for the schwa sound. Have the student write examples of the rule on the board. Review the definition of an open syllable from previous lessons. Give some examples on the board. *Words to teach the concept:* lus'ter, man'ner, numb'er, or'der, oth'er, sum'mer, win'ter. Have the student identify the pictures and read the words that match the pictures. Instruct the student to divide each word into syllables with a slash and to mark the accented syllable. Unknown words can be looked up in a dictionary.

Pictures:

  butch'/er, mo'/tor, slip'/per, sum'/mer
  bush'/el, hamp'/er, or'/der, win'/ter
  chil'/dren, sail'/or, num'/ber, doc'/tor
  jan'/i/tor, chap'/ter, slen'/der, trail'/er
  kitch'/en, let'/ter, help'/ful, bash'/ful

Activity 2. Have the student read the words. Instruct the student to circle the words where the underlined vowel makes the schwa sound.

Answers:
better
manner, wander, awful, flavor
other
whether, over

Activity 3. Instruct the student to select the word from Activity 2 that will correctly complete each sentence and write the word on the line. Unknown words can be looked up in a dictionary.

Sentences:
The silver car has a flat tire.
This is the last game whether we win or lose.
All the adults have freedom to vote.
Billy rode his bike in an unsafe manner .
Running a faucet for cool water is a wasteful practice.
This drink tastes awful!
The gem has a glimmer in the sunlight.
Watch the baby so she does not wander off and get lost.
Be careful with the sharp scissors.
She has a better way to cook the food.
The sick child laughed at the cheerful card.
Some people think that coffee has a bitter flavor.
The grateful child thanked his friend for the help.
Each morning we ponder the thought for the day.
She would like the picture on the other side of the window.
Sarah took her bike over the bump in the road.

Reading. Read and discuss the maxim for the Lesson.

Read the story *The Dream (continued)*. This is another chapter of the *A Little Princess* story.

---

2 Read the words with the *schwa* sound. Circle the words where the correct vowel with the *schwa* sound has been underlined.

(better)	silver	glimmer	wasteful
(manner)	(wander)	(awful)	(flavor)
(other)	grateful	ponder	freedom
careful	(whether)	cheerful	(over)

3 Complete the sentences with a word with the *schwa* sound from the words above.

The _____silver_____ car has a flat tire.
This is the last game _____whether_____ we win or lose.
All the adults have _____freedom_____ to vote.
Billy rode his bike in an unsafe _____manner_____ .
Running a faucet for cool water is a _____wasteful_____ practice.
This drink tastes _____awful_____ !
The gem has a _____glimmer_____ in the sunlight.
Watch the baby so she does not _____wander_____ off and get lost.
Be _____careful_____ with the sharp scissors.
She has a _____better_____ way to cook the food.
The sick child laughed at the _____cheerful_____ card.
Some people think that coffee has a bitter _____flavor_____ .
The _____grateful_____ child thanked his friend for the help.
Each morning we _____ponder_____ the thought for the day.
She would like the picture on the _____other_____ side of the window.
Sarah took her bike _____over_____ the bump in the road.
120   *Accented Syllables in Words with the Schwa Sound*

Preview the story and explain words or sentence structures that are not familiar to the student. With every story ask questions: who are the characters, what are they doing, what are they saying, where does the action take place, what is the order of events, what words are being used, what new information is given, what lesson can be learned?

Comprehension questions:
What did Erma start to notice about Sara?
Where did something happen that neither Sara or Erma saw?
What did they hear?
Why was the candle blown out?
What did Miss Minchin think Becky had done?
Who did Becky say was to blame for the missing food?

Assign. Lesson activities or reading that are to be completed as homework.

Lesson 136: Accented Syllables in Compound Words with -er

Overview:

- Use picture clues to read words
- Read words of three syllables
- Define an open syllable
- Recognize open syllables
- Divide words into syllables
- Apply the syllabication rules to words
- Identify the accented syllable in a word
- Auditory discrimination of the schwa
- Identify the vowel the schwa vowel in words of three syllables

Materials and Supplies:

- Teacher's Guide & Student Workbook 2
- White board or chalkboard
- Word cards (as necessary)
- Dictionary
- Reader: *A Little Princess & Other Classic Stories*

Teaching Tips:

Review for Mastery. Discuss and review any work from the previous lesson that was assigned as homework. Check for completion of the activities and orally quiz the student for comprehension. Review any reading that was assigned, discussing the characters, setting, plot, theme, language, sequence, etc.

Strengthen fluency and phonemic awareness by reviewing words and sentences from previous lessons. Build vocabulary skills by using some of the words in sentences.

Review the schwa and accents with Lesson 135, Activity 1. Use the words in phrases or sentences. Pay special attention to the accented syllables.

The *schwa* is the vowel sound in many lightly pronounced unaccented syllables in words of more than one syllable. It is the most common vowel sound in the English language.

Read the words. Divide the words into syllables. Circle the syllable with the *schwa* sound.

screw/driv/er, type/writ/er, wood/peck/er, salt/shak/er

news/pap/er, school/teach/er, step/lad/der, dog/catch/er

shoe/mak/er, sky/scrap/er, but/ter/fly, quar/ter/back

under/pass, door/knock/er, fish/er/man, over/coat

musk/mel/on, thun/der/bolt, gin/ger/bread, lum/ber/jack

Compound Words with the Schwa Sound 121

Activity 1. Review the rule for the schwa sound. Review the syllabication rules for compound words and affixes from previous lessons. Give some examples on the board. *Words to teach the concept:* bulldozer, icebreaker, kingfisher, matchmaker, painkiller, ringleader, sharpshooter, shoemaker, skyscraper, stockbroker, timekeeper, woodcutter, afterlife, giveaway, layover, lemongrass, letterhead, masterpiece, motherboard, riverboat, roundabout, stowaway, tenderfoot, wintergreen. Have the student identify the pictures and read the words that match the pictures. These are words of three syllables. Instruct the student to divide each word into syllables with slashes and circle the schwa syllable.

Pictures:

screw/driv/<u>er</u>, type/writ/<u>er</u>, wood/peck/<u>er</u>, salt/shak/<u>er</u>

news/pap/<u>er</u>, school/teach/<u>er</u>, step/lad/<u>der</u>, dog/catch/<u>er</u>

shoe/mak/<u>er</u>, sky/scrap/<u>er</u>, but/<u>ter</u>/fly, quar/<u>ter</u>/back

Horizons Phonics & Reading Grade 2 Teacher's Guide

Activity 1 continued:

un/<u>der</u>/pass, door/knock/<u>er</u>, fish/<u>er</u>/man, o/<u>ver</u>/coat

musk/mel/<u>on</u>, thun/<u>der</u>/bolt, gin/<u>ger</u>/bread, lum/<u>ber</u>/jack

Activity 2. Have the student read the words in the box. Sort some of the words to teach the concept from Activity 1. The student will sort the words by the syllable of the schwa sound and write them in the correct boxes.

Words:

Initial schwa	Middle schwa	Final schwa
aboveground	weatherman	dressmaker
aboveboard	silverware	stepmother
adulthood	letterhead	grasshopper

Activity 3. Have the student read the words and listen for the schwa. The student will underline the vowel is each word that has the schwa sound. Remind the student that the schwa can be in the first, second, or third syllable.

Words:

snapdrag<u>o</u>n, run<u>a</u>way, bandwag<u>o</u>n
stow<u>a</u>way, pil<u>o</u>thouse, cast<u>a</u>way
where<u>a</u>bout, lem<u>o</u>ngrass, give<u>a</u>way
hereaft<u>e</u>r, hide<u>a</u>way, mot<u>o</u>rboat
run<u>a</u>bout, roll<u>a</u>way, round<u>a</u>bout

Reading. Read and discuss the maxim for the Lesson.

Read the story *The Dream (continued)*. This is another chapter of the *A Little Princess* story. Preview the story and explain words or sentence structures that are not familiar to the student. With every story ask questions: who are the characters, what are they doing, what are they saying, where does the action take place, what is the order of events, what words are being used, what new information is given, what lesson can be learned?

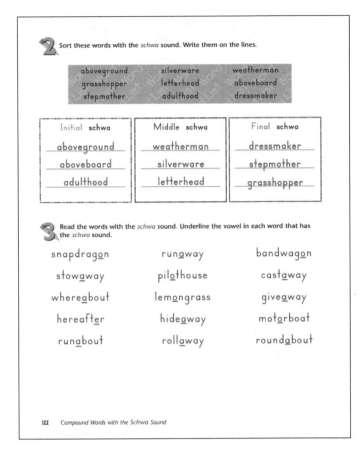

Comprehension questions:
Who stood up for Becky?
Who asked Sara if she was ever hungry?
What story did Sara tell to Erma?
What had Erma gotten that afternoon?
What did Erma offer to do?
Who did Sara and Erma agree to ask to the party?

Assign. Lesson activities or reading that are to be completed as homework.

Lesson 137: Antonyms

Overview:

- Add prefixes to root words
- Define the meaning of prefix **dis-**
- Define the meaning of prefix **un-**
- Read words with prefixes
- Define an antonym
- Match a word to its antonym

Materials and Supplies:

- Teacher's Guide & Student Workbook 2
- White board or chalkboard
- Word cards (as necessary)
- Dictionary
- Dictionary
- Reader: *A Little Princess & Other Classic Stories*

Teaching Tips:

Review for Mastery. Discuss and review any work from the previous lesson that was assigned as homework. Check for completion of the activities and orally quiz the student for comprehension. Review any reading that was assigned, discussing the characters, setting, plot, theme, language, sequence, etc.

Strengthen fluency and phonemic awareness by reviewing words and sentences from previous lessons. Build vocabulary skills by using some of the words in sentences.

Review the schwa with Lesson 136, Activity 1. Use the words in phrases or sentences. Sort the words by the position of the schwa syllable and look for similarities in spelling.

Activity 1. Review the rule and the meanings of the prefixes **dis-** and **un-**. When those prefixes are added to a word it means *not* or *the opposite*. Someone who is dishonest is the opposite of someone who is honest. A door that is unlocked is a door that is not locked. Read the base words with the student. Have him add the prefixes to make the words mean

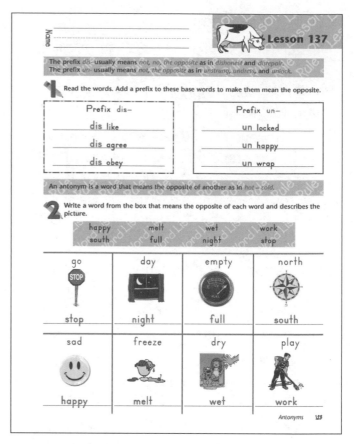

the opposite. Read the new words. Allow the student to use a dictionary to look up any unknown words.

Words:

Prefix dis-	Prefix un-
dislike	unlocked
disagree	unhappy
disobey	unwrap

Activity 2. Review the rule for an antonym and the example. *Words to teach the concept:* alive–dead, argue–agree, arrive–depart, awake–asleep, back–front, bad–good, beautiful–ugly, bent–straight, big–little, blunt–sharp, bottom–top, boy–girl, buy–sell, in–out. Assist the student as needed to read the words in the box. Review the word in each box and the picture clue. The picture clue is for a word that is the opposite of the word given in the box. Have the student find the word for the picture and write it on the line. Allow the student to use a dictionary to look up any unknown words.

Activity 2 continued:

Pictures:
   stop, night, full, south
   happy, melt, wet, work

Activity 3. Assist the student as needed with reading the words in each box. Instruct the student to find a word in the second box that means the opposite as a word in the first box and to draw a line to connect them. Allow the student to use a dictionary to look up any unknown words.

Word	Antonym
slow	fast
least	most
many	few
east	west
cold	hot
hill	valley
truth	lie
love	hate

Activity 4. Assist the student as needed with reading the words in the box. Instruct the student to find an antonym for each numbered word and write its letter on the blank. Allow the student to use a dictionary to look up any unknown words.

1. j. below
2. t. subtract
3. a. after
4. k. together
5. b. answer
6. l. worse
7. c. open
8. m. white
9. d. dark
10. n. hard
11. e. great
12. o. low
13. f. first
14. p. long
15. g. different
16. q. give
17. h. true
18. r. new
19. i. tame
20. s. no

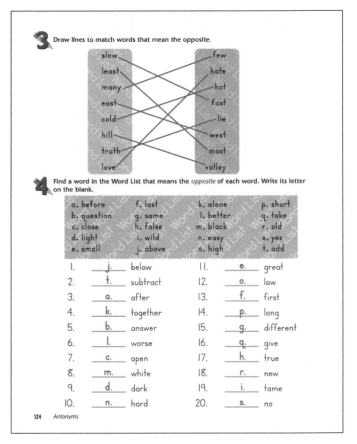

Reading. Read and discuss the maxim for the Lesson.

Read the story *The Dream (continued)*. This is another chapter of the *A Little Princess* story. Preview the story and explain words or sentence structures that are not familiar to the student. With every story ask questions: who are the characters, what are they doing, what are they saying, where does the action take place, what is the order of events, what words are being used, what new information is given, what lesson can be learned?

Comprehension questions:
   Why did Sara knock on the wall?
   What excited Becky when she got to Sara's room?
   What did Sara say never "quite" comes?
   What use did Sara come up with for Erma's shawl?
   What was Sara trying to think of?

Assign. Lesson activities or reading that are to be completed as homework.

Lesson 138: Synonyms

Overview:

• Define a synonym
• Complete sentences with synonyms
• Match a word to its synonym

Materials and Supplies:

• Teacher's Guide & Student Workbook 2
• White board or chalkboard
• Word cards (as necessary)
• Dictionary
• Dictionary
• Reader: *A Little Princess & Other Classic Stories*

Teaching Tips:

Review for Mastery. Discuss and review any work from the previous lesson that was assigned as homework. Check for completion of the activities and orally quiz the student for comprehension. Review any reading that was assigned, discussing the characters, setting, plot, theme, language, sequence, etc.

Strengthen fluency and phonemic awareness by reviewing words and sentences from previous lessons. Build vocabulary skills by using some of the words in sentences.

Review antonyms with Lesson 137, Activities 2-4. Use the words in a phrase or sentence.

Activity 1. Review the rule for a synonym. Have the student write examples of the rule on the chalkboard or white board. *Words to teach the concept:* aim–goal, call–shout, careful–cautious, cure–heal, divide–split, error–mistake, faith–trust, fat–plump, fix–repair, flat–level, gift–present, grateful–thankful, happy–glad, hard–difficult, hurry–rush, ill–sick, kill–murder, late–tardy, look–see, one–single, pair–couple, peak–top, thin–slim, weak–feeble. Assist the student as needed in reading the words in the lesson. Have the student read the

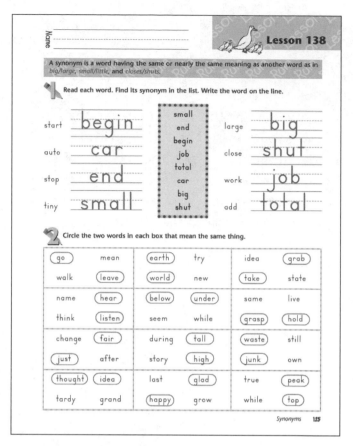

words and the words in the box aloud. The student will find a synonym in the box for each word and write it on the line. Allow the student to use a dictionary to look up any unknown words.

Words:

start – begin	large – big
auto – car	close – shut
stop – end	work – job
tiny – small	add – total

Activity 2. Have the student read the words in each box. Two of the words in each box are synonyms. Have the student circle the two words in each box that mean the same or nearly the same. Allow the student to use a dictionary to look up any unknown words.

Words:

go – leave	earth – world	take – grab
hear – listen	below – under	grasp – hold
just – fair	tall – high	waste – junk
thought – idea	happy – glad	peak – top

Activity 3. Assist the student in reading the sentences using the word printed under the blank to complete the sentence. Then help the student read the words in the box. Instruct the student to select a synonym in the Word List for the word under the blank that will correctly complete each sentence and write the word on the line. Unknown words can be looked up in a dictionary.

Sentences:
1. Please <u>place</u> the rug by the door.
2. Julie was <u>happy</u> when she saw her friend.
3. She will <u>hold</u> the stick in her hand.
4. He is a <u>fast</u> runner.
5. Mary is feeling <u>sick</u> today.
6. I will write the <u>reply</u> to the e-mail today.
7. Felix needs to paint the <u>border</u> of the picture.
8. I got 10 of the problems on the test <u>correct</u>.
9. Harry must <u>work</u> in the garden.
10. Mary Jo is ready to <u>complete</u> the race.

Reading. Read and discuss the maxim for the Lesson.

Read the story *The Dream (continued)*. This is another chapter of the *A Little Princess* story. Preview the story and explain words or sentence structures that are not familiar to the student. With every story ask questions: who are the characters, what are they doing, what are they saying, where does the action take place, what is the order of events, what words are being used, what new information is given, what lesson can be learned?

Read each sentence. Find a synonym for the word shown below the line in the Word List. Write the synonym on the line.

| work | fast | place | happy | sick |
| border | correct | complete | reply | hold |

1. Please __place__ the rug by the door.
   (put)
2. Julie was __happy__ when she saw her friend.
   (glad)
3. She will __hold__ the stick in her hand.
   (keep)
4. He is a __fast__ runner.
   (quick)
5. Mary is feeling __sick__ today.
   (ill)
6. I will write the __reply__ to the e-mail today.
   (answer)
7. Felix needs to paint the __border__ of the picture.
   (edge)
8. I got 10 of the problems on the test __correct__.
   (right)
9. Harry must __work__ in the garden.
   (labor)
10. Mary Jo is ready to __complete__ the race.
    (finish)

128   *Synonyms*

Comprehension questions:
Where did Sara look for things to decorate the table?
What was found in the old trunk?
What was the key to seeing the room as something that it was not?
What was the tissue paper turned into?
What other images did Sara create in her mind?

Assign. Lesson activities or reading that are to be completed as homework.

Lesson 139: Homographs & Homophones

Overview:

- Define a homonym or homophone
- Define a homograph
- Apply the spelling rules for sounds to read words that are homonyms
- Complete sentences with homonyms
- Identify homographs in a sentence
- Match a word to its homonym

Materials and Supplies:

- Teacher's Guide & Student Workbook 2
- White board or chalkboard
- Word cards (as necessary)
- Dictionary
- Reader: *A Little Princess & Other Classic Stories*

Teaching Tips:

Review for Mastery. Discuss and review any work from the previous lesson that was assigned as homework. Check for completion of the activities and orally quiz the student for comprehension. Review any reading that was assigned, discussing the characters, setting, plot, theme, language, sequence, etc.

Strengthen fluency and phonemic awareness by reviewing words and sentences from previous lessons. Build vocabulary skills by using some of the words in sentences.

Review antonyms with Lesson 138, Activities 1 & 2. Ask the student for an antonym for each word. Allow the student to use a dictionary to look up any words.

Review synonyms with Lesson 138, Activity 2. Ask the student for a synonym for some of the detractors given in the exercise. Allow the student to use a dictionary to look up any words.

Activity 1. Review the rule for homonyms. Have the student write examples of the rule on the chalkboard or white board. *Words to teach the concept:* air–heir, allowed–aloud, eye–I, bail–

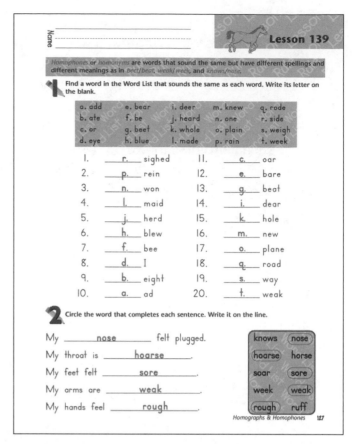

bale, band–banned, base–bass, berry–bury, berth–birth, bite–byte, billed–build, board–bored, brake–break, buy–by, ceiling–sealing, cell–sell, cent–scent, chord–cord, sight–site, coarse–course, creak–creek, dew–due, feat–feet, fair–fare, flour–flower, for–four, forth–fourth, grate–great, hair–hare, hart–heart, hay–hey, heal–heel, hear–here, hoarse–horse, hour–our, in–inn, peace–piece. Assist the student as needed with reading the words in the box. Instruct the student to find an homonym for each numbered word and write its letter on the blank. Allow the student to use a dictionary to look up any unknown words.

1. **r.** sighted		11. **c.** oar
2. **p.** rein		12. **e.** bare
3. **n.** won		13. **g.** beat
4. **l.** maid		14. **i.** dear
5. **j.** herd		15. **k.** hole
6. **h.** blew		16. **m.** new
7. **f.** bee		17. **o.** plane
8. **d.** I		18. **q.** road
9. **b.** eight		19. **s.** way
10. **a.** ad		20. **t.** weak

Activity 2. Assist the student in reading the homonyms in the box. Help the student read the sentences. Instruct the student to select the word from the box that will correctly complete each sentence and write the word on the line. Allow the student to use a dictionary to look up any unknown words.

Sentences:
My <u>nose</u> felt plugged.
My throat is <u>hoarse</u>.
My feet felt <u>sore</u>.
My arms are <u>weak</u>.
My hands feel <u>rough</u>.

Activity 3. Have the student read the words in each box. Two of the words in each box are homonyms. Have the student circle the two words in each box that are pronounced the same. Allow the student to use a dictionary to look up any unknown words.

Words:
witch–which	scene–seen	praise–prays
loan–lone	cheep–cheap	bred–bread
grown–groan	stare–stair	missed–mist
rays–raise	threw–through	write–right

Activity 4. Review the homograph rule. Write some examples on the board and discuss the meanings of the words. Assist the student in reading each sentence. Instruct the student to select the words in each sentence that are spelled the same but pronounced differently and underline the words. A dictionary can be used to look up word meanings.

Sentences:
<u>Wind</u> down the sail before the <u>wind</u> gets too strong.
The white <u>dove</u> <u>dove</u> to the branch of the tree.
Please <u>close</u> the door since you are <u>close</u> to it.
Bill will <u>present</u> the <u>present</u> to the teacher.
She will <u>lead</u> us down the path to the <u>lead</u> mine.
They will <u>record</u> the music for the <u>record</u>.
I <u>refuse</u> to let <u>refuse</u> clutter the road.
The man with the <u>bass</u> voice caught a large <u>bass</u> at the lake.
The <u>tear</u> in my new shirt brought a <u>tear</u> to my eye.

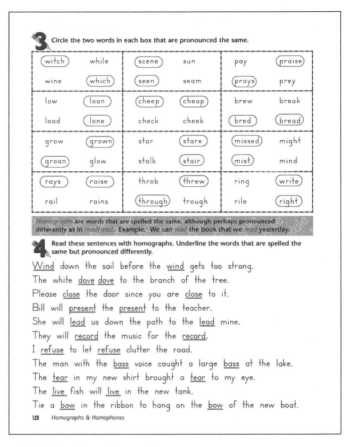

Activity 4 continued:
The <u>live</u> fish will <u>live</u> in the new tank.
Tie a <u>bow</u> in the ribbon to hang on the <u>bow</u> of the new boat.

Reading. Read and discuss the maxim for the Lesson.

Read the story *The Dream (continued)*. This is another chapter of the *A Little Princess* story. Preview the story and explain words or sentence structures that are not familiar to the student.

Comprehension questions:
What mental pictures did Sara draw for Erma?
What sudden thought came to Sara?
What did they hear just as they were starting to eat?
Who had guessed the secret and told on them?
What did Miss Minchin say to Becky?

Assign. Lesson activities or reading that are to be completed as homework.

Lesson 140: Review Antonyms, Synonyms, Homographs, & Homophones

Overview:

• Define an antonym
• Match a word to its antonym
• Define a synonym
• Match a word to its synonym
• Define a homonym or homophone
• Match homonyms to the definition
• Apply the spelling rules for sounds to read words that are homonyms
• Complete sentences with homonyms
• Identify homographs in a sentence
• Read sentences with homographs

Materials and Supplies:

• Teacher's Guide & Student Workbook 2
• White board or chalkboard
• Word cards (as necessary)
• Dictionary
• Reader: *A Little Princess & Other Classic Stories*

Teaching Tips:

Review for Mastery. Discuss and review any work from the previous lesson that was assigned as homework. Check for completion of the activities and orally quiz the student for comprehension. Review any reading that was assigned, discussing the characters, setting, plot, theme, language, sequence, etc.

Strengthen fluency and phonemic awareness by reviewing words and sentences from previous lessons. Build vocabulary skills by using some of the words in sentences.

Review homonyms with Lesson 139, Activity 2. Make up sentences for the unused words.

Review homonyms with Lesson 139, Activity 3. Circle the spellings for the vowels and/or consonants that have the same sounds for the homonyms.

Review homographs with Lesson 139, Activity 4. Code the vowels for the different pronunciations of the homographs.

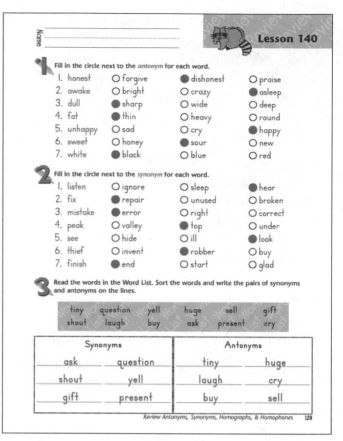

Activity 1. Review the rule for antonyms from previous lessons. Have the student read the words aloud. The student will select the antonym for each given word. Unknown words can be looked up in a dictionary.

Words:
1. honest—dishonest
2. awake—asleep
3. dull—sharp
4. fat—thin
5. unhappy—happy
6. sweet—sour
7. white—black

Activity 2. Review the rule for synonyms from previous lessons. Have the student read the words aloud. The student will select the synonym for each given word. Unknown words can be looked up in a dictionary.

Words:
1. listen—hear
2. fix—repair
3. mistake—error
4. peak—top
5. see—look
6. thief—robber
7. finish—end

Activity 3. Review the instruction and the words in the box with the student. The student is to sort the words into pairs of synonyms or antonyms and write them on the blanks. Unknown words can be looked up in a dictionary.

Words:

Synonyms	Antonyms
ask – question	tiny – huge
shout – yell	laugh – cry
gift – present	buy – sell

Activity 4. Review the rule for homonyms from previous lessons. Have the student read the definitions and words aloud. The student will select the correct spelling of the homonym to match the definition. Unknown words can be looked up in a dictionary.

Words:

1.	add	5.	hymn
2.	boy	6.	knot
3.	dough	7.	sea
4.	hare	8.	pail

Activity 5. Assist the student in reading the homonyms. Help the student read the sentences. Instruct the student to select the word that will correctly complete each sentence and fill in the circle next to the correct word. Allow the student to use a dictionary to look up any unknown words.

Sentences:

The squirrel had a bushy <u>tail</u>.
I like to smell a pretty <u>flower</u>.
My friend has a <u>horse</u> to ride.
Sally is <u>our</u> friend.
He will <u>buy</u> the ice cream.
There were <u>four</u> birds on the fence.
The light is on the <u>ceiling</u> of the room.

Activity 6. Review the Homograph Rule. Instruct the student to select the words in each sentence that are spelled the same but pronounced differently and read the sentences aloud. A dictionary can be used to look up word meanings.

Sentences:

1. A <u>live</u> plant cannot <u>live</u> without water.
2. The farmer will <u>sow</u> the grain so he can feed the <u>sow</u> in the pen.
3. She hung a <u>bow</u> made from ribbon on the <u>bow</u> of the ship.

Horizons Phonics & Reading Grade 2 Teacher's Guide

---

4 Fill in the circle for the *homonym* that matches the definition.

1. put two things together ○ ad ● add
2. a lad ● boy ○ buoy
3. used to make bread ○ doe ● dough
4. a rabbit ● hare ○ hair
5. a song ○ him ● hymn
6. tie a rope ○ not ● knot
7. the ocean ○ see ● sea
8. a bucket ● pail ○ pale

5 Fill in the circle for the spelling of the *homonym* that completes each sentence.

1. The squirrel had a bushy _____. ○ tale ● tail
2. I like to smell a pretty _____. ○ flour ● flower
3. My friend has a _____ to ride. ● horse ○ hoarse
4. Sally is _____ friend. ○ hour ● our
5. He will _____ the ice cream. ● buy ○ bye
6. There were _____ birds on the fence. ○ for ● four
7. The light is on the _____ of the room. ● ceiling ○ sealing

6 Underline the *homographs* in the sentences. Read the sentences to your teacher.

1. A <u>live</u> plant cannot <u>live</u> without water.
2. The farmer will <u>sow</u> the grain so he can feed the <u>sow</u> in the pen.
3. She hung a <u>bow</u> made from ribbon on the <u>bow</u> of the ship.
4. He <u>wound</u> the bandage around the <u>wound</u> on his leg.

190 *Review Antonyms, Synonyms, Homographs, & Homophones*

4. **He <u>wound</u> the bandage around the <u>wound</u> on his leg.**

Review for Test. The instructor should plan to use some time at the end of the class to review and prepare for the test that follows this lesson. Review as instructed in previous lessons.

Reading. Read and discuss the maxim for the Lesson.

Read the story *The Dream (continued)*. This is another chapter of the *A Little Princess* story. Preview the story and explain words or sentence structures that are not familiar to the student.

Comprehension questions:
How did Miss Minchin address Sara?
What was to be Sara's punishment?
What was Sara wondering again?
What did Sara miss by not looking at the skylight?
What was Sara thinking as she went to sleep?

Assign. Lesson activities or reading that are to be completed as homework.

Test 14
Lessons 125-134

Overview:

- Define the meaning of suffix **-y**, **-en**, **-able/-ible**
- Define the meaning of prefix **re-**, **un-**, **dis-**, **pre-**, **mis-**, **non-**
- Apply spelling rules to correctly add affixes to words
- Select the correct affix for a word
- Read words with affixes
- Identify the base word in words with affixes
- Divide words with affixes into syllables
- Use the rules for adding suffixes to separate words into the root and suffix
- Use the rules for adding affixes to separate words into the root and affix
- Form compound words
- Identify the schwa syllable in words
- Divide compound words into syllables

Materials and Supplies:

- Teacher's Guide & Student Workbook 2

Instructions:

Assessment Start-up. Read through the test with the student. Help the student with any words that he is still unsure of. The teacher should be available to answer any questions that the student may have during the test.

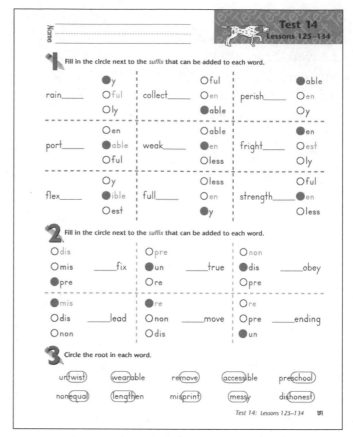

Activity 1. Review the words and the suffixes with the student. The student will select a suffix that correctly forms a new word from the root.

Words:

rainy	collectable	perishable
portable	weaken	frighten
flexible	fully	strengthen

Activity 2. Review the words and the prefixes with the student. The student will select a prefix that correctly forms a new word from the root.

Words:

prefix	untrue	disobey
mislead	remove	unending

Activity 3. Make sure the student can correctly read the words. The student is to circle the root in each word.

Words:

un<u>twist</u>, <u>wear</u>able, re<u>move</u>, <u>access</u>ible, pre<u>school</u>

non<u>equal</u>, <u>lengthen</u>, mis<u>print</u>, <u>messy</u>, dis<u>honest</u>

Activity 4. Make sure the student can correctly read the words. The student is to divide each word into syllables.

Words:

dis/grace, non/stick, weak/en, pre/view, mess/y

re/heat, stor/able, un/load, mis/step, sens/ible

Activity 5. Make sure the student can correctly read the phrases. The student is to form a compound word from words in the phrase.

Words:

1. raindrop
2. snowflake
3. bedtime
4. popcorn
5. mailbox

Activity 6. Make sure the student can correctly read the words. The student is to circle the syllable with the schwa sound.

Words:

doc/<u>tor</u>   man/<u>ner</u>   kitch/<u>en</u>   sal/<u>ad</u>

<u>a</u>/bove   fla/<u>vor</u>   ba/<u>con</u>   car/<u>rot</u>

Activity 7. Make sure the student can correctly read the compound words. The student is to divide the each word into syllables and mark the accented syllable.

Words:

crack'/down   head'/ache   off'/spring

play'/ground   key'/board   break'/fast

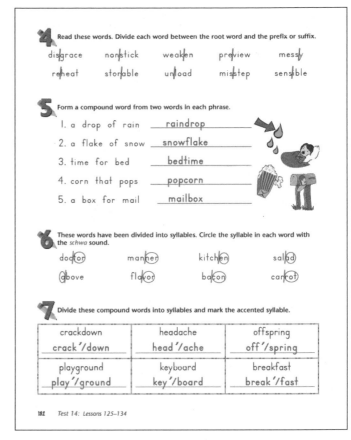

Assessment Follow-up. Every test is an important assessment of both the student's comprehension of the concepts and the instructional process. This makes follow-up after each test essential to the learning process. Review all of the errors made on the test with the student. Check for understanding of the concepts and of the problem instructions. Compare the errors made on the test to the test objectives to identify specific areas of weakness. If weak areas of understanding are detected it might be necessary to go back to those lessons to devise some enrichment activities for the concept.

The test results can be used to determine what concepts are reviewed during the daily time of classroom instruction. Devise enrichment activities that will provide development in those areas.

If time permits, choose a selection and have the student read it again. This can also be used as a catch-up time to complete unfinished selections.

Lesson 141: Spellings of Silent Double Consonants with t: ten, tle, ter

Overview:

- Recognize double consonants in words
- Match words to pictures
- Read words with a silent double consonant
- Divide words into syllables between double consonants
- Complete the spellings of words with double consonants
- Complete sentences

Materials and Supplies:

- Teacher's Guide & Student Workbook 2
- White board or chalkboard
- Word cards (as necessary)
- Dictionary
- Reader: *A Little Princess & Other Classic Stories*

Teaching Tips:

Review for Mastery. Discuss and review any work from the previous lesson that was assigned as homework. Check for completion of the activities and orally quiz the student for comprehension. Review any reading that was assigned, discussing the characters, setting, plot, theme, language, sequence, etc.

Strengthen fluency and phonemic awareness by reviewing words and sentences from previous lessons. Build vocabulary skills by using some of the words in sentences.

Review homonyms with Lesson 140, Activities 4 & 5. Use the detractors in a phrase or sentence.

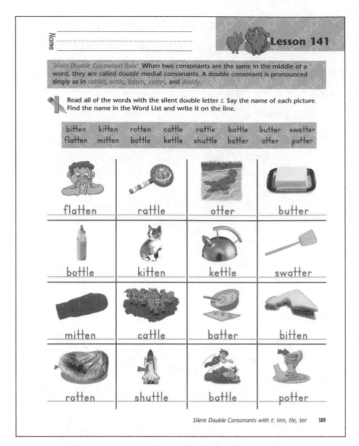

Activity 1. Review the Silent Double Consonants Rule. *Words to teach the concept:* little, settle, better, bitter, blotter, clatter, clutter, matter, shatter, sitter, hotter, quitter, squatter, twitter, wetter. Assist the student in reading the words in the box. Help the student identify the pictures and print the correct word underneath each picture.

Pictures:
  flatten, rattle, otter, butter
  bottle, kitten, kettle, swatter
  mitten, cattle, batter, bitten
  rotten, shuttle, battle, potter

Activity 2. Help the student read the sentences and the base words. Instruct the student to add an ending to the base word that will correctly complete each sentence and write the word on the line.

Sentences:
1. We will put the meat on the large <u>platter</u>.
2. Many men were hurt in the <u>battle</u>.
3. The apple under the tree was <u>rotten</u>.
4. We will buy a stamp for the <u>letter</u>.
5. A new fence in needed for the <u>cattle</u>.
6. The mother cat was kind to her <u>kitten</u>.
7. Shelley will be the next <u>batter</u>.
8. The dust in the air will soon <u>settle</u>.
9. Try to hit the fly with the <u>swatter</u>.
10. The good food will make the pig <u>fatter/fatten</u>.

Activity 3. Assist the student as needed to read these words. Have the student divide each of these double consonant words into syllables by making a slash between the double consonants.

Words:

brit/tle	bet/ter	smit/ten	tat/tle
lit/tle	lit/ter	writ/ten	knit/ter
quit/ter	shat/ter	scat/ter	flat/ter
mut/ter	bot/tle	got/ten	sit/ter
crit/ter	trot/ter	mat/ter	ut/ter
bit/ter	shut/tle	whit/tle	bit/ten

Reading. Read and discuss the maxim for the Lesson.

Read the story *The Dream (continued)*. This is another chapter of the *A Little Princess* story. Preview the story and explain words or sentence structures that are not familiar to the student. With every story ask questions: who are the characters, what are they doing, what are they saying, where does the action take place, what is the order of events, what words are being used, what new information is given, what lesson can be learned?

---

2 Add a *-ten*, *-tle*, or *-ter* ending to these base words to complete the sentences.

1. We will put the meat on the large _____ **platter** . `plat`
2. Many men were hurt in the _____ **battle** . `bat`
3. The apple under the tree was _____ **rotten** . `rot`
4. We will buy a stamp for the _____ **letter** . `let`
5. A new fence is needed for the _____ **cattle** . `cat`
6. The mother cat was kind to her _____ **kitten** . `kit`
7. Shelley will be the next _____ **batter** . `bat`
8. The dust in the air will soon _____ **settle** . `set`
9. Try to hit the fly with the _____ **swatter** . `swat`
10. The good food will make the pig _____ **fatter/fatten** . `fat`

VCCV Rule: When a word contains more than one vowel, it could follow the *VCCV* (vowel-consonant-consonant-vowel) pattern. The first step is to mark the vowels by writing a *v* under each vowel. Then mark the consonants by writing a *c* under them. Next, divide the word into syllables by drawing a line between the two consonants. Code the vowels and decide which syllable receives the accent (´).

3 Read these words with double consonants. Divide the words into syllables.

brit/tle	bet/ter	smit/ten	tat/tle
lit/tle	lit/ter	writ/ten	knit/ter
quit/ter	shat/ter	scat/ter	flat/ter
mut/ter	bot/tle	got/ten	sit/ter
crit/ter	trot/ter	mat/ter	ut/ter
bit/ter	shut/tle	whit/tle	bit/ten

194   *Silent Double Consonants with t: ten, tle, ter*

Comprehension questions:
How did Sara feel when she woke up?
What could Sara feel when she woke up?
What did Sara see when she woke up?
Did Sara think that what she saw was true?
What convinced Sara that the changes in the attic were true?
Whom did Sara wake up?

Assign. Lesson activities or reading that are to be completed as homework.

Lesson 142: Silent Double Consonants

Overview:

- Recognize double consonants in words
- Code vowels base on spelling
- Read words with a silent double consonant
- Divide words into syllables between double consonants
- Auditory discrimination of the schwa
- Identify unaccented syllables with the schwa sound
- Sort words using the Silent **e** and Open Syllable rules

Materials and Supplies:

- Teacher's Guide & Student Workbook 2
- White board or chalkboard
- Word cards (as necessary)
- Dictionary
- Reader: *A Little Princess & Other Classic Stories*

Teaching Tips:

Review for Mastery. Discuss and review any work from the previous lesson that was assigned as homework. Check for completion of the activities and orally quiz the student for comprehension. Review any reading that was assigned, discussing the characters, setting, plot, theme, language, sequence, etc.

Strengthen fluency and phonemic awareness by reviewing words and sentences from previous lessons. Build vocabulary skills by using some of the words in sentences.

Review double consonants with Lesson 141, Activity 1. Divide the words into syllables and read the words with silent **t** in the second syllable.

Activity 1. Review the VCCV Rule with the student. *Words to teach the concept:* abbey, bobbin, crabby, rubber, accrue, addict, addition, ladder, shoddy, coffee, offer, office, toffee, baggy, bugger, suggest, ballad, balloon, college,

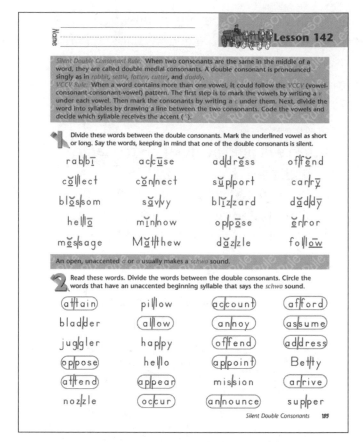

fellow, pulley, yellow, bummer, common, drummer, banner, funny, penny, winner, copper, slipper, supply, tissue, arrow, berry, burro, merry, surround, terror, assign, classic, essay, massive, scissor, bottom, button, kitty, nutty, buzzard, drizzle, fizzle, sizzle. Have the student divide each of these double consonant words into syllables by making a slash between the double consonants. Review the Silent **e** Rule, the Open Syllable Rule, and the CVC Short Vowel Rule. Code the underlined vowel in these words using the rule that applies. Read the words using the vowel sound coded by the student.

Words:

rab/bi	ac/cuse	ad/dress	of/fend
col/lect	con/nect	sup/port	car/ry
blos/som	sav/vy	bliz/zard	dad/dy
hel/lo	min/now	op/pose	er/ror
mes/sage	Math/thew	daz/zle	fol/low

Activity 2. Review the VCCV Rule with the student. Review the definition of double consonants and the Open, Unaccented Syllable Rule. In some of these words since the first double consonant is silent, they follow the Open Sylla-

ble Rule. *Words to teach the concept:* accrue, occasion, addict, addition, affair, offense, official, aggressive, applaud, array, assault, assort, assert, assign, attire, attorney. Point out the **a** or **o** initial letters in these words and the double consonants. Assist the student as needed to read these words. Have the student divide each of these double consonant words into syllables by making a slash between the double consonants. Review the CVC Short Vowel Rule. Instruct the student to circle the words that have an unaccented beginning syllable with the schwa sound. Using the words in a sentence of phrase will help identify the accented syllable.

Words:

at/tain	pil/low	ac/count	af/ford
blad/der	al/low	an/noy	as/sume
jug/gler	hap/py	of/fend	ad/dress
op/pose	hel/lo	ap/point	Bet/ty
at/tend	ap/pear	mis/sion	ar/rive
noz/zle	oc/cur	an/nounce	sup/per

Note: In some dictionaries, the **e** in *hello* is coded either as short or schwa.

Activity 3. Review the Silent **e** Rule and the VCVopen Rule. The second syllable of the words in this activity follow one of these rules. Assist the student in reading the words in the box. Have the student sort the words by the type of vowel they find in the second syllable.

Words:

Silent e Rule	VCVopen Rule
assume	coffee
diffuse	rabbi
accuse	toffee
oppose	daddy
commune	foggy
arrive	hello
commute	abbey
narrate	crabby
commode	berry
suppose	alloy
immune	baggy
corrode	hippie
appease	burro
pollute	lassie

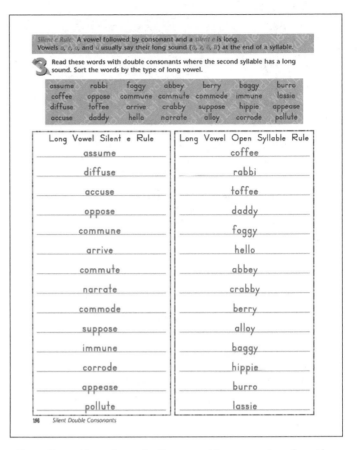

Reading. Read and discuss the maxim for the Lesson.

Read the story *The Visitor*. This is another chapter of the *A Little Princess* story. Preview the story and explain words or sentence structures that are not familiar to the student. With every story ask questions: who are the characters, what are they doing, what are they saying, where does the action take place, what is the order of events, what words are being used, what new information is given, what lesson can be learned?

Comprehension questions:
  What did Sara and Becky do?
  What was Becky's fear about the food, warmth, and things in the room?
  How did Sara conclude that this was not going to disappear?
  What were some of the things the other girls were talking about the next morning?

Assign. Lesson activities or reading that are to be completed as homework.

Lesson 143: Rhyming Words

Overview:

- Define words that rhyme
- Match words that rhyme
- Auditory discrimination of rhyming words
- Find words in a list that rhyme

Materials and Supplies:

- Teacher's Guide & Student Workbook 2
- White board or chalkboard
- Word cards (as necessary)
- Dictionary
- Reader: *A Little Princess & Other Classic Stories*

Teaching Tips:

Review for Mastery. Discuss and review any work from the previous lesson that was assigned as homework. Check for completion of the activities and orally quiz the student for comprehension. Review any reading that was assigned, discussing the characters, setting, plot, theme, language, sequence, etc.

Strengthen fluency and phonemic awareness by reviewing words and sentences from previous lessons. Build vocabulary skills by using some of the words in sentences.

Review double consonants with Lesson 142, Activity 2. Review the circled words. Ask the student how these words are similar. (The syllables all start with a vowel and are followed by double consonants.) Compare these to the uncircled words. (Those all have a CVC first syllable with a short vowel.) Review the words *pillow*, *allow*, *happy*, *hello*, *annoy*, and *Betty*. Note the open vowel ending to the second syllable.

Review double consonants with Lesson 142, Activity 3. Divide the words into syllables.

Activity 1. Review the rule for rhyming words and the examples. Write some practice lists of rhyming words on the chalkboard or white

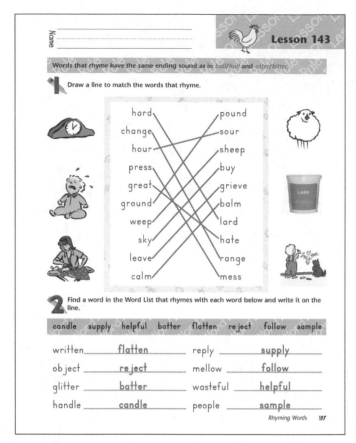

board. Review the definition of words that rhyme. Read the words and ask the student to identify the words that rhyme. Have the student read the words in each list of the activity aloud. The student will draw lines to match the words that rhyme.

Words:

hard	lard
change	range
hour	sour
press	mess
great	hate
ground	pound
weep	sheep
sky	buy
leave	grieve
calm	balm

Activity 2. Have the student read the words in the word box aloud and the other words in the activity. The student will write the word from the box that rhymes with the word and write it on the line.

Horizons Phonics & Reading Grade 2 Teacher's Guide

Activity 2 continued:

Words:

flatten	supply
reject	follow
batter	helpful
candle	sample

Activity 3. Help the student read the questions about the words that rhyme. Instruct the student to circle either **yes** or **no** to answer the question.

Answers:

1. yes
2. yes
3. no
4. yes
5. yes
6. yes
7. no
8. yes
9. no
10. yes

Activity 4. Have the student read the words in the word box aloud and the other words in the activity. The student will write the letter of the word from the box that rhymes with the numbered word on the line.

Answers:

1. m.	10. k.
2. o.	11. p.
3. g.	12. l.
4. i.	13. h.
5. c.	14. f.
6. j.	15. b.
7. r.	16. e.
8. d.	17. q.
9. a.	18. n.

Reading. Read and discuss the maxim for the Lesson.

Read the story *The Visitor (continued)*. This is another chapter of the *A Little Princess* story. Preview the story and explain words or sentence structures that are not familiar to the

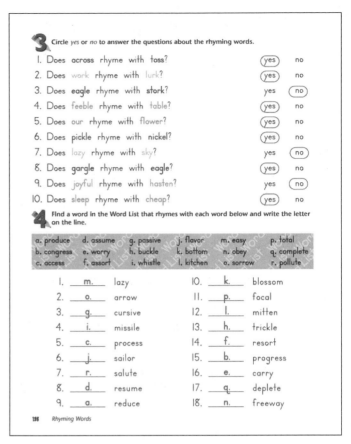

student. With every story ask questions: who are the characters, what are they doing, what are they saying, where does the action take place, what is the order of events, what words are being used, what new information is given, what lesson can be learned?

Comprehension questions:

How did the cooks look at Sara the next morning?

How did Sara speak to Becky in the kitchen?

What did Miss Minchin expect to see in Sara as she entered the schoolroom?

How did Sara come into the schoolroom?

Was Sara concerned that she was to have no food for the day?

Assign. Lesson activities or reading that are to be completed as homework.

Lesson 144: Words of Two Syllables with Accent on First

Overview:

- Read words of two syllables
- Divide words into syllables
- Identify words that have been correctly divided into syllables
- Code syllables with an accent
- Read two-syllable words with the correct accent
- Identify correct VCCV letter patterns in two-syllable words
- Label the VCCV letter patterns in two-syllable words

Materials and Supplies:

- Teacher's Guide & Student Workbook 2
- White board or chalkboard
- Word cards (as necessary)
- Dictionary
- Reader: *A Little Princess & Other Classic Stories*

Teaching Tips:

Review for Mastery. Discuss and review any work from the previous lesson that was assigned as homework. Check for completion of the activities and orally quiz the student for comprehension. Review any reading that was assigned, discussing the characters, setting, plot, theme, language, sequence, etc.

Strengthen fluency and phonemic awareness by reviewing words and sentences from previous lessons. Build vocabulary skills by using some of the words in sentences.

Review rhyming words with Lesson 143, Activity 1. Have the student identify the word endings that make the rhyming sound.

Review rhyming words with Lesson 143, Activity 3. Have the student suggest some rhyming words for the questions where the answer was no.

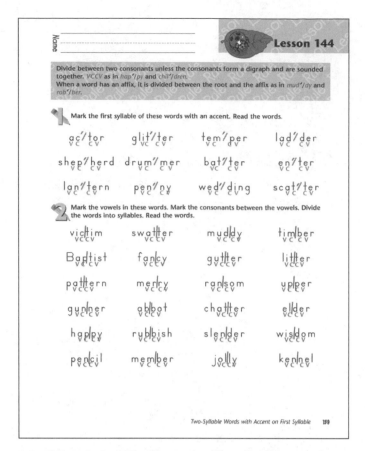

Activity 1. Review the rules for dividing VCCV words into syllables. *Words to teach the concept:* after, banter, cinder, conduct, factor, frantic, gander, hamlet, hermit, hundred, hunter, insect, jockey, kingdom, limber, lucky, perfect, pilgrim, render, sandy, serpent, signal, slumber, splinter, tender, under, velvet, victim. These words have been divided into syllables by the VCCV Rule to assist the student in reading the words correctly. Review the VCCV markings for each word and the slash between the double consonants that divide each word into syllables. Instruct the student to place an accent mark on the first syllable of all of these words. Assist the student as needed in reading the words with the correct accent.

Words:

ac'/tor, glit'/ter, tem'/per, lad'/der
shep'/herd, drum'/mer, bat'/ter, en'/ter
lan'/tern, pen'/ny, wed'/ding, scat'/ter

Activity 2. The student will mark the vowels in these words first. Then mark the consonants between the vowels and finally they are to

Horizons Phonics & Reading Grade 2 Teacher's Guide

divide each word into syllables by the VCCV Rule. After the words have been marked, have the student read the words with the correct syllabication and an accent on the first syllable.

Words:

vic/tim, swat/ter, mud/dy, tim/ber
Bap/tist, fan/cy, gut/ter, lit/ter
pat/tern, mer/ry, ran/som, up/per
gun/ner, ab/bot, chat/ter, el/der
hap/py, rub/bish, slen/der, wis/dom
pen/cil, mem/ber, jol/ly, ken/nel

Activity 3. These words have been marked by the VCCV Rule to assist the student in reading the words correctly. Not all of them have been marked correctly. Assist the student as needed in reading the words with an accent on the first syllable. Review the VCCV markings for each word and the VCCV Rule. Instruct the student to circle the words that have been marked correctly by the rule.

Answers:

mercy, offer
congress, sermon
only, number, common
bitter, pamper, ugly
children, tumbler, horrid
differ, seldom, angel

Activity 4. Review the syllable markings for each word and the VCCV Rule. Assist the student as needed in reading the words with an accent on the first syllable. Instruct the student to circle the words that have been divided into syllables correctly by the rule.

Answers:

car/rot, chop/per
gyp/sy
gal/lop, Bap/tist, chap/ter
sen/tence, blun'/der
sud/den
dan/ger, tal/ly, num/ber

Reading. Read and discuss the maxim for the Lesson.

Read the story *The Visitor (continued)*. This is another chapter of the *A Little Princess* story. Preview the story and explain words or sentence structures that are not familiar to the student. With every story ask questions: who are the characters, what are they doing, what are they saying, where does the action take place, what is the order of events, what words are being used, what new information is given, what lesson can be learned?

Comprehension questions:

Who was Sara going to tell about the dream that had come true?
Was Sara concerned about whether the meals continued?
What thought cheered Sara up?
What was the weather like?
What did Sara see when she finally returned to her room?
Who did Sara again share her good fortune with?

Assign. Lesson activities or reading that are to be completed as homework.

Lesson 145: Words of Two Syllables with Accent on First

Overview:

- Read words of two syllables
- Divide words into syllables
- Identify words that have been correctly divided into syllables
- Code syllables with an accent
- Read two-syllable words with the correct accent
- Label VCVopen letter patterns in two-syllable words
- Label VV letter patterns in two-syllable words
- Divide VV letter patterns into syllables

Materials and Supplies:

- Teacher's Guide & Student Workbook 2
- White board or chalkboard
- Word cards (as necessary)
- Dictionary
- Reader: *A Little Princess & Other Classic Stories*

Teaching Tips:

Review for Mastery. Discuss and review any work from the previous lesson that was assigned as homework. Check for completion of the activities and orally quiz the student for comprehension. Review any reading that was assigned, discussing the characters, setting, plot, theme, language, sequence, etc.

Strengthen fluency and phonemic awareness by reviewing words and sentences from previous lessons. Build vocabulary skills by using some of the words in sentences.

Review rhyming words with Lesson 143, Activity 2. Have the student suggest other words that rhyme with the words in the activity.

Review VCCV words with Lesson 144, Activity 2. Mark the accented first syllable in each word and read the words.

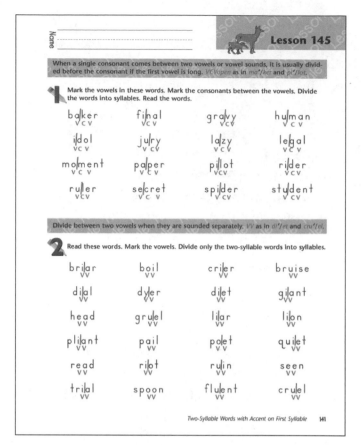

Review VCCV words with Lesson 144, Activity 3. Write the words that were labeled incorrectly on the board and have the student label the vowels and the consonants. Read the words.

Review VCCV words with Lesson 144, Activity 3. Write the words that were not correctly divided into syllables on the board. Have the student mark the VCCV patterns and correctly divide each word into syllables. Read the words.

Activity 1. Review the VCVopen Rule and the examples. *Words to teach the concept:* ruler, paper, student, signal, tutor, crazy, taper, final. The student will mark the vowels in these words first. Next, mark the consonant between the vowels and finally divide each word into syllables by the VCVopen Rule. After the words have been marked, have the student read the words with the correct syllabication and an accent on the first syllable.

Words:
  **ba/ker, fi/nal, gra/vy, hu/man
  i/dol, ju/ry, la/zy, le/gal
  mo/ment, pa/per, pi/lot, ri/der
  ru/ler, se/cret, spi/der, stu/dent**

Horizons Phonics & Reading Grade 2 Teacher's Guide

Activity 2. Review the VV Rule and the examples. *Words to teach the concept:* fuel, duel, fluent, suet, avian, burial, chia, defiant, denial, diagram, friar, media, Ohio, coed, Joey, Noel, radio. The student will mark the vowels in these words first. Next, divide each word into syllables by the VV Rule. After the words have been marked, have the student read the words with the correct syllabication and an accent on the first syllable.

Words:

bri'/ar, boil, cri/er, bruise
di/al, dy/er, di/et, gi/ant
head, gru/el, li/ar, li/on
pli/ant, pail, po/et, qui/et
read, ri/ot, ru/in, seen
tri/al, spoon, flu/ent, cru/el

Activity 3. Read the words. Then have the student divide each word into syllables by the VCVopen Rule. Instruct the student to mark the first syllable with an accent. Read the words again.

Words:

du'/ty, ci'/der, fe'/ver, glo'/ry
ho'/ly, i'/dol, o'/ver, la'/dy
ma'/ker, wa'/ges, vi'/per, va'/ry
tra'/der, to'/tal, stor'/ry, sha'/dy
ru'/by, ru'/ral, wa'/ger, stu'/pid
pre'/cept, sa'/cred, si'/lent, so'/ber

Activity 4. Read the words. Review the VCCV Rule, the VCVopen Rule, and the VV Rule. Review the syllable markings for each word. Instruct the student to circle the words that have been divided into syllables correctly by the rules.

Answers:

chil/ly, tri/al
fun/nel, pa/per
stu/dent, in/to, luck/y
pep/per, i/vy, li/on
tu/tor, tur/key
cra/zy, fi/nal

3 Read these words. Divide the words into syllables. Mark the first syllable with an accent.

du'ty	ci'der	fe'ver	glo'ry
ho'ly	i'dol	o'ver	la'dy
ma'ker	wa'ges	vi'per	va'ry
tra'der	to'tal	sto'ry	sha'dy
ru'by	ru'ral	wa'ger	stu'pid
pre'cept	sa'cred	si'lent	so'ber

4 Read the words. Circle the words that have been correctly divided into syllables.

(chil/ly)	(tri/al)	di/nner	rul/er
fe/rret	qu/iet	(fun/nel)	(pa/per)
(stu/dent)	(in/to)	(luck/y)	poet
(pep/per)	(i/vy)	si/gnal	(li/on)
gia/nt	si/lver	(tu/tor)	(tur/key)
(cra/zy)	diet	t/aper	(fi/nal)

142 *Two-Syllable Words with Accent on First Syllable*

Reading. Read and discuss the maxim for the Lesson.

Read the story *The Visitor (continued)*. This is another chapter of the *A Little Princess* story. Preview the story and explain words or sentence structures that are not familiar to the student. With every story ask questions: who are the characters, what are they doing, what are they saying, where does the action take place, what is the order of events, what words are being used, what new information is given, what lesson can be learned?

Comprehension questions:
Did the dream continue?
What was the result of the good food and warmth that Sara was getting?
What did Miss Amy say about Sara?
What had made Becky's life easier?
What came to the door one day?
To whom was the package addressed?
Who ordered Sara to open the package?

Assign. Lesson activities or reading that are to be completed as homework.

Lesson 146: Words of Two Syllables with Accent on Second

Overview:

- Read words of two syllables
- Identify prefixes
- Divide words into syllables
- Identify words that have been correctly divided into syllables
- Code syllables with an accent
- Read two-syllable words with the correct accent
- Label VCV letter patterns in two-syllable words
- Divide VCV letter patterns into syllables
- Identify silent **e** syllables
- Count vowels and syllables in two-syllable words
- Complete sentences

Materials and Supplies:

- Teacher's Guide & Student Workbook 2
- White board or chalkboard
- Word cards (as necessary)
- Dictionary
- Reader: *A Little Princess & Other Classic Stories*

Teaching Tips:

Review for Mastery. Discuss and review any work from the previous lesson that was assigned as homework. Check for completion of the activities and orally quiz the student for comprehension. Review any reading that was assigned, discussing the characters, setting, plot, theme, language, sequence, etc.

Strengthen fluency and phonemic awareness by reviewing words and sentences from previous lessons. Build vocabulary skills by using some of the words in sentences.

Review rhyming words with Lesson 143, Activities 3 & 4. Review the spellings that have the same sound, like the R-controlled vowels in *work* and *lurk* or the vowel digraphs in *sleep* and *cheap*. Contrast these to the sound of **y** in *sky* and *lazy*.

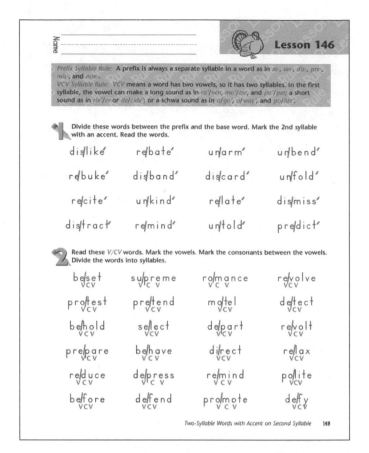

Review VCCV words with Lesson 144, Activity 3. Mark the accented first syllable in the words and read them.

Review VCCV words with Lesson 144, Activity 4. Mark the accented first syllable on the words that were divided correctly and read the words.

Review VCVopen words with Lesson 145, Activity 3. Label the vowels and consonant between them in the words. Read the words.

Review VCVopen words with Lesson 145, Activity 4. Review the VCVopen and the VV rules. Correct the syllabication of the words incorrectly marked in the activity. Read the words.

Activity 1. Review prefixes **dis-, re-, un-,** and **pre-.** Review the prefix rule for syllables. Instruct the student to divide these words with prefixes into syllables. Have the student mark the second syllable with an accent and read the words aloud.

Words:

   dis/like', re/bate', un/arm', un/bend'
   re/buke', dis/band', dis/card', un/fold'
   re/cite', un/kind', re/late', dis/miss'
   dis/tract', re/mind', un/told', pre/dict'

Activity 2. Help the student read the words with schwa, short, or long initial syllables and the accent on the second syllable. Review the VCV Syllable Rule. Instruct the student to mark the vowels, the consonant between them, and divide the V/CV words into syllables.

Words:

be/set, su/preme, ro/mance, re/volve
pro/test, pre/tend, mo/tel, de/tect
be/hold, se/lect, de/part, re/volt
pre/pare, be/have, di/rect, re/lax
re/duce, de/press, re/mind, po/lite
be/fore, de/fend, pro/mote, de/fy

Activity 3. Have the student read the words aloud. Review the Silent **e** Rule. Then have the student count the vowels, determine the numbers of syllables, and write the numbers in the boxes.

Vowels	Syllables	Vowels	Syllables	Vowels	Syllables
3	2	3	2	3	2
3	2	3	2	3	2
3	2	3	2	3	2
3	2	3	2	3	2
3	2	3	2	3	2

Answer to question: They are Final E or Silent E words.

Activity 4. Help the student read the sentences. Instruct the student to select a word from Activity 3 that will correctly complete each sentence and write the word on the line. Unknown words can be looked up in a dictionary.

Sentences:

1. The broken stair rail was <u>unsafe</u>.
2. To be ready for the program we must <u>prepare</u>.
3. Cold soup is something that I <u>dislike</u>.
4. It will be nice to tip the chair back and <u>recline</u>.
5. Mom will help us <u>decide</u> which puppy to buy.
6. Do not eat the pear that is <u>unripe</u>.
7. The teacher will <u>rebuke</u> the boy for telling a lie.
8. Next we will <u>define</u> the spelling words.

9. The new filter will <u>reduce</u> the dust in the air.
10. We can save money on the new toy with a <u>rebate</u>.

Reading. Read and discuss the maxim for the Lesson.

Read the story *The Visitor (continued)*. This is another chapter of the *A Little Princess* story. Preview the story and explain words or sentence structures that are not familiar to the student.

Comprehension questions:
What did Sara do with the items in the packages?
How did Miss Minchin feel about the package?
What was the reaction of the other girls when Sara came into the schoolroom?
What was troubling Sara?
What was Sara's plan for thanking the person who was doing the things for her?

Assign. Lesson activities or reading that are to be completed as homework.

Lesson 147: Words of Two Syllables with Accent on Second

Overview:

- Read words of two syllables
- Divide words into syllables
- Code syllables with an accent
- Read two-syllable words with the correct accent
- Label VCV letter patterns in two-syllable words
- Divide VCV letter patterns into syllables
- Label VCCV letter patterns in two-syllable words
- Divide VCCV letter patterns into syllables
- Complete sentences

Materials and Supplies:

- Teacher's Guide & Student Workbook 2
- White board or chalkboard
- Word cards (as necessary)
- Dictionary
- Reader: *A Little Princess & Other Classic Stories*

Teaching Tips:

Review for Mastery. Discuss and review any work from the previous lesson that was assigned as homework. Check for completion of the activities and orally quiz the student for comprehension. Review any reading that was assigned, discussing the characters, setting, plot, theme, language, sequence, etc.

Strengthen fluency and phonemic awareness by reviewing words and sentences from previous lessons. Build vocabulary skills by using some of the words in sentences.

Review VCVopen words with Lesson 145, Activity 1. Mark the accented first syllable and read the words.

Review VV words with Lesson 145, Activity 2. Mark the accented first syllable in the two-syllable words and read them.

Review V/CV words with Lesson 146, Activity 2. Mark the accented second syllable and read the words.

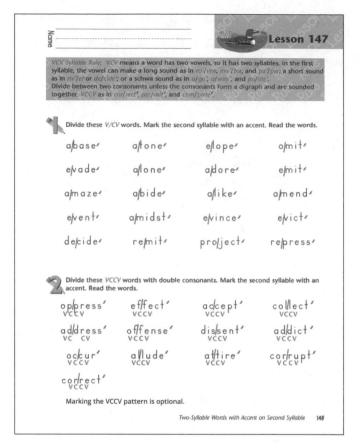

Review prefixes **re-, un-, pre-,** and **dis-** with Lesson 146, Activity 3. Sort the words by the prefix on the board.

Activity 1. Review the VCV Syllable Rule. The student will divide the V/CV words into syllables and mark the second syllable with an accent. After the words have been marked, have the student read the words with the correct syllabication and an accent on the second syllable.

Words:

  a/base', a/tone', e/lope', o/mit'
  e/vade', a/lone', a/dore', e/mit'
  a/maze', a/bide', a/like', a/mend'
  e/vent', a/midst', e/vince', e/vict'
  de/cide', re/mit', pro/ject', re/press'

Activity 2. Review the VCCV Rule. The student will divide each word into syllables by the VCCV Rule and mark the second syllable with an accent. After the words have been marked, have the student read the words with the correct syllabication and an accent on the second syllable.

Horizons Phonics & Reading Grade 2 Teacher's Guide

Activity 2 continued:

Words:

op/press', ef/fect', ac/cept', col/lect'
ad/dress', of/fence', dis/sent', ad/dict'
oc/cur', al/lude', at'tire', cor/rupt'
cor/rect'

Activity 3. Review the VCCV Rule. The student will mark the vowels and the consonants between them. After the words have been marked, have the student read the words with the correct syllabication and an accent on the second syllable.

Words:

mis/place', in/dent', com/plete', sub/mit'
in/struct', con/sume', ad/mit', mis/take'
per/spire', in/still', com/pute', en/tire'
trans/late', in/vert', sub/tract', as/pire'
con/tent', en/large', com/pel', in/vite'

Activity 4. Help the student read the sentences. Instruct the student to select the word from Activity 3 that will correctly complete each sentence and write the word on the line. Unknown words can be looked up in a dictionary.

Sentences:

1. The ticket will <u>admit</u> one person to the game.
2. I will <u>submit</u> my homework in the morning.
3. We will <u>enlarge</u> the circle to make it bigger.
4. <u>Subtract</u> the two numbers to get the answer.
5. Our work is <u>complete</u> so we can have recess.
6. When it is hot our skin will <u>perspire</u>.
7. There are 7 girls that I will <u>invite</u> to the party.
8. She will eat her <u>entire</u> sandwich for lunch.
9. It was a <u>mistake</u> to eat so much candy.
10. We must <u>translate</u> this Spanish letter.

---

3 Read the VCCV words with an accent on the second syllable. Mark the vowels. Mark the consonants between the vowels.

mis/place' in/dent' com/plete' sub/mit'
VC CV   VC CV   VC CV   VC CV

in/struct' con/sume' ad/mit' mis/take'
VC C V   VC CV   VC CV   VC CV

per/spire' in/still' com/pute' en/tire'
VC CV   VC CV   VC CV   VC CV

trans/late' in/vert' sub/tract' as/pire'
VC CV   VC CV   VC C V   VC CV

con/tent' en/large' com/pel' in/vite'
VC CV   VC CV   VC CV   VC CV

4 Complete these sentences with a word given above.

1. The ticket will ____admit____ one person to the game.
2. I will ____submit____ my homework in the morning.
3. We will ____enlarge____ the circle to make it bigger.
4. ____Subtract____ the two numbers to get the answer.
5. Our work is ____complete____ so we can have recess.
6. When it is hot our skin will ____perspire____.
7. There are 7 girls that I will ____invite____ to the party.
8. She will eat her ____entire____ sandwich for lunch.
9. It was a ____mistake____ to eat so much candy.
10. We must ____translate____ this Spanish letter.

140 *Two-Syllable Words with Accent on Second Syllable*

Reading. Read and discuss the maxim for the Lesson.

Read the story *The Visitor (continued)*. This is another chapter of the *A Little Princess* story. Preview the story and explain words or sentence structures that are not familiar to the student. With every story ask questions: who are the characters, what are they doing, what are they saying, where does the action take place, what is the order of events, what words are being used, what new information is given, what lesson can be learned?

Comprehension questions:

What happened to the letter during the day?
What did Sara hear outside the skylight?
How did Sara get the monkey into the attic?
Where did the monkey spend the night?

Assign. Lesson activities or reading that are to be completed as homework.

Lesson 148: Words of Three Syllables with Accents on First and Second

Overview:

- Read words of three syllables
- Divide words into syllables
- Read three-syllable words with the correct accent
- Match pictures to words
- Identify open syllables
- Sort words by the open second syllable

Materials and Supplies:

- Teacher's Guide & Student Workbook 2
- White board or chalkboard
- Word cards (as necessary)
- Dictionary
- Reader: *A Little Princess & Other Classic Stories*

Teaching Tips:

Review for Mastery. Discuss and review any work from the previous lesson that was assigned as homework. Check for completion of the activities and orally quiz the student for comprehension. Review any reading that was assigned, discussing the characters, setting, plot, theme, language, sequence, etc.

Strengthen fluency and phonemic awareness by reviewing words and sentences from previous lessons. Build vocabulary skills by using some of the words in sentences.

Review syllabication with Lesson 146, Activity 3. Label the vowels and the consonant or consonants between them. Divide the words into syllables.

Review V/CV words with Lesson 147, Activity 1. Mark the vowels and the consonant between them and read the words.

Three-Syllable Words with Full Accent on 1st and Weak Accent on 3rd   147

Review VCCV words with Lesson 147, Activity 2. Mark the vowels and the consonants between them and read the words.

Activity 1. Review the rule for words with three syllables and the examples with the student. *Words to teach the concept:* paradox, vagabond, calico, cannibal, pedigree, politic, vanity, felony. Have the student read the words aloud with an accent on the first syllable. The words have been divided into syllables to assist with reading them. Review the pictures with the student. The student will write the word for each picture on the line.

Pictures:
   vinegar, melody, animal
   ligament, monument, pyramid
   mariner, remedy, cabinet
   orator, family, canopy

Activity 2. Help the student read the words in the Word Box. Assist the student with identifying the open, unaccented second syllable in each word. Instruct the student to sort the words by the open vowel spelling of the second syllable.

Words:

Open a	Open e
senator	benefit
diamond	comedy
dialect	enemy

Open i

quality	capital
medical	similar
editor	citizen
typical	calico

Open o	Open u
memory	popular
ebony	document
colony	regular

Reading. Read and discuss the maxim for the Lesson.

Read the story *"It Is the Child!"* This is another chapter of the *A Little Princess* story. Preview the story and explain words or sentence structures that are not familiar to the student. With every story ask questions: who are the characters, what are they doing, what are they saying, where does the action take place, what is the order of events, what words are being used, what new information is given, what lesson can be learned?

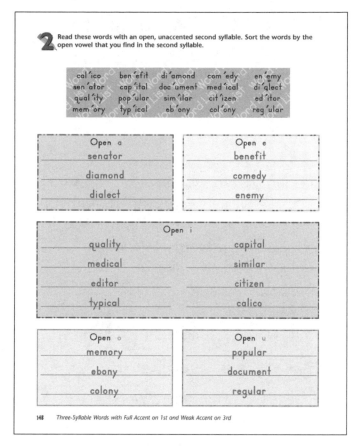

Comprehension questions:
  Who was sitting in Mr. Crawford's library?
  What was everyone in the library waiting for?
  What did the children call the girl who Mr. Crawford wanted to find?
  What had Donald noticed about Sara?

Assign. Lesson activities or reading that are to be completed as homework.

Lesson 149: Words of Three Syllables with Accents on First and Second

Overview:

- Read words of three syllables
- Divide words into syllables
- Read three-syllable words with the correct accent
- Match pictures to words
- Identify vowels in words
- Identify open syllables
- Read sentences
- Identify words that have three syllables

Materials and Supplies:

- Teacher's Guide & Student Workbook 2
- White board or chalkboard
- Word cards (as necessary)
- Dictionary
- Reader: *A Little Princess & Other Classic Stories*

Teaching Tips:

Review for Mastery. Discuss and review any work from the previous lesson that was assigned as homework. Check for completion of the activities and orally quiz the student for comprehension. Review any reading that was assigned, discussing the characters, setting, plot, theme, language, sequence, etc.

Strengthen fluency and phonemic awareness by reviewing words and sentences from previous lessons. Build vocabulary skills by using some of the words in sentences.

Review VCCVCCV words with Lesson 148, Activities 1 & 2. Divide the words written on the blanks into syllables. Review the rule for open, unaccented syllables that make the schwa sound.

Activity 1. Review the rule for words with three syllables and the examples with the student. *Words to teach the concept:* admiral, amnesty, classical, currency, decency, embassy, factory, faculty, family, festival, harmony, implement, industry, infidel, integer, justify, liberty, mystery, numeral, officer, permanent, summary, supplement, vacancy. Have the student read the words aloud with an accent on the first syllable. The words have been divided into syllables to assist with reading them. Review the pictures with the student. The student will write the word for each picture on the line.

Pictures:
   **calendar, butterfly, general
   ornament, library, cylinder
   embryo, ivory, crucifix
   reverend, continent, cinnamon**

Activity 2. Instruct the student to put a dot under each of the vowels that they find in these words. Help the student read the words. Review the meaning of an open syllable. Then have the student circle the words with an open first, second, or third syllable. Many of the words have more than one open syllable.

Answers:
   salary, comedy
   occupy, buttery
   element, origin, poetry
   accident, happiness
   penalty, quantity
   victory, practical
   enemy, diligent, vanity

Activity 3. Help the student read the sentences. Instruct the student to circle the words in each sentence that have three syllables.

Sentences:
1. She got a book of <u>poetry</u> from the <u>library</u>.
2. The <u>messenger</u> brings the letters on a <u>regular</u> basis.
3. A <u>victory</u> will make the team <u>popular</u> with the fans.
4. He can sing the <u>melody</u> from <u>memory</u>.
5. The <u>reverend</u> was a <u>minister</u> to the <u>citizens</u> of the <u>colony</u>.
6. The <u>popular</u> <u>senator</u> is a great <u>orator</u>.
7. The <u>general</u> will <u>occupy</u> <u>several</u> cities of the <u>enemy</u>.
8. I saw a <u>similar</u> <u>butterfly</u> in the <u>wilderness</u>.
9. The <u>accident</u> tore a <u>ligament</u> in his knee.
10. A <u>monument</u> <u>similar</u> to a <u>pyramid</u> was built to honor the <u>general</u>.

Reading. Read and discuss the maxim for the Lesson.

Read the story *"It Is the Child!" (continued)*. This is another chapter of the *A Little Princess* story.

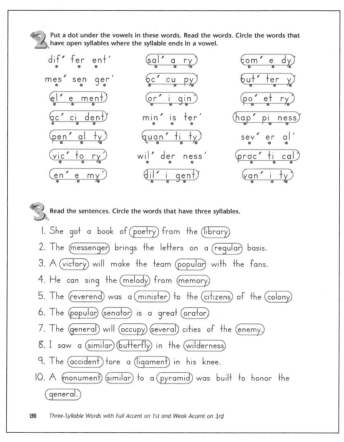

Preview the story and explain words or sentence structures that are not familiar to the student. With every story ask questions: who are the characters, what are they doing, what are they saying, where does the action take place, what is the order of events, what words are being used, what new information is given, what lesson can be learned?

Comprehension questions:
   What brought Mr. Mitchell home?
   What news did Mr. Mitchell have for Mr. Crawford?
   How did Mr. Crawford react to the news?
   What new plan did they make?
   Where did they decide to look for the girl first?

Assign. Lesson activities or reading that are to be completed as homework.

Lesson 150: Words of Three Syllables with Accent on Second

Overview:

- Read words of three syllables
- Divide words into syllables
- Read three-syllable words with the correct accent
- Match pictures to words
- Sort words by the final syllable
- Read sentences
- Identify words that have three syllables

Materials and Supplies:

- Teacher's Guide & Student Workbook 2
- White board or chalkboard
- Word cards (as necessary)
- Dictionary
- Reader: *A Little Princess & Other Classic Stories*

Teaching Tips:

Review for Mastery. Discuss and review any work from the previous lesson that was assigned as homework. Check for completion of the activities and orally quiz the student for comprehension. Review any reading that was assigned, discussing the characters, setting, plot, theme, language, sequence, etc.

Strengthen fluency and phonemic awareness by reviewing words and sentences from previous lessons. Build vocabulary skills by using some of the words in sentences.

Review VCCVCCV words with Lesson 148, Activity 1. Sort the words on the board by the spelling of the open, unaccented syllable.

Review VCCVCCV words with Lesson 149, Activity 1. Divide the words written on the blanks into syllables. Review the rule for open, unaccented syllables that make the schwa sound.

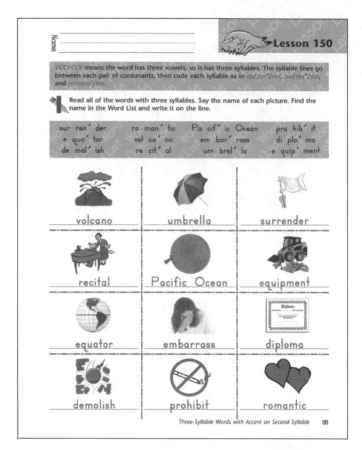

Activity 1. Review the rule for words with three syllables and the examples. Use the words in a sentence to help hear the accent. *Words to teach the concept:* abandon, accomplish, assembly, beginning, diminish, distemper, domestic, invalid, remember, subscriber, unmindful. Have the student read the words aloud with an accent on the second syllable. The words have been divided into syllables to assist with reading them. Review the pictures with the student. The student will write the word for each picture on the line.

Pictures:
**volcano, umbrella, surrender
recital, Pacific Ocean, equipment
equator, embarrass, diploma
demolish, prohibit, romantic**

Activity 2. Help the student read the words in the Word List. Instruct the student to sort the words by the final syllable and write them on the blanks.

Words:

Final -ment	Final -or
agreement	aggressor
amazement	collector
amendment	contractor
atonement	dictator
attachment	equator
confinement	protector
refreshment	spectator
enrollment	survivor
equipment	translator
detachment	impostor

Activity 3. Help the student read the sentences. Instruct the student to circle the words in each sentence that have three syllables.

Sentences:
1. They will <u>prohibit</u> a <u>spectator</u> to bring an <u>umbrella</u> to the <u>recital</u>.
2. A large <u>equipment</u> <u>contractor</u> will <u>demolish</u> the <u>attachment</u> to the building.
3. There is a <u>volcano</u> near the <u>equator</u> in the <u>Pacific</u> Ocean.
4. The blank <u>diploma</u> will <u>embarrass</u> the <u>impostor</u> who wants to be a <u>dictator</u>.

Review for Test. The instructor should plan to use some time at the end of the class to review and prepare for the test that follows this lesson. Review the objectives for the test and then look over the lessons that it will cover. If the student has struggled with any of the concepts that will be included in the test, some additional drill, practice, or review may be needed to adequately prepare him for the test.

Reading. Read and discuss the maxim for the Lesson.

Read the story *"It Is the Child!" (continued)*. This is another chapter of the *A Little Princess* story.

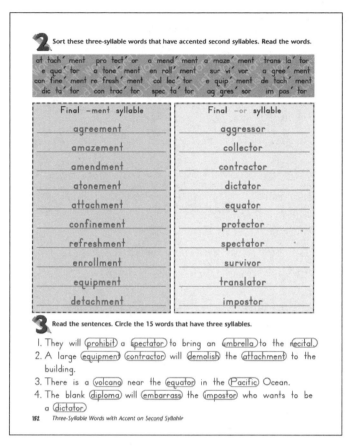

Preview the story and explain words or sentence structures that are not familiar to the student. With every story ask questions: who are the characters, what are they doing, what are they saying, where does the action take place, what is the order of events, what words are being used, what new information is given, what lesson can be learned?

Comprehension questions:
Who was coming to see Mr. Crawford?
What did Sara bring to Mr. Crawford?
How did Mr. Crawford know that Sara knew something about India?
Who was asked to question Sara?

Assign. Lesson activities or reading that are to be completed as homework.

Test 15
Lessons 135-144

Overview:

- Auditory discrimination of the schwa sound
- Recognize spellings of the schwa sound
- Divide words into syllables
- Match a word to its antonym
- Match a word to its synonym
- Match a homonym to its definition
- Divide words with double consonants into syllables
- Match words that rhyme

Materials and Supplies:

- Teacher's Guide & Student Workbook 2

Instructions:

Assessment Start-up. Help the student with any words that he is still unsure of. The teacher should be available to answer any questions that the student may have during the test.

Activity 1. Review the instructions and the words with the student. The student will circle the syllable with the schwa sound in each word and write the vowel that has the schwa sound on the blank by the word.

Words:

m<u>o</u>tor o	trail<u>er</u> e	kitch<u>en</u> e
aw<u>ful</u> u	free<u>dom</u> o	chil<u>dren</u> e
steplad<u>der</u> e	lumb<u>er</u>jack e	run<u>a</u>way a
<u>a</u>boveground a	un<u>der</u>pass e	newspap<u>er</u> e
bush<u>el</u> e	bash<u>ful</u> u	sil<u>ver</u> e

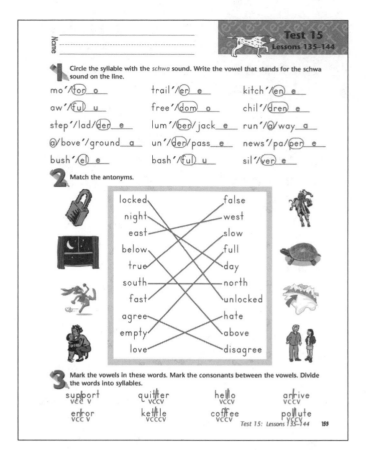

Activity 2. Review the words and the instructions with the student. The student will match each word with a word that means the opposite.

Words:

locked	unlocked
night	day
east	west
below	above
true	false
south	north
fast	slow
agree	disagree
empty	full
love	hate

Activity 3. Make sure the student can correctly read the words. The student is to label the vowels with a **v**, label the consonants between them with a **c**, and divide each word into syllables with a slash. The first word has been done as an example.

Words:

sup/port	quit/ter	hel/lo	ar/rive
er/ror	ket/tle	cof/fee	pol/lute

Activity 4. Review the words and the instructions with the student. The student will match each word with a word that means the same.

Words:

large	big
happy	glad
ill	sick
stop	end
close	shut
under	below
earth	world
answer	reply

Activity 5. Make sure the student can correctly read the word choices and the definitions. The student is to select the spelling for the homonym that matches the definition by filling in the circle.

Definitions:

1. an animal with four legs   deer
2. seven days   week
3. a number   eight
4. a sore throat   hoarse
5. a bunch of cattle   herd
6. put up your hand   raise
7. water in the air   mist
8. an insect   bee
9. a boy   son
10. to see with   eye

Activity 6. Review the words and the instructions with the student. The student will match each word with a word that rhymes.

Words:

sky	buy
batter	glitter
sample	people
kettle	rattle
pickle	nickel
helpful	wasteful

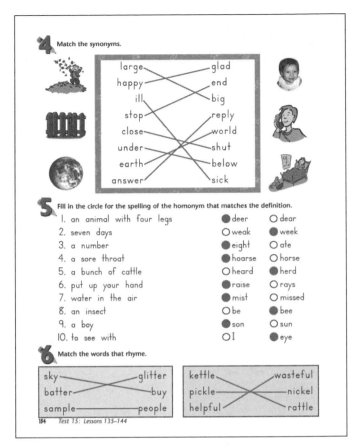

Assessment Follow-up. Every test is an important assessment of both the student's comprehension of the concepts and the instructional process. This makes follow-up after each test essential to the learning process. Review all of the errors made on the test with the student. Check for understanding of the concepts and of the problem instructions. Compare the errors made on the test to the test objectives to identify specific areas of weakness. If weak areas of understanding are detected it might be necessary to go back to those lessons to devise some enrichment activities for the concept.

The test results can be used to determine what concepts are reviewed during the daily time of classroom instruction. Devise enrichment activities that will provide development in those areas.

If time permits, choose a selection and have the student read it again. This can also be used as a catch-up time to complete unfinished selections.

Lesson 151: Words of Three Syllables with Accent on Second

Overview:

- Read words of three syllables
- Divide words into syllables
- Read three-syllable words with the correct accent
- Sort words by the final syllable
- Read sentences
- Identify words that have three syllables

Materials and Supplies:

- Teacher's Guide & Student Workbook 2
- White board or chalkboard
- Word cards (as necessary)
- Dictionary
- Reader: *A Little Princess & Other Classic Stories*

Teaching Tips:

Review for Mastery. Discuss and review any work from the previous lesson that was assigned as homework. Check for completion of the activities and orally quiz the student for comprehension. Review any reading that was assigned, discussing the characters, setting, plot, theme, language, sequence, etc.

Strengthen fluency and phonemic awareness by reviewing words and sentences from previous lessons. Build vocabulary skills by using some of the words in sentences.

Review VCCVCCV words with Lesson 150, Activity 1. Use the words in a sentence.

Review VCCVCCV words with Lesson 150, Activity 2. Read the sorted words. Pay special attention to the final syllable sound. Ask the student for the syllable that has the accent.

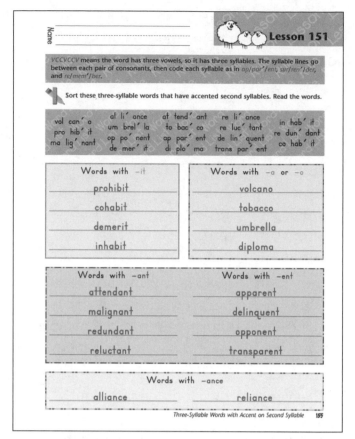

Activity 1. Review the rule for words with three syllables. Help the student read the words in the Word Box. Instruct the student to sort the words by the final syllable and write them on the blanks.

Words:

Final -it	Final -a or -o
prohibit	volcano
cohabit	tobacco
demerit	umbrella
inhabit	diploma

Final -ant	Final -ent
attendant	apparent
malignant	delinquent
redundant	opponent
reluctant	transparent

Final -ance	
alliance	reliance

Activity 2. Instruct the student to circle the words with an **-ish** ending. Then instruct them to draw a square around the words with an **-er** ending. Help the student read the words in each group.

Words:

Final -ish	Final -er
demolish	improper
establish	deliver
abolish	surrender
diminish	consider
accomplish	subscriber
admonish	remember
replenish	decanter
	bewilder

Activity 3. Instruct the student to draw a line under the words with an **-al** ending. Then instruct them to circle the words with an **-ic** ending. Help the student read the words in each group.

Words:

Final -al	Final -ic
arrival	pacific
recital	romantic
denial	specific
immoral	dogmatic
illegal	erratic
unequal	heroic

Activity 4. Help the student read the sentences. Instruct the student to circle the words in each sentence that have three syllables.

Sentences:
1. It was <u>apparent</u> that the <u>reluctant</u> <u>attendant</u> was <u>delinquent</u> on the rent.
2. <u>Remember</u> to <u>deliver</u> a <u>decanter</u> to the <u>subscriber</u>.
3. A <u>reliance</u> on <u>tobacco</u> may cause a <u>malignant</u> growth to <u>inhabit</u> the lung.
4. He made a <u>heroic</u> <u>arrival</u> at the <u>volcano</u>.
5. It is <u>illegal</u> and <u>immoral</u> to make a <u>denial</u> of the <u>specific</u> <u>alliance</u>.
6. A <u>demerit</u> will <u>admonish</u> the boy who did the <u>improper</u> act.

Reading. Read and discuss the maxim for the Lesson.

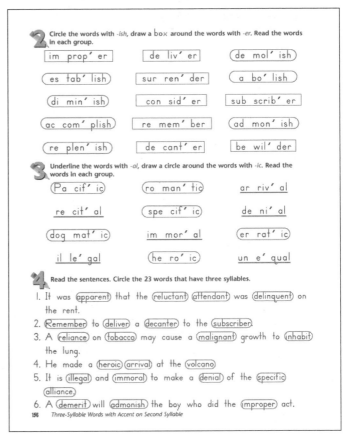

Read the story *"It Is the Child!" (continued)*. This is another chapter of the *A Little Princess* story. Preview the story and explain words or sentence structures that are not familiar to the student. With every story ask questions: who are the characters, what are they doing, what are they saying, where does the action take place, what is the order of events, what words are being used, what new information is given, what lesson can be learned?

Comprehension questions:
Why was Mr. Mitchell a good person to do the questioning of Sara?
Who was not very patient during Mr. Mitchell's questioning?
How did Mr. Crawford respond when Sara said that her father was Captain Crewe?
How did Sara react when she found out that she was the girl that Mr. Crawford had been looking for?

Assign. Lesson activities or reading that are to be completed as homework.

Lesson 152: Words of Three Syllables with Accents on First and Third

Overview:

- Read words of three syllables
- Divide words into syllables
- Read three-syllable words with the correct accents
- Match pictures to words
- Read sentences
- Identify words that have three syllables

Materials and Supplies:

- Teacher's Guide & Student Workbook 2
- White board or chalkboard
- Word cards (as necessary)
- Dictionary
- Reader: *A Little Princess & Other Classic Stories*

Teaching Tips:

Review for Mastery. Discuss and review any work from the previous lesson that was assigned as homework. Check for completion of the activities and orally quiz the student for comprehension. Review any reading that was assigned, discussing the characters, setting, plot, theme, language, sequence, etc.

Strengthen fluency and phonemic awareness by reviewing words and sentences from previous lessons. Build vocabulary skills by using some of the words in sentences.

Review previous lessons. Use the sorted words from Activity 1 of Lesson 151 in a sentence. Pay special attention to the final syllable sound. Ask the student for the syllable that has the accent. Use the sorted words written in Activities 2 & 3 of Lesson 151 in a sentence.

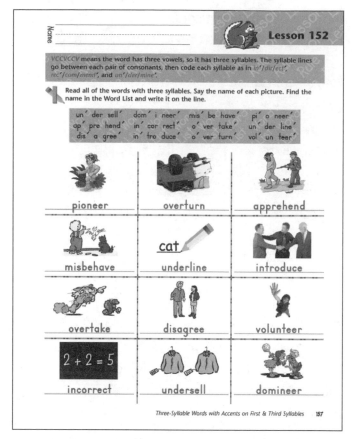

Activity 1. Review the rule for words with three syllables and the examples with the student. Use each example word in a sentence. Have the student read the words aloud with an accent on the first and third syllables. The words have been divided into syllables to assist with reading them. Review the pictures with the student. The student will write the word for each picture on the line.

Pictures:

    pioneer, overturn, apprehend
    misbehave, underline, introduce
    overtake, disagree, volunteer
    incorrect, undersell, domineer

Activity 2. Have the student read the words aloud. Pay special attention to the accents on both the first and third syllables. It may help to pronounce these words with a sing-song voice inflection.

Activity 3. Help the student read the sentences. Instruct the student to circle the words that have three syllables.

Sentences:
1. When two people <u>disagree</u>, they often <u>contradict</u> each other.
2. It is <u>immature</u> to <u>misbehave</u> in school.
3. The new <u>department</u> store will <u>undersell</u> the other stores.
4. A <u>volunteer</u> will help the <u>refugee</u> find a new home.
5. <u>Underline</u> the words in this story that you do not <u>understand</u>.
6. The stream of water may <u>undermine</u> the sign and cause it to <u>overturn</u>.
7. She will <u>introduce</u> the man who will <u>intercede</u> for the patient.
8. An <u>indirect</u> push on the side of the bike may cause it to <u>overturn</u>.
9. The tall boy will <u>domineer</u> on the <u>basketball</u> court.
10. She will <u>reconcile</u> the <u>incorrect</u> numbers on the chart.
11. The cop will <u>overtake</u> the bad man and <u>apprehend</u> him.

Reading. Read and discuss the maxim for the Lesson.

Read the story *"I Tried Not to Be."* This is another chapter of the *A Little Princess* story. Preview the story and explain words or sentence structures that are not familiar to the student. With every story ask questions: who are the characters, what are they doing, what are they saying, where does the action take place, what is the order of events, what words are being used, what new information is given, what lesson can be learned?

Comprehension questions:
   Who explained everything to Sara?
   What was Donald's regret?
   How did Sara react when she found out that Ram Dass and Mr. Crawford had been the ones who brought the things to her attic room?
   Why did Sara call Mr. Crawford her friend?
   Who needed to be informed that Sara's fortunes had changed?

Assign. Lesson activities or reading that are to be completed as homework.

Lesson 153: Difficult and Irregular Words of One Syllable

Overview:

- Read difficult one-syllable words
- Read words with different spellings of the same vowel sound
- Auditory discrimination of the long vowel sound
- Auditory discrimination of the short vowel sound
- Sort words by the vowel sound

Materials and Supplies:

- Teacher's Guide & Student Workbook 2
- White board or chalkboard
- Word cards (as necessary)
- Dictionary
- Reader: *A Little Princess & Other Classic Stories*

Teaching Tips:

Review for Mastery. Discuss and review any work from the previous lesson that was assigned as homework. Check for completion of the activities and orally quiz the student for comprehension. Review any reading that was assigned, discussing the characters, setting, plot, theme, language, sequence, etc.

Strengthen fluency and phonemic awareness by reviewing words and sentences from previous lessons. Build vocabulary skills by using some of the words in sentences.

Review VCCVCCV words with Lesson 152, Activity 1. Read the words in the activity. Pay special attention to the accents on both the first and third syllable.

Lesson 153

Read the words. Read left to right, then read top to bottom.

day	say	pray	way	stray
jail	rail	nail	ail	snail
maid	wear	brain	train	plain
vain	paint	claim	stage	bait
wait	graze	raise	shave	break
stay	slay	play	laid	paid
hair	pain	drain	faint	haste
waste	taste	strange	be	flea
leap	heap	feel	deal	peel
seal	steal	peal	peer	deer
near	clear	steer	cheer	sear
spear	feed	bead	read	heed
reed	bead	cream	steam	scream
team	feast	east	brief	deaf
beef	keep	fleece	tease	niece
grease	cheat	beat	heat	weak
squeak	shriek	seen	clean	queen
spleen	lean	heave	leave	freeze
cheese	seize	speech	beach	bleach
yield	field	leash	cry	buy
pie	high	sigh	light	right
slight	bright	rhyme	smile	wild

Difficult One-Syllable Words 159

The next few lessons will review many of the phonics concepts that have been covered in this course. Have the student write examples of different spellings that sound the same on the chalkboard or white board. Assist the student as needed in reading the words in the lesson.

Activity 1. Have the student read the words in this activity one row at a time. Discuss the vowel sound and the spelling. Look also for consonant blends and other spellings for sounds. After the words have been read by rows, read the words in a column. Assist the student in correctly pronouncing the words.

Activity 2. Have the student read aloud the words in each row. The student will circle the words in each row with a short vowel sound. Review the spellings of the sounds heard in each word.

Answers:
1. want
2. grass
3. bread
4. sketch
5. dead
6. deck

Activity 3. The student will read these words and sort them by the vowel sound.

Words:

ay	ear/air	a_e	ai
hay	stair	date	sail
lay	swear	shave	rain
may	wear	brave	frail
sway	bear	stage	strait
stray	tear	paste	laid
clay	lair	change	twain
bay	chair	haste	mail

Reading. Read and discuss the maxim for the Lesson.

Read the story *"I Tried Not to Be" (continued)*. This is another chapter of the *A Little Princess* story. Preview the story and explain words or sentence structures that are not familiar to the student. With every story ask questions: who are the characters, what are they doing, what are they saying, where does the action take place, what is the order of events, what words are being used, what new information is given, what lesson can be learned?

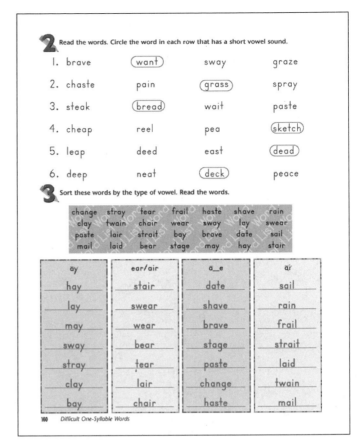

Comprehension questions:
  Did Sara return to the School?
  What gave Mr. Mitchell a chance to talk to Miss Minchin?
  Who told Miss Minchin where Sara had gone?
  Who told Miss Minchin that Sara was not going back to the School?
  How did Miss Minchin react when she heard that Sara was not coming back to the School?

Assign. Lesson activities or reading that are to be completed as homework.

Lesson 154: Difficult and Irregular Words of One Syllable

Overview:

- Read difficult one-syllable words
- Read words with different spellings of the same vowel sound
- Auditory discrimination of the long vowel sound
- Auditory discrimination of the short vowel sound
- Sort words by the vowel sound

Materials and Supplies:

- Teacher's Guide & Student Workbook 2
- White board or chalkboard
- Word cards (as necessary)
- Dictionary
- Reader: *A Little Princess & Other Classic Stories*

Teaching Tips:

Review for Mastery. Discuss and review any work from the previous lesson that was assigned as homework. Check for completion of the activities and orally quiz the student for comprehension. Review any reading that was assigned, discussing the characters, setting, plot, theme, language, sequence, etc.

Strengthen fluency and phonemic awareness by reviewing words and sentences from previous lessons. Build vocabulary skills by using some of the words in sentences.

Review difficult one-syllable words with Lesson 153, Activity 1. Read the words again, first by rows and then by columns. Make a list of the words that the student struggles with for additional review.

Read the words. Read left to right, then read top to bottom.

stride	guide	foe	owe	blow
snow	hoe	pole	roll	toll
stroll	most	more	floor	oar
boat	moat	soak	blown	told
load	soap	prose	coax	sworn
board	sword	due	sue	new
screw	crew	slew	chew	ewe
rude	crude	spruce	fruit	lure
lamb	limb	dense	fence	cash
gnash	bread	head	neck	speck
tense	drench	badge	hedge	pledge
twelve	valve	sweat	prism	guilt
drift	risk	spill	witch	fringe
spit	live	bolt	jolt	crumb
plump	church	judge	shrub	purge
purse	law	saw	claw	war
fort	caught	fought	naught	swarm
morn	yawn	broad	cause	torch
all	call	haul	crawl	wart
quart	scald	moss	fork	walk
stalk	wasp	balm	cask	mark
spark	shark	gasp	lard	launch

Difficult One-Syllable Words **161**

This lesson will continue to review many of the phonics concepts that have been covered in this course. Have the student write examples of different spellings that sound the same on the chalkboard or white board. Assist the student as needed in reading the words in the lesson.

Activity 1. Have the student read the words in this activity one row at a time. Discuss the vowel sound and the spelling. Look also for consonant blends and other spellings for sounds. After the words have been read by rows, read the words in a column. Assist the student in correctly pronouncing the words.

Activity 2. Have the student read aloud the words in each row. The student will circle the words in each row with a short vowel sound. Review the spellings of the sounds heard in each word.

Answers:

1. bench
2. brick
3. since
4. cross
5. young
6. dodge

Activity 3. The student will read these words and sort them by the vowel sound.

Words:

ea	ee	eer/ear	igh
pea	weed	rear	fright
meal	breeze	veer	sight
cheap	green	shear	might
peach	reef	year	height
sneak	seem	queer	flight
stream	steep	dear	tight
leaf	flee	deer	nigh

Reading. Read and discuss the maxim for the Lesson.

Read the story *"I Tried Not to Be"* (continued). This is another chapter of the *A Little Princess* story. Preview the story and explain words or sentence structures that are not familiar to the student. With every story ask questions: who are the characters, what are they doing, what are they saying, where does the action take place, what is the order of events, what words are being used, what new information is given, what lesson can be learned?

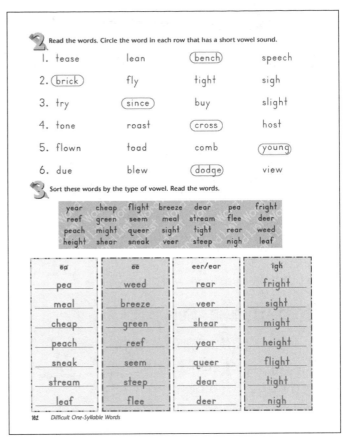

Comprehension questions:

Who explained to Miss Minchin that Sara's fortunes had changed?

What had made Sara rich?

How did Miss Minchin try to get Sara back to the School?

Did Miss Minchin know why Sara was not coming back to the School?

How did Miss Minchin try to make Sara come back to the School one final time?

Assign. Lesson activities or reading that are to be completed as homework.

Lesson 155: Difficult and Irregular Words of One Syllable

Overview:

- Read difficult one-syllable words
- Read words with different spellings of the same vowel sound
- Auditory discrimination of the long vowel sound
- Auditory discrimination of the short vowel sound
- Sort words by the vowel sound

Materials and Supplies:

- Teacher's Guide & Student Workbook 2
- White board or chalkboard
- Word cards (as necessary)
- Dictionary
- Reader: *A Little Princess & Other Classic Stories*

Teaching Tips:

Review for Mastery. Discuss and review any work from the previous lesson that was assigned as homework. Check for completion of the activities and orally quiz the student for comprehension. Review any reading that was assigned, discussing the characters, setting, plot, theme, language, sequence, etc.

Strengthen fluency and phonemic awareness by reviewing words and sentences from previous lessons. Build vocabulary skills by using some of the words in sentences.

Review difficult one-syllable words with Lesson 153 & 154, Activity 1. Read the words again, first by rows and then by columns. Make a list of the words that the student struggles with for additional review.

This lesson will continue to review many of the phonics concepts that have been covered in this course. Have the student write examples of different spellings that sound the same on the chalkboard or white board. Assist the student as needed in reading the words in the lesson.

Activity 1. Have the student read the words in this activity one row at a time. Discuss the vowel sound and the spelling. Look also for consonant blends and other spellings for sounds. After the words have been read by rows, read the words in a column. Assist the student in correctly pronouncing the words.

Activity 2. Have the student read aloud the words in each row. The student will circle the word in each row that has a different vowel sound. Review the spellings of the sounds heard in each word.

Answers:

1. stain
2. meal
3. bright
4. rude
5. stone
6. bench

Activity 3. The student will read these words and sort them by the vowel sound.

Words:

ow	oa	aw	R-controlled
tow	goal	straw	swerve
glow	coast	draw	fir
bowl	goat	jaw	carve
grow	coach	brawl	charge
flow	moan	drawl	verse
mown	toad	spawn	work
flown	croak	sawn	twirl

Reading. Read and discuss the maxim for the Lesson.

Read the story *"I Tried Not to Be" (continued)*. This is another chapter of the *A Little Princess* story. Preview the story and explain words or sentence structures that are not familiar to the student. With every story ask questions: who are the characters, what are they doing, what are they saying, where does the action take place, what is the order of events, what words are being used, what new information is given, what lesson can be learned?

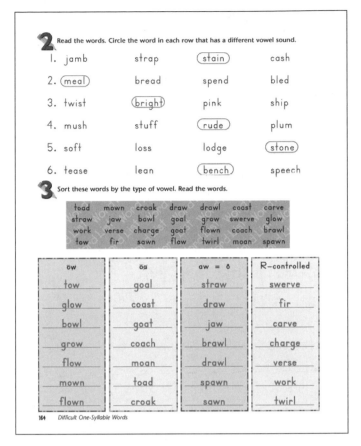

Comprehension questions:
  Who would not refuse Sara's wish to see her friends at the School?
  How did Miss Minchin say Sara must feel once again?
  Who spent time with Miss Minchin for the rest of the day?
  What change took place in Miss Amy?
  What was Miss Minchin going to miss the most about Sara's no longer being in her School?

Assign. Lesson activities or reading that are to be completed as homework.

Lesson 156: Contractions with will & not

Overview:

- Define a contraction
- Match two words to their contraction
- Apply the rules to write contractions from two words
- Replace two words in a sentence with a contraction

Materials and Supplies:

- Teacher's Guide & Student Workbook 2
- White board or chalkboard
- Word cards (as necessary)
- Dictionary
- Reader: *A Little Princess & Other Classic Stories*

Teaching Tips:

Review for Mastery. Discuss and review any work from the previous lesson that was assigned as homework. Check for completion of the activities and orally quiz the student for comprehension. Review any reading that was assigned, discussing the characters, setting, plot, theme, language, sequence, etc.

Strengthen fluency and phonemic awareness by reviewing words and sentences from previous lessons. Build vocabulary skills by using some of the words in sentences.

Review difficult one-syllable words with Lesson 153, 154, & 155, Activity 1. Read the words again, first by rows and then by columns. Make a list of the words that the student struggles with for additional review.

Activity 1. Review the definition of a contraction and the examples. Have the student read the words and the contractions aloud. The student will match the group of words to the corresponding contraction.

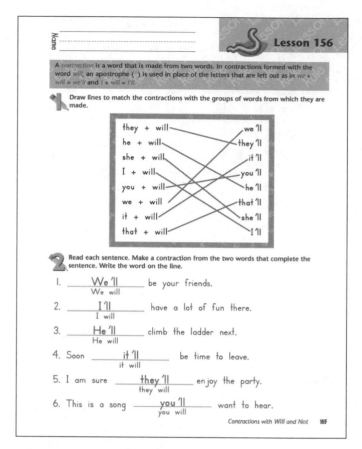

Activity 1 continued:

Words	Contraction
they will	they'll
he will	he'll
she will	she'll
I will	I'll
you will	you'll
we will	we'll
it will	it'll
that will	that'll

Activity 2. Help the student read each sentence using the words under the blank. Instruct the student to make a contraction from the words under the blank and write the contraction on the line. Read the sentences again.

Sentences:
1. <u>We'll</u> be your friends.
2. <u>I'll</u> have a lot of fun there.
3. <u>He'll</u> climb the ladder next.
4. Soon <u>it'll</u> be time to leave.
5. I am sure <u>they'll</u> enjoy the party.
6. This is a song <u>you'll</u> want to hear.

Activity 3. Review the definition of a contraction and the examples. Have the student read the words in the word box aloud. Discuss the contraction *won't* which is formed from the words *will* and *not*. Point out the word *cannot* which has *can't* as its contraction. The student will select the contraction for each word and write the contraction on the line.

Answers:

1.	hasn't	10.	wouldn't
2.	doesn't	11.	needn't
3.	weren't	12.	couldn't
4.	can't	13.	wasn't
5.	mayn't	14.	hadn't
6.	didn't	15.	won't
7.	isn't	16.	mustn't
8.	mightn't	17.	haven't
9.	aren't	18.	shouldn't

Activity 4. Help the student read each sentence using the words under the blank. Instruct the student to make a contraction from the words under the blank and write the contraction on the line. Read the sentences again.

Sentences:

1. They <u>shouldn't</u> eat the candy.
2. She <u>didn't</u> know the man at the store.
3. Somehow the toy <u>wasn't</u> in the box.
4. He <u>mightn't</u> like the new shirt.
5. I <u>can't</u> find the key for the lock.
6. This stove burner <u>shouldn't</u> be so hot.

Reading. Read and discuss the maxim for the Lesson.

Read the story *"I Tried Not to Be" (continued)*. This is another chapter of the *A Little Princess* story. Preview the story and explain words or sentence structures that are not familiar to the student. With every story ask questions: who are the characters, what are they doing, what are they saying, where does the action take place, what is the order of events, what words are being used, what new information is given, what lesson can be learned?

Comprehension questions:
  Who did Miss Minchin learn to respect?
  How did the girls in the school learn that Sara was not coming back to the School?
  Who got the letter from Sara?
  What did Erma say Sara would be more that ever?

Read the poem *The Table and the Chair*. Preview the poem and explain words or sentence structures that are not familiar to the student.

Comprehension questions:
  What did the table and the chair decide to do?
  How did the table and chair get safely back home?
  What words rhyme in the poem?

Read the poem *Time to Rise*. Preview the poem and explain words or sentence structures that are not familiar to the student.

Comprehension questions:
  Who taught the child a lesson in the poem?

Assign. Lesson activities or reading that are to be completed as homework.

Lesson 157: Contractions with have, has, had, & am

Overview:

- Define a contraction
- Match two words to their contraction
- Apply the rules to write contractions from two words
- Replace two words in a sentence with a contraction

Materials and Supplies:

- Teacher's Guide & Student Workbook 2
- White board or chalkboard
- Word cards (as necessary)
- Dictionary
- Reader: *A Little Princess & Other Classic Stories*

Teaching Tips:

Review for Mastery. Discuss and review any work from the previous lesson that was assigned as homework. Check for completion of the activities and orally quiz the student for comprehension. Review any reading that was assigned, discussing the characters, setting, plot, theme, language, sequence, etc.

Strengthen fluency and phonemic awareness by reviewing words and sentences from previous lessons. Build vocabulary skills by using some of the words in sentences.

Review contractions with the word *will* with Lesson 156, Activity 1. Write some of the contractions on the board and have the student write the base words.

Review contractions with the word *not* with Lesson 156, Activity 2. Write some of the base words on the board and have the student write the contraction.

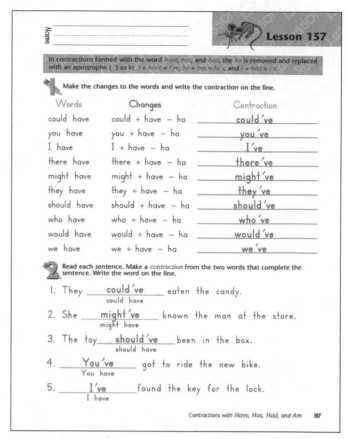

Activity 1. Review the definition of a contraction and the examples. Have the student read the words aloud and the changes that are being made Then have the student write the contraction that follows the changes on the line. Read the contractions. Some of these contractions may not be very common.

Words:

could've
you've
I've
there've
might've
they've
should've
who've
would've
we've

Activity 2. Help the student read each sentence using the words under the blank. Instruct the student to make a contraction from the words under the blank and write the contraction on the line. Read the sentences again.

Activity 2 continued:

Sentences:

1. They <u>could've</u> eaten the candy.
2. She <u>might've</u> known the man at the store.
3. The toy <u>should've</u> been in the box.
4. <u>You've</u> got to ride the new bike.
5. <u>I've</u> found the key for the lock.

Activity 3. Review the definition of a contraction and the examples. Have the student read the words and the contractions aloud. The student will match the group of words to the contraction for them.

Contractions	Words
it's	it has
he'd	he had
she's	she has
it'd	it had
they'd	they had
he's	he has
you'd	you had
I'm	I am
she'd	she had
I'd	I had
we'd	we had

Activity 4. Help the student read each sentence using the words under the blank. Instruct the student to make a contraction from the words under the blank and write the contraction on the line. Read the sentences again.

Sentences:

1. <u>Who'd</u> eaten the candy?
2. <u>What'd</u> the teacher asked you?
3. <u>There'd</u> been a mouse in the box.
4. It seems like <u>nobody'd</u> seen the new car.
5. I found the book <u>that'd</u> been lost.
6. <u>Somebody'd</u> touched the wet paint.
7. <u>I'm</u> going to the bank.
8. There is the CD <u>he's</u> wanted to buy.

Reading. Read and discuss the maxim for the Lesson.

Read the story *"I Tried Not to Be" (continued).* This is another chapter of the *A Little Princess*

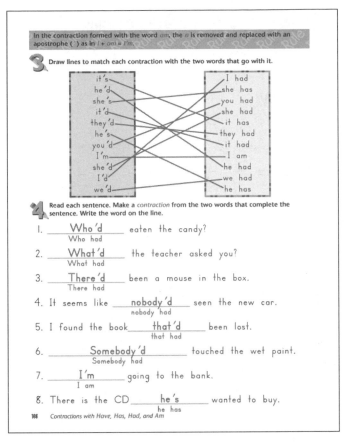

story. Preview the story and explain words or sentence structures that are not familiar to the student. With every story ask questions: who are the characters, what are they doing, what are they saying, where does the action take place, what is the order of events, what words are being used, what new information is given, what lesson can be learned?

Comprehension questions:

How late did the girls in the School continue to talk about Sara?

Why did Becky sneak up the stairs?

Who met Becky in the attic?

What did Ram Dass tell Becky?

Read the poem *Looking-glass River*. Preview the poem and explain words or sentence structures that are not familiar to the student.

What disturbs the quiet of the stream?

Who wishes they could live in a stream?

What brings quiet back to the stream?

Assign. Lesson activities or reading that are to be completed as homework.

Lesson 158: Contractions with is, are, & has

Overview:

- Define a contraction
- Write the two words that a contraction stands for
- Apply the rules to write contractions from two words
- Replace two words in a sentence with a contraction

Materials and Supplies:

- Teacher's Guide & Student Workbook 2
- White board or chalkboard
- Word cards (as necessary)
- Dictionary
- Reader: *A Little Princess & Other Classic Stories*

Teaching Tips:

Review for Mastery. Discuss and review any work from the previous lesson that was assigned as homework. Check for completion of the activities and orally quiz the student for comprehension. Review any reading that was assigned, discussing the characters, setting, plot, theme, language, sequence, etc.

Strengthen fluency and phonemic awareness by reviewing words and sentences from previous lessons. Build vocabulary skills by using some of the words in sentences.

Review contractions with the words *have*, *has*, and *had* with Lesson 157, Activity 1. Write some of the contractions on the board and have the student write the base words.

Review the contraction with the word *am* with Lesson 157, Activity 3. Write the base words on the board and have the student write the contraction.

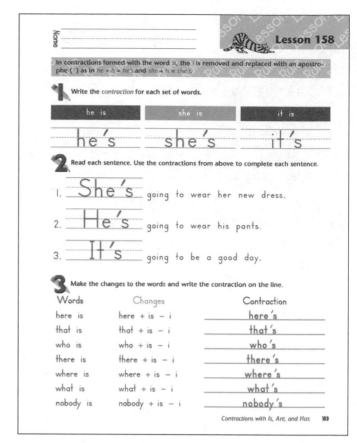

Activity 1. Review the definition of a contraction and the examples. Have the student read the words aloud. The student will write the contractions for each set of words on the line. Read the contractions.

Words:

he's, she's, it's

Activity 2. Help the student read the sentences. Instruct the student to write the correct contraction from Activity 1 to complete each sentence on the line.

Sentences:

1. She's going to wear her new dress.
2. He's going to wear his pants.
3. It's going to be a good day.

Activity 3. Have the student read the words aloud and the changes that are being made. Then have the student write the contraction that follows the changes on the line. Read the contractions.

Activity 3 continued:

Words:

here's
that's
who's
there's
where's
what's
nobody's

Activity 4. Review the definition of a contraction and the examples. The student will read each sentence and find the contraction. Have the student write the two words that the contraction stands for on the line.

Words:

1. **You are**
2. **We are**
3. **They are**
4. **Who are**

Activity 5. Have the student read the contractions aloud. Review the meaning of the **'s** when it is used in a contraction. The student will write the words that the contraction can stand for on the lines.

Words	Words
Sue is	Sue has
he is	he has
she is	she has
it is	it has
who is	who has
Bill is	Bill has
that is	that has
what is	what has

Reading. Read and discuss the maxim for the Lesson.

Read the story *Anne*. This is another chapter of the *A Little Princess* story. Preview the story and explain words or sentence structures that are not familiar to the student. With every story ask questions: who are the characters, what are they doing, what are they saying, where does the action take place, what is the order of events, what words are being used, what new information is given, what lesson can be learned?

In contractions formed with the word *are*, the *a* is removed and replaced with an apostrophe (') as in *you + are = you're* and *they + are = they're*.

4 Read each sentence. Write the two words that make up the contraction on the line.

1. You're going to the party. _____ You are
2. We're having a fun time. _____ We are
3. They're doing a good thing. _____ They are
4. Who're the boys in the photo? _____ Who are

5 In a contraction, the *'s* can stand for *is* or *has*. Read each contraction and write the two words that it can stand for. The first one is done for you.

Contraction	Words	Words
Pat's	Pat is	Pat has
Sue's	Sue is	Sue has
he's	he is	he has
she's	she is	she has
it's	it is	it has
who's	who is	who has
Bill's	Bill is	Bill has
that's	that is	that has
what's	what is	what has

170   *Contractions with Is, Are, and Has*

---

events, what words are being used, what new information is given, what lesson can be learned?

Comprehension questions:

What family was very happy that Sara had been found?

Why story did the Mitchell children enjoy hearing?

What did Sara call Mr. Crawford?

Why had Ram Dass suggested to Mr. Crawford that they help the girl in the attic?

Was Sara glad that Mr. Crawford had been her friend?

Read the poem *Pretty Is That Pretty Does*. Preview the poem and explain words or sentence structures that are not familiar to the student.

Who wears a plain dress?

Who works all day seeming to do nothing?

What things cannot be seen?

Assign. Lesson activities or reading that are to be completed as homework.

Lesson 159: Contractions with us, would, shall, will, & had

Overview:

- Define a contraction
- Match two words to their contraction
- Write the two words that a contraction stands for
- Apply the rules to write contractions from two words
- Replace two words in a sentence with a contraction

Materials and Supplies:

- Teacher's Guide & Student Workbook 2
- White board or chalkboard
- Word cards (as necessary)
- Dictionary
- Reader: *A Little Princess & Other Classic Stories*

Teaching Tips:

Review for Mastery. Discuss and review any work from the previous lesson that was assigned as homework. Check for completion of the activities and orally quiz the student for comprehension. Review any reading that was assigned, discussing the characters, setting, plot, theme, language, sequence, etc.

Strengthen fluency and phonemic awareness by reviewing words and sentences from previous lessons. Build vocabulary skills by using some of the words in sentences.

Review contractions with the words *is* and *are* with Lesson 158, Activities 1-4. Write some of the contractions on the board and have the student write the base words.

Review contractions with the words *is* and *has* with Lesson 158, Activity 5. Write the base words on the board and have the student write the contraction.

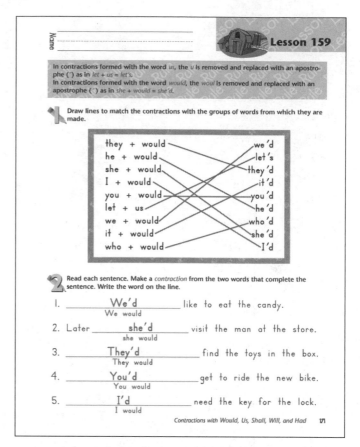

Activity 1. Review the definition of a contraction and the examples. Have the student read the words and the contractions aloud. The student will match the group of words to the contraction for them.

Words	Contractions
they would	they'd
he would	he'd
she would	she'd
I would	I'd
you would	you'd
let us	let's
we would	we'd
it would	it'd
who would	who'd

Activity 2. Help the student read each sentence using the words under the blank. Instruct the student to make a contraction from the words under the blank and write the contraction on the line. Read the sentences again.

Sentences:
1. <u>We'd</u> like to eat the candy.
2. Later <u>she'd</u> visit the man at the store.
3. <u>They'd</u> find the toys in the box.
4. <u>You'd</u> get to ride the new bike.
5. <u>I'd</u> need the key for the lock.

Activity 3. Have the student read the words aloud and the changes that are being made. Then have the student write the contraction that follows the changes on the line. Read the contractions.

Words:
 he'd
 there'd
 who'd
 it'd
 nobody'd

Activity 4. Review the definition of a contraction and the examples. Have the student read the contractions aloud. Review the meaning of the **'ll** when it is used in a contraction. The student will write the words that the contraction can stand for on the lines.

<u>Words</u>	<u>Words</u>
he will	he shall
she will	she shall

Activity 5. Have the student read the contractions aloud. Review the meaning of the **'d** when it is used in a contraction. The student will write the words that the contraction can stand for on the lines.

<u>Words</u>	<u>Words</u>
they had	they would
he had	he would
she had	she would
it had	it would
who had	who would
we had	we would
there had	there would
you had	you would

Reading. Read and discuss the maxim for the Lesson.

---

3 Make the changes to the words and write the contraction on the line.

Words	Changes	Contraction
he would	he + would − woul	he'd
there would	there + would − woul	there'd
who would	who + would − woul	who'd
it would	it + would − woul	it'd
nobody would	nobody + would − woul	nobody'd

In contractions formed with the word *shall*, the *sha* is removed and replaced with an apostrophe (') as in *he + shall = he'll* and *she + shall = she'll*.

4 In a contraction, the *'ll* can stand for *will* or *shall*. Read each contraction and write the two words that it can stand for.

Contraction	Words	Words
he'll	he will	he shall
she'll	she will	she shall

5 In a contraction, the *'d* can stand for *had* or *would*. Read each contraction and write the two words that it can stand for. Example: *I'd = I had* or *I would*.

Contraction	Words	Words
they'd	they had	they would
he'd	he had	he would
she'd	she had	she would
it'd	it had	it would
who'd	who had	who would
we'd	we had	we would
there'd	there had	there would
you'd	you had	you would

171 *Contractions with Would, Us, Shall, Will, and Had*

Read the story *Anne (continued)*. This is another chapter of the *A Little Princess* story. Preview the story and explain words or sentence structures that are not familiar to the student. With every story ask questions: who are the characters, what are they doing, what are they saying, where does the action take place, what is the order of events, what words are being used, what new information is given, what lesson can be learned?

Comprehension questions:
 How long did it take for Mr. Crawford to feel better?
 What did Mr. Crawford's wealth now give him?
 What story did Sara tell Mr. Crawford?
 What did Sara want to do to help the beggar children?

Assign. Lesson activities or reading that are to be completed as homework.

Lesson 160: Review Contractions

Overview:

- Define a contraction
- Match two words to their contraction
- Apply the rules to write contractions from two words
- Identify the letter(s) left out to write a contraction from two words
- Replace two words in a sentence with a contraction

Materials and Supplies:

- Teacher's Guide & Student Workbook 2
- White board or chalkboard
- Word cards (as necessary)
- Dictionary
- Reader: *A Little Princess & Other Classic Stories*

Teaching Tips:

Review for Mastery. Discuss and review any work from the previous lesson that was assigned as homework. Check for completion of the activities and orally quiz the student for comprehension. Review any reading that was assigned, discussing the characters, setting, plot, theme, language, sequence, etc.

Strengthen fluency and phonemic awareness by reviewing words and sentences from previous lessons. Build vocabulary skills by using some of the words in sentences.

Review contractions with the words *us* and *would* with Lesson 159, Activities 1-3. Write some of the contractions on the board and have the student write the base words.

Review contractions with the words *shall*, *will*, *had*, and *would* with Lesson 159, Activities 4 & 5. Write the base words on the board and have the student write the contraction.

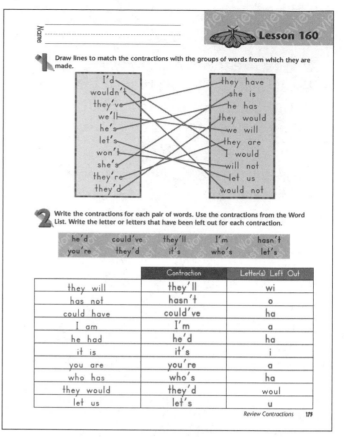

Activity 1. Review the definition of a contraction and the examples from previous lessons. Have the student read the words and the contractions aloud. The student will match the group of words to the contraction for it.

Contraction	Base Words
I'd	I would
wouldn't	would not
they've	they have
we'll	we will
he's	he has
let's	let us
won't	would not
she's	she is
they're	they are
they'd	they would

Activity 2. Help the student read the words in the box. Instruct the student to select the contraction from the words and write it on the line. Also the student is to write the letters left out to make the contraction on the line.

384

Activity 2 continued:

Contraction	Left Out
they'll	wi
hasn't	o
could've	ha
I'm	a
he'd	ha
it's	i
you're	a
who's	i
they'd	woul
let's	u

Activity 3. Have the student read the words in the box aloud. Have the student write the contraction for the base word on the line.

Words:

doesn't	hadn't	isn't
I'll	you'll	he'll
here's	we're	I'm
you've	I'd	what's
she'd	there'd	let's

Activity 4. Help the student read the sentences. Instruct the student to select the correct contraction from choices to complete each sentence.

Sentences:

1. <u>Let's</u> get ready to work.
2. I <u>don't</u> walk to school.
3. <u>It's</u> a long ride.
4. Stop, or <u>we'll</u> get run over!
5. <u>They're</u> coming home.

Review for Test. The instructor should plan to use some time at the end of the class to review and prepare for the test that follows this lesson. Review the objectives for the test and then look over the lessons that it will cover. If the student has struggled with any of the concepts that will be included in the test, some additional drill, practice, or review may be needed to adequately prepare him for the test.

Reading. Read and discuss the maxim for the Lesson.

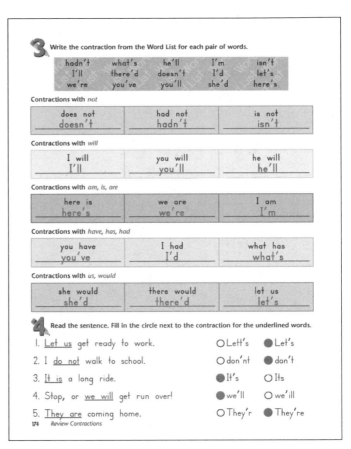

Read the story *Anne (continued)*. This is the final chapter of the *A Little Princess* story. Preview the story and explain words or sentence structures that are not familiar to the student. With every story ask questions: who are the characters, what are they doing, what are they saying, where does the action take place, what is the order of events, what words are being used, what new information is given, what lesson can be learned?

Comprehension questions:

Where did Mr. Crawford and Sara go in the buggy?
Did the lady at the bake shop remember Sara?
How had Sara's actions affected the lady at the bake shop?
Where was the beggar girl that Sara had helped?
Who did Sara suggest should be the one who gave the buns to the poor children?

Extension Activity. View a movie version of the *A Little Princess* story.

Test 16
Lessons 145-154

Overview:

- Read words of two syllables
- Divide words into syllables
- Identify words that have been correctly divided into syllables
- Read two-syllable words with the correct accent
- Label VCVopen letter patterns in two-syllable words
- Label VV letter patterns in two-syllable words
- Divide VV letter patterns into syllables
- Identify prefixes
- Identify words that have been correctly divided into syllables
- Match three-syllable words to the picture
- Count vowels and syllables in three-syllable words
- Sort words by the long vowel spelling

Materials and Supplies:

- Teacher's Guide & Student Workbook 2

Instructions:

Assessment Start-up. Read through the test with the student. Help the student with any words that he/she is still unsure of. The teacher should be available to answer any questions that the student may have during the test.

Activity 1. Review the instructions and the words with the student. The student is to mark the vowels, the consonants between the vowels, and divide each word into syllables.

Words:

fa/tal	pre/vent	lo/cal	pru/dent
i/cy	du/ty	pa/tron	wi/per
va/por	pa/per	gra/vy	se/cret

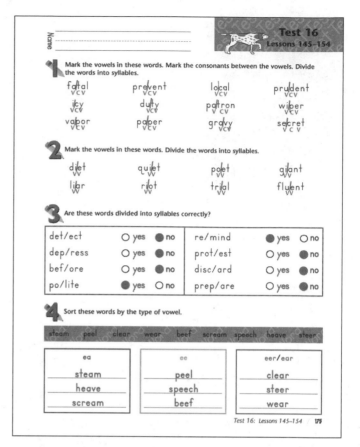

Activity 2. Review the instructions and the words with the student. The student is to mark the vowels and divide each word into syllables.

Words:

di/et	qui/et	po/et	gi/ant
li/ar	ri/ot	tri/al	flu/ent

Activity 3. Review the instructions and the words with the student. The student is to choose whether each word has been correctly divided into syllables.

Words:

det/ect	no
dep/ress	no
bef/ore	no
po/lite	yes
re/mind	yes
prot/est	no
disc/ard	no
prep/are	no

Activity 4. Review the instructions and the words with the student. The student in to sort the words by the vowel spelling.